BRIEF EDITION

TANYA MARIA GOLASH-BOZA
UNIVERSITY OF CALIFORNIA, MERCED

NEW YORK OXFORD OXFORD UNIVERSITY PRESS

Oxford University Press is a department of the University of Oxford.
It furthers the University's objective of excellence in research,
scholarship, and education by publishing worldwide.

Oxford New York
Auckland Cape Town Dar es Salaam Hong Kong Karachi
Kuala Lumpur Madrid Melbourne Mexico City Nairobi
New Delhi Shanghai Taipei Toronto

With offices in
Argentina Austria Brazil Chile Czech Republic France Greece
Guatemala Hungary Italy Japan Poland Portugal Singapore
South Korea Switzerland Thailand Turkey Ukraine Vietnam

For titles covered by Section 112 of the US Higher Education Opportunity Act, please visit www.oup.com/us/he for the latest information about pricing and alternate formats.

Published by Oxford University Press
198 Madison Avenue, New York, New York 10016
http://www.oup.com

Library of Congress Cataloging-in-Publication Data
Golash-Boza, Tanya Maria.
Race & racisms : a critical approach / Tanya Maria Golash-Boza,
University of California, Merced.—Brief ed.
pages cm
ISBN 978-0-19-023850-6
1. United States—Race relations. 2. Racism—United States. 3. Equality—United States.
4. United States—Emigration and immigration. 5. Race. 6. Racism. I. Title.
II. Title: Race and racisms.
E184.A1G5652 2016
305.800973—dc23

2015005991

Printing number: 9 8 7 6 5 4 3

Printed in Canada on acid-free paper

BRIEF CONTENTS

CONTENTS

PREFACE

This brief edition of *Race and Racisms* engages students in significant questions related to racial dynamics in the United States. In accessible, straightforward language, the text discusses and critically analyzes cutting-edge scholarship in the field.

FEATURES

This text includes several unique features that will be useful in teaching and learning about race and racism. Each of the following features appears consistently throughout the book:

- **Voices** boxes highlight individual stories about race and racism, bringing personal experiences to life.
- **Thinking about Racial Justice** boxes pose questions for students to consider in thinking about how racism could be addressed or alleviated.
- **Learning Objectives** point students to the key ideas in each chapter.
- **Check Your Understanding** questions at the end of the chapter tie back to the Learning Objectives and help students review.
- **Critical Thinking** questions guide students in interrogating their and others' assumptions about race and racism.

ORGANIZATION

Race and Racisms begins with a historical chapter on the origin and evolution of the idea of race. From there, it moves into an overview of racial ideologies and sociological theories of racism, and then to a historical and contemporary discussion of immigration. The next two chapters focus on racial ideologies in the media and colorism. The final five chapters explore racial inequalities across five key areas: education, the labor market, housing, the criminal justice system, and health and the environment. Each chapter uses an intersectional framework to guide our understanding of racial dynamics.

ANCILLARIES

Oxford University Press is proud to offer a complete supplements package to accompany *Race and Racisms: Brief Edition*. The Ancillary Resource Center (ARC) at www.oup-arc.com is a convenient, instructor-focused single destination for resources to accompany this book. Accessed online through individual user accounts, the ARC provides instructors with up-to-date ancillaries at any time while guaranteeing the security of grade-significant resources. In addition, it allows OUP to keep instructors informed when new content becomes available.

The ARC for *Race and Racisms: Brief Edition* contains a variety of materials to aid in teaching:

- PowerPoint-based lecture slides to aid in the presentation of course material
- Recommended readings that delve more deeply into the topics discussed in the chapter
- A test bank with multiple-choice, true/false, short answer, and essay questions

ACKNOWLEDGMENTS

Working on this brief edition has been a great pleasure largely because of the editors at Oxford University Press, particularly Sherith Pankratz, Acquisitions Editor, and Lauren Mine, Development Editor. Sherith's enthusiasm for this project has been unflagging, thus providing crucial inspiration to write and to finish this book. Thank you, Sherith, for being such a great cheerleader! Lauren and Sherith also worked assiduously with me and a team of reviewers to distill down the most important and relevant aspects of *Race and Racisms: A Critical Approach* into a brief edition. I am very grateful to the editorial staff at Oxford for all of their work on this brief edition and to the reviewers for their helpful suggestions. This collaborative effort has enhanced the quality of this book.

I did not write this book alone. In fact, many of these chapters were written in the company of fabulous colleagues. I'd like to extend a special thanks to my Write-on-Site colleagues in Merced who have been there through the duration of this project: Zulema Valdez, Christina Lux, Irenee Beattie, Susana Ramirez, Dalia Magaña, Jessica Blois, David Kaminski, Anne Warlaumont, Rick Dale, and Alexandra Main.

The Oxford Development team, led by Development Manager Thom Holmes, worked closely with me to fine-tune the content of the book. Lauren Mine helped immensely with the fluidity of the prose and the organization of the materials in this book.

I would also like to extend my sincere thanks to the rest of the team at Oxford University Press for their support in making this book a reality. Assistant Editor Katy Albis and Editorial Assistant Meredith Keffer were especially helpful in wrangling the photo, map, and figure program for the book. I thank the Oxford Production team, led by Managing Editor Lisa Grzan, for their encouragement and help in generating this book and shaping its final form. Other key production staff included Production Editor David Bradley and Copyeditor Debbie Ruel. Art Director Michele Laseau and Senior Designer Bonni Leon-Berman created the interior and cover design.

Special thanks to the reviewers who looked over the manuscript for this brief edition:

David Allen
Temple University

Amy Armenia
Rollins College

David Daniel Bogumil
California State University, Northridge

James L. Burnett Jr.
Urbana University

Ione Y. DeOllos
Ball State University

Johnnie M. Griffin
Jackson State University

Joachim S. Kibirige
Missouri Western State University

Karen McCormack
Wheaton College

Deirdre Oakley
Georgia State University

Mary Roaf
Northern Arizona University

Sarah Epplen Rusche
Minnesota State University, Mankato

Matthew Schneirov
Duquesne University

Damian T. Williams
Concordia University Chicago

1

THE ORIGIN OF THE IDEA OF RACE

CHAPTER OUTLINE

LEARNING OBJECTIVES

1.1 Define race and racism in the context of the history of the idea of race.
1.2 Examine how race is distinct from previous ways of thinking about human difference.
1.3 Describe the effects of the Indian Removal Act on Native Americans.
1.4 Examine how slavery influenced the writing of the U.S. Constitution.
1.5 Evaluate the role that early science played in the propagation of racism.

In the 1600s, European colonists, enslaved Africans, and Native Americans found themselves together in the New World. However, no one would have described the population in those terms at the time. They certainly would not have said that blacks, whites, and Indians were in the Americas. Instead, people identified themselves as Shawnee, Creek, or Iroquois. Others identified themselves as Scots or Irish. Still others identified themselves as Ashanti or Fante. How, then, did the Ashanti come to be known as "black," the Scots as "white," and the Creek as "Native American"? How and why was the idea of race created? What distinguishes it from previous ways of thinking about human difference? These are the questions we will consider in this chapter.

In the contemporary United States, one of the first things we notice about someone we meet is race. When we aren't sure of someone's race, we may get inquisitive or begin to feel uncomfortable (Dalmage 2000). It is as if, before interacting, we have to know if the other person is white, black, Asian, Native American, or something else. The perceived race of the other person affects how we treat one another and what we expect the other person to say and do.

In light of the importance of racial classifications in our society, it may be hard to imagine a time when the idea of race did not exist, when people did not think the world could be divided into discrete races. This time was not so long ago: humans have long used various factors to classify one another, but the idea of race as a classificatory system is a modern invention. Ancient Greeks and Romans, for example, did not think that the world could be divided into races. Their system of social classification was much different from ours. Race is a modern **social construction**, meaning that the idea of race is not based on biological differences among people, even though race has become important in determining how we interact. It is a particular way of viewing human difference that is a product of colonial encounters.

DEFINING RACE AND ETHNICITY

The word ***race*** refers to a group of people who share physical and cultural traits as well as a common ancestry. The idea of race implies that the people of the world can be divided into biologically discrete and exclusive groups based on physical and cultural traits. This idea is further linked to notions of white or European superiority that became concretized during the colonization of the Americas. As we will see in this chapter, the history of the idea of race is critical to an understanding of its meaning. ***Racism*** refers to both (1) the belief that races are populations whose physical differences are linked to significant cultural and social differences within a hierarchy, and (2) the practice of subordinating races believed to be inferior.

The idea of race is slightly different from the concept of ethnicity. Races are categories of people based on a hierarchical worldview that associates ancestry, descent, and phenotype with cultural and moral attributes. **Ethnicities**, on the other hand, are group identities based on notions of similar and shared history, culture, and kinship (Cornell and Hartmann 1998). Ethnicity also has a distinct historical trajectory from race. People self-identify as belonging to an ethnic group on the basis of a perceived shared history and a concomitant set of cultural attributes. In contrast to ethnicity, race is often an externally imposed category. In the United States, people are placed into races based on socially constructed, ascribed characteristics often related to physical appearance, such as skin color or hair texture, regardless of self-identification. Sociologist Eduardo Bonilla-Silva (1997:469) argues that "ethnicity has a primarily sociocultural foundation, and ethnic groups have exhibited tremendous malleability in terms of who belongs; racial ascriptions (initially) are imposed externally to justify the collective exploitation of a people and are maintained to preserve status differences."

Race is a social construction, an idea we endow with meaning through daily interactions. It has no biological basis. This might seem odd to read, as the physical differences between a Kenyan, a Swede, and a Han Chinese, for example, are obvious. However, these physical differences do not necessarily mean that the world can be divided into discrete racial groups. If you were to walk from Kenya to Sweden to China, you would note incremental gradations in physical differences between people across space, and it would be difficult to decide where to draw the line between Africa and Europe and between Europe and Asia. There may be genetic differences between Kenyans and Swedes, but the genetic variations within the Kenyan population are actually greater than those between Swedes and Kenyans (Smedley 2007). Although race is a social, as opposed to a biological, construction, it has a wide range of consequences in our society, especially when used as a sorting and stratifying mechanism.

Race is also a historical construction, meaning that the idea of race was formulated at particular historical moments and places. Of particular note in its development are the eras of **colonialism**—the practice of acquiring political control over another country, occupying it with settlers, and exploiting it economically—and slavery in the Americas. The idea of race involves classifying humans into distinct groups. Through this classification and the assignment of cultural and moral traits to each group, Europeans and their descendants have used the idea of race to justify exploitation, slavery, colonialism, and genocide.

RACE: THE EVOLUTION OF AN IDEOLOGY

The way we understand the idea of race today is distinct from previous ways of thinking about human difference. Before the conquest of the Americas, there was no worldview that separated all of humanity into distinct races (Smedley 2007; Montagu 1997; Quijano 2000). Understanding what race means today requires delving into the historical process through which the idea of race was created. Once we understand that thinking of people as belonging to specific racial categories is not "natural" but constructed, we can begin to think about why and how these categories were created. As this section makes evident, racial categories were created to justify mass genocide and brutal exploitation. This brutal history in turn raises the question of why we continue to use these categories.

Historical Precedents to the Idea of Race

Until the sixteenth century, Northern Europeans had very limited knowledge of the world beyond their immediate communities. Without this knowledge, it would have been difficult to develop a worldview that classified the people of the globe into various racial groups. Southern Europeans, in contrast, had much more contact with other peoples. People from the Mediterranean region have had extensive involvement with people from Asia, Africa, and the Arab world since time immemorial. These contacts, which range from Alexander the Great's travels to India and Greek exchanges with Ethiopia to the conquest of Spain by Islamic peoples, did not lead to a racial worldview. Ancient peoples did not divide the world into distinct races based on their physical and cultural traits. Instead, Greeks had great respect for the achievements of Ethiopians (Snowden 1970), and Muslims,

Christians, and Jews lived reasonably harmoniously together in Spain for hundreds of years (Smedley 2007).

Although the idea of race did not develop until later, these early interactions between Europeans and other groups did provide important precedents for current ways of conceptualizing human difference. The Spanish Inquisition is one example. When the Catholic Church began to consolidate its power in Spain under the reign of monarchs Ferdinand II of Aragon and Isabella I of Castile (1479–1504), Jews were expelled from Spain, and converted Jews were subject to scrutiny. In 1480, Ferdinand and Isabella established a tribunal called the Spanish Inquisition, which was intended to ensure the orthodoxy of people who had converted from Judaism and Islam to Catholicism. The monarchs issued royal decrees in 1492 and 1501 that ordered Jews and Muslims to convert or leave. During the Inquisition, Jews and Muslims were obliged to convert, but conversion did not ensure their safety, as they continued to be subject to scrutiny and suspicion. Moreover, people believed to be the descendants of Jews and Muslims also faced persecution. Discrimination against Jews and Muslims was more religious in nature than racial, yet the Inquisition's ideas regarding purity of blood set the stage for the European understanding of racial differences (Smedley 2007; Quijano 2000).

Another crucial precedent to the idea of race is the treatment of the Irish and later of the Native Americans by the English. England and Ireland were involved in centuries of conflict before the English first settled in North America, and English soldiers often portrayed the Irish as savage, sexually immoral, and resistant to civilizing forces. Because many English colonizers had been deployed to Ireland before settling in what would become the United States, the ideas the English developed about the Irish may have played a role in how English settlers perceived Native Americans (Allen 1994; Smedley 2007). The settlers perceived both the Irish and the Native Americans as savage and in need of civilizing. The concept of "savage" that the English developed to describe the Irish provided a framework for them to understand their relationship to Native Americans, shaped their interactions with them, and was a precursor to the idea that some humans were less fit for civilization than others.

Slavery before the Idea of Race

Slavery was not new to the Americas: the practice of enslaving people has existed since antiquity. In African, European, and Middle Eastern societies, conquered peoples often became slaves in the aftermath of war. As agricultural societies grew, so did the demand for labor, leading peoples such as the Greeks and Phoenicians to raid other societies for slaves. Slavery existed not only across societies but also within societies: people lacking the support of a family often had no place other than as slaves, and some people became enslaved as a means of paying off a debt or as punishment for a crime. Slavery of this latter form almost always involved persons of the same ethnic group as their masters.

The prevalence of slavery in ancient society is often thought of as proof that racism existed in antiquity. However, this equation of racism with slavery is misguided: although some ancient writings make reference to skin color, these references are very rarely derogatory and by no means represent the general ideology of any ancient society. On the contrary, Greeks and Romans held the Egyptians as well as the Ethiopians in high esteem and admired their culture and way of life. These ancient peoples developed no stereotypes of blacks as primitives or lacking in culture (Snowden 1983). Marriages between Egyptians and black Africans were commonplace in ancient times, and Muslim conquerors regarded anyone they succeeded in converting as brethren (Franklin 1974).

The status of slaves varied across societies. In some instances, slaves were adopted as kin after serving for a certain number of years; in other cases, slaves were permitted to marry and own property (Smedley 2007; Morgan 1975). Many slaves were granted rights not found in the system of slavery in the New World. These rights included access to education, the potential to obtain freedom for themselves and their children, the right to marry, and the right to own property. Until the eighteenth century, no society categorically denied the humanity of slaves. It was not seen as necessary to rationalize slavery by denying that slaves were fully human. Although slaves were at times treated

TIMELINE

The American Slave Trade

1492 Christopher Columbus lands in the Caribbean.

1619 First African slaves arrive in Jamestown.

1660 First slave codes enacted.

1676 Bacon's Rebellion.

1863 Abraham Lincoln issues the Emancipation Proclamation.

1865 Slavery is abolished in the United States.

voices

The Spanish Treatment of Indigenous Peoples

The following excerpts are from a 1519 report of Dominicans about the Spanish treatment of indigenous peoples in the Carib Islands.

> Some Christians encounter[ed] an Indian woman, who was carrying in her arms a child at suck; and since the dog they had with them was hungry, they tore the child from the mother's arms and flung it still living to the dog, who proceeded to devour it before the mother's eyes.
>
> When there were among the prisoners some women who had recently given birth, if the new-born babes happened to cry, they seized them by the legs and hurled them against the rocks, or flung them into the jungle so that they would be certain to die there.
>
> Each of them [the foremen] had made it a practice to sleep with the Indian women who were in his workforce, if they pleased him, whether they were married women or maidens. While the foreman remained . . . with the Indian woman, he sent the husband to dig gold out of the mines; and in the evening, when the wretch returned, not only was he beaten or whipped because he had not brought enough gold, but further, most often, he was bound hand and foot and flung under the bed like a dog, before the foreman lay down, directly over him, with his wife.

Source: Todorov 1984, 139.

brutally, the humanity of slaves was never put into question, and slavery was never attributed to racial inferiority (Smedley 2007).

European Encounters with Indigenous Peoples of the Americas

Before the arrival of the European colonizers, the Americas were home to over 100 million indigenous people. As a result of warfare, slavery, and disease, about 95 percent of this population was decimated during the first two centuries of colonization. The above excerpted accounts provide a small window into the depths of this massacre.

When Christopher Columbus encountered the native peoples of the Caribbean islands in 1492, he found them to be peaceable and

When Christopher Columbus encountered the native peoples of the Caribbean, he found them to be peaceable and generous.

generous. Despite the initial admiration the Spaniards expressed for the indigenous people, the relations between the two groups soon deteriorated, as it became clear that the Spaniards' primary motive was to extract gold from the Americas. Intent upon taking as much gold as possible, the Spaniards used their weaponry to overpower and enslave the people indigenous to the Americas in order to compel the natives to find gold and silver for the Spaniards to take back to Spain (Todorov 1984). The abuse of the Spaniards was devastating for the Caribbean peoples: the Arawaks of Santo Domingo were reduced from over 3 million people in 1496 to a mere 125 in 1570 (Jones 2003).

Reports of the Spaniards' extreme cruelty toward the indigenous people of the Americas made their way back to Spain and eventually became a subject of controversy. Fifty years after Columbus's arrival in the Caribbean islands, the enslavement of indigenous people was outlawed. The Spaniards continued to extract labor from indigenous people, however, by relying on other systems of forced labor (Wade 1997).

One of the most remarkable things about the conquest of the Americas is that many of the civilizations in the Americas were far more advanced than those from which the Europeans hailed. Europe in the sixteenth century was quite a ghastly place, with frequent famines and epidemic outbreaks of the plague and smallpox. Large cities were pestilent and dirty, with unsightly open sewers. Crime was rampant. Half of all children died before they turned ten. Thus, we can imagine the surprise and awe that the magnificent city of Tenochtitlán engendered in the Spaniards who arrived there. Tenochtitlán, an Aztec city in central Mexico, had about 350,000 inhabitants—many times the population of London or Seville at the time. When the Spanish explorer and colonizer Hernando Cortés (1485–1547) saw this city, he declared it to be the most beautiful city on earth. His companion and chronicler, Bernal Díaz (1492–1585), agreed, calling it a "wonderful thing to behold." Unlike European cities of the time, Tenochtitlán boasted clean streets, amazing floating gardens, a huge aqueduct system, and a market unlike any the Europeans had ever seen (Stannard 1993).

Despite their admiration, the Spaniards did not preserve this city. Moreover, the arrival of the Spaniards led to the destruction of not only this extraordinary city, but also many towns and cities across the Americas. The population of central Mexico was decimated in less than a century, declining from 25 million in 1519 to barely 1.3 million in 1595. This pattern continued throughout the Americas, so that nearly 95 percent of the native populations were destroyed in less than 200 years (Stannard 1993).

The Enslavement of Africans

Africans were present in the conquest of the Americas from the beginning, both as slaves and as sailors and explorers. Spain and Portugal were slaveholding societies long before Columbus set sail in search of the Indies. Many, but not all, of the slaves in Spain in the fifteenth century were Africans. Some African residents of Spain and Portugal—enslaved as well as free—accompanied Spaniards on their initial conquest voyages to the New World. Juan Garrido (ca. 1480–ca. 1547), for example, was born in Africa and later traveled to Portugal and then to Spain, where he joined an expedition to Santo Domingo. Juan Garrido also participated in the conquest of Puerto Rico, Cuba, and then Mexico. Juan García (ca. 1495–date of death unknown), in contrast, was born in Spain as a free mulatto and traveled to Peru as a colonist (Restall 2000).

The Spanish colonists—often called *conquistadores*—endeavored to subdue native populations and to convert them into Catholics and subjects of the Spanish Crown. Their main goal, however, was to extract as much wealth as possible from the Americas. This extraction of wealth required labor, and the Spanish colonists enslaved the native populations to this end. The harsh conditions of this enslavement led to massive declines in the native populations, and in 1550, the Spanish Crown outlawed the practice, although it continued to allow other forms of forced labor. The ban on enslavement of indigenous people did not end the need for labor, and the Spaniards turned to Africa in their search for workers. As they realized that agricultural exploitation, particularly the harvesting of sugarcane, could bring enormous wealth, they began to bring African slaves in very large numbers to their colonies in the Americas (Smedley 2007; Franklin 1974; Morgan 1975). Consequently, tens of millions of Africans were brought over between the early 1600s and the nineteenth century as slaves (Bowser 1974).

Whereas the Spaniards had had centuries of contact with Africans, the English who settled in North America had not had contact with Africans until the arrival of twenty Africans in Jamestown in 1619. Slaves did not become an essential part of the workforce in North America until much later.

The form of slavery that eventually emerged in the North American colonies was unique in several ways. First of all, slaves had no human or legal rights. They were seen only as property, not as people who could marry or own property themselves. Second, slavery was permanent and the slave status was inherited. Third, slaves were forbidden to learn to read or write, thereby ensuring their inferior social status. Finally, slavery in North America was unique insofar as nearly all Africans and their descendants were enslaved, and only this group could be enslaved. This unique system of human exploitation laid the groundwork for a new idea of human difference (Smedley 2007). Before delving further into this point, let's take a closer look at the English settlements in North America.

The Need for Labor in the Thirteen Colonies

In the late fifteenth century, Europeans began to explore parts of North America where indigenous peoples had lived for thousands of years. The English had heard of the great wealth the Spanish had accrued in the New World and were anxious to fill their coffers with riches as well. England first sent colonists to Roanoke in the late sixteenth century, but that attempt at settlement failed. The first permanent English settlement was at Jamestown in 1607. Similar to Columbus's reports from 1492, these English settlers reported that the local Native Americans were kind and generous and helped them to survive the unfamiliar conditions. Amicable trade relations did not last long, however, as it became clear that the Englishmen's intentions were not benign: they planned to take over indigenous land and resources (Zinn 2010; Morgan 1975).

European colonists and Native Americans engaged in constant warfare, with colonists often burning the native people's crops and lodging and enslaving entire Native American tribes. The English colonists justified their takeover of indigenous lands in religious terms. They interpreted their successes as God's will. For example, John Winthrop (1588–1649), a leader of the Massachusetts Bay Colony in the mid-seventeenth century, wrote that the death of so many American Indians as a result of smallpox showed that "the Lord hathe cleared our title to what we possess" (quoted in F. Wood 1991, 96). It is important to note that when the English colonists interacted with Native Americans, they did not see them as belonging to a separate race; this idea did not yet exist. Instead, the English saw themselves as superior in religious and moral terms. These religious justifications, however, laid the groundwork for racial distinctions that emerged later (Smedley 2007; Jordan 1968).

The first fifty years of the new settlement in Virginia were full of hardship and very high death rates of Native Americans as well as English colonists resulting from disease, starvation, and war. There were severe food shortages, partly because the first settlers did not plant enough corn. Morgan (1975) points out that most of the settlers in Virginia were not farmers but nobles or gentry who thought food cultivation was beneath them. Although the settlers were too proud to grow corn to eat, they were willing to take up the enterprise of growing tobacco to sell and expected to make their riches in this manner. As there was no shortage of land in this vast country, the only commodity lacking was labor power (Zinn 2010).

The English colonists were notoriously successful at decimating the Native American population, yet less so in their attempts to use Native Americans for labor. When the English realized they would not become rich instantaneously through gold or silver mining, as it appeared the Spaniards had done, they turned to agricultural production to seek wealth. For this, they needed labor—lots of it. The English were able to enslave Native Americans they captured in warfare, but most indigenous slaves either died or ran away, leaving the English in need of more labor in order to accumulate wealth (Zinn 2010).

The lack of success at enslaving Native Americans led the colonists to turn to Britain, where they recruited poor men, women, and children from the streets of cities such as Liverpool and Bristol. Englishmen also rounded up Irish and Scottish peasants who had been conquered in warfare, banished, or released from prison. Indentured servants from Europe who were willing to work for four to seven years to pay off their passage and debt soon became the primary source of labor for the colonies. The harsh treatment of European indentured servants needed no justification, as servitude was a way of life in Britain at the time (Smedley 2007; Zinn 2010).

Throughout the seventeenth century, indentured servants endured harsh conditions as laborers in the colonies. Hopeful laborers continued to come to the Americas, despite the difficult circumstances, because there were possibilities for social and economic advancement in North America that did not exist in England. The flow of English laborers began to decline, however, with the restoration of the monarchy in England in 1660, as King Charles II implemented policies that discouraged emigration (Smedley 2007).

In addition to bringing English laborers, colonists brought Africans to the colonies. Most African slaves brought to North America were from West Africa and were Yoruba, Igbo, Fulani, or Mada (Figure 1-1). In 1619, English colonists brought the first group of Africans to the North American colonies. These twenty Africans occupied nearly the same social status as European indentured servants and were soon joined by African slaves brought over by Dutch and Spanish slave ships. All of these early Africans were granted rights that were later denied to all blacks in Virginia. There is no evidence that African slaves during the period before 1660 were subjected to a more severe

FIGURE 1-1
REGIONS FROM WHICH CAPTURED AFRICANS WERE BROUGHT TO THE AMERICAS, 1501–1867

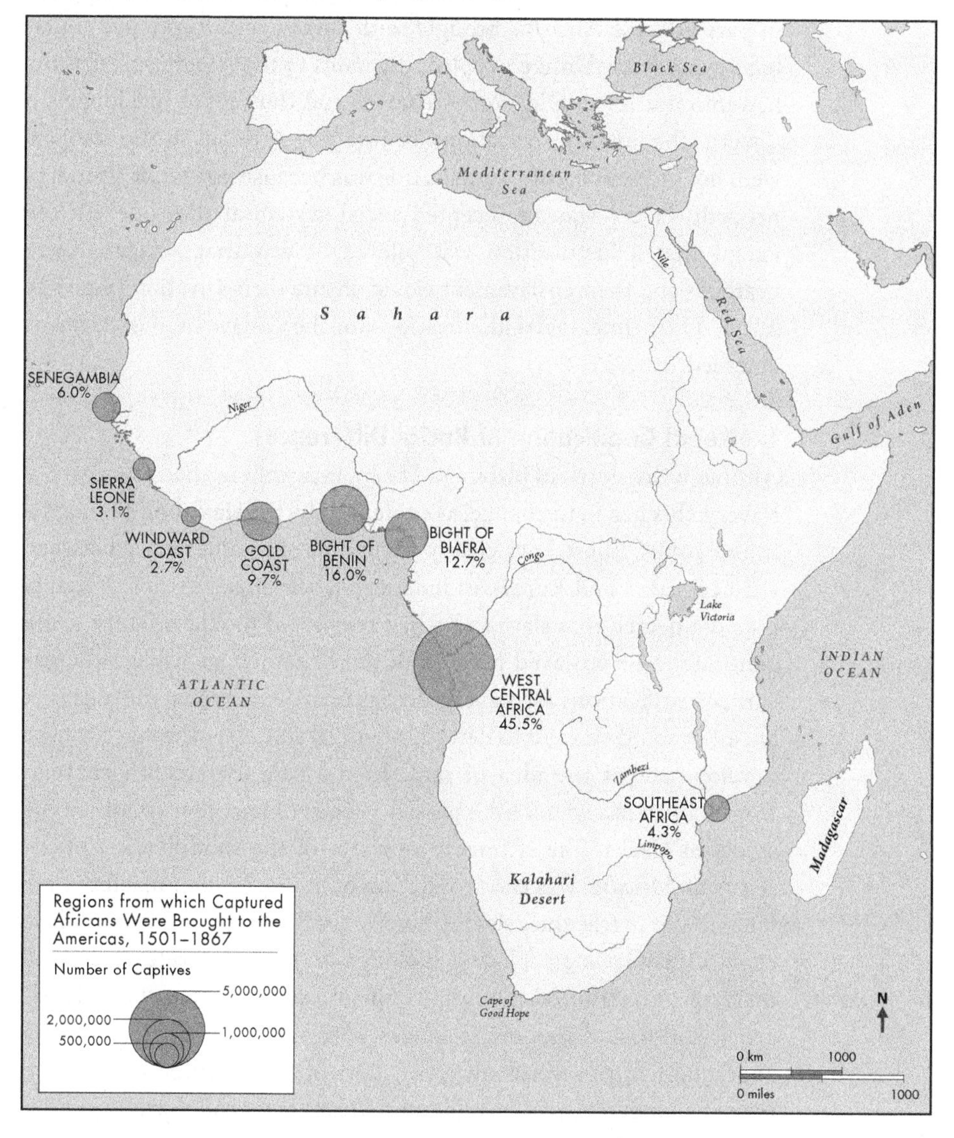

discipline than European servants. Some slaves were allowed to earn money of their own and to buy their freedom with it. There are several cases recorded in which masters set up conditions in their wills whereby Negro slaves would become free or could purchase their freedom after the master's death. The terms of these wills imply that the freed slaves would become regular members of the community (Morgan 1975; Smedley 2007; Zinn 2010).

The enslavement of Africans turned out to be particularly profitable, in part because Africans brought with them agricultural and craftsman experience. Unlike people indigenous to the Americas, Africans had immunities to Old World diseases and thus could live longer in slavery. The initial justifications for bringing Africans to the colonies were not racial in nature. In part, this was because no justification was needed: slavery was an accepted social system at the time. To the extent that a justification was offered, it was that Africans were heathens and their enslavement would ensure their salvation (Smedley 2007). Over time, racial justifications for the enslavement of Africans emerged.

The Legal Codification of Racial Differences

Although the status of blacks had been uncertain in the early years of slavery, this began to change, as evidenced by the **slave codes** enacted in the 1660s. These laws clearly spelled out the differences between African slaves and European indentured servants. In 1667, Virginia issued a decree that slaves who had converted to Christianity could continue to be enslaved because of their heathen ancestry. Whereas earlier justifications for slavery were primarily religious, the idea that ancestry could be used to determine social status set the stage for the development of the idea of race. In the late seventeenth century, Virginia and Maryland each passed a series of laws that solidified the status of blacks. The strongest indicator of the solidification of the status of Africans was the prohibition of manumission: masters were not allowed to free their slaves, thereby establishing a permanent slave class. Other laws established lifelong servitude, forbade interracial marriage, and limited the rights of blacks to own property and bear arms. These laws specific to blacks both reflected the social order and solidified the status quo. For most of the seventeenth century, European indentured servants and African slaves had shared a similar social status. The slave codes gradually changed this.

The shared social position of African and European servants and slaves in the early years of the colonies meant that these groups intermarried and fraternized. The fact that Africans and Europeans had amicable relations can be seen in the laws passed that forbade these relationships. In 1661, Virginia passed a law that imposed harsh conditions on English servants who ran away with African slaves. In 1691, Virginia passed another law that prohibited free whites from intermarrying with blacks and Native Americans. Had these groups been naturally disinclined to intermarry or to fraternize, these laws would not have been necessary. As the 1661 law shows, plantation owners were concerned that European indentured servants and African slaves would see that they shared a common interest in fighting for more rights and better conditions. As historian Howard Zinn puts it, "only one fear was greater than the fear of black rebellion in the new American colonies. That was the fear that discontented whites would join black slaves to overthrow the existing order" (2010, 37).

When Africans and Europeans first found themselves together in the Americas, sexual relations and even marriage between these two groups were not uncommon. African men and women married European men and women (Smedley 2007). Various laws were passed, however, both to prevent and to control these relationships. The aforementioned 1662 law made it clear that when African women had children, the child's status as slave or free would be in accordance with the condition of the mother. The law also indicated that when Christians—here meaning Europeans—had sexual relations with Africans, they would pay double the normal fine for adultery. The European men who wrote these laws perceived it to be important to prevent sexual relations between Europeans and Africans and to ensure that the children of enslaved African women would also be slaves. This law effectively prevented the formation of families by enslaved African women and European men.

Bacon's Rebellion, which occurred in September 1676, provides one example of what could happen when blacks and whites joined forces to fight for their interests. The rebellion itself was not particularly successful, but the coalition that emerged between poor whites and African slaves and freedmen became a cause for concern for the elite planter class, who depended on these groups for cheap labor. In Bacon's Rebellion, white indentured servants joined forces with African slaves and freedmen to protest their conditions. This massive rebellion, in which protestors demanding an end to their servitude burned Jamestown to the ground, was a clear threat to the status quo. One of the last groups to surrender was a mixed group of eighty black and twenty white servants. This multiracial coalition indicates that blacks and whites were willing to join forces to fight for their common interests as laborers. After Bacon's Rebellion, an official report arguing for the continued presence of British soldiers in Virginia stated: "Virginia is at present poor and more populous than ever. There is great apprehension of a rising among the servants, owing to their great necessities and want of clothes; they may plunder the storehouses and ships" (Zinn 2010, 37).

Howard Zinn and other historians argue that Bacon's Rebellion stirred up fear in the hearts of the elite planter class, and that this fear led these elites to pass laws that worked to divide blacks and whites. For example, in the aftermath of the rebellion, the Virginia Assembly gave amnesty to the white servants who had rebelled, but not to the blacks. By extending this and other privileges to whites that were denied to blacks, the elites succeeded in preventing future class-based alliances between blacks and whites that would threaten the social order.

Wealth in colonial North America was concentrated in the hands of a very few people. In 1700, there were about 250,000 colonists, most of whom lived in horrendous conditions. In Virginia, there were only about fifty wealthy families, who depended on the labor of the other 40,000 poor colonists. This imbalance of wealth made for a tenuous social order (Zinn 2010). The slave codes were enacted in an effort to subordinate blacks and prevent alliances between whites and blacks.

It soon became clear to the rich elite and the governing body that they could not continue to disregard the interests of the majority of the population. In 1705, a law was passed requiring masters to provide white servants whose indenture time was completed with ten bushels of corn, thirty shillings, a gun, and fifty acres of land (Morgan 1975, 344). This tactic of giving servants a piece of the American Dream was intended to avoid rebellion by convincing poor whites that the rich landowners were not extortionists or enemies, but protectors of their common interests. To reinforce this impression, it was further mandated that servants had the right to possess property, but that slaves did not (Morgan 1975, 333). The Virginia Assembly in 1705 also prohibited any Negro, mulatto, or Indian from raising his hand in opposition to any Christian, which meant any white man (Jordan 1968). By denying black slaves privileges extended to white servants, the first step was made in creating a division between blacks and whites (Zinn 2010).

In New York in 1708, a group of slaves was accused of murdering a farmer and his family. Shortly afterward, a law was enacted preventing the conspiracy of slaves. This meant, in effect, that slaves could not gather in private to talk about anything. In 1712, a slave rebellion involving about fifty slaves left nine whites dead and six others wounded. Immediately thereafter, New York's repressive laws were reinforced. For example, arson committed by a slave was made into a crime punishable by death (Szasz 1967).

One purpose of the slave codes was the prevention and deterrence of slave rebellions, which were becoming more and more of a real danger with the increasing number of slaves, especially in the southern colonies, where slaves often outnumbered whites. In 1730, in Virginia, the governor ordered that all whites should bring their guns with them to church on Sunday so that they would be prepared for a slave uprising in the event that slaves took advantage of their absence to conspire (Jordan 1968). The idea of a slave rebellion was even more distasteful to whites because of the widespread idea that any slave insurrection would have as its ultimate goal not only the emancipation of slaves but also the dominance of blacks over whites (Jordan 1968).

Eventually, the entire slave class was composed of black Africans and, as a result of manumission restrictions, most blacks were enslaved. The creation of this sort of color line, alongside the introduction of the concept of hereditary slavery, was an important step toward the solidification of the idea of race. Notably, it was not until the eighteenth century that negative beliefs about Africans became widespread among the English settlers. Even then, there is ample evidence that blacks and whites continued to fraternize. In 1743, a grand jury in Charleston, South Carolina, denounced "The Too Common Practice of Criminal Conversation with Negro and other Slave Wenches in this Province" (Zinn 2010).

The stories of Mary Peters and Daniel Dowdy elucidate the cruelty and dehumanization that were part and parcel of colonialism and enslavement in the Americas. These two phenomena—colonialism and slavery—have left a strong mark on the way people in the United States view the world. Our contemporary racial worldview is a relic of the systems of human classification that were first used in the context of the colonization of American Indian territories and the enslavement of Africans in the Americas. Although such brutal practices as those described previously are no longer morally or legally permissible, the ideas of racial difference that emerged from those practices persist.

voices

From *Bullwhip Days*

My mother's mistress had three boys—one twenty-one, one nineteen, and one seventeen. One day, Old Mistress had gone away to spend the day. Mother always worked in the house; she didn't work on the farm, in Missouri. While she was alone, the boys came in and threw her down on the floor and tied her down so she couldn't struggle, and one after the other used her as long as they wanted, for the whole afternoon. Mother was sick when her mistress came home. When Old Mistress wanted to know what was the matter with her, she told her what the boys had done. She whipped them, and that's the way I came to be here.

—Mary Peters describing the brutal circumstances of her own conception

I saw slaves sold. I can see that old block now. My cousin Eliza was a pretty girl, really good-looking. Her master was her father. . . . The day they sold her will always be remembered. They stripped her to be bid off and looked at. . . . The man that bought Eliza was from New York. The Negroes had made up 'nuf money to buy her off theyself, but the white folks wouldn't let that happen. There was a man bidding for her that was a Swedeland. He allus bid for the good-looking cullud gals and bought 'em for his own use. He ask the man from New York "What you gonna do with 'er when you git 'er?" The man from New York said, "None of your damn business, but you ain't got money 'nuf to buy 'er."

—Former slave Daniel Dowdy

Source: Mellon 2002, 287, 297.

SLAVERY AND THE IDEAL OF FREEDOM IN THE UNITED STATES

The Declaration of Independence famously begins by stating that all men are created equal. The question was, then, Why were some enslaved? Although the concept of liberty was at the core of the American Revolution, nearly half of the fifty-five men who made up the 1787 Constitutional Convention owned slaves, and most of the rest profited from slavery through their business practices. A prominent member, George Washington (1732–1799), was one of the richest men in the colonies and the owner of many slaves. These men struggled with the contradictions inherent in advocating for freedom in a slaveholding society, yet they were unwilling to outlaw slavery (Feagin 2001).

The writers of the founding documents of the United States were not willing to end slavery in part because most of them profited directly or indirectly from it. The wealth generated by slave labor in the United States had made the American Revolution possible: a significant amount of the funds that financed the American Revolution came from profits from slavery (Feagin 2001). The contradiction between the ideals of freedom and the prevalence of slavery led to justifications of slavery in terms of blacks' alleged racial inferiority. Writings by people such as Thomas Jefferson (1743–1826) validated the belief that people of African descent were less than human. In 1787, Thomas Jefferson wrote in *Notes on Virginia*: "Blacks, whether originally a distinct race or made distinct by time and circumstance, are inferior to whites in the endowment both of body and mind" (Jefferson [1787] 2004, 98–99).

Slavery was an immensely profitable enterprise for a small number of slaveholders. In 1860, the twelve wealthiest counties in the United States could all be found in the Deep South. The profits were not evenly divided: about 7 percent of Southerners owned three-quarters of the 4 million slaves in the South. This concentration of wealth meant that slaveowners constituted a powerful planter class that went to great lengths to protect its property, which included humans: slaveowners saw enslaved Africans and African Americans as an investment they did not want to lose. Additionally, many whites who did not own slaves profited indirectly from the slave system. In the southern United States, slavery was part of the economic and social fabric of society. There were fewer slaves in the northern states, but many Northerners had strong economic ties to slavery insofar as they consumed and manufactured products made on slave plantations. These strong economic interests in slavery meant that the practice was not ended in the United States until the victory of the North in the Civil War (C. Wilson 1996; Feagin 2001).

On January 1, 1863, President Abraham Lincoln (1809–1865) issued the Emancipation Proclamation, which freed the slaves held in the rebel states of the Confederacy. His willingness to issue this proclamation was not hindered by his belief that blacks were inferior to whites. Five years earlier, in 1858, Lincoln had declared: "I am not nor ever have been in favor of the social and political equality of the white and black races: that I am not nor ever have been in favor of making voters of the free negroes, or jurors, or qualifying them to hold office or having them to marry with white people. . . . I as much as any other man am in favor of the superior position being assigned to the white man" (quoted in Feagin 2001, 83–84).

In 1865, the United States finally abolished slavery. Slavery was one of the main reasons for the long and bloody Civil War that had pitted the North against the South. From the perspective of plantation owners in the South, slavery was a profitable institution that ensured the proper place of blacks in society. From the perspective of capitalists in the North, slavery gave southern capitalists an unfair competitive advantage (Feagin 2001). The end of slavery marked the end of an era of extreme exploitation. The racist ideologies that had justified the enslavement of Africans and the massacre and removal of American Indians, however, would endure.

THE INDIAN REMOVAL ACT: THE CONTINUATION OF MANIFEST DESTINY

Justifications for Indian removal often were couched in terms of whites' perception that Native Americans lacked civilization. American Indians would not use the land as well as whites would, the thinking went, and thus did not deserve to live on the land. Similarly, the supposed natural inferiority of Africans was used as a justification for slavery. In the late eighteenth century, these ideas would be used to carry out great injustices. Among them was Indian removal.

The **Indian Removal Act of 1830** enabled the administration of President Andrew Jackson to use military power to displace at least 70,000 Native Americans, killing tens of thousands in the process. Indian removal is often associated with the Cherokee of Georgia, but there were actually many more "**Trails of Tears**," including the forced displacement of the Apalachicola of Florida, the Peoria of Illinois, the Shawnee of Ohio, and a host of other tribes (Littlefield and Parins 2011). These removals violated treaties the United States had made with Native Americans, even though the Indian Removal Act contained a clause guaranteeing that "nothing in this act contained shall be construed as authorizing or directing the violation of any existing treaty between the United States and any of the Indian tribes" (quoted in Cave 2003, 1335). These forced displacements, which continued until 1859, when the Seminoles were removed from Florida, wreaked havoc on indigenous communities (Littlefield and Parins 2011).

During these treacherous journeys, tens of thousands of Native Americans died from disease, cold, starvation, and exhaustion. Approximately 17,000 Cherokee were forcibly removed, and nearly half of those who embarked on the Trail of Tears died in the process. Large numbers of indigenous people died in other removals: about 6,000 of the 40,000 Choctaw did not survive the journey, and only about half of the Creek and the Seminole peoples survived their removals (Churchill 2002).

The justifications for Indian removal were distinct from those used for slavery, as whites tended to see Africans as a vital source of labor. Native Americans, in contrast, were construed as hindering white expansion, and thus the racial ideologies surrounding Native Americans tended to explain and predict their gradual extinction. Notably, this extinction was imagined as occurring through both assimilation (marriage to whites) and natural selection (death from disease). Whereas colonists' ideas about Africans served to justify their hyperexploitation of slaves, whites' ideas about Native Americans aimed to justify those groups' assimilation and gradual extinction, enabling whites to appropriate Indian lands (Berger 2009). Ideas about racial inferiority emerged from the conditions of colonialism and slavery, yet they were reinforced by intellectuals who strove to quantify and measure these concepts.

THE RISE OF SCIENTIFIC RACISM

In the seventeenth century, people in the Americas developed and acted on folk ideas about differences among Africans, Europeans, and Native Americans that were based on daily interactions and the prevailing social order. The slow emergence of the idea of racial difference can be seen in the laws passed and the decisions made by religious leaders. However, the rise of science in the eighteenth century would fundamentally alter this conversation. The question of human difference began to move from the realms of religion and folk ideas to that of science.

European Taxonomies

Before the rise of science, Westerners primarily understood the world in biblical terms. Theology provided explanations for nearly everything. Thus, when Europeans encountered the Americas, they attempted to place these peoples into their understanding of the history of the world, as described in their scriptures. This led to debates over which of the three sons of Noah was the ancestor of the Native

Americans and even over whether Native Americans were fully human. The strong belief in the biblical scriptures carried over into scientific thought, which became the central arena for shaping understandings of race (Smedley 2007).

One of the key features of the rise of science was the emergence of taxonomy. Scholars endeavored to classify all flora and fauna known to them. Soon, scientists began to attempt to classify human beings into types. One of the first efforts to develop a classificatory system for humans appeared in a French journal in 1684. The author, François Bernier (1625–1688), divided humans into four groups: Europeans, Far Easterners, Negroes, and Lapps (people from Lapland in northern Scandanavia). His system used physical traits such as skin color and hair texture, which would later become prominent determinants of racial status, to categorize different groups. Other scholars worked on developing classificatory schemes, but it was not until 1735 that we begin to see the development of a comprehensive system of classification that resembles the modern concept of race (Eze 1997).

In 1735, the Swedish botanist Carolus Linnaeus (1707–1778) proposed that all human beings could be divided into four groups. These four groups are consistent with the modern idea of race in two ways: all of them are still used today, and Linnaeus connected physical traits such as skin color with cultural and moral traits such as "indolence." Linnaeus described these four groups, which correspond to four of the continents, in *Systemae Naturae* in 1735:

> Americanus: *reddish, choleric, and erect; . . . obstinate, merry, free; . . . regulated by customs.*
>
> Asiaticus: *sallow, melancholoy, . . . black hair, dark eyes, . . . haughty, . . . ruled by opinions.*
>
> Africanus: *black, phlegmatic, relaxed; women without shame, . . . crafty, indolent, negligent; governed by caprice.*
>
> Europaenus: *white, sanguine, muscular; inventive; governed by laws.*

Other European men elaborated on this schema. For example, Johann Blumenbach (1752–1840), a German professor of medicine, proposed a classificatory system that divided humans into five varieties that also were associated with geographical origins: Caucasian,

Mongolian, Ethiopian, American, and Malay. Both Blumenbach and Linnaeus endowed Europeans—their own group—with the most admirable qualities. It bears repeating that the idea of race is an idea that was initiated by European men and that, not surprisingly, consistently has been used to explain and justify European superiority. The Scottish philosopher David Hume (1711–1776), for example, asserted in 1748 that whites were the only "species" to have created civilized nations and to have developed arts and sciences. European explanations of white racial superiority espoused by Blumenbach, Linnaeus, and Hume soon reached the Americas, where they were used to explain and justify the enslavement of Africans and the continued takeover of indigenous lands (Eze 1997).

Scientific Racism in the Nineteenth Century

The nineteenth century was an age of emancipation from slavery and liberation from colonial powers; it saw the rise of industrial capitalism and the emergence of **scientific racism**—the use of science or pseudoscience to reproduce and/or justify racial inequalities. For intellectuals in the Americas and Europe, scientific racism was central to most human and social inquiries. Eighteenth-century scientists had developed elaborate systems of human classification. In the nineteenth century, scientists built on these classification systems by developing anthropometrics—tools designed to measure the qualities of humans.

With the publication between 1853 and 1855 of Comte Joseph-Arthur de Gobineau's four volumes entitled *Essays on the Inequality of the Human Races*, it is safe to say that by the mid-nineteenth century, the idea of race was fully in place. Gobineau (1816–1882) divided humanity into three races—white, yellow, and black—and argued that racial differences allow us to explain fundamental differences among people. Gobineau's thinking was in line with that of Herbert Spencer (1820–1903), who contended that the superiority of the European race explained its dominant position. He pointed to the natural inferiority of American Indians as an explanation for their decimation. Spencer's ideas of the "survival of the fittest" would hold great sway for many years to come. Both Spencer and Gobineau used ideas, arguments, and rudimentary evidence from travel accounts to make their claims. Other scientists, however, were developing anthropometric techniques that enabled them to measure differences between people (Gould 1996).

Samuel George Morton (1799–1851), a scientist and physician who worked in Philadelphia, amassed an impressive collection of human skulls. He began his collection in the 1820s and by the time of his death in 1851 had over 1,000 skulls. Morton used these skulls to test his hypothesis that brain size could be used to rank the various human races. In his initial efforts to measure brain size—a study known as **craniometry**—Morton filled the cranial cavity with mustard seed. Later, when he realized that mustard seed did not provide consistent measurements, he switched to lead shots with a one-eighth-inch diameter, which produced less variable results. Using both mustard seeds and lead shots, Morton's measurements consistently showed that Europeans had larger brains than Africans or American Indians. In 1977, evolutionary biologist and scientific historian Stephen Jay Gould re-analyzed Morton's raw data and found several examples of unconscious bias in his work (Gould 1996).

Morton found that American Indians had the smallest skull sizes. Gould explains that Morton arrived at this conclusion because he had included 155 skulls of Peruvian Incas, who had an average brain size of seventy-five cubic inches, yet only included three skulls of Iroquois people, who had, on average, a much larger skull size. In contrast, in the Caucasian group, Morton eliminated the Hindus, who had the smallest skulls, from his sample. Had Morton ensured equal representation from each of the American Indian and Caucasian groups, he would have found no significant differences in skull size.

Stephen Gould explains that skull size is related to body size yet contends that Morton never took body size into account when he measured skulls. As women tend to be smaller than men, women often have smaller skulls. When Morton compared the brain sizes of Africans and Europeans, his African sample was entirely female and his English sample entirely male. Of course, he found that Europeans had larger brains. What is remarkable about Morton's research is not just that it is full of unconscious bias, but also that his biases are consistently in favor of his expectations. Morton set out to prove, through science, that Europeans were superior. All of his miscalculations turned out in favor of his hypothesis. In this sense, Morton was similar to nearly all of his contemporaries: European and American male scientists of the nineteenth century developed a plethora of methods to measure human abilities and consistently found that white men were superior to all other groups.

Paul Broca (1824–1880), a French anthropologist, built on the work of Samuel Morton to develop more elaborate techniques to measure humans. Broca believed strongly that there was a direct correlation between brain size and intelligence and spent much of his career measuring the brains of dead people. Broca eventually ran into trouble with his arguments when he discovered, by measuring the brains of eminent scholars who had passed on, that many people considered to be highly intelligent turned out to have small brains. Broca, however, accounted for those anomalies by asserting that they died very old or that their brains had not been properly preserved. When a study of criminal brains revealed that criminals had abnormally large brains, Broca argued that their sudden death by execution meant that their brains did not atrophy, as did those of people who died of natural causes. Broca eventually went on to measure other characteristics of brains and bodies; however, his scientific measurements always showed what he set out to prove: that Europeans were superior to other groups (Gould 1996).

From Taxonomy and Skull Measurement to Intelligence Testing in the Twentieth Century

When nineteenth-century scientists compared the skulls of blacks to those of whites, they set out to use science to prove what they thought they already knew: that the white race was superior to all others. Nineteenth-century craniometry provided the first opportunity for scientists to bring massive amounts of data to bear on their ideas of human hierarchy. These data provided "scientific" proof of white superiority. Eventually, however, craniometry lost its appeal, and scientists looked for new ways to measure human difference and prove European supremacy. These new methods revolved around a hereditarian theory of intelligence. Rather than measuring brain size to infer intelligence, scientists endeavored to measure intelligence directly (Gould 1996).

In the United States **intelligence testing**—the attempt to quantify intellectual ability using scientific measures—became popular in the early twentieth century. Such tests were used in efforts to demonstrate the alleged superiority of not only Europeans and their descendants but particular groups of Europeans. The sudden popularity of these tests is revealing, as it coincided with the arrival of large numbers of immigrants from southern and eastern Europe (Gould 1996; Brodkin 1998).

Intelligence tests were not originally designed to find out which races were the most intellectually fit. Instead, the testing of mental ability was created to identify children who needed extra help in school. Alfred Binet (1857–1911), director of the psychology laboratory at the

Sorbonne in Paris, dedicated much of his scholarly career to the development of ways to measure children's intellectual ability with the goal of finding ways to enhance their educational experience. It was only when Binet's test was taken to the United States that it began to be used to determine which groups were innately superior or inferior. One of the first psychologists to use this test was H. H. Goddard (1866–1957), who adapted it for use in the Vineland Training School for Feeble-Minded Boys and Girls. Goddard firmly believed that feeblemindedness was inherited, attributing intelligence to a single gene. To provide evidence for his beliefs, Goddard took Binet's test to Ellis Island, where he administered the exam to arriving immigrants. He found that many received a low score, and instead of questioning the conditions under which he performed the exam—on recently arrived migrants who barely spoke English and had never before seen a test—he concluded that immigrants were of low intelligence and that immigration had to be curtailed. Later in his career, Goddard conceded that perhaps feeblemindedness could be cured through education (Gould 1996).

The next prominent psychologist to use intelligence testing was Lewis Terman (1877–1956), a professor of psychology at Stanford University. Terman modified the Binet test and developed the Stanford-Binet intelligence test, the precursor of the standardized tests we use today. Terman endeavored to standardize the test such that the average person would score 100. This number should sound familiar, as it is still used today as the mean for IQ—the intelligence quotient. Terman's colleague R. M. Yerkes (1876–1956) carried on Terman's work and developed the Army Mental Tests, which were designed to measure innate intelligence. Yerkes succeeded in convincing the U.S. Army to allow him to administer the tests to all of its recruits. This massive sample of over a million respondents gave significant quantitative weight to the emerging field of intelligence testing (Gould 1996).

Stephen Gould argues that the primary error in intelligence testing is that of reification—making intelligence into a scientific concept by measuring it. It is common knowledge that some people know more facts and trivia than others, that some are more quick-witted than others, that some can calculate sums in their heads faster than others, and that some are more eloquent in speech and writing than others. Intelligence tests attempt to take this wide range of abilities and measure them. The score on these tests is named an "intelligence quotient," or IQ. Gould contends that these tests are flawed and do not meet their stated goal of actually measuring intelligence. Moreover, instead of promoting the idea that each of these skills can be learned and nurtured, some social scientists have insisted that these talents are innate and passed on from generation to generation. Perhaps the ugliest manifestation of this idea came to fruition with the eugenics movement of the early twentieth century, during which time about 60,000 people were forcibly sterilized in the United States on the basis of their purported unfitness (M. Jacobson 1998).

The **eugenics** movement, which had its heyday from about 1900 to 1930, promoted the idea that not only intelligence but also alcoholism, laziness, crime, poverty, and other moral and cultural traits could be inherited. Based on this notion, eugenicists advocated the selective breeding of Americans and the sterilization of the biologically unfit as a way of creating a superior breed of people. During this period, many Americans believed that the American population was in decline as a result of immigration and the high fertility of poor people (Lindsay 1998).

One of the main proponents of eugenics was Madison Grant (1865–1937), a lawyer, historian, and physical anthropologist who was the author of *The Passing of the Great Race*. In much of his work, Madison Grant put forward the idea that Europe could be divided into three races: "Nordics," "Alpines," and "Mediterraneans." He forcefully argued that Nordics were the most fit of the three and that measures should be taken to ensure their racial purity and survival. His ideas made it into the mainstream both through his book and through his position as chairman of the U.S. Committee on Selective Immigration, which advocated for a reduction in the numbers of Alpines and Mediterraneans admitted into the United States. The views of Madison Grant and other eugenicists played an important role in the development of policy as well as court decisions in the 1920s, both through placing limits on the immigration of "undesirable" groups and through denying access to citizenship to non-whites (M. Jacobson 1998).

CONCLUSION AND DISCUSSION

The brutal, troubled history of the idea of race clearly demonstrates the power of ideologies about human difference. The idea that the world's population can be divided into discrete racial groups is a product of a specific series of events: colonialism, slavery, and the rise of scientific racism. Because Europeans wished to take land from indigenous peoples in the Americas and to extract labor from Africans, they developed ideologies of inferiority as justification.

Alongside this large-scale theft of land and exploitation of labor, science began to emerge as a field of study concerned largely with the classification of all objects and species into specific groups. Scientists rushed to develop taxonomies of flora and fauna, including classifications of humans. Europeans who proposed these classifications put their own group at the top of the hierarchy.

This subjective (and overt) bias of Europeans continued with the development of anthropometric and other measurement techniques in the nineteenth century. European scientists measured human skulls, brains, and every other imaginable part of the human body and arrived at the same conclusion: Europeans are superior. This recounting of history offers a revealing look at not only the past but also the present. We cannot simply look at the past and point fingers at those "racists" of yesteryear. Instead, we should also be compelled to explore the assumptions and ideologies that govern our behavior today.

THINKING ABOUT **RACIAL JUSTICE**

IN THIS CHAPTER, we have seen that the idea of race was created to justify mass genocide and brutal exploitation. We have also seen that there is as much or more diversity and genetic difference within any racial group as there is across racial groups. For many people, however, race is an important part of one's identity. How does what you learned in this chapter affect the way you think of yourself? Write a 500-word essay that provides (1) what your racial identity is and how you usually think of yourself; (2) evidence that race is a social construction and not a biological reality; (3) how this evidence affects how you think of your own racial identity; and (4) a reflection on how this knowledge might be used in the pursuit of racial justice.

Key Terms

Check Your Understanding

OBJECTIVE 1.1

Define race and racism in the context of the history of the idea of race.

- *Race* refers to a group of people who share physical and cultural traits as well as a common ancestry.
- Race is a social construction and has no biological basis.
- *Racism* refers to the belief that some races are superior to others, as well as the practice of subordinating races believed to be inferior.

Q Why do sociologists argue that race is a social construction?

OBJECTIVE 1.2

Explain how race is distinct from previous ways of thinking about human difference.

- There are historical precedents to the idea of race, including the Spanish Inquisition and the subjugation of the Irish by the English.
- Slavery existed long before the invention of the idea of race.
- When the Spanish colonists arrived in the Americas, they displayed extreme cruelty to the native people of the Americas.
- African slaves were brought to the Americas to meet labor needs.
- The idea of race emerged to justify slavery and colonization.

Q When was the idea of race invented? Why do sociologists argue that race is a historical construction?

OBJECTIVE 1.3

Describe the effects of The Indian Removal Act on Native Americans.

- The Indian Removal Act of 1830 resulted in the death of tens of thousands of Native Americans as a result of forced displacements.

Q How and why were the justifications for Indian removal distinct from those used for slavery?

OBJECTIVE 1.4

Explain how slavery influenced the writing of the U.S. Constitution.

- Although the Declaration of Independence declares that "all men are created equal," nearly half of the authors were slaveowners.

- Slavery was not abolished in the United States until 1865.

Q Why were slavery and freedom in tension during the writing of the Declaration of Independence?

OBJECTIVE 1.5

Describe the role that early science played in the propagation of racism.

- The idea of race was originally based on simple taxonomies. However, as science developed, scientists created more complex explanations of the differences among racial groups.
- In the nineteenth century, scientists measured skulls to assess differences among racial groups.
- In the early twentieth century, scientific racism continued. In an attempt to scientifically demonstrate the superiority of the white race, scientists used intelligence testing, and many promoted eugenics.

Q How did bias influence early scientific measurements of various racial groups?

Critical Thinking

1. Why is it important to clarify that the idea of race is a modern invention?
2. Can you imagine a world in which racial classifications had no importance? Why or why not?
3. What are today's prevailing racial ideologies in the United States? In what ways do those ideologies work to justify the current racial hierarchy?
4. How and why do racial ideologies related to Native Americans and African Americans differ?
5. What biases toward race might be present in today's sciences and social sciences?

2

RACISMS, RACIAL IDEOLOGIES, AND SOCIOLOGICAL THEORIES OF RACISM

CHAPTER OUTLINE

LEARNING OBJECTIVES

2.1 Explain how racism is connected to racial inequality.

2.2 Describe how systemic and structural racism create racial disparities.

2.3 Appraise various racial ideologies, and evaluate how racism has changed since the early twentieth century.

2.4 Evaluate and critique racial formation theory.

2.5 Examine the indigenous perspective on racism in the contemporary United States.

2.6 Examine how race, class, and gender oppression work together.

2.7 Evaluate the white privilege perspective.

Racial inequality is pervasive in the contemporary United States. We see it in the criminal justice system, where blacks and Latinos are several times more likely to go to prison than whites. We can find racial inequality in employment as well: audit studies have shown that blacks are less likely than whites to be interviewed and, once interviewed, to get a job. Once blacks have jobs, they are less likely to get promoted. Black business owners have more trouble getting contracts. In education, the picture is equally bleak. Many schools in the United States are racially segregated, and the quality of education is lower at primarily black and Latino schools. Within schools, white students are given preferential treatment. When white parents visit schools, they get more attention from staff members, and teachers are more likely to recommend white students for gifted programs. Sociologists and other researchers have carried out study upon study demonstrating such inequality. Yet how do we explain it?

This is where **sociological theories of racism** come into play; they are lenses that help make sense of patterns such as the over-representation of African Americans in the criminal justice system. Sociologists use evidence from their studies to develop explanations, known as theories, for how racial inequality is created and reproduced.

Before we begin an examination of these theories, what do you think? How would you explain the racial disparities in the criminal justice system, for example? Do you think blacks commit more crimes? Do you think police officers spend more time policing black communities? Do you think police officers are biased against African Americans? All of these questions can be translated into hypotheses that can be tested through scientific studies. First, let's look at how racism can be the basis of an explanation for racial inequality.

RACIAL PREJUDICE, DISCRIMINATION, AND INSTITUTIONAL RACISM

How is racism connected to racial inequality? Racism includes both prejudice and discrimination. Racial **prejudice** refers to racially biased beliefs, and racial **discrimination** involves practices or actions that reproduce racial inequality. For example, an employer can think African Americans are less competent than whites—this belief constitutes racial prejudice. When that employer decides to hire a white person instead of an equally qualified black person, that decision may be considered racial discrimination. Both prejudice and discrimination are widespread in U.S. society.

In one survey, Joe Feagin (2001) found that three-quarters of whites agreed with prejudicial statements about blacks, such as "blacks have less native intelligence" than whites (109). Eduardo Bonilla-Silva (2013) found that most whites use color-blind discourses that reproduce and justify racial inequality. In 1995, researchers conducted a study in which they asked participants to close their eyes for a second and imagine a drug user. Fully 95 percent of respondents reported imagining a black drug user (Alexander 2010). The reality is that African Americans account for only 15 percent of drug users in the United States and are just as likely as whites to use drugs. However, Americans have an unconscious bias against blacks and imagine them to be more likely than other groups to use drugs (Alexander 2010). These and other studies show the widespread nature of racial prejudice.

Many Americans, even those who do not believe they are racially prejudiced, have implicit biases that operate at the level of the subconscious. It is hard to avoid these biases because of the barrage of racialized messages we receive in the media and through our personal networks. Racial prejudice and implicit biases inevitably lead to racial discrimination. (Curious about your own implicit bias? Take the Implicit Association Test at https://implicit.harvard.edu/implicit/.)

In this chapter, we will focus on theories of race and racism. There is another set of scholars whose work focuses more on ethnicity, often through the lens of **assimilation**—understood as the incorporation of ethnic minority groups into the mainstream. This body of work considers how cultural characteristics, the labor market, and U.S. immigration policies shape the incorporation patterns of ethnic minorities (Portes and Rumbaut 2006). These scholars explain ethnic minority incorporation primarily as the result of the ethnic features and traits of a group and that group's unique "context of reception" (Portes and Rumbaut 2006; Valdez 2011).

As Howard Winant (2000) explains in an article on race theory, there are clear limits to approaches that focus on ethnicity. These include obstacles to integration and the undesirability of assimilation. As we will see in this chapter, approaches that place race and racism at the center of their analyses allow us to perceive these obstacles more clearly and to understand how and why racial hierarchies persist.

Assimilation theories can be further distinguished from race theories in that they tend to focus on group-level factors, whereas race theories look primarily at the individual or the social structure. Most theories of race and racism emphasize the social structure. However, as we will see in the next section, understandings of racial discrimination at the individual level continue to be crucial.

Individual Racism

Discrimination can occur at the individual level when one person discriminates against another. Audit studies have consistently shown that blacks are less likely to be interviewed for jobs than whites, and that blacks and Latinos face housing discrimination on a regular basis (Feagin 2001). Racially discriminatory actions by individuals such as not calling back an interviewee for a job because of his race or telling a person on the phone that the apartment is taken because he or she has a Spanish accent constitute **individual racism**. Individual acts of racial discrimination and bigotry are commonplace in our society and help to reproduce racial inequalities.

How widespread is individual racism? Researchers have consistently found that racial discrimination is pervasive. One study of Department of Defense employees revealed that nearly half of the black employees had heard racist jokes in the previous year. Another survey conducted by Feagin and McKinney (2003) revealed that 80 percent of black respondents had encountered racial hostility in public places. One African American secretary detailed the consequences of constant discrimination as follows: "I had to see several doctors because of the discrimination, and I went through a lot of stress. And, then, my blood pressure . . . went on the rise" (82). This woman, like many other African Americans interviewed in this study, displayed high levels of stress as a result of her mistreatment in the workplace and consequently developed health issues.

It is remarkable that individual racism is widespread in a society that usually condemns overt acts of racism. If a television announcer were to make a racially charged or overtly racist statement such as "African Americans are inherently more violent than whites," we can be sure that the following day, critics would come from all over to condemn the racist statement. If racial discrimination is frowned upon, how can it be so widespread?

One way that individual racism persists, even in a society that decries racism, is through **racial microagressions**—daily, commonplace insults and racial slights that cumulatively affect the psychological well-being of people of color. The consequences of these microaggressions can be severe, and studies of African Americans, Latinos, and Asians have uncovered the continued prevalence of microaggressions. One recent study of African Americans on college campuses, for example, found that white students and professors consistently doubted the academic potential of African Americans. One black student was presumed to have cheated after getting an "A" on a difficult math quiz. Another black student found that people assumed his scholarship was for sports, when in fact it was for his academic achievements. These students reported that the cumulative effect of these slights was to make them tired, discouraged, and frustrated—especially since they had expected more from their professors and peers (Solorzano, Ceja, and Yosso 2000).

African Americans are not the only group to experience microaggressions. In a study of Asian Americans' experiences of discrimination, Derald Wing Sue and his colleagues found that Asian Americans experienced a wide variety of microaggressions, ranging from the assumption of foreignness to exoticization of Asian women to invisibility. For example, Asian Americans reported that white Americans consistently asked them questions such as "Where are you from?" or made comments such as "You speak good English," when the only indication that they might not be from the United States was their Asian appearance. Other Asian Americans pointed out that people presumed they were good at math, and that men presumed Asian women would be submissive lovers. Asian Americans also reported that people presumed that they didn't face discrimination. The Asian Americans in this study recounted that the constant barrage of microaggressions angered them, but that they also felt disempowered to respond, as any single event could seem inconsequential by itself (D. Sue, Bucceri, Lin, Nadal, and Torino 2007).

Kevin Nadal and his colleagues conducted a study of multiracial people's experiences of microaggressions and found them to be pervasive (Nadal et al. 2011). These studies of both Asian Americans and multiracial individuals reveal that well-intentioned whites often deliver microaggressions because of their insensitivity toward and ignorance about non-whites. This can be seen, for example, when a white person speaks Japanese to a Chinese American or tells a biracial woman with a black mother and a white father that being half-white makes it easier to get along with her. In the first instance, the white person may be trying to show a cultural interest in Asian people, although her act simultaneously tries to erase the differences between Japanese and Chinese people and reasserts the presumed foreignness of Asian Americans. In the second instance, this assertion reinforces white supremacy by implying that the biracial woman is better than other blacks because she has a white parent.

Microaggressions and other forms of individual racism continue to pose a problem on college campuses. We might expect college

voices

Microaggressions

Individuals who have had the following experiences and consider them to be racial microaggressions posted these reports on the website microaggressions.com. How do you feel as you read these? What would you say if you overheard such a comment? What would you say if someone directed one of these comments at you?

- Often when I have dinner at people's houses, they ask me if I would prefer chopsticks, regardless of the meal!
- I am a registered nurse and always get told that I speak English so well. I was born in Australia and I am of Filipino background. I don't think about my appearance until a patient or their family member points it out and they are quite amazed/baffled that someone who appears Asian "speaks so well" and could be considered a "real Australian."
- I always get asked to be an interpreter for patients who are not native English speakers, specifically for those of Asian background. Because I am of Asian background as well, there is this assumption that I speak every language in Asia or that there is only one language/country in Asia. Unbelievable.
- "Sorry, that must be my black coming out." [Said by] my biracial friend (African American and Mexican). Whenever she does or says something negative she blames it on the "Black" side of her. Makes me feel angry, belittled, resentful.

The presumption that Asian Americans use chopsticks at every meal is based on an idea of inherent cultural differences. We don't see these same presumptions applied to third-generation Italian Americans or Irish Americans.

voices *continued.*

Microaggressions

- I express that my brother attends a private university. Immediately a girl in the car responds in a very sure voice "Oh, he plays football?" This is the second time this has happened. As if a young black male can only attend a prestigious private college on a football scholarship.
- "You're really un-intimidating for a black guy." Said by white male. I am a freshman in college. Made me feel as though I should be intimidating because I'm black.
- Substitute teacher: Quiet down! You're acting like a bunch of wild Indians!
- At my school, the Introduction to Native Americans class, which covers the history of Native Americans from pre-Contact to present day, does not count towards the United States History general education requirement.
- Oh, but you're Latin, so you must love the heat! While discussing the summer weather. I'm from Bogotá—the average temperature is 60°F. I feel like nobody in the States bothers to understand that Latinos are not just one monolithic entity.

Source: microaggressions.com.

campuses to be relatively free of racial tensions—after all, they are filled with youth, who tend to be open-minded, and staff, teachers, and administrators encourage students to respect diversity and celebrate difference. However, studies have consistently found that individual acts of bigotry are commonplace on college campuses (Harper and Hurtado 2007). In a recent study (Harper et al. 2011), higher education researchers interviewed fifty-two African American male resident assistants (RAs) on five college campuses and found that many of the participants reported that supervisors and fellow students consistently doubted their competence and stereotyped them as potential thugs or gangsters. The frequency of individual acts of racism on college campuses has led a number of scholars to argue that many primarily white campuses have hostile climates that are not conducive to learning for non-white students (Harper and Hurtado 2007).

Institutional Racism

Individual racism can be distinguished from **institutional racism**—the policies, laws, and institutions that reproduce racial inequalities

(Ture and Hamilton 1967). Understanding the framework of institutional racism is essential for understanding racism in the United States, as racism amounts to more than individual acts of discrimination. An individual police officer, for example, may have prejudicial beliefs that blacks are more likely to be violent than whites. Based on this prejudice, the officer may be more likely to racially discriminate against blacks and more likely to use more physical force against blacks. What do we call it, though, when this happens over and over again? Almost all victims of police brutality are black or Latino—97 percent, according to one study (Feagin 2001). How do we explain this?

Have individual prejudices, biases, and acts of discrimination alone created a penal system that disproportionately affects black men? In overwhelmingly black neighborhoods in Washington, D.C. and Chicago, nearly three-quarters of black men have been incarcerated. In some states, black men go to jail on drug charges at fifty times the rate of white men. In seven states, blacks constitute over 80 percent of drug offenders sent to prison (Alexander 2010). These extraordinary disparities cannot be explained by individual acts of discrimination alone.

Instead, it makes sense to argue that racial discrimination has become institutionalized in the criminal justice system. This is because racial discrimination happens at every single level of this system. The laws are written in ways that discriminate against blacks—the disparities in sentences for possession of crack and possession of cocaine are one example. Police officers are consistently more likely to pull over and arrest black men than they are white men. Blacks are more likely to get harsher sentences or even the death penalty. When we look at the system as a whole and see that the criminal justice apparatus more harshly affects blacks than whites, and when we can see that racial discrimination is consistent and systematic, we can say that the criminal justice system is a prime example of institutional racism. Institutional racism also exists in other institutions, including the educational system, housing, and corporations.

SYSTEMIC AND STRUCTURAL RACISM

Since the 1960s and 1970s, many thinkers have enhanced Hamilton and Ture's conceptual models and developed more complex and integrative ways of thinking about institutional racism. In this section, we explore two of these approaches: systemic and structural racism.

Systemic Racism

Sociologist Joe Feagin defines **systemic racism** as "a diverse assortment of racist practices; the unjustly gained economic and political power of whites; the continuing resource inequalities; and the white-racist ideologies, attitudes, and institutions created to preserve white advantage and power" (2001, 16). He explains that systemic racism encompasses daily microaggressions, deep-seated inequalities, and anti-black ideologies. Taken together, systemic racism includes:

- Patterns of unjust impoverishment of non-whites
- Vested group interests of whites to maintain racism
- Omnipresent and routinized discrimination against non-whites
- The rationalization of racial oppression
- An imbalance of power whereby whites are able to reproduce inequality through control of major political and economic resources

Systemic racism theory gives primacy to history: Feagin explains that systemic racism exists because of the history of the United States as a slaveholding nation. Racial oppression was foundational to and is deeply ingrained in our nation's history. The legal system of the United States—based on the Constitution and Supreme Court cases—is rife with examples of entrenched racism. Systemic racism in history and the present day has created a "white racial frame" that shapes individuals and institutions in the United States. Feagin emphasizes that racism and racial inequality were created by whites and continue to be perpetuated by white individuals and white-owned institutions (2001).

The unjust enrichment of whites through slavery and privileged access to resources since the beginning of the United States is at the core of an understanding of systemic racism. This unjust enrichment on the one hand has led to unjust impoverishment of African Americans. Past and continuing discrimination has created a situation in which African Americans have been denied resources many whites have come to take for granted, including good jobs, great schools, and nice neighborhoods (Feagin and McKinney 2003; Feagin 2001). The pervasiveness of everyday acts of discrimination, combined with a legacy of unequal distribution of resources throughout every aspect of U.S. society, constitutes systemic racism.

Structural Racism

Proponents of the idea of **structural racism** take a slightly different approach in their analysis of racial inequality. As we have seen, institutional racism focuses on practices within institutions, and systemic racism focuses on accumulated acts of racism across history and throughout one's lifetime. Structural racism differs by pointing to inter-institutional interactions across time and space. For example, racial inequality in housing leads to racial inequality in schooling, which in turns leads to racial inequality in the labor market. Across generations, this chain of events becomes a cycle, because parents who are less well-positioned in the labor market cannot afford housing in the better neighborhoods, which means that their children will be less likely to attend better schools. A structural understanding of racism underscores the "structural relationships that produce racialized outcomes" (powell 2008, 798). This emphasis on the relationships among structures of institutional inequality provides new insights into how racial inequality is reproduced across generations.

Eduardo Bonilla-Silva proposes the concept of "racialized social systems." By this, he means "societies in which economic, political, social, and ideological levels are partially structured by the placement of actors in racial categories" (1997, 469). Bonilla-Silva places particular emphasis on racial hierarchies and points to how these hierarchies influence all social relations. Societies that have racialized social systems differentially allocate "economic, political, social, and even psychological rewards to groups along racial lines" (442). Bonilla-Silva's framework reflects a structural racism perspective because he focuses on structures of inequality, hierarchies, and social relations and practices that reproduce and justify racial disparities.

Melvin Oliver and Thomas Shapiro (2006) offer a keen analysis of the role of structural racism in reproducing wealth inequalities. Today, whites have twenty times the wealth of African Americans and eighteen times the wealth of Latinos (Kochhar, Fry, and Taylor 2011). Oliver and Shapiro (2006) explain that wealth inequality "has been structured over many generations through the same systemic barriers that have hampered blacks throughout their history in American society: slavery, Jim Crow, so-called de jure discrimination, and institutionalized racism" (12–13). Oliver and Shapiro (2006) point to three instances of structural inequalities that work together: (1) blacks' transition from slavery to freedom without a material base, (2) the suburbanization of whites and the ghettoization of blacks, and (3) contemporary institutional racism in the lending and real estate markets. These three inequalities work together to create a situation in which

FIGURE 2-1

MEDIAN NET WORTH OF WHITE, HISPANIC, AND BLACK HOUSEHOLDS, 2009

Whites have twenty times the wealth of blacks.

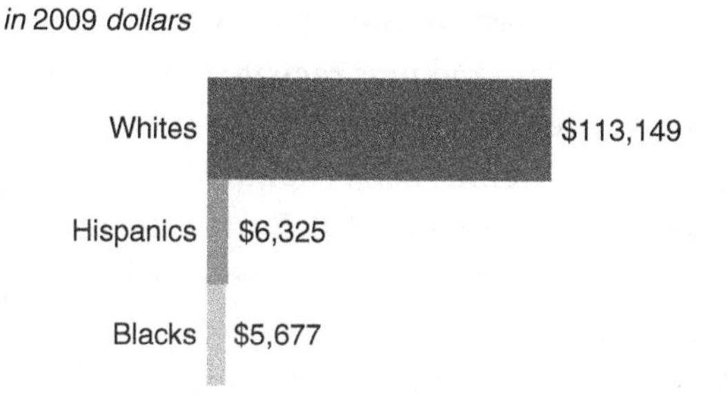

Source: Kochhar, Fry, and Taylor (2011); based on Pew Research Center Data.

blacks and Latinos have, on average, one-twentieth the wealth of whites (Figure 2-1).

Oliver and Shapiro (2006) explain how laws and policies, even those that do not mention race, can still work to enhance racial inequality. Our tax policies provide one example. In the United States, capital gains are taxed at a lower rate than income, and tax deductions are offered for home mortgages. These policies are ostensibly designed to help the middle class and encourage economic growth. However, they provide many more advantages to whites than to blacks because blacks rarely have capital gains income, are less likely to own a home, and, when they do own a home, have houses that are worth less than whites (Shapiro 2004). These state policies work to enhance the wealth gap between blacks and whites by providing advantages to those who are already wealthier, and who are more likely to be white.

RACIAL IDEOLOGIES

Whereas prejudice involves individual beliefs, an ideology involves a set of principles and ideas that embodies the interests of a societal group. A **racial ideology**, then, is a set of principles and ideas that (1) divides people into different racial groups and (2) serves the interests of one group. Ideologies are usually created by the dominant group and reflect the interests of that group. Both historically and today, the dominant racial group in the United States includes whites (Feagin 2001). Our individual prejudices and acts of discrimination are directly related to our acceptance (conscious or unconscious) of racial ideologies.

Many scholars make a distinction between old racism—which permitted the internment of the Japanese and the enslavement of Africans, for example—and **new racism**. In this new ideology, it is no longer acceptable to make overtly racist statements, yet racial inequality persists (P. Collins 2004; Bonilla-Silva 2013; Logan 2011; Harvey Wingfield and Feagin 2010). Racism did not disappear with the dismantling of slavery and **Jim Crow laws**, nor did the civil rights era mark the end of racism.

Racial inequality persists today both because of our history and because of ongoing practices of discrimination and exclusion. The new racism is an outgrowth of past racial inequality that continues to be propagated today. New racism relies on mass media and popular beliefs to "help manufacture the consent that makes the new racism appear to be natural, normal, and inevitable" (P. Collins 2004, 34). Racial inequality in the United States has become naturalized. We have come to think of it as normal that African American men are overrepresented among prisoners and that white men are overrepresented among the elite, even though we would never accept laws that overtly discriminate against African Americans.

In the United States, most people do not consider themselves to be racist, and we have laws in place that prevent overt acts of discrimination. Despite this massive change in attitudes and laws over the past century, racial inequality persists. African Americans have, on average, a mere 10 percent of the wealth that whites have (Oliver and Shapiro 2006). African American men are seven times more likely than white men to go to prison (Feagin 2001). On almost any measure, blacks and Latinos are doing worse socially and economically than whites in the United States (Logan 2011). How do we explain the persistence of racial inequality despite the social stigma on being a racist? One way is by looking at how different forms of racism operate. This allows us to see how some forms of racism are more acceptable than others, even though all racial ideologies serve the same purpose: to explain, justify, and normalize racial inequality and injustice.

Biological Racism

Biological racism is the idea that whites are genetically superior to non-whites. This idea has its origins in the scientific racism of the nineteenth century, which set out to prove whites' superior innate intelligence. In the 1920s, the American lawyer Madison Grant argued that Nordics were the "master race" and that the United States should pass laws banning interracial marriages and ensuring the sterilization of inferior races. In the twenty-first century, it would be difficult to find people who openly advocate for the sterilization of blacks because of their biological inferiority. Nevertheless, these ideas have not completely disappeared.

One of the most prominent examples of biological racism in recent decades is a 1994 book called *The Bell Curve*. In this book, Richard Herrnstein and Charles Murray argue that intelligence is quantifiable. They measured what they perceived to be IQ through intelligence testing and found differences in intelligence across racial groups. For Herrnstein and Murray, as for a century of intelligence testers before them, the fact that blacks scored lower on intelligence tests than whites provided support for the idea that blacks are innately inferior to whites. More recently, Frank Miele and Vincent Sarich argued in their 2004 book, *Race: The Reality of Human Differences*, that races are a biological reality and that there are measurable intellectual differences among racial groups. The publication of *The Bell Curve*, *Race: The Reality of Human Differences*, and other books and articles in this vein provide evidence of the persistence of the belief that whites are genetically or biologically superior to non-whites. However, most academics reject these views, and few Americans openly express such opinions in public spaces today. Biological racism still exists, but it is waning and is subject to virulent criticism whenever expressed.

Cultural Racism

Cultural racism is a way of thinking that attributes disadvantaged racial groups' lack of prosperity to their behavior and culture, rather than to structural factors. Unlike biological racism, which claims that some races are inferior because of lower intelligence, cultural racism is the standpoint that a particular culture—African American or Latino culture, for example—inhibits success.

The seed for many of the ideas inherent in cultural racism were planted in 1965 with the publication of a report by the American politician Daniel Patrick Moynihan (1927–2003). The document, which has come to be known as the Moynihan Report, acknowledged the pervasiveness of poverty in the black community yet pointed to the breakdown of the black family as one of the principal causes of this poverty. Moynihan argued that the history of slavery and racism had had detrimental consequences for the black family. He made the gendered argument that the central problem of black America was that there were too many single black mothers who were incapable of raising children on their own. His proposed solution to black poverty was that black men be restored to their rightful place as breadwinners and heads of families. For Moynihan, the solution to black poverty was to "fix" black families. This stance—which ignores structural factors such as discriminatory employment policies and practices—is typical of cultural racism. The cultural racism argument points to the behavioral patterns of African Americans as the primary cause of their poverty. This perspective continues to be propagated today when pundits blame blacks' educational failures on dysfunctional families or parenting styles rather than on failing schools and pervasive poverty.

Cultural racism also takes another form: teachers perceive children who invoke African American language and style as less intelligent than those who conform to dominant culture. Ann Arnett Ferguson (2001) found in her research in an elementary school that black students were more likely to get into trouble at school because of the way teachers and school administrators responded to their body language, oral expressiveness, manners, and styles. She found that children who conformed to white, middle-class cultural norms were less likely to get into trouble and more likely to do well in school, and that the use of "Black English" or African American forms of expressiveness in school was grounds for punishment. Ferguson also argues that when children are white or behave in a white middle-class way, they are perceived to be self-disciplined and good, while children who "behave black" are perceived as troublemakers. Ferguson's findings point to the persistence of cultural racism: whereas white, middle-class children are rewarded for behaving in school as they and their parents do at home, working-class and poor black children are punished for speaking and acting as their parents do. When a teacher tells a child who is speaking in the Black English that his mother taught him that he is not talking properly, she is also telling him that his mother does not speak properly.

Cultural racism also affects other racialized groups in the United States. Latinas are often portrayed as "pregnant breeders" who plan to have "anchor babies" in the United States (Hondagneu-Sotelo 1995). Asians feel the brunt of the "model minority" stereotype, and Native Americans are perceived alternatively as "savages" or "wise men." The racialized sterotypes of Native Americans, Asian Americans, and Latinos and Latinas are discussed further in Chapter Four.

Color-Blind Racism

Sociologist Eduardo Bonilla-Silva offers a framework for understanding how widespread racial inequality exists even though no one wants to be called a racist. In his work, Bonilla-Silva (2013) presents the notion of **color-blind racism**, a racial ideology that explains contemporary racial inequality as the outcome of nonracial dynamics, such as market dynamics, naturally occurring phenomena, and non-whites' supposed cultural limitations. This racial ideology ignores or marginalizes people of color's distinctive needs, experiences, and identities. Bonilla-Silva argues that although race is a social construction, the idea of race is real in a social sense and has produced a racial structure that systematically privileges whites.

How is it possible to have widespread racial inequality when most whites claim there is no racism and that they are not racist? Bonilla-Silva offers an explanation in his book *Racism Without Racists* (2013). His research team interviewed whites and asked them questions about their views on race in the United States. He found that whites use several "frames" of color-blind racism to justify and reproduce racial inequality.

One frame Bonilla-Silva mentions is **abstract liberalism**. This frame involves using liberal ideas such as equality of opportunity or freedom of choice to explain or justify racial inequality. For example, when presented with the fact that African Americans still live in underserved, poorer neighborhoods than whites do, a person using this frame would explain this inequality by saying that people live in such neighborhoods because they choose to do so. Nothing prevents them from leaving, so their situation is not because of racism, but because of individual choices. This response, however, ignores the structural factors that both have created segregation and continue to perpetuate it. Similarly, the **naturalization** frame permits people to explain racial phenomena as if they were natural. The explanation for segregation would be that people like to be around others who are like them. Again, segregation is not because of structural factors, but because it's normal or natural.

The aforementioned frames represent explanations that whites consistently offered in interviews about their racial attitudes. In addition, Bonilla-Silva found that whites used specific **rhetorical strategies**, or ways of expressing ideas, to justify their own racial prejudices and discriminatory actions. These rhetorical strategies permit whites to reproduce racism without being labeled as racists. Bonilla-Silva argues that because post–civil rights racial norms do not permit the open expression of racial views, whites have developed concealed ways of voicing them.

As Bonilla-Silva found, one common rhetorical strategy is to preface discriminatory claims with "I am not a racist, but . . . ." Alternatively, whites would say, "Some of my best friends are black, but . . . ." For example, when asked if they would mind if their daughter married a black man, a white person would respond, "I am not a racist, but I don't think interracial marriages work." Or they might use another rhetorical strategy called projection, according to which they would respond: "I don't mind if my daughter marries a black man, but you have to think about the children." These rhetorical strategies allow whites to express discriminatory or prejudiced ideas without seeming racist.

In his research, Bonilla-Silva found that color-blind racial ideology is used in everyday speech patterns to *justify* racial inequality. It influences rhetorical strategies, stories, and etiquette that allow whites to explain why we have racial inequality even though most people are not racist. In addition to justifying racial inequality, color-blind racism *reproduces* racial inequality by permitting people to engage in discriminatory actions without being labeled as racists.

RACIAL FORMATION

Whereas analyses of structural and systemic racism focus on racism itself, Michael Omi and Howard Winant consider racial meanings (1994). They introduce the concept of **racial formation** to help us understand how racial dynamics work in the United States. Omi and Winant define racial formation as "the sociohistorical process by which racial categories are created, inhabited, transformed, and destroyed," and as a "process or historically situated project" (56). They argue that the state (i.e., national government) is the primary site where race is constructed and contested. According to this theory, the state can reproduce or alleviate racial inequality through its institutions and policies. Omi and Winant explore "how concepts of race are created and changed" and argue that "concepts of race structure both state and civil society" (vii).

When Omi and Winant's book was first published in 1986, it was a welcome change from earlier works that studied race as some variation of ethnicity, class, or nation. Instead, Omi and Winant presented race as a topic worthy of study in itself. Their groundbreaking work has greatly enhanced our understanding of how race works in the United States.

Omi and Winant (1994) draw from the Italian theorist Antonio Gramsci to argue that racial dynamics in the United States have changed from domination to hegemony. Domination refers to direct rule by coercion, whereas hegemony involves rule by both coercion and consent. For example, Omi and Winant contend that the United States prior to the civil rights era could be characterized as a racial dictatorship in which racial inequality was enforced through domination. During slavery and the Jim Crow era, white domination was legal, state-enforced, and difficult to contest openly. In the current era, racial stratification and white dominance are achieved more subtly through coercion and consent. Omi and Winant argue that the United States is undergoing a slow, gradual, and contentious transition from a racial dictatorship to a racial democracy.

The concept of racial formation blends an understanding of social structures with an understanding of cultural representations. Omi and Winant use the concept of a **racial project**, which they define as being "simultaneously an interpretation, representation, or explanation of racial dynamics, and an effort to reorganize and redistribute resources along particular racial lines" (1994, 56). Racial projects give meaning to racial categories through cultural representations while also organizing our social world on the basis of race through social structures. Cultural ideas and social structures work together in racial formation projects.

For Omi and Winant, a racial project is defined as racist if it "creates or reproduces structures of domination based on essentialist categories of race" (1994, 71). They are careful to distinguish between race and racism and to point out that not all racial projects are racist.

Projects are racist only when they reproduce structures of domination and hegemony. Omi and Winant argue that every state institution is a racial institution. They don't go so far as to say that every state institution is *racist*. This is because they believe the state can also use racial schemas to promote racial equality.

WHITE SUPREMACY AND SETTLER COLONIALISM

What if we consider present-day racism in the United States from the perspective of indigenous studies? From this perspective, our focus shifts significantly. We are forced to contend with questions related to the meaning of white control of lands that once belonged to indigenous people. What would the end of racism look like for indigenous people? We can imagine that indigenous people have an entirely different set of claims than do African Americans.

Andrea Smith (2012) argues that there are three pillars of white supremacy: (1) anti-black racism, (2) genocide, and (3) orientalism (Table 2-1). Anti-black racism defines people as property, thereby justifying slavery and current forms of exploitation, and is rooted in a logic of capitalism. Genocide is rooted in colonialism. This is the idea that native people are disappearing and must disappear, and that therefore non-native people have a right to everything that once belonged to native people. Orientalism is rooted in the idea that certain nations or peoples pose a permanent threat to Western civilization and is thereby used to justify war.

Although the United States is no longer engaged in the mass murder and expulsion of Native Americans, many indigenous scholars contend

TABLE 2-1
Pillars of White Supremacy

	Anti-Black Racism	Genocide	Orientalism
BASIS	Capitalism	Colonialism	Security
POSITION	People can be property.	Native people are disappearing and must disappear.	Certain nations or peoples pose a permanent threat to Western civilization.
CONCLUSION	Slavery and current forms of exploitation are justified.	Non-native people have a right to all that once belonged to native people.	War against such nations or peoples is justified.

Source: Based on Smith 2012.

Students graduating from Haskell Indian Nations University in Lawrence, Kansas.

that the logics of genocide and settler colonialism endure (Smith 2012). Native Americans continue to have a unique legal position in the United States: they are citizens both of the United States and of the tribes to which they belong. Scholars such as Andrea Smith (2012) contend that capitalist ideas of property ownership and white supremacist ideas of indigenous inferiority work together to justify the expropriation (seizure) of indigenous lands. From this perspective, simply returning lands to Native Americans would not solve the problem of indigenous expropriation. The more fundamental problem is the nation-state itself and the idea that people can control territory and keep other human beings out of it.

Once we recognize that the United States is a nation rooted in white supremacy, it becomes clear that the state will never grant native peoples self-determination. For some indigenous scholars, this recognition means that the struggle against racism requires a challenge to the very existence of the United States as an illegitimate state (A. Smith 2012).

Joe Feagin (2001), in his systemic racism framework, contends that anti-black oppression is at the center of U.S. society even though the United States was formed through genocide. Andrea Smith (2012) contests this framework, arguing that the United States exists precisely because of the disappearance of indigenous people and that this genocide continues today. One's framework for understanding the experience of native peoples is critical, because it shapes how we view racial progress or regression. Smith points to the example of high rates of intermarriage between Native Americans and whites. Is this progress? Or is it a continuation of a pattern of genocide?

Using these perspectives, we can see how frameworks shape research questions and answers. From the perspective of settler colonialism, one might argue that the United States is an illegitimate state founded on genocide and must be dismantled. From a systemic racism perspective, one can argue that the United States is founded on a history of racism and that the Constitution must be rewritten. From a racial formation perspective, the United States is headed in the right direction and through more struggles for justice and civil rights will complete the transition from racial dictatorship to racial democracy.

INTERSECTIONAL THEORIES OF RACE AND RACISM

In what ways do race, class, and gender oppression work together? Some race scholars argue that we need to develop a concrete understanding of how race and racism work before we can understand other forms of oppression. Feminist scholars, however, often contend that we must look at race and gender oppression simultaneously—a concept known as **intersectionality**.

Kimberlé Crenshaw (1991) uses this concept in her work, making her point with the example of a group of black and Latina women in a battered women's shelter. Taken together, the factors of race, class, and gender elucidate how these women ended up in the shelter. The women faced abuse in part because of gender oppression, but their economically vulnerable situation and race also help us understand their situation. If they had the economic resources, they likely would have gone elsewhere—not to a shelter. If they were white, they wouldn't face racial discrimination in employment, meaning they may have had more resources. If they were men, their chances of being battered would be much lower. Any proposed method of helping these women must pay attention to their gender, class-based, and racial oppression. A narrow lens that focuses on just race, gender, or class would miss crucial aspects of these women's situations.

Similarly, Priya Kandaswamy (2012) contends that an intersectional perspective helps us better understand welfare policies. She argues that race scholars, Marxists, and feminists often look past one another. In contrast, she takes an intersectional perspective to shed light on the 1996 welfare reforms.

Interconnected ideas of gender, sexuality, race, and class influence public opinions about who deserves state assistance and who does not. The subtext of the "welfare queen" in the successful passage of the 1996 welfare reforms was due to raced, class-based, gendered, and heteronormative ideas. The 1996 welfare reforms, which dramatically reduced public aid, did not mention race specifically. In contrast, the writers of the legislation had no qualms about promoting heteronormative ideas of appropriate families: the first line of the 1996 law is: "Marriage is the foundation of a successful society." The 1996 law explicitly embraced marriage, was based on a public discussion of family values and personal responsibility, and was designed to reform the "welfare queen," a stereotypical figure who is often imagined as a black woman. Priya Kandaswamy (2012) explains how the idea that race is historically produced and constantly changing can complicate our understanding of intersectionality, as it forces us to look at how race and gender "are constituted in and through each other" (26). Race is a socially constructed idea that has developed in conjunction with ideas about gender, class, and sexuality. In this examination of welfare policy, Kandaswamy explains concretely how a racial formation perspective can be enhanced by the adoption of an intersectional perspective.

WHITE PRIVILEGE

Whereas most studies of racism focus on oppression, those scholars who use a white privilege framework focus on privilege—the opposite side of oppression. **White privilege** refers to the advantages associated with being categorized as white. The concept derives from earlier work by African American sociologist W. E. B. DuBois (1868–1963), who observed that white workers in the United States over time came to see themselves as white like their bosses, as opposed to developing working-class solidarity with recently freed black slaves. DuBois argued in 1936 that white workers received a psychological "**wage of whiteness**" by aligning with the dominant group; they were poor, but at least they were white. Additionally, by reserving certain segments of the labor market for whites only, white laborers were able to reap material rewards from their whiteness. Other scholars, mostly historians, have built on DuBois's insights to explain how waves of European immigrants learned to be white and to reap the privileges of whiteness (Allen 1994; Jacobson 1998; Roediger 1999).

European immigrants who arrived in the United States in the early twentieth century did not think of themselves as white prior to coming to the United States. And, in some cases, people in the United States did not see them as white. Irish immigrants learned to capitalize on their whiteness by forming unions and excluding blacks from them. And although Jews faced discrimination during and after World War II, as whites, they were able to reap the benefits of the GI bills and Federal Housing Administration and Department of Veterans Affairs mortgages that were denied to blacks, which propelled many whites into the middle class (Brodkin 2005). Whereas these European immigrants had to learn to be white, most whites today never have to think about whiteness.

In the contemporary United States, whiteness is an unmarked identity. Whereas blacks, Latinos, Asians, and Native Americans are constantly reminded of their race, whites easily can forget that they too have a race (Dalton 2005). When we talk about race (or, more recently, diversity), the focus is usually on non-whites, as if white were not also a race (A. Lewis 2004). When we think of race in the United States, whiteness usually is not the first thing that comes to mind. The reason is that whiteness has become normalized—"whiteness makes itself invisible precisely by asserting its normalcy" (Frankenberg 1997, 6).

Privilege is often hard to notice. If you are white, it can be difficult to notice that you are not being followed around the store; that people are smiling at you on the street instead of clutching their purses; that no one asks you if you speak English; that you are not asked for identification when paying with a credit card. Instead, you are likely to think that these things are normal—that this is simply how things are. To notice these privileges as a white person, you likely would have to walk down the street with an African American friend or accompany a Latino friend to get a driver's license. Few whites notice that they are treated better than non-whites, and most are unlikely to attribute that better treatment to privilege. Privilege works so well in part because it is largely invisible to those who have it.

When thinking of white privilege, it is also important to realize that white privilege doesn't simply exist—it is enacted. When shopkeepers are not suspicious of white shoppers, the white shopper is the beneficiary of the privilege, but only because the shopkeeper has accepted the racist idea that whites are less likely to shoplift. White privilege, then, is related to white supremacy: white privilege exists because of past and current practices that reproduce racism.

However, we can also ask whether racism can be harmful to whites even though white privilege exists. Tim Wise, for example, contends that "the price we pay to stay one step ahead of others is enormous" (2005, 120). The vast majority of working people could earn higher wages and have better benefits if whites and non-whites worked together to demand them as a common goal. Whites are less likely to go to prison than blacks or Latinos, yet the enormous amount of resources our country invests in the prison-industrial complex are resources that don't go into better schools, parks, libraries, and universities. For these reasons, DuBois and others refer to the "psychological wage of whiteness": racism makes all whites *think* they are getting a better deal, but the reality is that racism affects all of us, albeit in different ways. DuBois argues that the psychological wage of whiteness drives a wedge between white and black laborers who otherwise share an interest in working together to fight for better material conditions. Think about it: What are some ways that our society would be better for whites if racism weren't pervasive?

It is important to think about white privilege for several reasons. First of all, if we want to understand racial oppression, it is crucial to understand how it looks from the other side. Second, white privilege often remains invisible, and by bringing it to light we can develop a better understanding of how racism works in our society. Nevertheless, it is important to keep in mind that all whites do not experience white privilege in the same way.

CONCLUSION AND DISCUSSION

Theories of systemic, structural, and institutional racism provide us with different frameworks to understand the deep-seated nature of racial inequality in the United States. These analyses place the emphasis on racism and are exemplified by Feagin and Elias (2013), who argue that only through an understanding of racial oppression can we grasp the true nature of racial meanings. In contrast, racial formation theory focuses on how race is constructed, and it uses these analyses to understand racism (Omi and Winant 1994). Analyses of white privilege focus on privilege to show how racial oppression works. Still other scholars invoke settler colonialism as the primary framework for understanding racial oppression. Who is right?

There is no right answer to this question. Instead, it depends on the kind of question you are asking. An understanding of why African Americans and Latinos are faring worse economically than whites in the aftermath of the Great Recession would likely benefit from an analysis based on systemic or structural racism (Kochhar, Fry, and Taylor 2011). A consideration of why Indonesian women use whitening creams yet insist they have no desire to be Caucasian might get a more nuanced treatment when approached from a racial formations perspective (Saraswati 2010). Both of these studies are grounded in the field of racial and ethnic studies, but they have different research questions and goals and thus draw from different frameworks.

The frameworks set forth by indigenous and feminist scholars can also be more or less useful, depending on the kinds of questions you decide to ask. A consideration of Mayan migration to Houston would likely benefit from Andrea Smith's (2012) indigenous-settler framework, and an analysis of violence in youth gangs in Oakland would likely be enriched by an intersectional perspective that focuses on race, class, gender, and sexuality. A study of whiteness and class in an economically diverse white neighborhood would do well to interrogate the white privilege perspective. No theory can be expected to shed light on every aspect of our society. Moreover, sociologists and other thinkers continue to develop ways for us to understand inequality. Readers of these texts can decide for themselves which frameworks are most useful for understanding the questions that are important to them. What about you? What frameworks do you find most compelling, and why?

THINKING ABOUT RACIAL JUSTICE

THE UNITED STATES has one of the highest incarceration rates in the world. African American men are seven times more likely than white men to go to prison. Explain this statistic using two different perspectives from this chapter (e.g., cultural racism, institutional racism, structural racism, white privilege). Can either of these perspectives help us to understand this disparity? Is either of these perspectives useful in terms of racial justice?

Key Terms

sociological theory of racism 32
prejudice 32
discrimination 32
assimilation 33
individual racism 34
racial microaggression 34
institutional racism 37
systemic racism 39
structural racism 39
racial ideology 41
new racism 42
Jim Crow laws 42
biological racism 43
cultural racism 43
color-blind racism 45
abstract liberalism 45
naturalization 45
rhetorical strategies 46
racial formation 46
racial project 47
intersectionality 50
white privilege 51
wage of whiteness 51

Check Your Understanding

OBJECTIVE 2.1

Explain how racism is connected to racial inequality.

Prejudice, discrimination, and institutional racism are interconnected and thus should not be studied in isolation. Prejudice refers to beliefs about racial difference; discrimination refers to actions; and institutional racism describes the larger context in which prejudice and discrimination occur.

Q How widespread is individual racism, and how does it persist?
Q What are some examples of racial microaggressions?
Q What is the relationship between individual and institutional racism?

OBJECTIVE 2.2

Describe how systemic and structural racism create racial disparities.

Systemic racism and structural racism are two theoretical frameworks that both aim to explain how racism is deeply rooted in society. While systemic racism focuses on accumulated acts of racism across history and throughout one's lifetime, structural racism points to inter-institutional interactions across time and space.

Q What is one key difference between systemic racism and structural racism?
Q How does structural racism explain wealth inequalities?

OBJECTIVE 2.3

Appraise various racial ideologies, and evaluate how racism has changed since the early twentieth century.

A racial ideology is a set of principles and ideas that (1) divides people into different racial groups and (2) serves the interests of one group. Racism has changed over the years yet continues to benefit whites.

- What is an example of racism pre-1965?
- What is an example of racism post-1965?
- What are the differences among biological, cultural, and color-blind racisms?

OBJECTIVE 2.4

Evaluate and critique racial formation theory.

Racial formation is one of the most influential theories of race and racism in the United States. It focuses on racial meanings—how racial categories are "created, inhabited, transformed, and destroyed," as Omi and Winant (1994) describe.

- What do Omi and Winant mean when they say the United States is transitioning from a racial dictatorship to a racial democracy?
- What is an example of a racial project?

OBJECTIVE 2.5

Examine the indigenous perspective on racism in the contemporary United States.

Another way to consider how racism works is to examine it from the perspective of indigenous studies. This leads us to consider settler colonialism theory, which offers a broad critique of racism and capitalism.

- What are the three pillars of white supremacy?
- Why is it important to understand genocide in relation to contemporary race relations?

OBJECTIVE 2.6

Examine how race, class, and gender oppression work together.

Ideas of race, gender, class, and sexuality all shape how racism works, and intersectional scholars take these factors seriously as they build their frameworks.

What is an example of a scenario that intersectional theory helps us to understand?

OBJECTIVE 2.7

Evaluate the white privilege perspective.

White privilege refers to the advantages associated with being categorized as white and can be a useful analytic in terms of understanding racial oppression.

Q Who benefits from white privilege, and why?

Critical Thinking

1. Think of an issue related to racial inequality and use one of the frameworks discussed in this chapter to explain it. Justify your selection of this framework over the others.
2. What are some of the key differences between systemic racism and structural racism, and how might they shape your research agenda?
3. Most of the scholars cited in the section on intersectionality are women of color. Why do you think these scholars have been at the head of these debates and discussions?

3

RACISM AND NATIVISM IN IMMIGRATION POLICY

CHAPTER OUTLINE

LEARNING OBJECTIVES

3.1 Examine the racialized history of U.S. immigration policy.

3.2 Describe U.S. policy responses to undocumented immigration.

3.3 Analyze the relationship between nativism and racism in the twenty-first century.

As of this writing in 2015, over 30,000 men, women, and children behind bars in the United States are not waiting for a trial and are not serving time for a crime. These people are not citizens of the United States and are held in preventive detention, mostly waiting to find out if they will be deported to their countries of birth. Some have already been ordered deported and are waiting for the day of their deportation. Many are asylum seekers, fleeing persecution in their home countries.

The detention of immigrants in the United States is just one aspect of our immigration law enforcement system. Today, as in the past, our harsh immigration policies primarily affect people who are considered non-white. This chapter considers the history of immigration policy in the United States and the extent to which racist and nativist sentiments have played a role in U.S. immigration legislation. Although the country's immigration policy has shifted dramatically over the years, two trends have remained constant: (1) nativism has always been an integral part of debates over immigration policy, and (2) the consequences of immigration policy have been more disadvantageous to people considered non-white than to those considered white. What has changed over time is the removal of explicitly discriminatory language from U.S. immigration laws. This chapter explores how immigration laws can have racially disparate consequences, even when the laws do not mention race. Whereas racism presumes the superiority of a racial group, **nativism** presumes the superiority of native-born citizens, favoring the allocation of resources to them over immigrants and promoting a fear of foreign cultures.

As Robert Bautista's story below makes clear (see Voices on p. 60), U.S. immigration policy can be draconian—even long-term legal residents can have their rights stripped away for minor transgressions of the law. In this chapter, we explore the history of U.S. immigration policy, as well as present-day laws and policies. The historical overview shows how lawmakers have used immigration policy to influence the racial and ethnic make-up of the nation. In this process, racism and nativism often have become indistinguishable.

Immigration policy continues to be at the forefront of the political agenda in the United States today. It is hard to imagine a time when the country had no immigration policy, yet just one hundred years ago, there was no Border Patrol, and passports and visas were not required

voices

Robert Bautista—Denied Due Process

In 2009, immigration agents arrested Robert Bautista as he was returning from vacation in the Dominican Republic, his country of birth. Once arrested, Mr. Bautista was placed in detention without the possibility of a bond hearing. He had been a legal permanent resident of the United States for twenty-five years, had been married for over a decade, had three school-age children, and was the owner of a successful business in Pennsylvania. His mandatory detention caused his business to be destroyed and his family to lose their home. His children, all of whom are U.S. citizens, had to bear witness to their father being treated as if he were a criminal, but without the procedural protections normally accorded to people charged with crimes.

Mr. Bautista's immigration detention was not pursuant to any criminal convictions. In 2002, Mr. Bautista had been found guilty of third-degree attempted arson for carrying a container of gasoline near his own vehicle, but by 2009 he had completed his parole. When immigration agents arrested him, it was not because he was being charged with a new crime. Instead, he was detained because the Department of Homeland Security (DHS) ruled that his 2002 conviction was a crime involving moral turpitude (CIMT). Because of this prior conviction, Mr. Bautista was considered to be seeking admission to the United States, as if he were not present in the country and as if he had not been living and working in the country for over two decades. As a person not technically inside the United States, Mr. Bautista was not protected by the Constitution.

Just one hour before his immigration hearing, DHS made an additional argument: that third-degree attempted arson is also an aggravated felony, meaning that Mr. Bautista would be subject to mandatory detention and deportation without judicial review. In such a case, it does not matter if you have lived in the United States for three decades, if you have three children, if you have no relatives in your country of origin, or if your family depends on you for their survival. Non-citizens convicted of aggravated felonies are not given a fair and reasonable hearing of the sort that would meet international human rights standards.

In October 2011, the Board of Immigration Appeals (BIA) heard Mr. Bautista's case and decided that third-degree attempted arson is an aggravated felony, as DHS had charged. This determination means that Mr. Bautista could not challenge his deportation on the basis of his ties to the United States. Instead, he faced mandatory deportation to the Dominican Republic, where he would be labeled a criminal deportee and face a bleak future. The Dominican government treats arriving criminal deportees as if they are criminals. They are booked at the city jail, and their deportation is recorded on their criminal record, making it nearly impossible to secure employment.

(continued)

voices *continued.*

Robert Bautista—Denied Due Process

If Mr. Bautista had been afforded the due process protections we give to criminals, he would have had a bond hearing and likely would not have been detained for two years, he would have had the opportunity for a trial in which a judge could weigh the equities in his case, and he may have been eligible for a public defender. Instead, he remained behind bars until December 2011, when the Third Circuit Court of Appeals reversed the previous decision, finding that his conviction did not constitute an aggravated felony.

Source: Golash-Boza 2011b and Immigration Law Group @ Baurkot & Baurkot 2011.

to enter the United States. When the United States began to pass immigration laws governing the entry and residency conditions of the foreign-born at the end of the nineteenth century, the laws were overtly racialized and expressed a clear preference for people from Northern and Western Europe.

THE RACIALIZED HISTORY OF U.S. IMMIGRATION POLICY

The history of U.S. immigration policy is a reflection of societal racism and nativism. As various scholars have noted (e.g., Lippard 2011; Sanchez 1997; K. Johnson 2004), racist nativism is a prominent feature of contemporary American society: the fear of foreigners is clearly racialized, and nativist sentiments are directed at particular racial groups, such as Mexicans and people from the Middle East. Through an examination of the history of immigration policy and nativist responses to immigration, we will see how nativism and racism have been intertwined in U.S. history and how nativism today is distinct from that of the past.

Race and the Making of U.S. Immigration Policies: 1790 to 1924

The United States was a sovereign nation for a full century before immigration restrictions became a subject of political debate, let alone law. Although the country did not begin to pass immigration laws until the late 1800s, Congress passed an important piece of legislation in 1790 related to people born abroad. The **Naturalization Act of 1790** was not an immigration policy in that it did not regulate entry; instead, it stated that only free white persons who had lived in the United States for at least two years were eligible for citizenship. This first piece of legislation related to the foreign-born is particularly notable because it contained a racialized provision, defining citizenship as accessible solely to whites. The purpose of this clause was to deny citizenship to African-descended slaves, and it was later used to deny Asians **naturalization**, or the granting of citizenship after birth.

When large numbers of immigrants began to arrive on the shores of the United States fifty years after the passage of the Naturalization Act of 1790, the question of who was white gained importance. Between 1846 and 1855, over 3 million immigrants came to the United States, including 1,288,307 from Ireland and 975,311 from Germany. There is no reason to believe that the millions of Irish who came to the United States in the mid-nineteenth century thought of themselves as "white" when they lived in Ireland. In a context in which everyone is Irish, whiteness has little meaning. As each of these groups integrated into the United States, they experienced both a process of *assimilation*, through which Irish, Italians, and Germans became Americans, and a process of *racialization*, through which Celts, Hebrews, and Mediterraneans became white. This process was not smooth, as Irish faced discrimination, and Italians and Jews were lynched in the South alongside African Americans (M. Jacobson 1998). Racialized fears of European and Asian immigrants eventually translated into laws that ended these immigration flows.

TIMELINE

U.S. Immigration and Deportation Policy

1790	Naturalization Act
1882	Chinese Exclusion Act
1924	Immigration Act (Johnson–Reed Act)
1924	Oriental Exclusion Act
1924	Creation of Border Patrol
1942–1964	Bracero program
1943	Repeal of Chinese Exclusion Act
1950–1954	Operation Wetback
1965	Immigration and Nationality Act
1986	Immigration Reform and Control Act
1996	Anti-Terrorism and Effective Death Penalty Act (AEDPA)
1996	Illegal Immigration Reform and Immigrant Responsibility Act (IIRIRA)
1996	Personal Responsibility and Work Opportunity Reconciliation Act (PRWORA)

The first major piece of immigration legislation was the **Chinese Exclusion Act**, signed into law in 1882. This act denied entry to one specific group: Chinese laborers. In specifically excluding a group because of race and class, the Chinese Exclusion Act set the stage for twentieth-century immigration policy, which had both overt and covert racial and class biases (E. Lee 2002). Although the Chinese Exclusion Act was repealed in 1943, the court cases that stemmed from it continue to shape how we treat immigrants today.

An 1893 landmark Supreme Court case, *Fong Yue Ting v. United States*, involved three Chinese nationals who claimed they deserved constitutional protections in their deportation cases. The court held that the power to deport non-citizens was inherent in the nature of sovereignty and that constitutional protections, including the right to a trial by jury, did not apply. This case defined deportation as simply an administrative procedure and not a punishment. The idea of deportation as a nonpunitive action was based on a distinction between deportation and banishment. Banishment removes a person from a country where he or she belongs, whereas deportation returns a person to where he or she belongs and thus is not considered a punishment. According to the *Fong Yue Ting* decision, which still holds in court today, deportation is a procedure to ensure that people abide by the terms of their visas. When they do not, they face the possibility of being returned to where they belong. It is remarkable that this court decision, which was made in the context of strong anti-Chinese sentiment, continues to hold the status of legal precedent today.

The Chinese Exclusion Act was passed in the midst of a great wave of immigrants from both Europe and China. In the 1840s, the United States began to experience large-scale immigration for the first time since its founding. This influx dramatically changed both the country's cultural landscape and its official stance toward immigrants. Between 1841 and 1850, 1.7 million immigrants arrived in the United States (see Figure 3-1), and in the following decade, 2.6 million arrived. In 1870, immigrants constituted nearly 14 percent of the total population. Each subsequent decade until 1924, millions continued to arrive. Toward the end of this wave of immigrants in the early twentieth century, the United States began to implement policies governing the entry of the foreign-born.

FIGURE 3-1

IMMIGRANTS AS TOTAL NUMBER AND AS A PERCENTAGE OF THE U.S. POPULATION, 1850 TO 2011

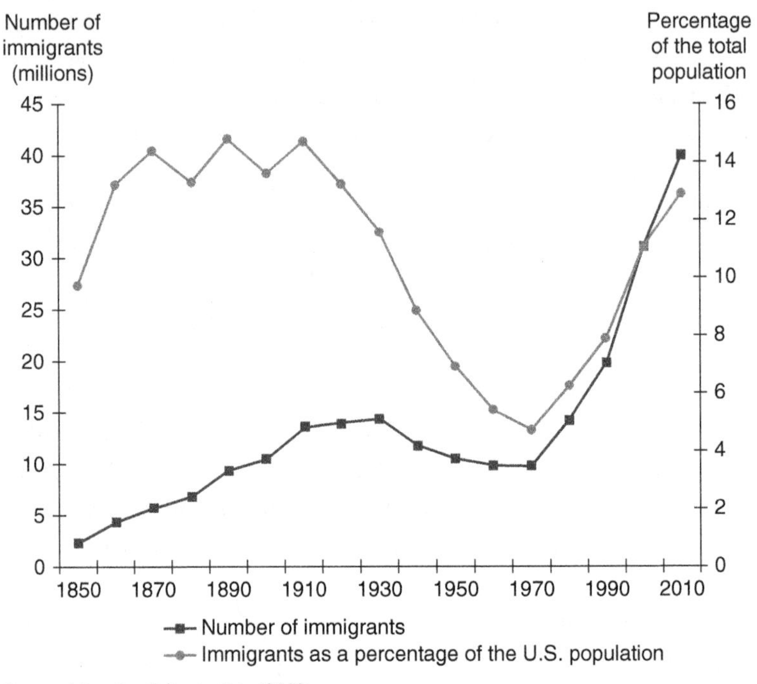

Source: Migration Policy Institute (2012).

In 1924, the U.S. Congress implemented three restrictive measures that effectively cut off immigration from most countries. The first of these was the overtly racialized **Immigration Act of 1924**, or the **Johnson–Reed Act**, which greatly reduced immigration from southern and eastern Europe by introducing quotas, or limits on the number of people from these countries who were allowed to enter the United States. The Johnson–Reed Act was implemented due to lobbying efforts by the *eugenics* movement (see Chapter 1). Eugenicists advocated the selective breeding of Americans, the sterilization of the biologically unfit, and selective immigration policies as a way of creating a superior breed of people.

The next major piece of immigration legislation was the 1924 **Oriental Exclusion Act**, which expanded the Chinese Exclusion Act and prohibited most immigration from Asia. The motivation for both of these laws passed in 1924 was to improve the racial stock of the United States by restricting immigration to "Nordics." The final measure implemented in 1924 was the creation of the Border Patrol to prevent illegal entry into the United States. These restrictive measures were effective: immigration dropped drastically and did not pick up again until the 1960s, when the national origin quotas were expanded and the overtly racial nature of the immigration laws was rescinded.

Nativism Between 1924 and 1964

The period between 1924 and 1964 was an exceptional period in U.S. history in that the country welcomed relatively few immigrants. The 1924 measures significantly curbed the flow of immigrants until the 1965 overhaul of U.S. immigration laws. These trends are evident both in Figure 3-1 and in Figure 3-2, which displays the number of people who attained legal permanent resident status by decade. A **legal permanent resident** is a foreign national granted the right to remain in the United States and who will be eligible for naturalization after a period of three to five years. To become a U.S. citizen today, a legal permanent resident must have been a permanent resident for at least five years if he or she is not married to a U.S. citizen or at least three years if he or she is the spouse of a U.S. citizen. The applicant must also be a person of good moral character; have basic knowledge of U.S. history and government; and, in most cases, be able to read, write, and speak basic English. In addition, the applicant must pay the filing fees, which were $680 in 2014.

FIGURE 3-2

NUMBER OF PEOPLE TO ATTAIN LEGAL PERMANENT RESIDENT STATUS IN THE UNITED STATES BY DECADE, 1820–2009

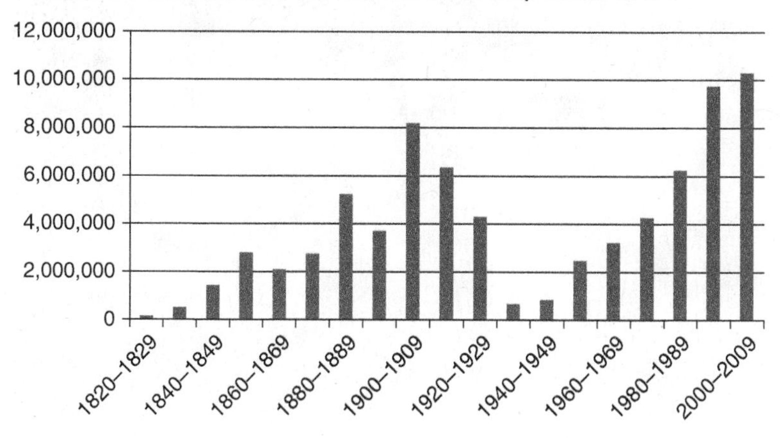

Source: U.S. Department of Homeland Security, Office of Immigration Statistics (2010).

Mass Deportation of Mexicans

Mexicans have a long history of immigration to the United States. The first group of Mexicans to enter the United States were not immigrants, however, but became Americans following the U.S. takeover of large swaths of Mexican land under the 1848 Treaty of Guadalupe Hidalgo. The first substantial wave of Mexican immigrants came between 1910 and 1930, when the Mexican immigrant population tripled from 200,000 to 600,000. This wave was due largely to instability caused by the Mexican Revolution and to the growth of agribusiness in the United States (Massey, Durand, and Malone 2002; Ngai 2004; K. Hernandez 2010).

The second wave of Mexican immigration came during the **bracero program** (1942–1964). Under this program, created by the U.S government to meet the labor shortages caused by World War II, 4.6 million Mexicans, called *braceros* (a Spanish term that can be roughly translated as "farmhands"), came to work in agriculture in the United States. Mexicans also continued to immigrate to the United States illegally, because not all workers qualified for the bracero program, and the costs associated with immigrating as a bracero were prohibitive to some.

Mexican workers in a flax field, 1946.

U.S. deportations of Mexicans also came in two waves during this period. The first was on the heels of the U.S. stock market crash of 1929, which triggered the onset of the Great Depression. In the context of double-digit unemployment rates, the Immigration and Naturalization Service, in cooperation with local officials, mounted a repatriation campaign, under which over 400,000 people of Mexican origin were returned to Mexico (Ngai 2004).

The second wave of deportations occurred in the 1950s, when the U.S. Border Patrol deported over a million Mexican immigrants in a series of roundups known as **Operation Wetback**. World War II had created a Mexican American middle class, and during this time Mexicans were also accorded an improved social standing in the borderlands. By the late 1940s, "No Mexicans Allowed" signs had disappeared, and high schools were increasingly integrated. At the same time, the Border Patrol became more firmly entrenched as part of the federal government, meaning that its policies often reflected Washington's interests more than local interests along the border. This shift created tensions, as ranchers and farmers in Texas wanted to employ undocumented Mexicans, whereas it was the duty of Border Patrol agents to stop immigrants from crossing over (K. Hernandez 2010).

One example of an Operation Wetback raid happened on July 30, 1952. At dawn, about one hundred Border Patrol agents began to arrest Mexicans by the hundreds in an area near Brownsville, Texas. By the end of the day, they had made 5,000 arrests and had transported all of those people to the bridge that led back to Mexico. These sorts of roundups continued through 1954. In October 1954, the Border Patrol announced it had deported more than one million Mexican immigrants. These mass arrests created fear and tension in immigrant communities, as Mexicans were forced to leave their loved ones, their belongings, and their lives in the United States and return to Mexico (K. Hernandez 2010).

The McCarran Internal Security Act

Mexicans were not the only target of nativism during this period; at the same time, the United States was gripped by a pervasive fear of communism, and communism was portrayed as a product of foreign influence. The **McCarran Internal Security Act**, signed into law in 1950, was designed to combat communism, both outside and within the borders of the United States. Anyone in the United States who was affiliated with the Communist Party was required to register with the federal government. In addition, this act allowed for the deportation of foreign nationals who were members of the Communist Party. Between 1946 and 1966, deportation proceedings were initiated against 15,000 foreign nationals on ideological grounds (primarily because they were Communists or suspected Communists), and 253 people were deported. Deportation for ideological reasons remained legal until the Immigration Act of 1990 repealed these provisions (Torok 2004). The McCarran Internal Security Act was followed by the **Immigration and Nationality Act of 1952**, also known as the **McCarran–Walter Act**. This Act repealed some of the earlier national origin provisions yet focused on denying immigrants entry for political and social reasons such as affiliation with radical politics. This act also set the stage for the major legislative change of 1965.

The 1965 Immigration and Nationality Act and the Changing Face of Immigration

One of the most significant changes to U.S. immigration law in the twentieth century was the **1965 Immigration and Nationality Act**, also called the 1965 **Hart–Cellar Act**. This act put an end to the racially biased quotas set forth in the 1924 Oriental Exclusion Act and the Immigration Act of 1924. In the spirit of the civil rights movement, the 1965 act set a universal quota of 20,000 immigrants for every country in the world. Each country could send up to 20,000 qualified immigrants a year, with no racial restrictions. Potential immigrants could now qualify for entry based on either family ties to the United States (relatives could petition for their entry) or their skills (employers could request immigrants based on their skills and education). The 1965 act had two main consequences: (1) it increased immigration from Asia, Latin America, and the Caribbean; and (2) it increased undocumented immigration from Mexico.

Asian Immigration

Historically, immigrants from India, China, Japan, the Philippines, and Korea had come to the United States to work as laborers. However, the longstanding prohibitions on Asian immigration between 1882 and 1965 greatly decreased Asian immigration. The 1965 act opened up the possibility of immigration to Asians by removing racial quotas, and large numbers of Asians began to migrate to the United States once again.

Between 1820 and 1849, only 210 people came to the United States from Asia as legal permanent residents. In the 1850s, 36,080 people from Asia became legal permanent residents. Asian immigration peaked in the first decade of the twentieth century, with nearly 300,000 people from Asia becoming legal permanent residents. After the passage of the 1924 Immigration Act, this number dropped off, and only 19,231 Asians gained legal permanent residency in the 1930s. Asian immigration again increased in the 1950s to 135,000 and then increased exponentially to nearly 1.5 million in the 1970s, 2.4 million in the 1980s, and 2.9 million in the 1990s (see Figure 3-3). In the first decade of the twentieth century, almost 3.5 million Asians became legal permanent residents. The most prominent countries of origin of Asian immigrants today are China, the Philippines, India, Korea, and Vietnam—each with its own history of immigration to the United States.

Immigration from Asia increased dramatically with the passage of the 1965 Immigration and Nationality Act. Asians did not come from every country in the region, but specifically from countries with which the United States had longstanding ties. In fact, with the exception of Vietnam, those Asian countries that send large numbers of immigrant

FIGURE 3-3

NUMBER OF ASIANS TO ATTAIN LEGAL U.S. PERMANENT RESIDENT STATUS, BY DECADE

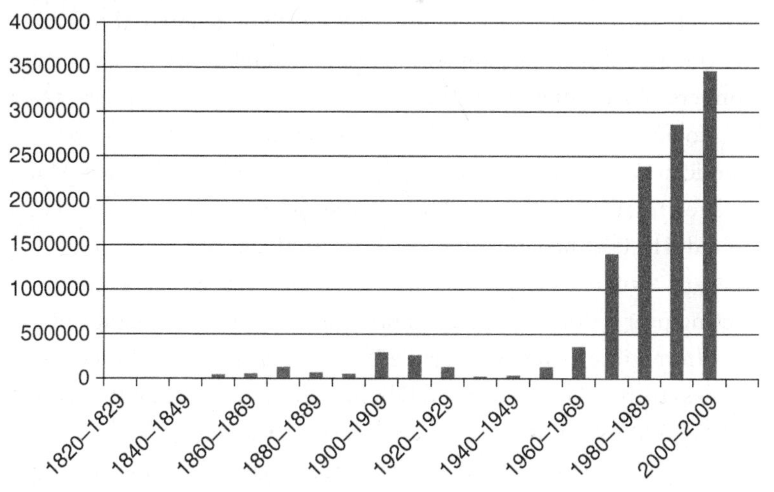

Source: U.S. Department of Homeland Security, Office of Immigration Statistics (2010).

to the United States today are the same countries that sent substantial numbers of immigrants in the late nineteenth and early twentieth centuries. These immigration patterns can be directly linked to both the family ties and high skills provisions in the 1965 Immigration and Nationality Act.

Chinese immigrants to the United States predate many other immigrant groups; the large-scale migration of Chinese to the United States began when U.S. contractors recruited laborers to build railroads in the mid-nineteenth century. Around the same time, recruiters in Hawaii (which would not become a U.S. state until 1959) brought tens of thousands of Chinese to work in agriculture and other industries. Chinese immigration peaked in the 1870s, with 133,000 Chinese becoming legal permanent residents of the United States. Following the Chinese Exclusion Act of 1882, however, immigration dropped off dramatically and did not begin to rise again until decades after the act was repealed in 1943.

Following the 1943 repeal of the Chinese Exclusion Act, Chinese immigration to the United States slowly began to pick up again. The presence of Chinese immigrants and their descendants in the United States facilitated future waves of immigration. In the 1980s, 171,000 Chinese immigrated to the United States. Chinese immigration increased in the next decade to 342,000 and to 592,000 in the first decade of the twenty-first century.

The United States has a longstanding relationship with the Philippines, as well as a protracted migration history. This helps to explain why this relatively small (with a population of 88 million, compared to China and India's billion-plus people) and quite distant country sends large numbers of its nationals to the United States. The Philippines was a U.S. colony from 1898 until 1946. From 1898 to 1934, Filipinos were American nationals and could freely come to the United States. Many were recruited as laborers by Hawaiian sugar plantations, and by 1931, around 113,000 had migrated to Hawaii alone. Manufacturers and vineyard owners in California also recruited Filipinos as workers, attracting over 5,000 to the mainland by 1920. With the passage of the 1924 Immigration Act, which ended the flow of Japanese laborers, agribusiness turned to Mexican and Filipino labor, such that by 1930, there were 56,000 Filipinos on the West Coast. As the numbers of Filipinos began to increase in the 1920s, whites increasingly began to see Filipinos as a problem and a threat. In 1929, the California legislature asked

Congress to restrict Filipino immigration. Congress eventually responded by passing the Tydings–McDuffe Act in 1934, which limited Filipino immigration to an annual quota of fifty—the smallest of any country. The onset of World War II and racial violence on the West Coast also contributed to slowing Filipino immigration. Between 1946 and 1965, 33,000 Filipinos immigrated to the United States, nearly half of whom were wives of U.S. servicemen (Liu, Ong, and Rosenstein 1991; M. White, Biddlecom, and Guo 1993; Ngai 2004).

As with other countries, the 1965 Immigration and Nationality Act changed immigration patterns from the Philippines to the United States. Between 1965 and 1985, about 667,000 Filipinos obtained visas to come to the United States. These Filipino migrants consisted of two groups of people. The first group, which constituted about two-thirds of Filipino immigrants, came on family reunification visas from the networks of the pre-1965 migrants. The second included migrants who obtained employment visas, mostly as professionals and other highly trained individuals (Liu et al. 1991).

India is another country that sent large numbers of immigrants to the United States prior to the passage of the Johnson–Reed Act. As with other Asian countries, immigration from India resumed after 1965. Between 1966 and 1981, 215,640 Asian Indians came to the United States. This rate of 14,376 immigrants per year is twenty times higher than the rate at the previous peak in the period just before World War I. The majority of these new immigrants were professionals, with less than 1 percent working in farm labor occupations (Gonzales 1986).

The pattern is similar for Korea. Over 7,000 Koreans migrated to Hawaii to work on sugar plantations between 1903 and 1905. Korean migration was cut off, first as a result of restrictions placed on emigration by the Japanese imperial power, and later by the 1924 restrictions. These restrictions were lifted in the aftermath of the Korean War (1950–1953), and more than 3,000 Koreans were admitted between 1950 and 1965, the vast majority of whom were wives of U.S. servicemen stationed in Korea. With the passage of the 1965 Immigration and Nationality Act, Koreans quickly became one of the largest immigrant groups in the United States. In 1965, 2,165 Koreans entered the United States. In 1970, 9,314 came. And in 1977, 30,917 entered (Reimers 1981; Min 1990). Between 1975 and 1990, Korea sent more immigrants to the United States than any other country, with the exception of Mexico and the Philippines. Korean immigrants were relatively highly educated, and 30 percent in the 1970s came on skills-based visas. The remaining 70 percent came on family reunification visas (Min 1990).

Vietnam is distinct from the other Asian countries in that there were almost no Vietnamese in the United States in the early twentieth century, or even prior to the Vietnam War. Today, however, there are over one million Vietnamese in the United States. The first wave came as refugees; between 1971 and 1980, 150,000 Vietnamese were admitted to the United States (M. White et al. 1993). The reunification provisions of the 1965 act led to the growth of the Vietnamese population in the United States well after the Vietnam War ended (G. Kelly 1986). Those Vietnamese who were in the United States already had the right to bring their family members to the country under the family reunification provisions of the Immigration and Nationality Act. Legal immigration through family reunification policies, combined with illegal immigration, led to the continued growth of the Vietnamese population. The 2000 census reported the presence of over one million Vietnamese, nearly a quarter of whom had been born in the United States (Hoefer, Rytina, and Campbell 2007).

In 2010, Vietnam came in at number nine in the list of the top twenty countries sending legal permanent residents to the United States, with 310,000 Vietnamese legal permanent residents in the country (Rytina 2011). Three other countries in Asia had larger populations of legal permanent residents in the United States: the Philippines (560,000), China (550,000), and India (500,000). Figure 3-4 shows the population of undocumented immigrants in the United States. The ten countries displayed in the graph account for 85 percent of all undocumented migrants. Of these ten countries, six are in Latin America and four are in Asia.

Latin American and Caribbean Immigration

The 1965 Immigration and Nationality Act instituted quotas of 20,000 immigrants per country. At first glance, this blanket quota may seem fair. However, most of the 180-plus countries in the world do not send 20,000 immigrants per year to the United States, and a handful of countries send many more. Mexico is a case in point. Prior to 1965, there were no limits on the number of immigrants that could be admitted from Mexico, and tens of thousands of Mexicans came to the

FIGURE 3-4

COUNTRY OF BIRTH OF UNDOCUMENTED IMMIGRANTS RESIDING IN THE UNITED STATES, 2011

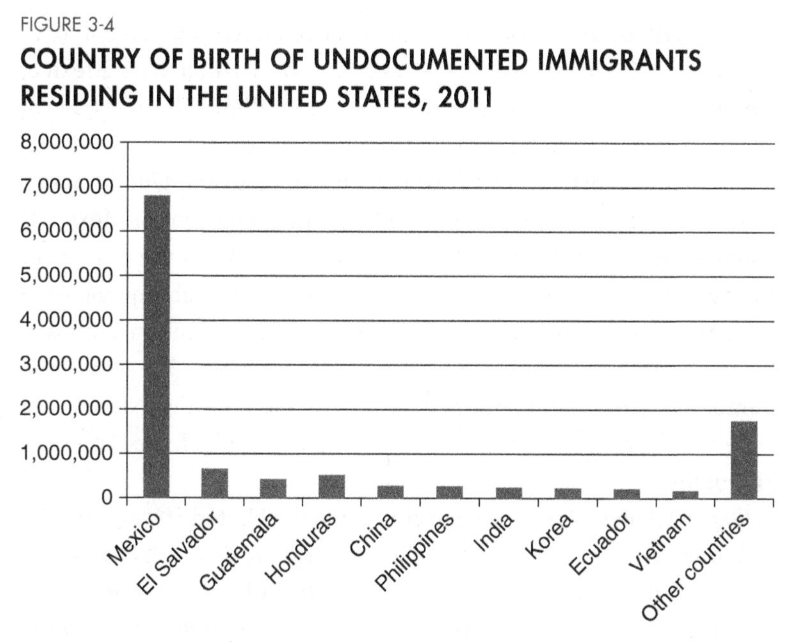

Source: U.S. Department of Homeland Security, Office of Immigration Statistics (2010).

United States each year. The 1965 act initially established a ceiling of 120,000 immigrant visas for the entire Western hemisphere. In 1976, the law came fully into effect, and a quota of 20,000 immigrants per year was extended to all countries in the Western hemisphere, including Mexico (Joppke 1998). The imposition of a quota of 20,000 immigrants from Mexico was unrealistic in the 1970s because of the need for Mexican labor and the desire of many Mexicans to work in the United States.

The restrictions on the number of immigrants from countries in the Western hemisphere did not end large-scale migration from Mexico. Because many employers depended on Mexican labor to thrive, workers came illegally to the United States. At this time, there were hardly any Border Patrol agents, and it was easy for Mexicans to enter the United States illegally. Thus, Mexicans continued to arrive. The imbalance between the quota and the need for Mexican labor to sustain economic growth in the United States led to increased undocumented immigration (Massey et al. 2002).

The first Mexicans who came to be part of the United States never crossed a border. In 1848, the United States and Mexico signed the Treaty of Guadalupe Hidalgo, which resulted in Mexico's loss of almost half of its territory. Mexico surrendered its control over California, Nevada, Utah, Texas, and parts of Arizona, New Mexico, Colorado, and Wyoming in exchange for $15 million. The first wave of Mexican migrants came in the early twentieth century. Up until the 1970s, over 80 percent of Mexicans who came to the United States were temporary farm workers. By 1997, only 40 percent of Mexicans could be described as such (Massey et al. 2002). With the passage of the 1965 Immigration and Nationality Act and the subsequent 1986 mass legalization laws, increasing numbers of Mexicans have chosen to reside permanently in the United States. Figure 3-5 shows the number of people who obtained legal permanent resident status who were from Latin America and the Caribbean (all of the Americas except for Canada).

Central Americans have been coming to the United States since the late nineteenth century, but they did not begin to arrive in large numbers until the 1960s, with the passage of the 1965 Immigration and Nationality Act. Around 8,000 Central Americans entered the United States legally between 1900 and 1910; this number increased to 17,000 in the next decade, around 6,000 in the 1930s, 21,000 in the 1940s, and about 45,000 in the 1950s. In the 1960s, the presence of U.S. companies in Central America increased, with a concomitant increase in

FIGURE 3-5

PERSONS FROM THE AMERICAS ATTAINING LEGAL PERMANENT RESIDENT STATUS, 1820–PRESENT

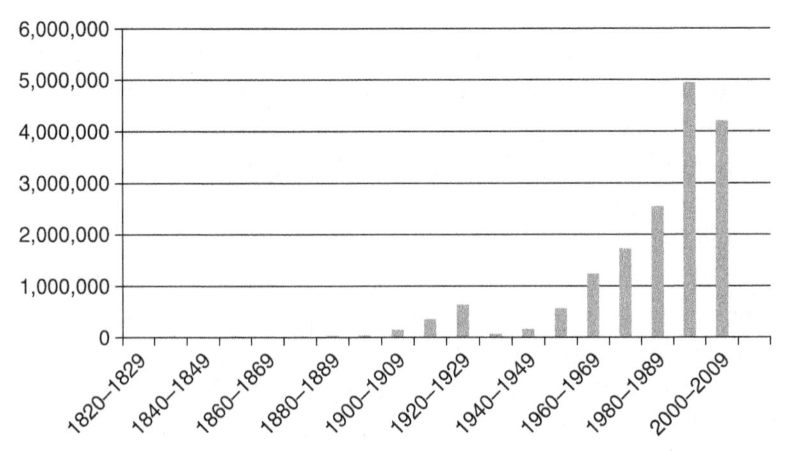

Source: U.S. Department of Homeland Security, Office of Immigration Statistics (2010).

the presence of Central Americans in the United States. Between 1971 and 1980, more than 130,000 Central Americans legally entered the United States (Hamilton and Chinchilla 1991).

In the 1980s, immigration to the United States from El Salvador and other Central American countries increased rapidly as a result of both political violence in Central America and the economic setbacks that this violence entailed (Hamilton and Chinchilla 1991). In neighboring Nicaragua, the U.S. Central Intelligence Agency financed and organized a counterrevolution against the Sandinista government. In El Salvador, the U.S. government supplied military equipment to the government in the 1980s, which was used to kill thousands of civilians (Hamilton and Chinchilla 1991). As part of its Cold War strategy, the U.S. government also supplied the Salvadoran government with more than $6 billion in military and economic aid between 1980 and 1992 (Quan 2005). The civil war in El Salvador caused massive population displacements, and many of those displaced came to the United States. While the conditions in El Salvador were the motivation for leaving, the nation's longstanding ties to the United States turned the latter country into a preferred destination when Salvadorans began to seek refuge (Menjívar 2000).

Immigrants have been coming to the United States from the Caribbean as long as the nation has been keeping records. Between 1820 and 1900, nearly 90,000 people from the Caribbean came to the United States. Immigration from this region reached a peak in the first three decades of the twentieth century, when 300,000 people from the Caribbean became legal permanent residents. In the last three decades of the twentieth century, 2.5 million people from the Caribbean became legal permanent residents of the United States. Another million migrated legally in the first decade of the twenty-first century (Golash-Boza 2012). Since the passage of the 1965 Immigration and Nationality Act, large numbers of immigrants from the Dominican Republic, Cuba, and Jamaica have entered the country.

The United States has been heavily involved in the affairs of the Dominican Republic and has been the destination of many immigrants as a consequence of this close relationship. Between 1961 and 1968, for example, the United States was closely entangled in the Dominican Republic's presidential elections, to the point of ensuring that the democratically elected leftwing president Juan Bosch was ousted in 1965. This time of intense involvement in the Dominican Republic coincided with the passage of the 1965 Immigration and Nationality Act, which paved the way for Dominicans to enter the United States. During this time, more people from the Dominican Republic entered the United States than from any other country in the Western hemisphere except Mexico. Emigration from the Dominican Republic continued to rise through the 1970s, when an average of 16,000 Dominicans immigrated per year, to the 1980s, when an average of 30,000 immigrated annually. In 1991 and 1992, the number of Dominicans arriving in the United States exceeded 40,000 each year (Garrison and Weiss 1979; R. Hernández 2004).

Cuba is another Caribbean country that has had a longstanding relationship with the United States. In the early twentieth century, more than 20,000 Cubans lived in the United States, and by the end of the 1950s, that number was about 50,000. This population continued to increase following the 1959 victory of Fidel Castro in the Cuban Revolution. By the end of the 1980s, there were nearly one million Cubans in the United States (Perez 2003). Cubans enjoy a special status in U.S. immigration policy. Cubans who are found at sea attempting to come to the United States are sent back to Cuba, while those who manage to land on U.S. soil are nearly always welcomed into the United States. The exiles who came in the early 1960s came because of a long history of U.S. military interventions into Cuba, with the expectation that the U.S. government would assist in ousting Castro's government. Those migrants who come today come more often for economic than political motives, and because of ties they have in the United States, in the context of an immigration policy that is generally favorable toward Cubans (Eckstein and Barberia 2002; Perez 2003; Pew Hispanic Center 2006).

Relatively few Jamaicans came to the United States prior to 1965, in part because Jamaicans were primarily emigrating elsewhere: to Central America, other islands, and Great Britain. However, just as Great Britain passed a series of restrictive immigration laws in the 1960s, the United States passed the 1965 Immigration and Nationality Act, which facilitated the increased immigration of Jamaicans on skills- and family-based visas. By 2009, there were about 637,000 Jamaican migrants in the United States (Glennie and Chappell 2010). Nearly half of Jamaicans in the United States live in New York City, and another 28 percent live in southern Florida. There are also significant populations in Connecticut,

New Jersey, Washington, D.C., and Atlanta (Vickerman 1999). Notably, over half of Jamaican migrants to the United States are women (Foner 2008; Glennie and Chappell 2010).

ILLEGAL IMMIGRATION AND POLICY RESPONSE

In the 1970s, undocumented immigration reached unprecedented levels and became a matter of public debate for the first time. During the 1980s, public opposition to undocumented immigration grew, and politicians began to get tough on immigration. Eventually, another major legislative change took place in 1986.

The Immigration Reform and Control Act of 1986 (IRCA) and Nativism

At the beginning of the twenty-first century, it is hard to imagine that there was ever a time when illegal immigration was not seen as a problem. Remarkably, this issue did not figure on the national political agenda until the 1980s, when the tightening economy, combined with the arrival of increasing numbers of Latin Americans, generated waves of nativism and anti-immigrant sentiment. The concern over large numbers of undocumented migrants often had a racial tenor: the debates made it clear that the "problem" with immigration was the high and increasing numbers of Mexicans in the United States (Inda 2006).

The debates leading up to the passage of the **Immigration Reform and Control Act of 1986 (IRCA)** invoked racialized sentiments about Mexicans taking jobs from Americans, overusing welfare, and refusing to assimilate, despite evidence to the contrary. As Pierrette Hondagneu-Sotelo (1994) argues, the debates surrounding IRCA were not so much about the presence of Mexicans as about the reality that increasing numbers of Mexicans were settling in the United States. Hondagneu-Sotelo (1994) contends that the nativism pervading the debates over the IRCA focused on three claims: (1) allegations that immigrants were stealing jobs from Americans, (2) concerns that immigrants were overusing the welfare system, and (3) worries that the newcomers were too different and "unassimilable." By the end of the twentieth century, immigration restrictionists were no longer concerned about the inability of southern and Eastern Europeans to assimilate. Now, the target was Mexicans.

The passage of IRCA involved a series of compromises and constituted the last mass legalization of the twentieth century. As the name implies, IRCA included immigration reform and control provisions. The twin prongs of IRCA were (1) to offer a legalization option for people who lived in the United States but did not have the proper authorization to work in the country, and (2) to impose sanctions on employers who hired people not authorized to work in the United States. The imposition of sanctions was meant to deter employers from hiring undocumented workers. Instead, these sanctions ultimately created an industry that produced fraudulent documentation, making it easy for anyone to obtain the (false) documents they needed to work (Fragomen and Bell 2007).

One of the major consequences of IRCA was to encourage the permanent settlement of Mexican immigrants, who had formerly come primarily as temporary workers. Until the 1970s, over 80 percent of Mexican immigrants were temporary workers who came to the United States to work in the agricultural sector for a few months and then returned to Mexico with their savings. By 1997, only 40 percent of Mexican migration was for temporary work in the agricultural sector (Avila, Fuentes, and Tuirán 2000). The legalization of temporary workers encouraged more migrants to settle permanently in the United States and to bring their families with them (Massey et al. 2002). Once migrants obtained legal residence or citizenship, they were able to bring over family members under family reunification provisions. As increasing numbers of Mexicans settled permanently in the United States, racialized fears of immigrants intensified.

Proposition 187 and the Lead-Up to the Illegal Immigration Reform and Immigrant Responsibility Act of 1996 (IIRIRA)

Fear of immigrants often has racial undertones. As Kevin Johnson (2004) points out, the vast majority of immigrants to the United States are people of color—less than 20 percent of immigrants come from Europe, Canada, or Australia. Thus, any discourse about immigration today has the subtext of minority incorporation into society. The racialization of immigrants, and especially of undocumented immigrants, became clear in the campaign to push forward Proposition 187 in California, a ballot initiative that would deny social services and educational opportunities to the undocumented.

When Proposition 187 was being debated in the early 1990s, California was on the verge of becoming a majority-minority state, and demographic changes were at the center of the fears expressed by Proposition 187 supporters. For example, in Robin Dale Jacobson's interviews with supporters, one of her respondents told her that the proposition was a response to the "Mexican impact on the state of California." Another interviewee was more forthright: "So, I just wanted something to be done about too many Mexican people all of a sudden" (R. Jacobson 2008, 39). These fears about the increase in the Mexican population were exacerbated by the conflation of Mexicans with "illegals" and "criminals." Supporters of the proposition often took the fact that undocumented migrants had crossed the border illegally or overstayed their visas to indicate that they were prone to criminal activity more generally. Governor Pete Wilson fanned the flames of this fire by "widely publicizing the estimated costs of keeping illegal aliens in prison" (R. Jacobson 2008, 55). In addition to criminalizing undocumented immigrants, much of the discourse surrounding Proposition 187 racialized undocumented immigrants as Mexican. Thus, many of its supporters interpreted the "invasion" of undocumented workers as a racial takeover of California (R. Jacobson 2008, 117).

The political campaigns that promoted the passage of Proposition 187 drew on racial imagery. Television ads supported by Governor Wilson "showed shadowy Mexicans crossing the border in large numbers" (K. Johnson 2004, 43). Johnson argues that the Proposition 187 campaign was a clear manifestation of the racial fears of white Californians. While it would have been politically unsavory to launch an overtly racist attack on people of color, targeting undocumented immigrants without mentioning race directly was permissible.

In the context of an economic downturn, job losses, and state cutbacks in social services, many Californians found undocumented immigrants to be appropriate scapegoats for their economic troubles, and in 1994 Proposition 187 was passed (Alvarez and Butterfield 2000). Although there was no clear connection between the presence of a large undocumented population and the hard economic times, gubernatorial and state legislature candidates in California were able to use the presence of undocumented people to their advantage by advocating for harsh policies that were not guaranteed to improve the fiscal health of the state. Politicians used undocumented immigrants as scapegoats by blaming them for the poor economic conditions, and their promises to get tough on illegal immigration helped them win elections. In California, 60 percent of voters voted in favor of Proposition 187. The bill was not implemented, however, as it was found to be unconstitutional in 1997 (Diamond 1996).

Although Proposition 187 was found to be unconstitutional, the debates surrounding it set the stage for the passage of three laws in 1996 that negatively affected immigrants: the **Anti-Terrorism and Effective Death Penalty Act (AEDPA)**, the **Illegal Immigration Reform and Immigrant Responsibility Act (IIRIRA)**, and the **Personal Responsibility and Work Opportunity Reconciliation Act (PRWORA)**.

The PRWORA was designed to "end welfare as we know it." It also had nativist provisions that denied services to non-citizens. Contrary to popular belief, undocumented migrants have never been eligible for welfare services such as cash benefits, Medicaid, food stamps, or public housing. The root of the myth that undocumented migrants benefit from need-based programs such as food stamps is that their U.S.-citizen children are eligible for the same set of benefits as any other U.S. citizen. When PRWORA was passed, it extended the limitations on welfare benefits to legally present immigrants. Touted as a money-saving measure, PRWORA denied most benefits to legally present migrants, at least for the first five years of their stay in the United States (Tumlin and Zimmerman 2003). Now, let's turn to the other two laws passed in 1996.

The 1996 Laws and the Detention and Deportation of Black and Latino Immigrants

In 1996, Congress passed two laws that fundamentally changed the rights of all foreign-born people in the United States: the Anti-Terrorism and Effective Death Penalty Act (AEDPA) and the Illegal Immigration Reform and Immigrant Responsibility Act of 1996 (IIRIRA). These laws were striking in that they eliminated judicial review of some deportation orders, required mandatory detention for many non-citizens, and introduced the potential for the use of secret evidence in certain cases. Some of the most pernicious consequences of these laws are related to the deportation of legal permanent residents, commonly referred to as "green card holders."

Under IIRIRA, legal permanent residents face mandatory deportation if they are convicted of "aggravated felonies." These include crimes for which a person is sentenced to at least one year in prison, regardless of whether the sentence is served or suspended. These crimes can also be relatively minor, such as the theft of baby clothes from a department store or two counts of minor drug possession. These cases do not require judicial review, meaning that people do not have the right to have a judge hear the specifics of the case or consider the ties that a person has to the United States. Furthermore, the law can be applied retroactively. This means that any legal permanent resident charged with a crime at any time during his or her stay in the United States could be subject to deportation. For example, a person could have come to the United States legally at age two, been convicted of resisting arrest at age eighteen, and—twenty years later, after the passage of IIRIRA—be subject to deportation at age thirty-eight. Even adopted children of U.S. citizens have faced deportation under these laws, in those cases in which parents failed to naturalize their children prior to age eighteen (Morawetz 2000; Master 2003). In light of the heavy policing of black and Latino neighborhoods, and of black and Latino youth in particular, immigrants from Latin America and the Caribbean are more likely to face deportation because of these laws.

The 1996 laws are punitive and harsh. Moreover, they have disproportionately affected blacks and Latinos. Kevin Johnson (2004) argues that since the vast majority of immigrants who come to the United States each year are people of color, the differential treatment of non-citizens in U.S. legal practices amounts to racial discrimination. As discussed in the previous chapter, Joe Feagin (2001: 31) defines systemic racism as "a diverse assortment of racist practices; the unjustly gained economic and political power of whites; the continuing resource inequalities; and the white-racist ideologies and attitudes created to preserve white advantage and power." He further contends that "one can accurately describe the United States as a 'total racist society' in which every major aspect of life is shaped to some degree by the core racist realities." The system of deportation and detention of immigrants is no exception: it is clearly shaped by the "core racist realities" of the United States.

As described in Chapter Nine, the criminal justice system systematically disadvantages black and Latino men. Even though black and white men have similar levels of criminal activity, black men are seven times more likely than white men to be imprisoned, and Latinos are

voices

Hector, a Guatemalan Deportee

Hector moved to the United States with his mother when he was three years old, in 1984. They joined his father, who had been there since he was a newborn. In 1990, his parents applied for political asylum, as Hector's mother had worked for the Guatemalan government and could be subject to persecution if they returned. They were issued work permits and waited for their cases to be heard. In 1999, Hector and his family were able to legalize under the Nicaraguan Adjustment and Central American Relief Act (NACARA). Hector became a legal permanent resident of the United States.

Hector spent most of his childhood in the San Fernando Valley, where he completed elementary, middle, and high school. He did well in high school and attended the University of California. After he finished college in 2004, his first job was on campus as a coordinator for a smoking prevention and cessation program.

While working on campus, Hector also began to work part time at a computer company. When the grant funding his university job ran out, he switched over to full-time work at the computer company. There, he quickly moved up from entry- to mid-level management. Things were going well for him. He was earning good money at the company and was promoted several times.

Hector frequently traveled back to the San Fernando Valley to visit his parents and old friends. It was there he reconnected with some people who encouraged him to join them in a credit card fraud scheme. Hector and his friends were caught forging credit cards, and he was sentenced to eighteen months in jail. After finishing his time, Hector faced automatic deportation to Guatemala.

At Hector's deportation hearing, it did not matter that he had come to the United States when he was three years old, that he was a legal permanent resident, that he had a college degree, and that he had no immediate family in Guatemala. The only consideration the judge could take into account was the fact that he had been convicted of an aggravated felony. With this on his record, the judge had no choice but to order Hector deported to Guatemala, where he had to remake his life from the ground up.

Source: Golash-Boza 2012.

four times as likely (P. Collins 2004; Feagin 2001; Western 2006). In the case of drug offenses, the data are particularly striking. In the United States, black men are sent to prison on drug charges at thirteen times the rate of white men, yet five times as many whites use illegal drugs as blacks (Alexander 2010). Although whites use drugs more frequently than blacks, blacks are much more likely to end up incarcerated. These data are important for understanding deportations, as about a third of all deportees are deported for drug charges, and most criminal deportees are men (Golash-Boza 2012).

Racism in the criminal justice system has severe implications for black and Latino/a immigrants. Many Jamaicans, Dominicans, and Haitians experience the same set of resource deprivations and racist ideologies and practices that lead to the mass incarceration of black men. Immigrants from Latin America often live in Latino neighborhoods that are heavily policed. This means that immigrants of African and Latin American descent are more likely to be jailed and eventually deported than immigrants of European or Asian descent who are not subject to the same set of prejudices and discriminatory actions. Whereas the immigrant population includes many whites and Asians, blacks and Latinos almost exclusively make up the group of detainees and deportees. Black and brown people from Latin America and the Caribbean are substantially more likely to be deported than are whites or Asians; over 90 percent of people deported on criminal grounds between 1997 and 2007 were from countries that have a Caribbean coast (Human Rights Watch 2009).

Earlier in this chapter, we looked at the five countries of origin from which most legal permanent residents in the United States come: China, India, Mexico, the Philippines, and Vietnam. With the notable exception of Mexico, these are not the countries to which we send most deportees. The top five countries of origin of deportees in 2009 were Mexico, Honduras, Guatemala, El Salvador, and the Dominican Republic. These five countries alone accounted for over 90 percent of all people deported in 2009. Table 3-1 lists the top ten countries to which deportees were sent in 2008. These ten countries represent 95.21 percent of people deported in 2009. These data call attention to a glaring fact: Asians are prominent among immigrants overall, whereas Latin Americans and Caribbean nationals are overrepresented among deportees. At this point, it will be useful to take a closer look at the numbers. As Figure 3-6 shows, even when we take into account the relative numbers of undocumented migrants in the country, Latin Americans are still much more likely to be deported than Asians.

Deportation policy also has gendered effects. Nearly 90 percent of all deportees are men, even though about half of all immigrants are men (Golash-Boza and Hondagneu-Sotelo 2013). This disparity is due to the

TABLE 3-1
Top Ten Countries to Which Deportees Were Sent, 2009

Country	Total	Percent	Cumulative Percent
Mexico	282,666	71.87%	71.87%
Guatemala	29,182	7.42%	79.29%
Honduras	26,849	6.83%	86.12%
El Salvador	20,406	5.19%	91.31%
Dominican Republic	3,464	0.88%	92.19%
Brazil	3,407	0.87%	93.05%
Colombia	2,443	0.62%	93.68%
Ecuador	2,303	0.59%	94.26%
Nicaragua	2,098	0.53%	94.79%
Jamaica	1,615	0.41%	95.21%
Total # of Deportees	393,289		

Source: U.S. Department of Homeland Security, Office of Immigration Statistics (2009).

way criminal and immigration laws are enforced. Men are more likely than women to be in public places—driving, walking, or standing on the corner—and thus are more likely to come to the attention of the authorities. Although more men are deported than women, deportation policy does not affect only deportees—it also affects their families. When a person is deported, a family often loses a breadwinner.

FIGURE 3-6

RATIO OF UNDOCUMENTED MIGRANTS TO DEPORTEES, 2009

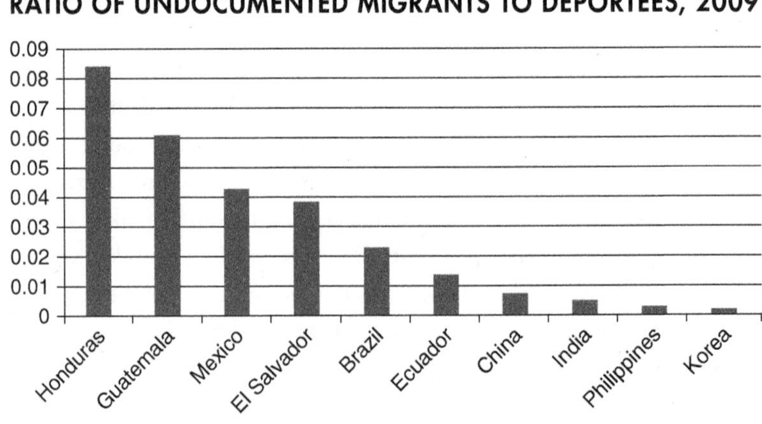

Source: U.S. Department of Homeland Security, Office of Immigration Statistics (2009).

Current immigration laws, practices, and policies further enhance the extent to which our society is riddled with racism and repression. The general climate of strict enforcement of immigration laws in the post–9/11 era has further exacerbated the situation. A recent nationally representative survey of Hispanics found that nearly one in ten Latinos had been stopped by authorities and asked about their immigration status, and a similar percentage had experienced discrimination in housing. Remarkably, 15 percent of all Latinos between the ages of eighteen and twenty-eight said they had experienced some form of discrimination. It is thus no wonder that the majority of those Latinos surveyed said that they worry about deportation (Lopez and Minushkin 2008). These numbers indicate that the racial profiling of Latinos is widespread and that Latinos are targeted in immigration enforcement efforts.

The 1996 deportation laws were punitive. Moreover, they have had a disproportionate effect on people of color. This pattern is consistent with other patterns of systemic racism in this country. This point of view allows us to see that the racism embedded in immigration policy is not an isolated case but a foreseeable byproduct of a society that systematically denies the dignity and humanity of people of color. The criminalization of black men leads to the deportation of a disproportionate number of Dominicans and Jamaicans. The stereotype of Mexicans, and of those who look "Mexican," as "illegals" leads to the targeting of Mexicans and Central Americans in immigration enforcement efforts.

These practices and policies do not simply isolate and remove immigrants of color, but they also have detrimental effects on their families, who are, in most cases, also people of color. Those children, spouses, and parents who witness their loved ones being mistreated and banished are also victims of this systematic denial of human rights. In light of patterns of segregation, there are whole communities of Mexicans and Mexican Americans in which children are growing up not only experiencing structural racism in terms of resource provisions, but also witnessing their mothers, fathers, brothers, sisters, neighbors, and community leaders being told that they have no right to be here and, in many cases, being forcibly removed from their communities. Just as African American children often grow up knowing that blacks are more likely than other groups to be "locked up," Mexicans and other Latin American and Caribbean people grow up knowing that people like them are being expelled from this country at the rate of nearly 1,000 people a day (Golash-Boza 2012).

The DREAM Act

The DREAM Act (Development, Relief, and Education for Alien Minors) was first introduced in the Senate on August 1, 2001, by Senators Dick Durbin and Orrin Hatch. As of this writing in 2015, despite widespread support, the DREAM Act still has not made it through Congress. The DREAM Act would allow undocumented youth who finish high school in the United States to apply for legalization and a path to citizenship. According to the Pew Hispanic Center, 86 percent of Latinos in the United States believe that migrants to this country—even unauthorized ones—deserve a chance to become citizens. This belief is shared by 72 percent of all Americans. In 2012, DREAMers were able to successfully pressure President Obama into providing deferred action and work permits to undocumented youth. In June 2012, the president issued the Deferred Action for Childhood Arrivals (DACA) memorandum, which protects youth from deportation for two years. To qualify, undocumented immigrants must have been under the age of thirty-one on June 15, 2012; have arrived in the United States before the age of sixteen; and be currently enrolled either in school or in the armed forces or already have completed high school. A path to citizenship and full inclusion into the country many of them call home, however, remains elusive.

NATIVISM IN THE TWENTY-FIRST CENTURY

At the end of the twentieth century, the United States witnessed a surge in nativism not seen since the 1920s. Because this nativism was directed primarily at new immigrants—Asians and Latin Americans—it can be difficult to disentangle it from racism.

Historian George Sanchez (1997) suggests that there are three factors that distinguish the racialized nativism of today from that of a century ago:

- The rise of extreme antipathy toward languages other than English. This is exemplified in a campaign some people have launched against having to "press 1 for English" when trying to reach customer service or townspeople's insistence that libraries not purchase books in languages other than English.
- The concern that Asian, Caribbean, and Latin American immigrants are taking advantage of affirmative action programs

designed to help native-born minorities, especially African Americans. This can be seen in conversations regarding the high numbers of West Indians entering Ivy League schools.

- The worry that immigrants are draining public resources through the overuse of welfare, education, and health care services. This sentiment persists even though laws passed in 1996 severely limit immigrants' access to welfare and health services. The Supreme Court decided in *Plyler v. Doe* in 1982 that any child in the United States has the right to an education. It is indicative of the strong sense of nativism that exists in the United States today that a politician or pundit can suggest that the children of foreigners are draining our funds by attending public schools, instead of seeing the education of children—both immigrant and native-born—as an investment in the future of this country.

The rise of nativism is also closely tied to economic restructuring in the United States. Nativism in the 1920s was connected to a difficult transition from a primarily agricultural economy to a massively industrialized one. At the end of the twentieth century, the United States experienced rapid deindustrialization and the rise of a service-oriented economy. These structural changes in the economy produced economic uncertainty, especially among the working class and poor. Moreover, as native-born blacks, whites, and Latinos/as have been displaced from factory jobs, immigrants have come in to fill jobs in the service sector. As the economy has shifted, native-born workers have not always been able to retool their skill sets or displace themselves to areas of high growth. The widespread perception that immigrants are "taking our jobs" is intimately tied to the rise of nativism. The lack of evidence that immigrants are taking jobs from the native-born can be seen in the aftermath of restrictive immigration policies passed in Alabama. When Alabama passed laws restricting the rights of undocumented people, the state experienced a massive outflow of immigrants. These immigrants left jobs behind that went unfilled. The reason for this is that immigrants in Alabama who picked tomatoes for a living could not easily be replaced by the urban unemployed. Native-born urban workers are unlikely to see the benefit of moving from the city to the countryside to pick tomatoes. The idea that Alabama could simply rid itself of undocumented workers and thereby fix its unemployment problem was ill conceived and riddled with nativist logic.

The law passed in Alabama that scared away thousands of immigrants was called House Bill (HB) 56, the Alabama Taxpayer and Citizen Protection Act. It is similar to Georgia's HB 87, the Illegal Immigration Reform and Enforcement Act of 2011, and Arizona's Senate Bill (SB) 1070, the Support Our Law Enforcement and Safe Neighborhoods Act.

Arizona SB 1070 went into effect on July 29, 2010; its passage sparked national debate, protests, and boycotts. When Arizona governor Jan Brewer signed SB 1070 on April 23, 2010, the law required local law enforcement agents to determine the immigration status of any person with whom they interacted during the course of their duties. This meant, for example, that if a police officer responded to a call for domestic violence, he would be required to check the immigration status of both the perpetrator and the victim, if he had reason to believe that either might be in the country unlawfully. SB 1070 was subsequently modified with the enactment of HB 2162 on April 30, 2010, which changed the language such that police officers would only be required to check the immigration status of people during a lawful stop, detention, or arrest. With these modified provisions, SB 1070 only required intervention in those cases in which a person was suspected of violating state laws. These modifications relieved some concerns that the law would make victims of crimes more unlikely to contact law enforcement officials, yet the possibility of racial profiling remained a substantial problem. According to an amicus brief filed by the American Immigration Lawyers Association (AILA) (2010, page 5), "there is simply no unbiased means of implementing the term 'unlawful presence,' because as a legal status there are no observable characteristics of 'unlawful presence,' or readily available means by which a police officer could discern 'unlawful presence' in any stop, detention, or investigative encounter." Regardless of the final outcome of these court cases, these laws make it clear that nativism is alive and well in the twenty-first century.

CONCLUSION AND DISCUSSION

How far have we come since 1882, the year of the passage of the Chinese Exclusion Act? The immigration laws passed since 1965 in the United States do not have overt racial provisions like the 1882 Chinese Exclusion Act or the 1924 Oriental Exclusion Act. We also have not seen anything as egregious as the 1954 Operation Wetback.

Laws with these names or provisions would be untenable in the twenty-first-century United States. Nevertheless, we continue to see both the racially uneven consequences of immigration laws and racialized sentiments directed at particular national-origin and racial groups.

This chapter has shown that U.S. immigration policy has been racialized from the beginning. At the same time, the way these policies have been racialized has changed over time, as racial ideologies have shifted. Throughout history, nativism has also consistently reared its head, although in different ways over time.

Harvard professor Aristide Zolberg titled his 2009 book on immigration policy *A Nation by Design,* hinting at the ways that immigration policy has been deployed with the goal of creating an ideal populace. In 1882, the Chinese Exclusion Act was passed to end the influx of Chinese laborers. The 1924 Immigration Act was designed to recruit immigrants from northern and Western Europe and to exclude immigrants from the rest of the world. The 1965 Immigration and Nationality Act was passed in the name of civil rights and ostensibly to create a diverse society yet ended up creating a large undocumented Mexican population. The 1986 laws were passed with the hope of ending immigration. When that did not work, the 1996 laws made life more difficult and precarious for immigrants. The current state laws are designed with the hope that immigrants will self-deport.

Each of these laws was proposed because of a vision lawmakers had for society. But the United States is a changing nation. Soon, the country will no longer have a white Anglo majority. As the United States changes, whites could either become more accepting of differences or reject those differences more forcefully. What do you think will happen? What do you think should happen?

THINKING ABOUT **RACIAL JUSTICE**

The United States has a long history of immigration from around the world and an equally long history of welcoming some immigrants while barring or discouraging others. Since the 1960s, the vast majority of immigrants to the United States have been non-white. In this context, is it possible to have laws that discriminate against immigrants without being racially discriminatory?

Key Terms

nativism 59
Naturalization Act of 1790 62
naturalization 62
Chinese Exclusion Act 63
Immigration Act of 1924/ Johnson–Reed Act 64
Oriental Exclusion Act 64
legal permanent resident 65
bracero program 66
Operation Wetback 67
McCarran Internal Security Act 67
1952 Immigration and Nationality Act (McCarran–Walter Act) 68
1965 Immigration and Nationality Act (Hart-Cellar Act) 68
1986 Immigration Reform and Control Act (IRCA) 77
Anti-Terrorism and Effective Death Penalty Act (AEDPA) 80
Illegal Immigration Reform and Immigrant Responsibility Act (IIRIRA) 80
Personal Responsibility and Work Opportunity Reconciliation Act (PRWORA) 80

Check Your Understanding

OBJECTIVE 3.1

Examine the racialized history of U.S. immigration policy.

- Nativism and racism have been intertwined in U.S. immigration policies since the beginning of the nation's history. The first piece of immigration legislation was the Chinese Exclusion Act in 1882. Laws continued to be racialized over the course of the twentieth century.

Q What is the significance of the Chinese Exclusion Act and the court cases that stemmed from it?

Q Why was Operation Wetback important?

Q How have immigration flows and quotas changed since the 1850s?

OBJECTIVE 3.2

Describe U.S. policy responses to undocumented immigration.

- The passage of the 1965 Immigration and Nationality Act and subsequent 1986 Immigration Reform and Control Act created the problem of illegal immigration. Since then, more restrictive laws have been passed.

Q What were some major changes brought about by the 1965 Immigration and Nationality Act?

Q What legislative changes sparked Asian and Latin American immigration in the late twentieth century?

Q What restrictive immigration laws were passed in the late twentieth century?

OBJECTIVE 3.3

Analyze the relationship between nativism and racism in the twenty-first century.

- When most immigrants are people of color, racism and nativism are difficult to disentangle.

Q How has nativism changed from previous historical periods?

Critical Thinking

1. How have economic circumstances played a role in the passage of immigration laws?
2. How have U.S. colonial and imperial relationships with other countries affected migration flows?
3. Are IRCA and IIRIRA related to racialized sentiments? How so?
4. Why are Latin American immigrants the most likely to be deported?

THE SPREAD OF IDEOLOGY

"Controlling Images" and Racism in the Media

CHAPTER OUTLINE

LEARNING OBJECTIVES

4.1 Examine racial stereotypes propagated in popular culture today.
4.2 Examine racial stereotypes found in new media.
4.3 Assess how media images serve to justify racial inequality.
4.4 Demonstrate how media representations are raced, classed, and gendered.

If you were to watch the films of the early twentieth century, you would find that non-whites are portrayed almost exclusively in stereotypical roles: Native Americans are represented as silent Indian chiefs, Arabs play the roles of desert sheikhs, Latinas appear as sexy ladies, and African Americans play roles of mammies and buffoons. Fast-forward to the twenty-first century, and we find more nuanced depictions. However, there are still traces of these historical stereotypes in film, television, and even new media.

Moreover, these stereotypes are not harmless: they have real and enduring consequences. Representations of blacks and Latinos as poor and as lawbreakers, for example, reinforce popular notions about black and Latino cultural deficiencies. The pervasiveness of these images makes us less likely to question why African Americans earn less than whites and why blacks and Latinos are more likely to be incarcerated than whites. Many people in the United States think that blacks and Latinos are more likely to be incarcerated than whites because they commit more crimes (P. Collins 2004; Feagin 2001). This stance ignores evidence to the contrary, as well as the racially discriminatory nature of the criminal justice system, yet it makes sense to people who constantly see images of blacks and Latinos shooting and robbing on television. Just as past stereotypes about black laziness served to justify slavery, current representations of blacks as criminals work to justify the high rates of incarceration of African Americans. Representations of people of color on television are modern versions of the stereotypical images created to justify slavery, segregation, genocide, colonialism, and exclusion.

In this chapter, we will focus on racial ideologies propagated in the media. How do these ideologies play a role in normalizing and justifying racial inequality? Why do racial segregation and inequality remain prevalent in spite of laws against racial discrimination? An understanding of how the media reproduces racial stereotypes will help us answer these questions. More pointedly, this examination will show how media portrayals may partly explain why so little is being done about racial disparities in a nation that values equality and democracy.

PORTRAYALS OF PEOPLE OF COLOR ON TELEVISION AND IN OTHER MEDIA

In 2012, people in the United States watched, on average, 2.8 hours of television a day, making television viewing the most common leisure activity in the country (Bureau of Labor Statistics 2013a). Given that Americans spend so much time in front of the small screen, it is no wonder television has a great influence on how we see the world. Think, for example, of two popular shows: *Friends* and *Sex and the City*, both of which were set in the extraordinarily diverse New York City. According to the 2010 U.S. census, over one-third of the population of New York City is foreign-born, and the city's population is less than half white. In these two shows, however, all of the main characters were white, and the tremendous racial and ethnic diversity of their city was largely unnoticeable, even when the characters were in public. By presenting primarily white people in primarily white spaces, representations in shows such as these naturalize racial segregation. It thus seems perfectly natural to many white Americans that they themselves would live in primarily white neighborhoods and send their children to primarily white schools, even when they too live in multiracial urban areas (Orfield 2009). Racial segregation thus becomes completely normal and desirable.

Because television shapes how we see the world, it is important to consider how various groups are portrayed in television shows. First, let's consider how much diversity there is on television, given the United States' multiracial society. Television, it turns out, is mostly black and white. Overall, whites and blacks are overrepresented, and all other groups, including Asians, Latinos, and Native Americans, are underrepresented (Kopacz and Lawton 2011a; Monk-Turner, Heiserman, Johnson, Cotton, and Jackson 2010; see Figures 4.1a and 4.1b).

Portrayals of Blacks

Prior to the civil rights era, portrayals of blacks on television and in popular culture were uniformly stereotypical. Shows such as *Amos 'n' Andy* featured African Americans who appeared almost exclusively as maids, cooks, "mammies," con artists, or deadbeats. These representations served to legitimate the racial order of overt white dominance. The logic of the era was that African Americans were incapable of self-governance and thus were well served by the racial order of the

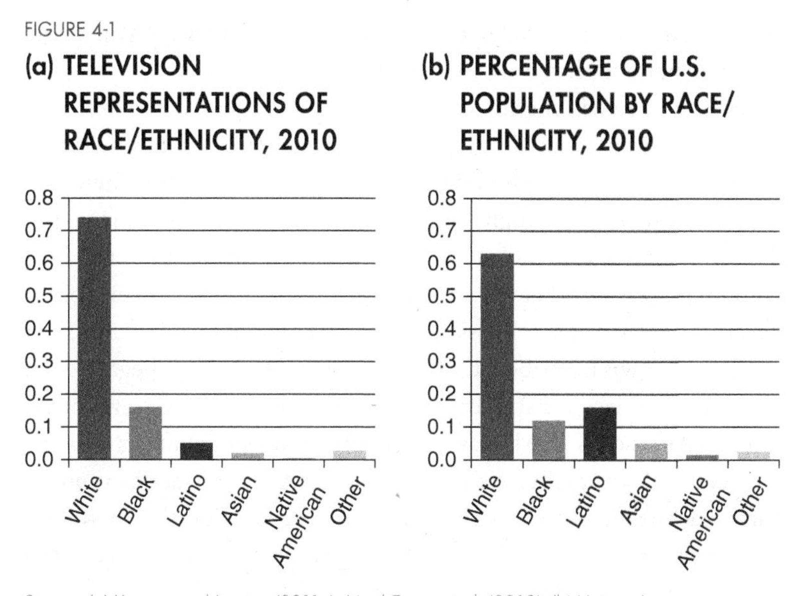

FIGURE 4-1

(a) TELEVISION REPRESENTATIONS OF RACE/ETHNICITY, 2010

(b) PERCENTAGE OF U.S. POPULATION BY RACE/ETHNICITY, 2010

Source: (a) Kopacz and Lawton (2011a); Monk-Turner et al. (2010); (b) Humes, Jones, and Ramirez. 2011.

day. Whites were reassured that while blacks were often good servants and entertainers, they were not capable of assuming the responsibilities of full citizenship. The NAACP contended that *Amos 'n' Andy* exclusively represented blacks as lazy, stupid, loud, thieving, and dishonest and promoted racial prejudice against blacks; it eventually leveled a lawsuit against CBS because of these portrayals. The lawsuit was successful and resulted in *Amos 'n' Andy* being taken off of the air in 1953 (Gray 1995; Hunt 2005).

In the 1980s, a completely different kind of show became popular. Instead of presenting blacks as deadbeats or servants, *The Cosby Show* had a central cast of successful black characters. It reached the top of television viewers' rankings and remained there for most of its eight years on prime time television (Hunt 2005). The show, which first aired in 1984, was about a middle-class African American family made up of Cliff Huxtable, a doctor; his wife, Clair, a lawyer; and their five children. The family lived in a spacious brownstone in New York City and was successful economically, socially, and educationally. The depictions could not be further from those of *Amos 'n' Andy*. However, even though *The Cosby Show* did not reinforce negative stereotypes of blacks, it still worked to reproduce what communications scholars Sut Jhally and Justin Lewis (1992) call **enlightened racism**: the idea that the United States is a land of opportunity and that African Americans could do better if they only tried harder.

Jhally and Lewis conducted fifty-two focus groups with white and black Americans about *The Cosby Show* and found that white Americans were able to accept the Huxtable family as people like them. There was a catch, however: although white Americans were happy to have the Huxtables in their living rooms each week, the show did not reduce stereotypes about other African Americans. Instead, the depiction of successful blacks on television reinforced "enlightened racism," as Jhally and Lewis described it. Moreover, white Americans began to see themselves as less racist because they liked the Huxtables and other African Americans who behaved similarly. Whites attributed any negative feelings they might have had about other African Americans not to their blackness, but to how they behaved. The fact that the Huxtables never experienced racism further reinforced the idea that racism is the direct result of how African Americans behave.

In the media today, we see another seemingly positive image of African Americans: the black athlete. African Americans dominate U.S. sports, and Americans of all hues idolize black athletes. The idolization of black athletes might make it seem as if the media tend to portray these athletes in a positive manner. However, scholars who analyze the portrayal of black athletes point out that these portrayals also reinforce stereotypes and that the media portray black and white athletes quite differently (King and Fruehling Springwood 2001). For example, when black athletes transgress moral or legal boundaries, the media are quick to home in on the stories—especially those that reinforce stereotypes. One example King and Fruehling Springwood give is of Christian Peter, a white football player, and Lawrence Phillips, a black football player, both of whom played at the University of Nebraska. When Peter was accused of assaulting a white woman, the incident received attention only in Lincoln, Nebraska. When Phillips, however, was charged with beating his white ex-girlfriend, it received intense national coverage, including a segment on *60 Minutes*. King and Fruehling Springwood also juxtapose athletes Kobe Bryant and Drew Henson. They argue that when Kobe Bryant, who is black, decided not to attend college full-time, the media commentary suggested that Bryant needed refinement, training, and discipline, and that this was a bad decision. In contrast, when Drew Henson, who is white, made a similar decision, the conversation in the media did not revolve around his maturity or his possibilities for upward mobility.

African American women also continue to be portrayed in stereotypical ways. A recent study by Melissa Harris-Perry (2011) revealed that stereotyped caricatures of black women—as Mammies, Sapphires, and Jezebels—continue to be prominent. A **Mammy** is a stereotypical image of a black maid, encapsulated by the "Aunt Jemima" icon and taking its name from "Mammy" in *Gone with the Wind.* **Sapphire** was one of the main characters on *Amos 'n' Andy* and is a caricature of an angry black woman. **Jezebel** is a name with biblical origins that has come to signify an oversexed or hypersexual black woman. Harris-Perry (2011) found that these three stereotypes about African American women have been prominent in political and popular culture since the Civil War and influence how black women perceive themselves and are perceived by others.

Although representations of African Americans on television have improved in response to complaints levied by the NAACP and other groups, we still can find traces of enduring stereotypical images. African Americans continue to be portrayed disproportionately as welfare mothers, mammies, athletes, thugs, rapists, and sidekicks (P. Collins 2004). In the following sections, we will consider the extent to which this continues to be true for other groups.

Portrayals of Latinos/as

Latinos/as are both underrepresented and misrepresented in the U.S. media (Monk-Turner, Heiserman, Johnson, Cotton, and Jackson 2010; Rodriquez 2000). During prime time of the fall 2001–2002 season, two-thirds of all Latino characters were males, and they were most often portrayed as either law enforcement officers or criminals. Latinas most often were portrayed as nurses, clerical workers, or domestic workers. Eleven percent of all Latino male appearances on prime-time television in the 2001–2002 season were of criminals (National Hispanic Foundation for the Arts 2001).

In a study of prime-time television realized during March 2007, Monk-Turner and colleagues found that overall, Latinos were the group most likely to be portrayed negatively on television (2010). For example, their analyses revealed that none of the Latino characters were depicted as articulate, whereas 25 percent of black and 30 percent of white characters were depicted as articulate. Half of all African

American actors were depicted as intelligent, compared with 43 percent of whites and 27 percent of Latinos. Finally, the researchers found that only 2 percent of white actors were portrayed as immoral, compared to 9 percent of African Americans and 18 percent of Latinos, and 3 percent of whites were portrayed as despicable, compared to 9 percent of African Americans and 18 percent of Latinos.

Latino men are often stereotyped into specific roles: gangbanger, bandit, drug trafficker, police officer, janitor, gardener, and the Latin lover. Latinas are most likely to be portrayed as either hot-blooded women anxious for sexual fulfillment or as maids anxious to please (Rodriguez 1997).

Prime-time television shows starring Latinos are few and far between. One exception is *Ugly Betty*, which made its debut in 2006 and ran for four seasons. Based on the Colombian soap opera *Yo Soy Betty, La Fea*, it was the story of a twenty-two-year old Latina from Queens and her efforts to make it in the publishing industry. The main character, Betty Suarez, was given considerable depth and was quite likable. Her family, however, fit well into the stereotypes that many Americans have about Latino/as. Her father was in the United States illegally and had escaped Mexico wanted for murder, her sister was a single mother who dressed provocatively, and the family lived in Queens in a clearly working-class household. Salma Hayek, the show's producer, also appeared on the show as Sofia Reyes, a famous author. Sofia was very smart and capable but displayed characteristics of the stereotypical hot-blooded Latina.

Another show on prime time, *Desperate Housewives*, played strongly to Latino/a stereotypes. It starred two Latinos—Eva Longoria as Gabrielle Solis, and her husband, Carlos Solis, played by Ricardo Antonio Chavira. In this show, Eva was an unfaithful wife who could not keep her hands off of the sixteen-year-old gardener. In addition, she constantly used her sex appeal in attempts to manipulate her husband and other men. Carlos appeared at first to be a loving husband but turned out to be a criminal and was sent to prison. Upon his return, he had an affair with the maid, and he and Gabrielle got divorced. *Desperate Housewives* was on prime-time television for eight years, from 2004 to 2012.

The main problem with Latino/a representation on television continues to be underrepresentation. With such a limited number of representations, it is hard to avoid stereotypes. Some of the most prominent Latinas on television in recent years have been Gabrielle Solis as an adulteress housewife, Hilda Suarez as a single mother, and Betty Suarez as a misfit, with many of the rest appearing as maids. For Latinos, we see Ignacio Suarez as an undocumented immigrant, George Lopez as a factory supervisor, and Carlos Solis as a former convict, with the majority of the rest being criminals or cops. This limited variety of representations is not surprising given the small number of Latinos on television. However, it still serves to mold the images of Latinas as hot-blooded, subservient, and dependent, and of Latinos as criminally inclined and working-class.

Portrayals of Arabs and Arab Americans

Although there are large numbers of Arab Americans in this country, Arabs are overwhelmingly portrayed on television as foreign. Arab women are usually seen veiled or as exotic figures, and Arab men as terrorists or billionaires. In very recent years, this has begun to change, and we now occasionally see Arab Americans on prime-time television. One of the most popular representations of Arab Americans on television is as the targets of racial discrimination. Evelyn Alsultany (2008) points out that in the aftermath of September 11, some television shows took up the question of whether it was fair to discriminate against Arab or Muslim Americans in the name of national security. Alsultany contends that this representation leads to the conclusion that Americans have to choose between protecting the nation and discriminating against Arabs and Arab Americans (who are, according to the subtext, prone to being dangerous). Although more nuanced than previous representations of Arab men, this representation ultimately reinforces the idea that Arabs are terrorists, and thus that it is legitimate to discriminate against them in the name of national security.

Portrayals of Asians and Asian Americans

Darrell Hamamoto (1994) analyzed representations of Asians and Asian Americans on television between 1950 and 1990. He found that Asian men were often represented as foreign, sinister, unidimensional, effeminate characters. But whereas Asian men are often presented in U.S. media as asexual or effeminate, Asian women are often portrayed as hypersexual. There are two primary ways that Asian women are presented: as the **Dragon Lady** or as the **Butterfly** (Rajgopal 2010). The Dragon Lady is a sinister, crafty, and destructive seductress. The

Butterfly is a demure, devoted, submissive wife who is eager to please whites and men in general.

There seems to have been some gains in the representation of Asian women on television. One example is Dr. Christina Yang, a central character in *Grey's Anatomy*. Yang is a beautiful and competent doctor. Her character has substantial depth and defies the "generic Asian" stereotype by making it clear she is both Korean American and from Beverly Hills—not Korea. However, as Rajgopal (2010) points out, Christina Yang's character does not have the feminine qualities of white characters in the show, such as Meredith Grey. She remains enigmatic and cold, showing hints of the Dragon Lady stereotype as well as the "inscrutable Oriental" stereotype. Another example is Ling Woo, Lucy Liu's character in the television series *Ally McBeal*. Similar to Christina Wang, Ling Woo was no Butterfly. Her character was even colder, blunter, and more sexualized than that of Christina Yang. Ling Woo is the quintessential Dragon Lady—the evil seductress.

Portrayals of Native Americans

In the early years of the United States, when white settlers were endeavoring to take over Indian lands in the newly formed nation, the most popular depictions of Native Americans were of savages. Over time, the "captivity narrative"—in which white women and children were captured by savage natives—became a staple in American fiction throughout the eighteenth, nineteenth, and twentieth centuries. Alongside this depiction of Native Americans as primitive and savages, an alternative depiction emerged: that of the Native American wise man or medicine man. Depictions of Native American men tend to fall into either of the two categories of the savage or the wise man (Kopacz and Lawton 2011a; Bird 1999; F. White 2012).

In popular culture in the United States, American Indian men are often eroticized and portrayed as the object of white women's illicit lust. To enhance this eroticization, American Indian men are frequently portrayed as nearly naked. At the other end of the spectrum is the Native American wise man, who is often stoic and far from being a sex object. His wise advice is most often given to white heroes, and he often is a loner without a family of his own. A similarity between these two stereotypical representations is that they both often are placed in the service of whites. The lustful, erotic savage often provides sexual pleasure to white women, and the wise man often reserves his best spiritual advice for white men. In both cases, sexuality and family life among Native Americans is largely invisible (Bird 1999).

Representations of American Indian women also tend toward a duality: as either an American Indian princess or a lustful savage. Pocahontas is the quintessential representation of a Native American woman: she is beautiful, erotic, noble, and fully dedicated to her white lover. At the other end of the spectrum is the squaw, who has sex indiscriminately with both whites and Indians (Kopacz and Lawton 2011a). Similar to the depictions of American Indian men, these depictions are from a white point of view. Native American male and female characters often have the primary purpose of serving white interests—by providing sexual satisfaction, as well as intimate knowledge of nature and other sacred things, and by helping to convince other Indians of the importance of assimilation (Bird 1999).

Johnny Depp plays Tonto in *The Lone Ranger* (2013).

In a survey of Native American stereotypes on television, Frederick White (2012) found that television producers almost exclusively show American Indians as shamans, wise men, sidekicks, Indian princesses, and matriarchs. Today, Native Americans are most commonly represented on television in brief appearances on popular sitcoms. In these appearances, Native Americans are usually presented as the stereotypical wise men who offer advice to white protagonists (Tahmahkera 2008). There are very few representations of Native Americans on television as recurring main characters. Two exceptions were the television shows *Northern Exposure* and *Dr. Quinn, Medicine Woman*. These shows were unique in featuring a prominent cast of Native Americans. However, even these shows relied on stereotypes such as the medicine man and the wise man and woman (Bird 1999; F. White 2012).

Racial Stereotypes in Films

Hollywood films continue to be a major source of entertainment for people in the United States. Although the Internet and global trade give us access to films from every country that produces them, Americans continue to primarily consume Hollywood films. Seventy percent of Americans watch at least one movie a week. The most popular way to watch movies is at home on broadcast, cable, or satellite television; the second most popular is home viewing on DVD or pay-per-view (Pew Research Center 2006). With the majority of the population consuming films on a regular basis, it is likely that the stereotypes portrayed in films also affect how Americans perceive different racial groups.

Films have a much longer history than television, and the earliest films of the twentieth century set the stage for stereotypes that persist today. The representation of Arabs as living in desert kingdoms dominated by tents and camels goes back to the 1920s, with films such as *The Sheik* (1921) and *The Desert Bride* (1928). Early twentieth-century films generally portrayed Asian men as threatening foreigners (Fu Manchu), Americanized detectives (Charlie Chan), and laundrymen. African Americans appeared in stereotypical roles as mammies, loyal slaves, brutes, and violent men in *Birth of a Nation* (1915) and in a host of films afterward (Guerrero 1993). Early representations of Latinas were often sexualized, such as the lusting harlot played by Linda Darnell in *My Darling Clementine* (1946) and the exotic Mexican dancer played by Dolores del Rio in *In Caliente* (1935). Latinos also were portrayed stereotypically as *bandidos,* as in *Broncho Billy and the Greaser* (1914), and as "Latin lovers," as in *The Sheik* (1921) (Berg 2002). Although we no longer see non-whites confined to specific roles, these stereotypical representations have had a lasting legacy.

Arab stereotypes continue to be a staple of Hollywood films. Women in Arab countries are often portrayed as victims of sexism and religious oppression, in need of rescue by enlightened Westerners. There is an intriguing duality of representation whereby Arab women are presented as either "half-naked, belly-dancing sirens" or "*burqua*-covered victims of the Taliban" (Rajgopal 2010, 151). In both cases, women are portrayed as being in need of rescue, often by Western men. The stereotypical image of the Arab man in the United States is well known: he is either a turbaned, sinister terrorist or an immoral billionaire or desert sheikh. Arabs play prominent roles as terrorists in films such as *Black Sunday* (1975), *Frantic* (1988), and *The Siege* (1988). More recently, especially since the bombing of the World Trade Center in 1993 and again in 2001, representations of Arabs as terrorists in films have proliferated. In 1994, these stereotypes were present in the film *True Lies,* and the television series *Homeland,* which continues to air at the time of this writing in 2015, consistently features Arab terrorists as characters. In the twentieth century, there were almost never any representations of Arabs in film or television beyond these stereotypes and rarely any representations at all of Arab Americans. Arabs have been portrayed as perpetually foreign (Shaheen 1997).

Asians also continue to be a fixture of popular culture in the United States. More recently, the representation of Asians as corrupt businessmen and skilled martial artists has emerged. Jane Chi Hyun Park's (2010) recent work points to a character type called the **biracial buddy**—a Westernized Asian man who uses ancient Japanese or Chinese knowledge to help whites. Examples of this character type can be found in films such as *The Karate Kid* and *The Matrix*.

In television and film, we see that the representations of non-whites today are certainly less stereotypical and offensive than they were in the 1950s, 1960s, and 1970s. Stereotypes persist, however, and it is hard to find non-white characters who are given the depth typical of white characters. We find similar trends in other media.

NEW MEDIA REPRESENTATIONS

In 2013, the amount of time Americans spent online surpassed television viewing for the first time—the average adult spent five hours per day online (eMarketer 2013). The amount of time that Americans spend watching television makes it a key site for understanding the proliferation of stereotypes. However, it is also important to consider new media, where we can note many of the same trends.

Video Games

With the advent of new technology, we can no longer restrict our analysis of visual media to film and television. About 90 percent of children between the ages of eight and seventeen regularly play video games. Moreover, instead of being passive viewers, video game players are actively engaged and thus potentially more susceptible to stereotypes. Anna Everett and S. Craig Watkins (2008) carried out a study in which they explored how youths' interactions with video games affected how they thought about race. The researchers argue that the interactive nature of the games enhances the potential for the games not only to perpetuate stereotypes—but also to counter them. Additionally, as technology has improved and permitted video games to be more realistic, game creators have been able to produce what they perceive to be more real and authentic places in video games. This increased realism has led, for example, to the creation of urban spaces that are dominated by African American and Latino young men.

Studies of video games have revealed consistent stereotyping—Latinos are overrepresented in sports games, Asians are almost exclusively portrayed in fighting games, and Arabs are typically portrayed as targets of violence (Saleem 2008; Burgess, Dill, Stermer, Burgess, and Brown 2011). A study of video games by Melinda Burgess and her colleagues (2011) revealed that black characters were more likely than white characters to be portrayed as thugs, athletes, and gun-toting figures. This study demonstrated that African American men continue to be portrayed as criminals and athletes, even in newer forms of media. Burgess and colleagues also found that black women were largely absent from video games.

Social Media

Films, television, and video games are all produced by large corporations. In contrast, social media can be produced and consumed by individuals. In the United States, it is not very difficult to gain access to the technology to create a Twitter account, a Facebook account, a blog, or even a YouTube video. For example, on March 31, 2012, one of the students in my sociology class posted a video on YouTube called "I Am Not Trayvon Martin" in which she argues that middle-class white activists have more in common with George Zimmerman than Trayvon Martin. She contends that whites must work hard to resist the stereotypes that led George Zimmerman to attack Trayvon Martin. Zimmerman's reaction to Martin was based on racial stereotypes about black men (even though Martin was a boy when he was killed). Her video quickly went viral and, as of September 2013, had received over 700,000 views.

This statement is just one example of how social media can be produced by people with low budgets and few connections. It also shows the power of social media to counter, instead of reinforce, stereotypes. But how often does this happen? Are people using social media to counter stereotypes, or are they simply reproducing them?

Kopacz and Lawton (2011b) conducted an analysis of YouTube videos and found that, in contrast to mainstream media, many YouTube videos in which Native Americans played central roles and were depicted as both modern members of society and active agents against discrimination. Their findings indicate that user-generated videos such as those found on YouTube have the potential to counteract stereotypes. To uncover whether these videos did in fact counter stereotypes, Kopacz and Lawton (2011a) assessed audience reactions to these videos. This second study had two central findings: (1) users preferred videos that adhered to stereotypical depictions of Native

voices

I Am Not Trayvon Martin

I AM NOT TRAYVON MARTIN. I AM NOT TROY DAVIS.

and to the middle class, white, socially concerned activist who wears a shirt emblazoned with those slogans, you are wrong.

I know you wear that shirt to stand in solidarity with Trayvon, Troy, and other victims of injustice. The purpose of those shirts is to humanize these victims of our society, by likening them to the middle class white activist wearing it. And once we've humanized the victims, this proves to us the arbitrariness of their deaths and thereby the injustice at play.

Student Emma Halling gives her monologue, "I Am Not Trayvon Martin."

But the fact of the matter is that these men's deaths are anything but arbitrary. The fact that the real Troy Davis and Trayvon Martin and countless other victims of oppression are buried under 6 feet of cold dirt while we middle class white activists are alive, marching, and wearing their names is an indication that our societal system is working exactly as it's intended.

A more accurate t-shirt to display on my white body would be "I AM GEORGE ZIMMERMAN." Zimmerman and I were indoctrinated in the same American discourse where we learned that the "other," particularly black men like Trayvon and Troy, were less human and were to be feared. Society taught me that as a little white girl, I must preserve my purity and goodness, and that the presence of young single males threatened it. Society taught me that being in the presence of a BLACK man compounds that threat exponentially. I have been taught that male, black, bodies are an immediate threat to my safety and the well-being of society as a whole, and Zimmerman was taught the same damn thing. We're all taught it.

I look at George Zimmerman and think, "there, but for the grace of god, go I." Had it not been for a decent education, intense critical thinking, and some truly excellent parenting, I would never have questioned the societal norms that Zimmerman and I were both taught, and I would have ended up feeling his attack on Trayvon was justified, just as he did, and the state of Florida does.

If we are to effect real change in the wake of Trayvon's murder, we have to realize this. Realizing that you more closely resemble a homicidal oppressive force than a helpless victim is a really uncomfortable thing to do. I know. But wanting to identify with the victim is weak, and immature when it is not an accurate representation of reality. Real change is effected when we own up to our actions, our privilege, and our complicity with the system that murdered Trayvon and countless others.

(continued)

voices *continued.*

I Am Not Trayvon Martin

Us privileged activists have to realize just how easy it is to be Zimmerman, and work to change this. Subvert stereotypes. Make it harder for others to buy into the bullshit that we're fed our whole lives about race, class, gender, and other people by identifying and critiquing these messed up norms. Force adults to confront these norms, and raise children without indoctrinating them with the same old bullshit. Use your privilege to actively dismantle this messed up system. Listen to marginalized people like Trayvon's family and Troy's family and insure them access to the discourse. Listen to them, stand in solidarity with them. But do not, I repeat, DO NOT claim to be them.

Source: "I Am Not Trayvon Martin" http://www.youtube.com/watch?v=TBRwiuJ8K7w.

Americans, such as the wise elder and the doomed warrior; and (2) viewers also favored videos that countered stereotypes and offered accurate depictions of Native American tribal diversity and activism. Whereas previous research had only shown that viewers prefer stereotypical portrayals, this study of user-generated videos found that there is also a positive audience reception to counter-stereotypical portrayals. Their study suggests that social media do have the potential to work in positive ways to counter stereotypes.

Another social media case worthy of exploration is the "successful black guy" **meme** (a meme is an idea, image, video, or phrase that spreads in a culture). This meme shows an image of a well-dressed, light-skinned, handsome African American man, with a message that first triggers a stereotypical reaction and then changes course to show that, in fact, the man is saying something harmless or even helpful. This meme, which has become very popular, is another example of social media being used to reveal and counter stereotypes. As of September 2013, the meme had received over a million views and had been online for three years.

The other side of social media is that creators can be anonymous, and since anyone can create social media, these realms also can become venues for racial stereotypes to emerge and be validated. Sociologist Jessie Daniels studies online hate speech and has found in her research that people in the United States who have created websites with overt hate speech often go unpunished. In many cases, these website creators are protected by free speech laws and can post overtly racist messages on their own site without facing any legal troubles. Daniels (2008) also has found "cloaked" websites that seek to deceive Web users by appearing to have a neutral stance but actually give false information supporting a white supremacist outlook. One example of such a website is www.martinlutherking.org, which at first glance appears to be a tribute to civil rights leader Dr. Martin Luther King, Jr., but in fact aims to undermine him and other civil rights leaders.

In the digital era, racialized messages can also emerge through social media such as Twitter. In March 2012, the much-awaited film *The Hunger Games* was released, based on the novel with the same title. The movie was a box-office success and exceeded expectations. However, some viewers were surprised about the race of the characters and made their feelings public. In the book, author Suzanne Collins describes several of the main characters as having "dark brown skin." When viewers went to the premiere and saw that several of the main characters were African American—Amandla Stenberg as Rue, Lenny Kravitz as Cinna, and Dayo Okeniyi as Thresh—some were disappointed and made their views known on Twitter. Tweets such as the following appeared over the weekend:

> *"why does rue have to be black not gonna lie kinda ruined the movie"*
>
> *"for the record, im still pissed that rue is black"*
>
> *"rue is too black for what I pictured"*
>
> *"call me racist but when i found out rue was black her death wasn't as sad"*
>
> *"why did the producer make all the good characters black smh [shaking my head]"*
>
> *"ewwww rue is black?? I'm not watching"*
>
> *"awkward moment when Rue is some black girl and not the little blonde innocent girl you picture"*

These tweets make it evident that some viewers would like to keep their heroes white. These viewers were able to share their views via social media. However, these tweets soon caught the attention of bloggers, who called the tweeters out on their statements. Resistance to and reproduction of racial stereotypes in new media is an emerging area of sociological inquiry, and future studies will further demonstrate how racial stereotypes are reproduced and contested in this realm.

An excellent example of resistance to racial stereotypes through social media is the hashtag #iftheygunnedmedown, developed by Twitter user @CJ_musick_lawya in the aftermath of the police shooting of unarmed Michael Brown in Ferguson, Missouri on August 9, 2014. The day after the shooting, NBC News posted a photo of Michael Brown wearing a Nike Air jersey and flashing a sign with his fingers which could be misconstrued as a gang sign—although others argue that it was actually a peace sign. Activists questioned why NBC news chose to use that picture instead of a widely available picture of Brown in a cap and gown. In response, social media users began to post tweets with two pictures of themselves—one in a military uniform or cap and gown alongside another with athletic clothing on, drinking, smoking, or in otherwise less flattering attire, and used the hashtag #iftheygunnedmedown along with the question: "Which picture would they use?" The original tweet by @CJ_musick_lawya was retweeted over two thousand times and the hashtag used over 200,000 times in less than a week. In response, NBC took down the picture.

MEDIA IMAGES AND RACIAL INEQUALITY

Pop culture representations of people of color have evolved over time yet continue to propagate old racial ideologies. While the seventeenth-century representation of black men as lazy served to justify slavery, the current representation of black men as thugs serves to justify the astonishingly high rates of incarceration of black men today. And while the eighteenth-century representation of the black woman as sexually depraved served to justify the common practice of raping black women, the current representation of the "ho" in films and other media serves to justify cuts in social services to primarily black inner cities by deeming poor black women unworthy of such aid. Sociologist Patricia Hill Collins argues that such justifications rely heavily on mass media representations of African Americans. She defines and describes a **new racism**, which reflects "the juxtaposition of old and new—in some cases, a continuation of long-standing practices of racial rule and, in other cases, the development of something original.

The new racism reflects sedimented or past-in-present racial formations from prior historical periods" (2004, 55).

Modern-day representations of African Americans as thugs and whores are some examples of what Patricia Hill Collins calls **controlling images** (2004, 165), or gendered depictions of African Americans in the media that shape people's ideas of what African Americans are and are not. Throughout U.S. history, blacks have been represented as grotesque, physically resistant, and hypersexual. These representations create a fascination with blackness, but they also define what whites are not. In this way, every representation of non-whites also defines whiteness. If blacks are represented as embodying physical strength, then whites can see themselves as embodying intelligence—brawn versus brain. The same could be said of stereotypes of other groups: for example, representations of Latinos as gangbangers and gardeners send the message that whites are not gangbangers or gardeners. These stereotypical representations not only shape how people in the United States view one another but also work to justify rampant inequalities.

Representations of Latinos as drug kingpins, gangbangers, and petty criminals serve to justify the disproportionate rates of imprisonment for Latinos. In the United States, 97 percent of all victims of police brutality are either black or Latino (Feagin 2001, 147), and these sorts of media representations serve to reinforce the idea that Latinos are prone to criminality. The representation of the Latina as possessing uncontrolled sexuality serves to justify cuts in welfare and restrictions on immigration. And the representation of Latinas as maids serves to reinforce the idea that Latinas are destined for-low wage occupations. With the exception of the criminal, the majority of the representations of Latinos/as portray these individual as in service to whites or to the very system that exploits them. The Latin lover's primary role is to sexually please white women. The hot-blooded Latina fulfills the sexual desires of her lovers and the fantasies of others. The maid and the gardener keep the well-to-do neighborhoods looking nice. And the law enforcement officials keep the streets safe for everyone.

These stereotypes also work to justify foreign interventions. Hollywood has played an important role in portraying the Arab world as an exotic place that requires white Westerners to civilize its people and drag them into the twenty-first century. Shoba Sharad Rajgopal argues that representations of Arab women as veiled, traditional, and oppressed work to reinforce the stereotype that Western culture is "dynamic, progressive, and egalitarian," whereas Arab cultures are "backward, barbaric, and patriarchal" (2010, 145). She further contends that these stereotypes reinforce the idea that Americans need to go to Iraq and Afghanistan to rescue women from themselves and, in particular, from their brutal and oppressive Arab husbands.

Insofar as media depictions shape our perceptions and portray white characters as having more depth and redeeming qualities than non-white characters, they work to justify the fact that whites tend to do better in American society on nearly any social measure than non-whites. In a similar fashion, the depiction of Americans as saviors of the world helps to shape our perception of the United States as the beacon of democracy, even as the U.S. military wreaks havoc on Iraq and Afghanistan.

RACED, CLASSED, AND GENDERED MEDIA IMAGES

As we have seen increasing numbers of people of color in popular culture, we also have become able to find a variety of representations across class lines. African Americans, for example, are no longer portrayed only as mammies or con artists. Instead, many are doctors and lawyers. Portrayals of people of color on television are raced, gendered, and classed—meaning that the representations vary by race, class, and gender, and that they influence how we think about various racial groups in this country. Patricia Hill Collins's (2004) concept of "controlling images" argues that the media produce class- and gender-specific depictions of people of African descent in popular culture. She further contends that "mass media has generated class-specific images of Black women that help justify and shape the new racism of desegregated, color-blind America." Collins's analysis of the representations of black men and women in popular culture is useful, and I describe it in detail later in this chapter. In addition, Collins's idea of controlling images can be extended to other groups, including Latinos, Native Americans, Asians, and Arabs.

Collins contends that the vast majority of representations of blacks on television fall into the raced and classed categories presented in Table 4-1.

TABLE 4-1
Raced and Classed Categories of Black Representations on Television

	Working-Class	Middle-Class
WOMEN	**BITCH:** Aggressive, loud, rude, and pushy **BAD BITCH:** Materialistic, sexualized; iconized in hip-hop culture; modern version of the Jezebel **BAD BLACK MOTHER (BBM):** Mother who neglects her children; characterized by bad values; welfare queen **FEMALE ATHLETE:** Feminized; focuses on the family; lesbianism erased	**MODERN MAMMY:** Loyal female servant; focuses on work and subservience to white male boss **BLACK LADY:** Designed to counter images of black women's promiscuity; focuses on the home **EDUCATED BLACK BITCH:** Has money, power, and jobs; is beautiful; success depends on her being tamed by men
MEN	**ATHLETE:** Physically strong; harsh temper; needs to be controlled by coaches **THUG OR GANGSTA:** Inherently physical and, unlike the athlete, his physicality is neither admired nor easily exploited for white gain **BLACK PIMP:** Involved in illegal activity; hustler; uses women for economic gain; refuses to work; promiscuous **BLACK RAPIST:** Hypersexual, desirous of white women;	**SIDEKICK:** Black buddy in service to whites; origins lie in Uncle Tom; loyal to whites; asexual, nonviolent, safe, nonthreatening **SISSY:** Effeminate and derogated black masculinity; gay characteristics, a queen; reinforces heterosexuality of others

Based on P. H. Collins 2004.

Collins argues that these images influence how blacks treat each other and how others treat them. However, this does not mean that these images *determine* how blacks are treated. Instead, their pervasive nature means that they affect all people in our society. Faced with these images, we can: (1) internalize them and accept them as reality, (2) resist them and develop our own ideas about black masculinity and femininity, or (3) ignore them. Any of these reactions requires some action on our part and will affect how we think of ourselves and others.

Collins primarily restricted her analyses to African Americans. The idea of controlling images can be applied to other groups, however, as it is evident that stereotypical representations vary by gender. Table 4-2 lists some examples of prominent gendered stereotypes of Arabs, Native Americans, Latinos/as, and Asians. As with African Americans, these controlling images account for the vast majority of representations of these groups. It is hard to find characters in popular culture who do not fit into these stereotypes. Moreover, each of these depictions also defines what whites are not. White men are not terrorists or savages; they are peaceful and civilized. White women are not exotic or hot-blooded; they are reserved and ethical.

TABLE 4-2
Prominent Gendered Stereotypes by Racial/Ethnic Group

	Men	Women
ARABS	Terrorist Immoral billionaire Haggler	Veiled victim Exotic seductress Maiden
NATIVE AMERICANS	Savage Sidekick Wise elder Doomed warrior	Squaw Princess Matriarch
LATINOS/AS	Latin lover Greaser/bandito Gangbanger Gardener Buffoon	Hot-blooded Latina Maid Abuela (grandma) Mexican spitfire
ASIANS	Buddy Threatening foreigner Martial artist Corrupt businessman	Butterfly Dragon Lady

Based on Rajgopal 2010; Kopacz and Lawton 2011a; 2011b; Rodríguez 1997.

Each of these representations is gendered. Arab women are rarely portrayed as terrorists, and men are almost always the perpetrators, not the victims, of gendered violence (Rajgopal 2010). Native American men are usually portrayed either as savages (cruel and primitive men who brutalize white people), as wise elders who use their knowledge to help whites, or as warriors who are romanticized but know that their tribe will ultimately meet its doom. In contrast, Native American women are usually portrayed as either princesses who fall in love with a white hero or as promiscuous squaws (Kopacz and Lawton 2011a). When Latino men on television are not involved in urban violence as either criminals or police officers, they are most likely to be found in unskilled labor occupations such as janitor or gardener. This portrayal of Latinos as subservient is complemented by the portrayal of the Latin lover, who, despite his success in meeting the sexual desires of the Anglo woman, ends up being the "Latin loser" when his lover is in turn conquered by an Anglo man (Rodríguez 1997). Latinas, in contrast, tend to be portrayed as hot-blooded women, maids, or *abuelas* (grandmothers) who are out of touch with modern life (Berg 2002). Asian women tend to be portrayed either as Dragon Ladies or as Butterflies, both of which highlight their sexuality. In contrast, Asian men are usually desexualized and emasculated. These gendered stereotypes reinforce prevalent stereotypes about people of color in the United States and also work to define whites as morally superior.

CONCLUSION AND DISCUSSION

Within the television industry, debates over the representation of people of color often revolve around a sort of "chicken and egg" question: Do the media create or simply reflect popular stereotypes? For example, would a film that portrayed black women as demure intellectuals and white women as gangbangers be unsuccessful because it would seem unrealistic?

The stereotypical portrayals we see in the media today certainly were not invented by the media. Instead, they are part of our history and were created decades or even centuries ago. In this chapter, we have seen both how these stereotypes have evolved and how they continue to be part and parcel of popular media. We have also seen some of the consequences of these stereotypes: how they work to reproduce and justify racial inequalities. This raises the question of whether the media have a responsibility to try to alter stereotypes.

One recurring complaint about representations of people of color in the media is that they lack the depth that white characters have. One way that this could change is through the inclusion of people of color as writers and producers of popular media. In 2012, Shonda Rhimes, the creator of the popular series *Grey's Anatomy, Private Practice,* and *Scandal,* was the sole prominent African American woman with a significant role in creating television shows in the United States. Rhimes's shows have garnered praise both for including more characters of color and for giving those characters more depth than we are used to seeing on other shows. Thus, with the inclusion of more people of color in Hollywood as creators of media, we will perhaps see fewer stereotypes.

However, one of the most prominent African American male showrunners is Tyler Perry, who is widely criticized for his use of stereotypical depictions of black women in his works, including *House of Payne, Diary of a Mad Black Woman, Madea Goes to Jail,* and many other television shows, films, and stage plays. Although Tyler Perry has the ability to portray black women in a nuanced fashion, he is still beholden to the fact that the primary motive for the entertainment industry is making a profit. For Perry, it is clear that making fun of African Americans sells. In 2011, *Forbes* magazine named Tyler Perry the highest-paid man in entertainment—with five movies and two television series, Perry earned $130 million between May 2010 and May 2011 (Pomerantz 2011). Perry's body of work shows that simply having black producers is not enough if the goal is to reduce stereotypes.

To return to the question of the media's responsibility for reproducing stereotypes, there are two sides to this issue. On the one hand, you could argue that the media are responsible to the public, as the public constitutes their customer base. On the other hand, you could contend that the media are simply responding to market forces and giving their customers what they desire. What do you think?

THINKING ABOUT **RACIAL JUSTICE**

Can you think of a positive representation of a person of color in film, television, or new media today? Describe the character and explain the extent to which they conform to the stereotypes mentioned in this chapter. To what extent do positive representations of people of color contribute to a more racially just society?

Key Terms

enlightened racism 95
Mammy 97
Sapphire 97
Jezebel 97
Dragon Lady 99
Butterfly 99
biracial buddy 103
meme 106
new racism 108
controlling images 109

Check Your Understanding

OBJECTIVE 4.1

Examine racial stereotypes propagated in popular culture today.

- Common stereotypes of various racial and ethnic groups are perpetuated on television and in other media.

Q How have media representations of African Americans, Latinos/as, Arabs, Asians, and Native Americans changed since the 1950s?

OBJECTIVE 4.2

Examine racial stereotypes found in new media.

- Old stereotypes prevail even in new media such as video games and social media, which have an increasingly important influence.

Q How are stereotypes changing as a result of user-generated media and social media?

OBJECTIVE 4.3

Assess how media images serve to justify racial inequality.

- Media images are not harmless: they justify racial inequalities by shaping stereotypes about racial and ethnic minorities as well as about whites.

Q What is an example of a stereotype that is used to justify racial inequality?

Q To what extent are controlling images prominent in the media today?

OBJECTIVE 4.4

Demonstrate how media representations are raced, classed, and gendered.

- Media images vary not only by racial group but also by race and class.

Q Why does Patricia Hill Collins argue that media representations are race-, class-, and gender-specific?

Critical Thinking

1. New media include a large portion of user-generated content—material produced by everyday people with access to rudimentary technology. Do you think that new media have the potential to counter racial stereotypes, or do you think that they are providing an arena for the proliferation of stereotypes? Use at least one example from new media to make your case.
2. Television shows change constantly. Thus, the shows mentioned in this chapter may or may not be familiar to you and may or may not still be on the air. Do the stereotypes mentioned in this chapter apply to the shows you watch? Why or why not? Pick one popular show on television and assess the extent to which the non-white characters fit into stereotypical roles. Are the Latina characters portrayed as hypersexual? Are the Asians and Native Americans stoic? Describe at least two characters in a popular television show and then assess the extent to which those characters fit into the controlling images for their group.

5

COLORISM AND SKIN-COLOR STRATIFICATION

CHAPTER OUTLINE

LEARNING OBJECTIVES

5.1 Examine when and how colorism originated.
5.2 Evaluate the global color hierarchy and how colorism differs across societies.
5.3 Illustrate how skin color relates to gender and beauty.

We have already seen that racism is an ideology with material consequences. In this chapter, we will learn about a related yet distinct ideology: **colorism**. Whereas racism relies on the belief that some races are better than others, colorism is the idea that, within races, lighter is better. Whereas racism is based on the worldview that the people of the world can be divided into discrete categories and judged on that basis, colorism gives differential value to people in the same racial group, based on a continuum from light to dark. Colorism primarily refers to skin color but also encompasses physical characteristics that are related to skin color, such as eye color, hair texture and color, and facial features (Nakano Glenn 2009).

The prevalence of colorism has led to **skin-color stratification**, in which resources such as income and status are distributed unequally according to skin color. In the United States, lighter-skinned people generally have higher incomes and education than their darker-skinned counterparts and are more likely to own homes and marry. Darker-skinned people generally have longer prison sentences and lower job statuses on average than lighter-skinned people (Hochschild and Weaver 2007). Verna Keith (2009) has found that lighter-skinned African Americans have advantages over their darker-skinned counterparts in terms of earnings, education, and occupations. Eduardo Bonilla-Silva and David R. Dietrich (2009) contend that the United States is a **pigmentocracy**—a society in which blacks, Asians, and Latinos have different social statuses according to their skin color.

Skin-color stratification is also evident among U.S. immigrants from Africa, Asia, and Latin America. Using data from the 2003 New Immigrant Survey, Joni Hersch (2008) found that darker-skinned immigrants generally earn less than their lighter-skinned counterparts. This nationally representative survey included interviews with people who had recently been granted legal permanent residence in the United States. Each interviewee's skin color was rated on a scale of 1 to 10, with 1 being the lightest and 10 the darkest. Overall, Hersch found that for immigrants from these regions, light skin color is associated with higher wages across the spectrum. There is a pay disparity of 17 percent between the lightest-skinned immigrants and the darkest-skinned immigrants, even if we take into account gender, education, English-language skills, visa type, and occupation. This pay disparity indicates that discrimination on the basis of skin color likely does occur in the United States.

THE HISTORY OF COLORISM

When and how did colorism originate, not only in the United States but also around the world? Some scholars argue that the preference for light skin stems from the history of slavery and genocide in the Americas. Their argument is that the preference for light skin is fundamentally a preference for whiteness, and thus that colorism has the same history as racism (Hunter 2005, 2007). For these thinkers, colorism is a modern phenomenon. Scholars who focus on Asia (Rondilla and Spickard 2007; Saraswati 2010, 2012) attribute the preference for light skin to earlier ideas that equated leisure with light skin and work with dark skin. Most scholars of colorism would agree that colorism is a global phenomenon, with a long history and distinct manifestations around the world.

The Origins of Colorism in the Americas

Colorism has existed in the United States since the colonial era. The Africans who were brought to the North American colonies as slaves were primarily dark-skinned. Soon after the arrival of Africans in the Americas, the progeny of blacks and whites became a new class of mixed-race people, known as **mulattos**, who were darker than whites but lighter than blacks. At first, mulattos were officially recognized as a distinct category in the United States. In fact, the United States census included a mulatto category from 1850 to 1910. However, eventually both law and social custom changed, and **hypodescent**—the idea that having any amount of black ancestry makes you black—became more prevalent. Each state had the authority to define which people would be classified as black. In some states, an individual was legally black if one of his or her grandparents was black (i.e., if he or she was one-quarter black). In other states, an individual was black if his or her great-grandparents were black. In still other states, an individual was considered black if he or she was one-thirty-second black. These laws were eventually abolished in the 1960s (Telles 2004). However, they have had a lasting impact, in that people with relatively little African ancestry (and thus very light skin) can be considered black. The existence of a wide color spectrum in the black community is one factor that has enabled colorism to flourish.

Skin-color stratification was prevalent during the era of slavery: lighter-skinned slaves were more likely to work in the house instead of the fields, to be taught to read, and to be manumitted (freed). The manumission of some led to a small class of freedmen, who tended to be lighter in skin tone than their enslaved counterparts. These lighter-skinned blacks eventually formed the core of the black elite in the United States, meaning that skin color has been mapped onto social status in the African American community for centuries (Hunter 2005).

The association of light skin with elite status continued into the twentieth century. Jewish American anthropologist Melville Herskovits conducted a study of blacks in Harlem in the 1920s and found that the black elite was disproportionately light-skinned and that black men preferred light-skinned partners. His study revealed that whereas only 9 percent of the Harlem black elites were very dark-skinned, 28.9 percent of the elites were very light-skinned. Herskovits also found that in over half of Harlem couples, wives were lighter than husbands, revealing that men often preferred lighter-skinned women and that women were able to marry higher-status darker-skinned men. Within the black community, lighter skin was valued more highly than dark skin. Additionally, light skin became associated with elite status. Thus, the desire to be light was connected both to the idea that white was better and to the idea that light skin meant higher class.

In Harlem in the 1920s, the black elite were disproportionately light-skinned.

Consequently, skin bleaches and hair straighteners were very common in Harlem in the 1920s. Skin bleaches that promised to provide women with "light skin that men can't resist" formed a substantial portion of the cosmetics products sold in Harlem at the time (Dorman 2011). The practice of skin bleaching persists today: Christopher A. D. Charles (2011) found that pharmacies and beauty supply stores in Harlem were still selling bleaching products in 2010. Moreover, the labels on these products devalued black skin by promising to help customers with "problems" associated with dark skin.

In Latin America, a skin-color hierarchy has existed for centuries. During the period that Latin American countries were Spanish colonies, the Spaniards developed a system of *castas*—an elaborate system based on ancestry that determined one's social and legal ranking in society. By the end of the colonial period in 1821, there were over one hundred possible categories that were memorialized in a series of *casta* paintings. The categories included *españoles* (Spaniards), *indios* (indigenous people), ***mestizos*** (persons with one Spanish and one indigenous parent), *castizos* (persons with one *mestizo* parent and one Spanish parent), and *mulatos* (persons with one African parent and one Spanish parent). The categories went on to divide people up into over one hundred different possible mixtures, each with its own name. These categories were based on ancestry, not color. Nevertheless, we can say that, as a general rule, more Spanish ancestry meant both lighter skin and more prestige. These categories are no longer used in Latin America, but the inequalities that stemmed from them persist (Telles and Steele 2012).

Brazil, in contrast to the United States and Spanish America, never had a system of official classification whereby a person with a certain amount of African ancestry would be legally considered black. Instead, in Brazil, usually only a person who looks black is considered black, whereas a person who looks white is considered white, regardless of his or her actual ancestry. The Brazilian census classifies people as white, ***pardo*** (brown), and black, and the term *mulatto* is used in everyday language to describe people who are neither black nor white. There is a certain amount of fluidity between these categories, and many families report blacks, whites, and *pardos* in their households on the Brazilian census. Although Brazil has never had laws that mandated racial segregation, this does not mean that there is no racial inequality in Brazil. There is racial inequality, and privilege is mapped along color lines, with lighter-skinned people generally having more education and income (Telles 2004). The presence of skin-color stratification in Brazil today is a relic of colonialism.

Does Colorism Predate Colonialism? The Origins of Colorism in Asia and Africa

The preference for light skin in the Americas seems to have its roots in the period of colonization. In contrast, Asia has a longer history of colorism. As early as the late ninth century, the ancient Sanskrit text *Ramayana* featured light skin as ideal. Ayu Saraswati (2010) explains that in both the Indian and Indonesian versions of this text, beautiful women are described as having white faces that shine like the full moon. Aryan Indians spread their preference for white skin to the rest of South and Southeast Asia. In Indonesia, this predilection for light skin was reinforced during the Dutch colonial period in the nineteenth century. Colonial authorities granted preferential treatment to persons of mixed Dutch-Indonesian ancestry. When the Japanese became the colonial power in Indonesia in 1942, they also brought their fondness for lightness with them. And U.S. popular culture is currently making its mark in Indonesia through advertising, with blue-eyed blonds staring out of images in this primarily non-white country. In Indonesia today, dark-skinned people continue to be seen as unattractive and undesirable. As in other places, this social pattern has clear gendered dimensions: women feel more pressure than men to alter their appearance and lighten their skin (Saraswati 2012).

What about in Africa? Was there preference for light skin in this region prior to the arrival of Europeans? There are people of every skin shade on the African continent, with lighter-skinned people living in the North and those with darker skin living close to the Equator and in the south. Anthropologist Peter Frost (2006) has reviewed the evidence from several African tribes and found that there is some evidence that a preference for lighter skin predates colonialism in Africa. In many tribes, women with brown or reddish skin are seen as more beautiful than those with very dark skin, and there are indications that these preferences are deeply rooted in these societies. For example, many tribes' languages include value-laden terms that distinguish between skin color, and early twentieth-century anthropologists found preferences for lighter skin even among older Africans who were born before the arrival of Europeans in their communities (Frost 2006). Whether or not the preference for light skin predates colonialism is an open question. However, it is clear that the obsession with light skin increased with colonization and the presence of large numbers of Europeans in Africa. In South Africa, for example, skin lighteners have been available since the 1930s (Thomas 2009).

The preference for light skin seems nearly universal. Despite varying local histories, these preferences have converged in the current era as a result of cultural globalization and the spread of transnational corporations that tend to promote whiter or lighter beauty ideals.

THE GLOBAL COLOR HIERARCHY

How does colorism differ across societies? Consider a 2012 commercial from India for a product called Clean and Dry Intimate Wash. In the commercial, a light-skinned couple sits down for a cup of coffee. The woman is visibly distressed, and her male partner ignores her. She takes a shower. From there, the screen flashes to the shower, and a drawing of a brown vagina is shown. The vagina then is cleaned off and is shown to be sparkly white. Next, the woman (who has emerged from the shower) saunters back into the living room with confidence, and her partner is clearly much more interested in her. He swings her around, and the screen fades back to the product—which claims to not only clean, but also lighten, the vagina. This commercial demonstrates that in India, there is a market for whitening every part of the body—particularly the female body.

Skin-whitening creams are prevalent not only in Asia but also in Latin America, Africa, and the United States. They are evidence of a **global color hierarchy**, in which white (or light) skin is privileged and people—especially, but not exclusively, women—strive to become lighter. These dynamics play out differently in distinct areas of the world.

In this section, we will examine this hierarchy in three areas of the world: Asia, Latin America, and Africa, as well as the **diaspora**, or dispersion, of their populations in the United States.

Asia and Asian Americans

The privileging of light skin in Asia and among Asian Americans has its roots in ancient Aryan Indian beauty ideals, Japanese and Chinese ideas of white skin as a sign of leisure, and colonial domination of India and Indonesia by European powers. Today, women from Thailand, South Korea, Vietnam, Japan, China, the Philippines, Indonesia, and India use skin-whitening creams in an effort to make their skin as light as possible and even undergo eyelid surgery to widen their eyes (Saraswati 2010, 2012). In India, the preference for light skin is also connected to the caste system. Although it is not the case that all high-caste members (Brahmins) are light, a pattern can be seen whereby higher-caste people

voices

The Fair-Skin Battle

Fair & Lovely, a skin-lightening cream from India.

I will admit: I've avoided the sun so I wouldn't get darker. I've gone swimming at night instead of during the day to avoid tan lines. It's completely and utterly ridiculous. I should enjoy the sun's warm rays and get some exercise! But where do these thoughts come from? We weren't born with the innate ability to distinguish between skin colors and assign meanings to them. But for some women, the fair skin battle draws them into deeper depths than just avoiding sunshine during the day.

In South Asian tradition, a light-skinned woman is supposedly more beautiful than a dark-skinned woman. This belief can be traced back to early invasions of India by the Turks and British. As light-skinned people inhabited India and wielded their authority, natives who sought power and beauty likened fair skin with power and status. Some say the Caste System also contributed to these attitudes, with light-skinned higher-caste members dominating the lower-caste members with darker skin. Additionally, history might indicate that lighter-skinned people enjoyed a more fanciful life, while darker-skinned people worked in the fields.

For an even more blatant and modern perpetuation of this stereotype, watch any Bollywood movie's actors and actresses. The movies tend to feature ultra-fair-skinned heroes and heroines, while villains and village women tend to be portrayed by darker-complexioned actors.

Can this be a realistic depiction of South Asian people? Do South Asian women strive to appear like the beautiful women seen in the movies? The majority of South Asians are not as fair skinned as the movies portray. They range in hues from ivory to caramel, from mocha to ebony.

(As a humorous side note, check out some of the matrimonial ads seeking fair maidens.)

Furthermore, the South Asian skin product market is littered with skin lightening products. Everything from our aunt's Fair and Lovely to our dermatologist's hydroquinone is being consumed for the purpose of a fair complexion. Some of these crèmes are harmful for the skin, and can lead to irritation. It's amazing to observe the lengths some women will go to, sometimes dangerous lengths, just to achieve a slightly lighter shade.

However, Fair and Lovely is now the topic of controversy in South Asia nowadays, where a movement led by the All India Democratic Women's Association finally begins to bring some justice to the issue of skin color.

This issue doesn't just concern South Asians. African American celebrities like Beyoncé, Rihanna, and Halle Berry are so beautiful and talented in their genres, but in all actuality,

(continued)

voices *continued.*

The Fair-Skin Battle

they're considerably fair! In fact, an MSNBC article posed the question of whether *Vanity Fair* lightened Beyoncé's skin for a cover photo (which they vehemently denied). A darker-skinned woman like Fantasia Barrino doesn't get nearly the same spotlight, despite her enormous talent. Some African American bloggers speak of similar sentiment concerning skin color in their communities as well.

It's clear that American Desi girls feel the fair-skin pressure because of the media coming at them from both sides of the world. Both Desi culture and American culture subconsciously allude towards the idea that a lighter complexion is more beautiful than a darker one. It's not easy living in a society where vanity and visual appearance speak volumes before a woman even speaks!

The vast diversity in our skin colors is just one of the visual aspects of our heritage. And there's so much wonder woven into our heritage to fret over skin color! So, feel free to bask in the sun and be proud of your glow!

Source: Mohideen 2009.

in India tend to be lighter than those of lower caste. In addition, the term for caste, *varna*, literally means "color," and there has been some historical association of Brahmins with whiteness and the untouchables with blackness. In and across Asia, there are historical and present-day advantages associated with light skin, especially for women (Parameswaran and Cardoza 2009).

These preferences for light skin in Asia have carried over to Asian Americans in the United States. Research by Joanne Rondilla and Paul Spickard (2007) reveals a fascinating aspect of skin-tone discrimination among Asian Americans: the preference for light skin is omnipresent, yet Asian Americans do not want to be *too* white. The researchers tell the stories of a Vietnamese American woman who uses a destructive skin-whitening cream because she feels excluded by her ethnic group and a Filipina woman who stays out of the sun to avoid being called "dark." On the flip side, they also describe a Chinese woman whose great-grandmother was French who is excluded from social groups because her freckles and reddish hair make her look too white, as well as a woman whose mother is Japanese and father is white who struggles to feel accepted in either community. Based on these interviews and other evidence, Rondilla and Spickard argue that light skin is preferred in Asian American communities, but that this does not signal a desire for whiteness.

Latin America and Latinos/as

In Latin America, people of mixed ancestry have historically been considered mulattos (when they have African and European ancestry) or *mestizos* (when they have European and indigenous ancestry). *Mestizo* is an official classification in Mexico, Peru, and other countries, and *pardo* (brown) is an official classification in Brazil. Within this system, only people who are very dark-skinned are considered to be black, and only those who both are dark-skinned and display indigenous cultural features are considered indigenous (Golash-Boza 2011a). Thus, you could find a family in which one child is considered black, another mulatto, and still another white. In these families, it is often the case that the lighter-skinned children are given preferential treatment (Twine 1998). Latin Americans often strategically choose romantic partners who are lighter in skin tone than themselves, with the hope that their children will be lighter and thus better positioned in society. In Spanish, this strategy is called *mejorando la raza*, or improving the race, and is common across Latin America (C. Sue 2009).

Latin American countries are marked by a skin-color hierarchy, in which lighter-skinned people possess a disproportionate share of the resources. Because of the existence of intermediate categories, we can say that whites are often at the top of the hierarchy, mestizos and mulattos in the middle, and blacks and indigenous people at the bottom (Telles and Steele 2012).

Edward Telles and Liza Steele (2012) conducted a study in which they compared skin color and educational attainment across Latin America. They wanted to know whether or not lighter-skinned Latin Americans are more likely to complete high school and go to college than darker-skinned Latin Americans. Using a recent and innovative dataset that contained information about skin color and education for nearly 40,000 people in twenty-three Latin American countries, they were able to explore the relationship between skin color and each respondent's educational attainment. These data allowed them to ask if lighter-skinned people were able to complete more years of schooling on average than darker-skinned people. In most Latin American and Caribbean countries, they found that lighter-skinned people were more likely to have higher educational attainment than darker-skinned people. This trend was most prominent in Andean countries such as Peru and Bolivia, where darker-skinned people receive an average of eight years of schooling, as compared to the thirteen years received by lighter-skinned people. In all the countries except four—Panama, Suriname, Belize, and Guyana—their study revealed that lighter-skinned people had more years of education than darker-skinned people. Educational attainment is an important indicator of socioeconomic success. Thus, this study makes it clear that a pigmentocracy continues to be prevalent in Latin America.

The prevalence of skin-color stratification in Latin America raises the question of whether this stratification is also present among Latin American immigrants in the United States. Do lighter-skinned Latinos in the United States have more education, income, and resources?

Having light skin has real, material rewards for Latinos in the United States in terms of education and income. Social scientists have conducted a few quantitative studies that measured skin color is measured and tested whether light-skinned people tend to have higher incomes and education. In 1996, Edward Murguia and Edward Telles published a study based on the 1979 National Chicano Study. They found that whereas only 7 percent of light-skinned Mexican Americans had less than five years of schooling, 10.2 percent of them had finished college. By comparison, about 19 percent of medium- and dark-skinned Mexican Americans had less than five years of schooling, but only about 5 percent of them had finished college. Murguia and Telles's analyses also revealed that skin color still influenced educational outcomes even when parents' education was taken into account. This means that skin color had an independent effect on the likelihood that Mexican Americans would attain high levels of education.

Margaret Hunter (2005), using data from the 1979 National Chicano Study as well as the 1980 National Study of Black Americans, also found that skin color predicted educational outcomes for Mexican American and African American women. Those with lighter skin generally had higher educational levels, even controlling for their own class backgrounds. Hunter also found that lighter-skinned African American women earned higher incomes than their darker-skinned counterparts. However, she did not find skin color to be a significant predictor of income for Mexican American women. For black women, light skin translated into a higher likelihood of marrying a better-educated spouse. Hunter's findings show that there are clear advantages to being lighter-skinned for African American and Mexican American women.

You might wonder if things have changed since 1979 and 1980, the years from which the data used in these studies were drawn. The findings of more recent studies are, not surprisingly, similar. In 2004, Korie Edwards, Katrina M. Carter-Tellison, and Cedric Herring published a study based on marriage data from 1992 to 1994. This study drew on data from several urban areas across the United States and included data on skin tone for blacks, Latinos, and Asians. The researchers found that across the board, darker-skinned men and women were less likely to marry than their lighter-skinned counterparts. Another study, based in Boston, found that Latinas with light skin were more likely to be married than dark-skinned Latinas (C. Gomez 2008).

Africa and the African Diaspora

Jemima Pierre (2008) describes a scene in downtown Accra, Ghana, where large billboards that feature a very light-skinned African woman to advertise *Gel Eclaircissant*—a bleaching treatment—are plastered across the town. Pierre asks how Ghana, "a proud black postcolonial African nation with an established history of Pan-Africanism," can have such blatant anti-black advertisements. To answer this question, Pierre argues that skin-bleaching practices are a reflection of the ways that processes of racialization are alive and well in postcolonial Ghana. Thus, even though Ghana is a proud, black nation, it is not immune to global white supremacy. It is through global white supremacy that Ghana and other African nations are connected to the African diaspora, where a preference for light skin is prevalent. Additionally, many African countries are marked by a hierarchy in which lighter-skinned, mixed-race people occupy more positions of power and have more economic resources than darker-skinned people (K. Lewis, Robkin, Gaska, and Njoki 2011).

Skin bleaching has become common throughout Africa. Studies have revealed that as many as 25 percent of women in Mali; 30 percent of women in Tanzania; 52 percent of women in Dakar, Senegal; 66 percent of people in Brazzaville, Congo; 75 percent of people in Lagos, Nigeria; and 60 percent of women in Zambia use skin-bleaching products (K. Lewis et al. 2011; Kpanake, Munoz Sastre, and Mullet 2009).

Why? In Tanzania, a team of scholars (K. Lewis et al. 2011) interviewed forty-two women to ask them why they used skin-bleaching products, even though these products are known to cause severe skin damage, skin cancer, and brain disease. Tanzanian women gave six primary reasons for why they bleached their skin: (1) to remove acne, (2) to have soft skin, (3) to be more white, (4) to remove dark patches, (5) to attract men, and (6) to impress peers. Women gave a variety of reasons for why they used these creams, but the desire to look better was at the center of all of them. For many, the desire to look better was connected to looking whiter. One woman said she started bleaching "to be beautiful and to look like Arabians or Europeans and attractive to people especially men" (33). In a similar study in Togo, Kpanake and his colleagues (2010) interviewed 300 men and women who reported using skin-bleaching creams and found that they gave a variety of reasons for doing so, including wanting to be considered important, civilized, and attractive, and to have lighter and softer skin. The prevalence of skin bleaching in a variety of African countries demonstrates that Africans continue to privilege light skin.

In a study of skin bleaching in Jamaica, Christopher A. D. Charles (2009) interviewed thirty-six women and twenty-two men who bleached their skin. He found that most of them bleached their skin either to remove facial blemishes, to lighten their skin, or to look more beautiful. Although more than 90 percent of Jamaicans are black, light skin is viewed as socially desirable among both men and women. For this reason, people who bleached their skin often thought that having lighter skin would make them more attractive. Similar to Ghana, Jamaica is also considered to be a proud, black nation. It is thus surprising that large numbers of Jamaicans wish to lighten their skin.

In the United States, skin bleaching was common among African Americans in Harlem in the 1920s and 1930s. Since then, we have seen the rise of the "black is beautiful" movement and an embrace of blackness among African Americans. There is some evidence that these social movements have alleviated colorism among black Americans. However, colorism has not completely dissipated.

A study by JeffriAnne Wilder (2010) reveals the extent to which colorism continues to be embedded in the African American community.

Wilder conducted focus groups with fifty-eight African American women in which she probed them about skin-color labels and their meanings. Wilder found that there are a wide variety of labels used to describe light-skinned blacks, quite a few used to describe darker-skinned blacks, and just four used to describe those of medium skin tone. The wide variety of labels used indicates the importance of skin tone in the African American community. Whereas the terms used to describe medium skin—brown, milk chocolate, caramel, and pecan tan—were neutral, those used to describe light and dark skin were not. Terms for light skin included "house nigga" and "pretty skin," while those for dark skin included "jigaboo" and "tar baby." The association of lightness with "pretty skin" is an indication of the fact that many African Americans view light skin to be more beautiful than dark skin. At the same time, the use of the term "house nigga" is a reference to slavery and to the implication that those with light skin may be less authentically black. Wilder found in her focus groups that many African Americans view lighter-skinned women as more beautiful, intelligent, and refined than their darker-skinned counterparts, indicating that colorism continues to be prevalent in the African American community.

voices

Colorism and Creole Identity

Creole identity is a complicated thing in Louisiana, says Kristina Robinson, 29, of New Orleans.

It's an ethnicity, a cultural designation for people descended from colonial settlers in Louisiana, mainly of French and Latin lineage.

The term Creole was claimed by the French and Spanish settlers in colonial times but it also referred to Africans and people who were a mixture of races. Those mixed-race descendants became a unique racial group and sometimes even included Native American heritage.

But in popular representation, Robinson says Creole has come to be defined as skin color.

She doesn't want to deny the rich Creole history but she doesn't identify as such if it means moving away from her blackness.

(continued)

voices *continued.*

Colorism and Creole Identity

Black people think that her embrace of Creole means a rejection of being black.

"I never wanted to distance myself from my black ancestors," says the creative writing graduate student at Dillard University.

"They are the ones who claim me."

Kristina Robinson identifies more as black than as Creole.

In her light skin, Robinson understands the insidious ways of colorism, a system in which light skin is valued more than dark skin.

"Colorism is a major problem within the Creole community and the black community," she says. "It's underdiscussed. It's perplexing and vexing how to work out this idea. I can see how the one drop rule is why we have so much colorism in our society.

"One drop is a lie," she says. "Black plus white doesn't equal black or it doesn't equal white. It equals black plus white."

She calls herself black. But other people think she is from India or the Middle East, especially in her academic work environment, where she does not have black colleagues.

"The assumption is I am not black," she says.

Ultimately, she believes environment plays a big role in identity.

Few people, she says, think that of her sister. One reason may be that her sister has more of a button nose. But another reason is that she works in a field with more black people, whereas Robinson finds herself in academic settings where she is the sole black woman.

Robinson acknowledges her lighter skin gives her privilege in a color-conscious society.

"But in those situations where you have to identify yourself and you choose to identify yourself as white—there's a big denial going on there.

"I do think it's troublesome when someone who is of mixed race chooses to deny that part of them that was oppressed," she says.

Source: Basu 2009.

There is evidence that these preferences for light skin are connected to real, material rewards for being light. In the United States, historically, lighter-skinned African Americans have had more resources than darker-skinned African Americans and have tended to pass those resources down to their children. Ongoing discrimination exacerbates these inequalities. Colorism is a prominent aspect of inequality for African Americans in the criminal justice system: studies have shown that darker-skinned blacks get longer prison sentences than blacks with lighter skin, and that darker-skinned blacks are more likely to receive the death penalty. The preference for light skin also plays out in hiring decisions: one experimental study showed that white employers were more likely to hire a lighter-skinned African American over a darker-skinned African American (Hochschild and Weaver 2007).

SKIN COLOR, GENDER, AND BEAUTY

How does skin color relate to gender and beauty? Colorism is evident in the U.S. entertainment industry, especially for women of color. Many of the most prominent Latina stars—Salma Hayek, Jennifer Lopez, and Eva Longoria—are very light-skinned. The same can be said for prominent female African American stars such as Halle Berry and Beyoncé, who are both very light-skinned. In 2012, *People* magazine featured Beyoncé on its cover as the World's Most Beautiful Woman. She was the first black woman to land this cover issue since Halle Berry was featured in 2003. Jennifer Lopez—named Most Beautiful in 2011—is the only Latina to have ever been granted that title. It is not a coincidence that very light-skinned black and Latina women are the only ones who have graced this cover: it is a direct reflection of the fact that light skin is seen as more beautiful in the United States. It is thus not surprising that the first black woman to be crowned Miss America was Vanessa Williams, a light-skinned African American woman who won the title in 1983.

Light-skinned artists of color are more likely to rise to fame, because light skin is associated with beauty both in the United States and around the globe. Margaret Hunter (2005) explains that beauty, like colorism, is an ideology that can be used as a tool to maintain **patriarchy**, or male dominance in a society. Beauty divides women through competition and diverts their attention to their physical appearance and away from other oppressive forces in their lives. In the

Beyoncé on the cover of *People* magazine as the "World's Most Beautiful Woman." Many prominent female African American stars are very light-skinned.

United States, light skin, long hair, light eyes, and straight noses are all associated with beauty—and with whiteness. When a woman is called "fair," this label refers both to light skin and to physical attractiveness. Thus, African American women with long, straight hair and light skin are often perceived to be more attractive than their darker-skinned counterparts. Of course, there is individual preference and variation. However, studies have consistently shown that dark-skinned women are devalued both by their co-ethnics and by whites (Hunter 2005).

Hunter (2005, 70–71) introduces the concept of a **beauty queue** to explain "how sexism and racism interact to create a queue of women from the lightest to the darkest, where the lightest get the most resources and the darkest get the least. The lightest women get access to more resources because not only are they lighter-skinned and therefore racially privileged, but their light skin is interpreted in our culture as more beautiful and therefore they are also privileged as beautiful women." For African American, Asian, and Latina women, having lighter skin brings privileges. For women, beauty is an asset that can lead to better jobs, better pay, and more status. Because lighter women are seen as more beautiful, they can be considered to have **skin-color privilege**, even if they belong to a disadvantaged racial group.

Siobhan Brooks (2010) uses the concept of **erotic capital** to explain how skin color relates to beauty for women of color. Doing research with strip club workers, Brooks found that white women often earned more than black and Latina women, but that light-skinned black and Latina women were able to use their erotic capital—their attractiveness and sensuality—to earn more than darker-skinned black women. Whereas lighter-skinned black and Latina women were seen as exotic, dark-skinned black women were perceived as hypersexual and thus devalued. Similar to Hunter (2007), Brooks found evidence of a beauty queue, in which white women earned the most, followed by lighter-skinned blacks and Latinas, and then darker-skinned women. In the case of strip clubs, being whiter or lighter had material advantages.

Although there are clear advantages to being light-skinned, there is also evidence that women of color do not necessarily want to be white, even if they prefer lighter skin. Dionne Stephens and Paula Fernández (2011) interviewed thirty-four Hispanic women to shed light on their perspective about the relationship between skin color and attractiveness. The researchers found that "having 'some color' was viewed as an important symbol of [the women's] 'authentic' Hispanic identity" (85). The women they interviewed specifically stated that they did not desire white skin, but that they preferred to be tan and viewed being tan as being attractive and sexy. Notably, the women also did not want to be "black" or too dark.

This research is also relevant for Asian Americans. Rondilla and Spickard (2007) interviewed ninety-nine Asian Americans about their skin-color preferences. They found that respondents widely agreed that lighter skin was better in that it was associated with beauty, intelligence, and high class. Women and men recalled being told by their parents not to marry too dark so they could have light-skinned children. As part of the interview process, the researchers showed interviewees a picture of three conventionally beautiful Asian American women and asked them to make up a story about each woman. One woman had light skin, hair, and eyes; another was medium-toned and had black hair; and the third was dark-skinned. The stories about the medium-toned women were the most positive: she was seen as smart, wealthy, and stylish. In contrast, the dark-skinned woman was seen as likely an immigrant, poor, and hardworking. The stories about the lightest woman were not positive either: interviewees saw her as confused about her identity, lazy, a partygoer, and unhappy. These findings reveal that Asian Americans have an abstract desire for whiteness but do not desire features that make them look too Caucasian. In her later work, Joanne Rondilla (2009) argues that Asian women do not use skin lighteners in an attempt to become white; instead, they use them out of a wish to become a better version of themselves.

This research has parallels with work conducted in other parts of the world. Aisha Khan (2009) argues that although there is a color hierarchy in Indo-Trinidadian society, the ultimate desire is to become light, but not white, as whiteness signifies cultural loss. Lynn Thomas (2009) points out that in South Africa, women use skin lighteners not to become white, but to attain a lighter shade of black. Christina Sue (2009) contends that people in Veracruz, Mexico, use *mestizaje* as a whitening strategy to become lighter mestizos, not to become white. Evelyn Nakano Glenn (2009) argues that Filipinas associate light skin with modernity and social mobility, not necessarily with whiteness. And Ayu Saraswati (2012) finds that Indonesian women use skin whiteners to become lighter, but not to become Caucasian or to attain the light skin of Chinese women. Instead, they prefer Indonesian whiteness.

In a study of beauty pageants in Nigeria, Oluwakemi M. Balogun (2012) examined two beauty pageants: the Queen Nigeria pageant, which focuses primarily on Nigeria, and the Most Beautiful Girl in Nigeria pageant, which is geared to a more international audience and is connected to the Miss Universe and Miss World pageants. Balogun found that beauty pageant directors viewed dark skin as more authentically African and light skin as having more global mass appeal, and that they selected contestants on both of these bases. Directors of beauty pageants did not ignore skin color, nor did they give universal preference to light skin. Instead, they chose dark-skinned women when their goal was to find an authentic African woman to represent their country to the world and a lighter-skinned one when they were searching for a woman with global mass appeal as a beautiful woman.

Most of these works on skin color focus on women, as colorism is a gendered dynamic. Skin-color valuations more heavily affect women's lives than men's. Jyostna Vaid (2009) highlights the increasing salience of skin color, as well as the gendered nature of judgments based on skin color, for Indians in India and the diaspora. Vaid found that Indian women are twice as likely as men to mention skin color in marriage ads, signaling that skin color is more important in marriage negotiations for women than for men. Evelyn Nakano Glenn (2009) conceptualizes light skin as a form of symbolic capital and makes the case that this form of capital is more important for women than for men. Ayu Saraswati (2012) interviewed forty-six Indonesian women about their use of skin-whitening creams and found that many of the

Ad in Indian Newspaper for a Groom in the 1990s

Wanted: a professionally qualified boy for an extremely beautiful, fair Punjabi Khatri girl, 24/160, B.Com, C.A. (Group 1 passed) employed girl from a respectable family.

From: Sethi 2000.

women had experienced discrimination and denigration because of their dark skin color. Many had received comments on their skin color when they were girls and used skin-whitening creams to hide what they viewed to be a deficiency—their dark skin. Whereas dark skin can be seen as masculine, and thus appropriate, for men, Saraswati found that women in Indonesia overwhelmingly preferred light skin. Moreover, women around the world feel more pressure than men to be beautiful, as a woman's beauty is one of her most important assets (Hunter 2005).

In India, it continues to be common for people to use advertisements to find spouses, and these advertisements make it clear that fair skin makes women more marriageable. Parameswaran and Cardoza (2009) report that men are much less likely than women to report their own skin color in these advertisements, and that men are much more likely to indicate a preference for light skin in a partner. These researchers consistently found ads written by men that sought a "fair" bride and even report one advertisement by a father who laments the fact that his daughter's skin is not fair. These preferences have generated a market for skin-lightening creams in India. By 2003, skin-lightening solutions constituted the largest market share of the cosmetics and toiletries market in India, with Hindustan Lever's Fair & Lovely facial cream at the top of the market. Companies that make these products also use advertising to reinforce the idea that lighter women are more marriageable. One ad for Fair & Lovely Fairness Cold Cream shows a young woman with a beaming smile. The caption reads: "This winter, I discovered the only cold cream that also made me fairer. (And *he* discovered me)" (Parameswaran and Cardoza 2009). A consistent theme in Indian advertisements for whitening creams is that women who wish to be more beautiful can use these creams to become more fair, and thus more desirable to men.

Transnational corporations have taken advantage of the widespread desire for fair skin around the world and used it to generate immense profits. Through advertising, large transnational corporations have not only reinforced the idea that light skin is essential for success, but they also have profited immensely from selling products that promise to save women from the pain and rejection associated with dark skin. Lynn Thomas (2009) underscores the importance of transnational entanglements for the global preference for lighter skin, as most companies that sell whitening products are transnational. In Indonesia, for example, transnational corporations such as Unilever, L'Oréal, and Shiseido are the main sellers of skin whiteners. And out of all the products in the cosmetics industry, it is skin-whitening products that are the most profitable in Indonesia, which is the fourth–most populous country in the world (Saraswati 2012).

Given the widespread use of skin whiteners, you might wonder about the use of skin-tanning products by white women in the United States—a practice that is also harmful to the skin, and that can even lead to skin cancer. In an article on skin-whitening advertisements, Ayu Saraswati (2010: 34) also examines skin-tanning advertisements. She finds that the "color tan is advertised *without* undermining the supremacy of the Caucasian white race." Unlike the whitening ads, the tanning ads never use the words "blackening" or "browning." Instead of making your skin brown, these products will make your skin "deep bronze." Additionally, the skin-tanning ads use an explicit language of choice, telling customers they can customize their color. Whitening ads, by contrast, tell consumers they can detox their skin color. Thus, although the skin-tanning ads would seem to celebrate dark skin, in reality, they permit white-skinned people to imagine controlling their color just enough to appear as if they have been on a lovely tropical vacation.

CONCLUSION AND DISCUSSION

As we have seen in this chapter, skin-color valuations have been pervasive throughout history and around the world. The preference for whiteness or lightness can be found in Africa, Asia, Latin America, and the United States. There are local variations on these preferences, yet they also have many aspects in common and are closely related to gender and sexuality. Colorism, it turns out, is a manifestation of racism that further splits fractured groups into an internal hierarchy related to color. At the same time, since race is closely tied to identity, there are costs to being perceived as too light or, especially, too white. Examining colorism around the world allows us to perceive both commonalities and differences in terms of racial stratification.

This examination also sheds light on the gendered nature of colorism: the color hierarchy has different meanings for men and women. Although some men use skin-whitening creams and dark men may find it more difficult to find romantic partners than light men, the evidence is overwhelming that women are much more likely to use skin-bleaching products. Darker skin makes it more difficult for women to find a husband than it does for men to find a wife. Physical attractiveness serves as capital for both men and women, but patriarchy has created a situation in which women must depend more than men on their physical appearance. To the extent that light skin is viewed as more desirable around the world, this aspect of the human body more heavily influences women's lives than men's. And skin color is something over which we really have no control. We are born with a certain pigmentation and must live with the consequences of that coloring for the rest of our lives. Of course, many people endeavor to change their natural coloring. However, the costs of doing so are remarkably high—skin-bleaching creams can in fact be fatal.

THINKING ABOUT **RACIAL JUSTICE**

Racial justice is the creation of a society free of racial oppression. How might a consideration of colorism affect how we think about racial justice? Explain how the presence of colorism could challenge our thinking about racial justice. Reflect on how we might overcome that challenge.

Key Terms

colorism 118
skin-color stratification 118
pigmentocracy 118
mulatto 119
hypodescent 119
mestizo 121
pardo 121
global color hierarchy 123
diaspora 123
patriarchy 132
beauty queue 133
skin-color privilege 133
erotic capital 133

Check Your Understanding

OBJECTIVE 5.1

Examine when and how colorism originated.

- Colorism has a long history and distinct manifestations around the world.

Q What is the difference between colorism and skin-tone stratification?

Q What is the history of colorism in Asia and Africa?

OBJECTIVE 5.2

Describe the global color hierarchy and how colorism differs across societies.

- Skin-whitening creams, evidence of a global color hierarchy, can be found from the United States to Latin America to Asia to Africa.

Q What is a "beauty queue"?

Q What are some indicators of skin-color stratification in the United States?

Q How long has colorism been a factor in the African American community?

Q How is skin-tone stratification in Brazil related to colonialism?

OBJECTIVE 5.3

Explain how skin color relates to gender and beauty.

- Skin-color stratification and colorism are more prominent for women, and this disparity is largely related to beauty norms.

Q What are some of the privileges related to light skin in the United States?

Q How does skin color privilege vary by racial group?

Critical Thinking

1. In what ways is colorism "gendered"?
2. What are some distinctions between a desire to be white and a desire to have light skin?
3. Why might it be important to understand whether colorism predates colonialism?

EDUCATIONAL INEQUALITY

CHAPTER OUTLINE

LEARNING OBJECTIVES

6.1 Examine the history of educational inequality in the United States.

6.2 Analyze the dimensions of racial inequality in our educational system.

6.3 Evaluate the continuing gap in the educational achievements of white, Asian, black, Native American, and Latino students.

Education is meant to be the great equalizer. Every child in the United States, regardless of race, gender, or citizenship status, has the right to attend free public school up until the twelfth grade. With these educational opportunities, any child should be able to be successful. Nevertheless, there are tremendous gaps in educational achievement in the United States. And these gaps fall along racial and ethnic lines.

Historically, educational opportunities in this country have not been equal. Enslaved Africans and their children were forbidden to learn how to read or write. Chinese immigrants were banned from public schools. African American, Asian American, and Mexican American children were relegated to separate and unequal schools. Prior to 1954, U.S. laws prevented many non-white children from accessing the best educational opportunities.

Today, seventy years later, some things have changed. There are no longer any all-white universities in the United States. The best colleges and universities now seek out diverse students, and many offer scholarships to students who can contribute to campus diversity. Elite private high schools offer similar incentives to attract students who are neither white nor from privileged backgrounds. Yet non-white children still do not have equal access to the opportunities available to their white counterparts.

In this chapter, we will look at the history and current state of educational inequality in the United States. We will see how far we have come and how far we must go to achieve equality in educational opportunities and outcomes for all children in the United States.

THE HISTORY OF EDUCATIONAL INEQUALITY

In the United States, the idea of equal opportunity holds great weight, even as the reality has fallen short of the ideal. Before the ***Brown v. Board of Education*** decision of 1954, children who were not white were systematically prevented from attending white schools under a doctrine called "separate but equal."

During slavery, many African Americans were prevented from learning to read and write, sometimes by law. Free blacks were not permitted to enroll in the few public schools that existed in southern states. With emancipation came freedom to learn and to teach.

African Americans across the South started schools wherever they could—in fields, in one-room schoolhouses, and in people's homes. Southern blacks who managed to learn to read and write taught others in their community. They also recruited Northerners as teachers. By the end of the nineteenth century, states across the South were able to ensure free public schooling for all children (Span 2002).

Beginning in the early twentieth century, racial tensions heightened. African Americans lost the right to vote in several southern states. In this context, school segregation was implemented and enforced in both the North and the South. With segregation, black children were often left with few educational resources. Their communities regularly had to make do with one-room schoolhouses provided by the state, or else pool their own funds to build better schools. Community-established schools provided some of the first educational opportunities to black children in the South, but they were gravely under-resourced (Span 2002).

For much of the twentieth century, many African American and Mexican children were required to attend segregated schools in their home communities, and many Native American children were sent to Indian boarding schools. The history of segregated and unequal schools in this country stretches over many decades and continues to have implications today.

Indian Schools

In the late nineteenth and early twentieth centuries, U.S. government officials enacted policies to ensure that Native Americans would leave behind their traditional ways and assimilate into American society. One of the measures aimed at the task of obliterating native cultures was the creation of Indian schools.

There were three main types of schools designed for Native Americans: (1) boarding schools located outside of reservations, (2) boarding schools located on reservations, and (3) day schools on reservations. In addition, starting in 1819, there were federally subsidized mission schools, which focused on teaching Native American children about Christianity. All of these schools were designed to assimilate Native Americans into mainstream society (Watras 2004).

The first boarding school was the Carlisle Indian School in Pennsylvania, established in 1879. The philosophy of the school's founder, Richard Henry Pratt, was that by fostering assimilation, the

Students in cadet uniforms at the Carlisle Indian School, ca. 1880.

school could "kill the Indian and save the man." By 1926, about 70,000 of the 84,000 Native American children in the United States were attending a government-created school (Watras 2004). In 1930, there were 707 Indian schools across the United States, with 52 in Montana alone (Noel 2002).

Some Native American children attended boarding schools by choice, often with the hope that they would be provided for materially and would learn skills that would help them survive in mainstream society. There is evidence, however, that many children were forced or coerced to attend these schools (Noel 2002). Once there, students who tried to run away were often harshly punished. At Chemawa School in Oregon, for example, there were forty-six runaway attempts in 1921 and seventy in 1922. At this school, runaways, called deserters, were forced to stand in the hallway with their arms and legs tied. If they tumbled over because they fell asleep, the matron would whip them and make them stand again (Marr n.d.). At Haskell Indian School, there were 53 runaways in September 1910, and another 35 in October. If runaways were returned to the school, they would face physical punishment for their behavior (Stout 2012).

When children arrived at these schools, they were often renamed. A young man named Raining Bird, for example, was renamed Arthur Raining Bird. If the boys had long hair, it was cut. American Indian children were forbidden from speaking in their native languages and from practicing their own religions. Children who spoke in their native languages were often physically punished if the teacher overheard them. Native languages, dress, and hairstyles were forbidden in order to inculcate Native American children in the ways of white Americans (Noel 2002).

The children spent half of the day in classes learning English, reading, and mathematics, and the other half of the day doing industrial, agricultural, or domestic work, which was framed as "productive activities." The girls were assigned to kitchen duties, sewing, laundry, ironing, and cleaning, while the boys were required to do farm labor, gardening, groundskeeping, and carpentry (Noel 2002). In some cases, once Native American girls learned how to keep house, they were sent to local white homes to work as servants (Trennert 1982).

Native American children who went to boarding schools were often homesick. Many of them were underfed at the schools and became ill. Many died. In 1926, a comprehensive study of Indian schools showed that the boarding schools' budget for feeding children was only eleven cents a day—$1.41 a day in today's currency, and not nearly enough to provide a reasonable diet. Because of undernourishment, the children often succumbed to diseases such as tuberculosis (Watras 2004). Many boarding schools across the United States today have burial grounds for Indian children who died while at school.

The boarding schools became a bit more tolerable after 1933, when assimilation programs were officially ended, the schools were reformed, and many schools were closed. The repercussions of these institutions, however, continue to be felt today. Genevieve Williams, who is nearly ninety years old, went to an Indian school as a young girl. She remembers being forced to scrub floors on her hands and knees and being beaten for speaking in her native language. She recalls girls being flogged for wetting the bed. When she returned home at age fourteen, she no longer recognized her mother. Having never bonded with her own mother, Williams found it hard to nurture her own children. Her husband had been physically abused at school, and this also affected his ability to raise their children (M. King 2008). This story is just one example of the many ways the effects of the Indian boarding schools continue to be felt today.

Segregation and Landmark Court Cases

Prior to 1885, Chinese American students were not allowed to attend public schools in California. Between 1896 and 1954, it was legal for states to deny African Americans, Mexican Americans, American Indians, and Asian Americans access to public schools and other facilities designated for whites (Wollenberg 1974). Segregation was deemed legal in an important court case, *Plessy v. Ferguson* (1896), which determined "separate but equal" facilities to be constitutional (as discussed in Chapter Three). This court decision was used to justify the existence of separate educational facilities for white and non-white students. By 1931, more than three-quarters of the school districts in California practiced segregation (Wollenberg 1974). At that same time in Texas, 90 percent of the schools were racially and ethnically segregated (Godfrey 2008).

The schools established for non-whites were inferior to those that served whites in many ways. Schools for Mexican American children were designed to "Americanize" them through instruction in cooking, hygiene, English, and civics. In these segregated schools, children were punished for speaking Spanish, and girls were taught home economics so that they could work in the homes of whites (Wollenberg 1974).

In the 1930s and 1940s, Mexican Americans in Texas and California initiated protests against these separate and inferior schools. In Texas, the League of United Latin American Citizens (LULAC), founded in 1929, led the protests. The first case brought by LULAC was *Independent School District v. Salvatierra*, in 1931. The court decided that segregation was permissible, because it was not based on race but on language and academic abilities. Advocates of educational equality in Texas continued to be unsuccessful through a series of similar court cases over the next two decades.

One of the first victories of the civil rights movement came in 1946 with the case of *Mendez v. Westminster*, when a federal circuit court in California ruled that the segregation of children of Mexican and Latin American descent was unconstitutional. The *Mendez* case was a critical forerunner to the landmark 1954 Supreme Court decision in the case of *Brown v. Board of Education*, which overturned the *Plessy v. Ferguson* ruling.

Mendez began when Gonzalo Mendez, a Mexican American naturalized U.S. citizen, and his Puerto Rican wife, Felicítas, attempted to enroll their three children in the 17th Street Elementary School in Orange County, California. Although Gonzalo Méndez had attended the school himself as a boy, his children were turned away, because the school no longer allowed Mexican Americans to attend. Méndez initially approached the school board, but his complaints fell on deaf ears. Thus, in 1945, he, along with 5,000 other people, filed suit against several Orange County school districts. Their court case was successful, and the Supreme Court ruled that segregation on the basis of a Spanish surname was unconstitutional (Ruiz 2001).

For African Americans, the landmark case regarding educational segregation was *Brown v. Board of Education* in 1954, which was a compilation of four separate cases from four different towns. It involved two rural communities—Clarendon County, South Carolina, and Prince Edward County, Virginia, and two urban districts—Topeka, Kansas, and Wilmington, Delaware. African Americans in each of these communities perceived that the education their children received was inferior to that given to white children. Indeed, local governments spent less money on the education of black children. Nationally, prior to 1950, the average expenditure for black students was less than two-thirds of that for white students (Siddle Walker 2000). (In 1951 in Clarendon County, for example, the annual average expenditure was $44.32 per black student, compared with an average of $166.45 per white student. Additionally, white children did not have to pay for their school materials, whereas black students did [Anderson and Byrne 2004]). These unequal expenditures meant that African Americans had access to fewer educational resources (Siddle Walker 2000). Parents in Clarendon County got together to protest this tremendous inequality, and their case became one of the four cases heard in *Brown v. Board of Education*.

Despite tremendous obstacles, African Americans in the pre–civil rights era worked hard to ensure that their children had educational opportunities. Parents often provided equipment and spaces when they could. Communities mobilized to ensure educational opportunities. At exemplary high schools such as Dunbar High School in

Washington, D.C., 60 percent of graduates of this primarily black school went on to attend college in the 1950s. At this same high school, several of the teachers had doctorates from elite institutions (Siddle Walker 2000).

The rulings in *Mendez v. Westminster* and *Brown v. Board of Education* were only the beginning of the long process of school desegregation. In Prince Edward County, Virginia, for example, the *Brown* decision led to the closing of all public schools so that white students would not have to integrate. In 1964, a Supreme Court decision forced the county to reopen public schools (Orfield and Lee 2004).

The Persistence of Racial Segregation in the Educational System

In Texas in 1968, about 40 percent of Mexican-origin students were attending schools that were 80 percent or more Mexican American (San Miguel 1983). Little has changed in the intervening years: in 2001, 40 percent of Latino students and 31 percent of black students in the South attended schools that were less than 10 percent white (Orfield and Lee 2004).

Segregation persists in part because little has been done to prevent it. Schools are no longer allowed to prevent non-white children from attending, but proactive measures to prevent de facto segregation are lacking. School busing is one proactive measure that was successful at integrating school districts. In the 1970s, courts often ordered schools that continued to be racially segregated to bus children in from across town. This strategy worked because even though neighborhoods were segregated, busing meant that schools did not have to be. However, busing was short-lived (McNeal 2009). In 1991, the Supreme Court decided in *Dowell v. Oklahoma City* that schools were not obliged to desegregate. This decision meant that many school districts abandoned desegregation programs. Once children began to attend schools in the neighborhoods where they lived (as opposed to being bused to other neighborhoods), schools rapidly became resegregated (see Figure 6-1).

In the South in 1954, there were no black students in majority-white schools. That percentage barely shifted until 1967, when pressure from the civil rights movement led to school integration. By 1970, a third of black students in the South attended majority-white schools. With busing, that percentage peaked at 43.5 percent in 1988. However, the

FIGURE 6-1

PERCENT OF BLACK STUDENTS IN MAJORITY WHITE SCHOOLS IN THE SOUTH, 1954–2001

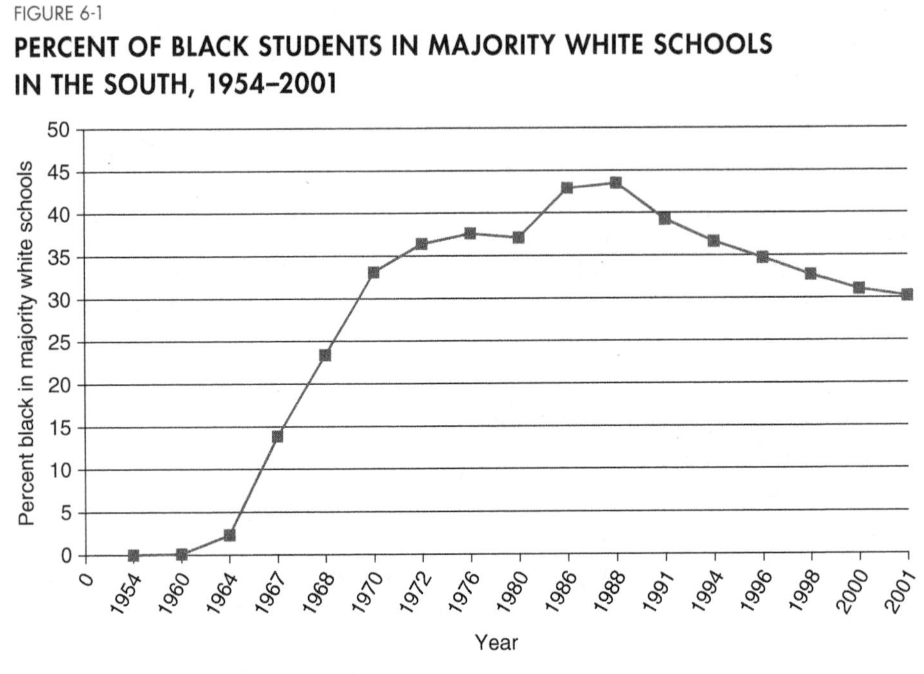

Source: Adapted from Orfield and Lee (2004).

number of black students in majority-white schools has decreased since 1991 as a result of the end of busing programs. By 2001, there were fewer black students in majority-white schools in the South than there had been in 1970.

This high level of racial segregation is often associated with poverty: in 2001, 88 percent of schools that were over 90 percent non-white were also majority-poor schools, with over 50 percent of the student body living below the poverty line (Orfield and Lee 2004). There is a direct relationship between the percentage of black and Latino students in a school and the percentage of poor students (Orfield and Lee 2004). A recent study of Florida schools found that more than 80 percent of students in primarily black schools were impoverished, compared with 50 percent of students in integrated schools and 43 percent of students in primarily white schools. This study also found that only 32 percent of fifth-graders at the primarily black schools had passed a basic test, compared with about 55 percent of those at the primarily white and integrated schools. Students at schools that were over 90 percent black fared the worst on standardized tests (Borman et al. 2004).

Affirmative Action in Higher Education

Racial diversity in schools is a contentious issue at the university level as well. Title VI of the 1968 Civil Rights Act enabled colleges and universities to take **affirmative action** in order to enhance racial diversity on campus. Affirmative action encompasses policies and procedures designed to combat ongoing discrimination in schools and in the workplace. In higher education, it has meant giving preferential treatment to people who are members of historically disadvantaged groups. In schools with affirmative action programs, admissions committees can consider the racial diversity of applicants as one factor in their decision to admit a student to a university.

In 1965, only 2 percent of medical students in the country were African American. In response to this underrepresentation, the University of California at Davis Medical School set aside sixteen of its one hundred admission slots for underrepresented minority students. In 1978, a white applicant named Allan Bakke was denied admission to the medical school. Bakke believed that in the absence of these racial quotas, he would have been admitted. He therefore filed a class-action lawsuit alleging that UC Davis had discriminated against him on the basis of his race. In the *Regents of the University of California v. Bakke* (1978) case, the Supreme Court ruled that the preferential racial quotas did deny equal protection to white students and thus were unconstitutional. However, the Supreme Court also ruled that race could still be used as one factor in determining admission. With this ruling, racial quotas were no longer permissible, but diversity could continue to be used as a factor in determining admission. The *Bakke* decision thus ended the relatively short history of racial quotas in university admissions, leaving us today with more ambiguous options for promoting diversity. The University of California system, for example, can argue that a student or job candidate would contribute to the diversity of the campus, yet they cannot say that they did or did not offer a position because of racial or ethnic identity (Yosso, Parker, Solorzano, and Lynn 2004).

After the *Bakke* decision, affirmative action programs continued to come under attack across the United States. In 1996, California voters passed Proposition 209, which banned the consideration of race in higher education admissions. As a consequence, admission rates of black, Latino, and Native American students to the University of California system fell dramatically. Between 1997 and 1998—the year the ban took effect—admissions of underrepresented students fell 61 percent at UC Berkeley and 36 percent at UCLA. These disparities continue today: black, Latino, and Native American students made up 54 percent of all California high school graduates in 2012, but just 27 percent of all UC freshmen in that same year (Murphy 2013).

Proponents of affirmative action also argue that **legacy admissions**—giving preference to the children and siblings of alumni—enhance the need for affirmative action. Legacy applicants are three times as likely to gain admission to highly selective colleges and universities as other applicants. Insofar as the vast majority of these legacy admissions are white and upper middle class, some people call legacy admissions "affirmative action for the rich" (Hurwitz 2011; Kahlenberg 2010).

EDUCATIONAL INEQUALITY TODAY

At all levels of schooling, educational achievements in the United States vary by racial or ethnic group. In 2010, over half of Asians had a bachelor's degree or higher—well above the national average of 27.9 percent. In contrast, only 13 percent of American Indians, 13 percent of Hispanics, and 17.7 percent of blacks had a bachelor's degree (Figure 6-2). The data are similar if we look at professional degrees.

FIGURE 6-2

PERCENTAGE OF POPULATION 25 YEARS AND OVER WITH A BACHELOR'S DEGREE OR HIGHER, 2006–2010

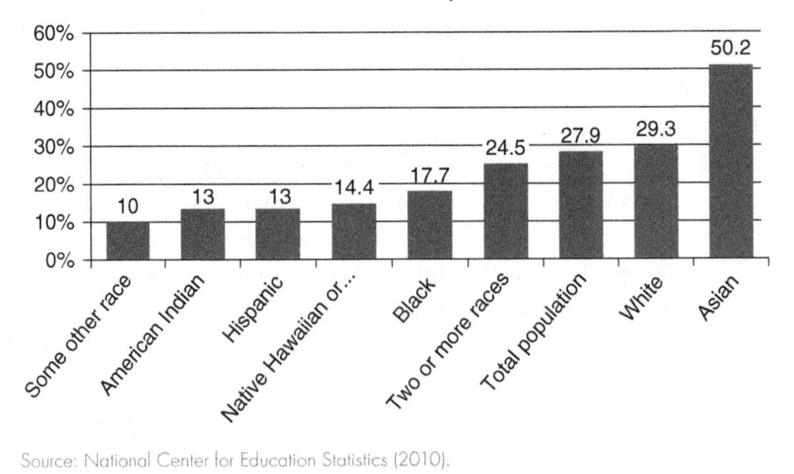

Source: National Center for Education Statistics (2010).

FIGURE 6-3

AVERAGE GPA BY RACE/ETHNICITY, 2008–2009

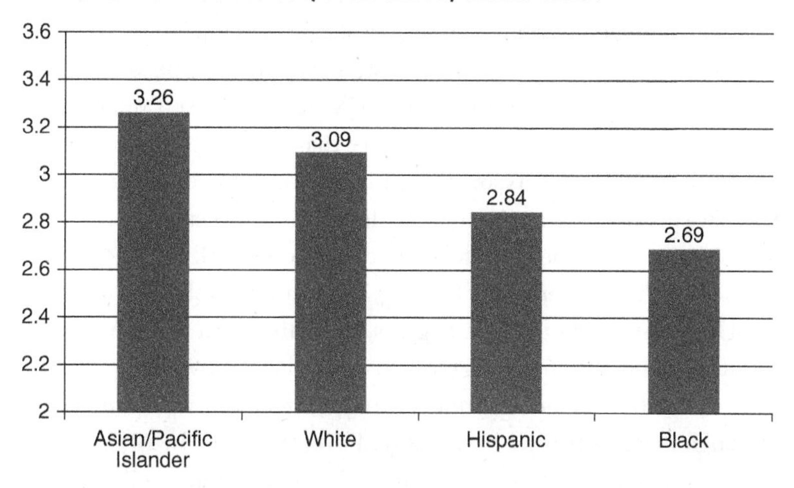

Source: National Center for Education Statistics (2010).

Grade point averages (GPAs) also vary by race and ethnicity. In 2008–2009, the average GPA among Asian American students was 3.26, compared with 3.09 for whites, 2.84 for Hispanics, and 2.69 for blacks (Figure 6-3).

Although disparities in educational outcomes persist, it is undeniable that they have lessened over the course of the past hundred years in the United States. Legal segregation has been banished, American Indian children are no longer forced to attend boarding schools, standard curricula now include multicultural components, nearly all youth have achieved literacy, and high school graduation rates for all racial groups are converging. Between 1971 and 1996, the gap in reading test scores between blacks and whites shrank by almost one-half (Kao and Thompson 2003). In 2012, 84 percent of Asians, 69 percent of Hispanics, 67 percent of whites, and 63 percent of blacks who graduated from high school immediately enrolled in college. There are still some significant disparities among racial groups, but they are not as pronounced as they were even ten years ago, when 28 percent of Hispanic youth dropped out of high school, compared with only 14 percent in 2012 (Fry and Taylor 2013).

In aggregate data, it becomes apparent that Asian students are outperforming all other students in test scores and high school and college completion rates. These achievements have led to a **"model minority" myth**, according to which Asians are widely perceived as the racial minority group that has "made it" in the United States. As we saw earlier, Asians have not always been viewed as a model minority. In fact, they were prevented from attending public schools in California in the late nineteenth century. The current stereotype did not become prevalent until the late twentieth century (Wing 2007). And today, even though Asians perform better on average than other groups, it is not the case that every single Asian student is an overachiever. Additionally, when we break the Asian population down into national-origin groups, we can see a more complex story (Ngo and Lee 2007). In 2004, for example, less than 10 percent of Hmong, Laotian, or Cambodian adults in the United States had college degrees, compared with about half of all Chinese and Pakistani adults (Museus and Kiang 2009).

There continue to be disparities in college attendance and completion, although these disparities have changed over the years. In 2012, Asians were the most likely racial or ethnic group to attend college, with 84 percent of Asian recent high school graduates enrolled in college. Seventy-nine percent of these students were enrolled at a four-year college or university, and 91 percent were enrolled full time (Fry and Taylor 2013). In 2012, 69 percent of Latino high school graduates enrolled in college, compared to 67 percent of white high school graduates. Latinos, however, were less likely to attend a four-year college than white students. In 2012, 56 percent of Latino college students were at a four-year college, compared with 72 percent of white students. In addition, Latinos were less likely than whites to attend a selective college, to be enrolled in college full time, and to complete a four-year degree (Fry and Taylor 2013).

Educational disparities among racial and ethnic groups are evident at each level of the educational system. In the next section, we will explore these disparities in more detail and look at the various explanations sociologists offer for them. Before we proceed with sociological explanations, pause and think about why black, Latino, and Native American students are faring less well than white and Asian students in the educational system. What have we learned so far that might inform your explanations?

THE ACHIEVEMENT GAP: SOCIOLOGICAL EXPLANATIONS FOR PERSISTENT INEQUALITY

What explains persistent disparities in educational outcomes by race and ethnicity? Sociologists describe the disparate educational outcomes of whites, Asians, blacks, Latinos, and Native Americans as the **achievement gap**. There are a variety of sociological explanations for this gap, and we will explore a few of these in this section.

The first thing to note when discussing educational disparities is that public education in the United States depends heavily on local property taxes. Inequalities in housing values translate into inequalities in schools. Relevant factors include widespread racial segregation in housing, the concentration of black and Latino families in impoverished inner cities, and the flight of middle-class white families to wealthier suburbs (Walters 2001).

Parental Socioeconomic Status

In the United States, parental education, income, and wealth are not distributed evenly. A major factor that can help us understand racial and ethnic inequality in education is overall socioeconomic inequality. For example, one study tracked the college completion rates of youth who were sophomores in high school in 1980. Over half of the youth whose family incomes were in the top 25 percent had earned a college degree by 1992, compared with only 7 percent of those whose family incomes were in the lowest 25 percent. The chances of college completion for the higher-income group were thus seven times higher than the chances for the lower-income group. Overall, differences in family income can explain about one-third of the test score gap between blacks and whites and nearly all of the differences in college completion rates (Gamoran 2001).

In addition to family income, parental education matters. Children with parents who have college degrees, for example, are much more likely to attend college than children whose parents have not completed high school. Parental education is one factor that explains Asians' relatively high educational attainment. In 1990, 65 percent of immigrants from India had college degrees, as did 63 percent of immigrants from Taiwan. However, it is important to recognize the variety in the Asian American experience: less than 5 percent of Cambodian and Laotian immigrants had a college degree in 1990 (Kao and Thompson 2003).

Children from working-class backgrounds tend to fare less well in school than children from middle-class or wealthy families. The fact that African Americans and Latinos are, on average, less wealthy than white students helps explain some of the inequalities in educational outcomes. In one study, sociologists Vincent Roscigno and James Ainsworth-Darnell (1999) found that family socioeconomic status could explain about half of the difference between the test scores of black and white children. What explains the other half? Why do black and Latino children fare less well in school than white children who have the same family structure and income levels? Sociologists offer a few explanations, which we will consider next.

Cultural Explanations: "Acting White" and Other Theories

Sociologists and other social scientists have long conducted research on the extent to which culture plays a role in the achievement gap. Culture is a broad analytic concept and can refer to a wide variety of factors, ranging from teachers' failure to recognize the cultural norms of Native American students to the distinct discipline styles of East Asian parents.

Scholars of education have spent much ink trying to understand why black students perform more poorly in school and have lower test scores than white students. One explanation that gained currency in the 1980s and 1990s is the **oppositional culture** thesis, credited to anthropologists Signithia Fordham and John Ogbu (1986). This thesis has two basic components. The first is that African American children do not do well in school because they equate school success with "**acting white**," behaving in ways associated with white people. The second is that African American children have responded to widespread discrimination by developing an identity in opposition to dominant white culture, and thus in opposition to school success. The basis of this argument is that black children receive signals from both the white and black communities that lead them to reject schooling as a route to success. Fordham and Ogbu contend that black students' and their parents' experiences with discrimination lead them to distrust white authority figures and institutions. Additionally, they argue that black students develop anti-achievement attitudes to avoid peer sanctions. They found that black students equate "working hard to get good grades in school" (186) with acting white. Fordham and Ogbu's thesis is based on a study with only thirty-three students, and it gained an inordinate amount of media attention.

The idea that black students do not do well in school because they have antischool attitudes was widely accepted and publicized because it resonated with the popular belief that black people do not value education. However, a series of subsequent studies have shown that it is simply not true that black students consciously underachieve or equate academic success with acting white. For example, using a nationally representative sample of nearly 17,000 students, Ainsworth-Darnell and Downey (1998) found that black students had more positive attitudes toward school than white students. They also found that black students reported being more popular when they did better in school, refuting the claim that black students experience peer pressure to reject school. They did not find support for the claim that black students perceive lower returns from education than white students; instead, black students were more likely than white students to agree with the statement that education is important to getting a job.

In a qualitative study of seventy-two black students from the southeastern part of the United States, Karolyn Tyson (2002) found that black third- and fourth-graders were consistently very excited about school and about learning. In her study, students were proud when they excelled and disappointed when they got answers wrong or were not allowed to participate in classroom activities. Instead of experiencing high achievement as a burden, as Fordham and Ogbu (1986) have argued, Tyson (2002, 1174) found that black youth experience a "burden of low achievement," in which students experienced emotional distress when they did not do well.

Tracking

Even when schools are ostensibly integrated, there is often internal segregation. A well-known book by Beverly Daniel Tatum is titled *Why Are All the Black Kids Sitting Together in the Cafeteria?* (2003). There are many answers to this question, but one response is that schools are internally segregated, with white students being the most likely to be in the more advanced classes. When children are in different classes, it is not surprising that they would not spend time together during social hours. In his memoir, *High Price,* African American neuroscientist Carl Hart (2014) explains that he often felt torn between the opportunities to learn more when he was in primarily white advanced classrooms and socializing more when he remained in the exclusively black remedial classrooms.

From elementary to high school, students in U.S. schools are placed in different classes based on ability groups, or "tracks." Many studies have found that non-white children are more likely to be placed in low-ability groups, beginning in elementary school, whereas white children are more likely to be placed in college-bound tracks in high school. Kao and Thompson (2003) discuss data from 1997 which reveals that nearly half of whites and Asians were in college preparatory tracks, compared with about a third of Latino and Asian students and less than a quarter of Native American students. Another study, based on 1998 data, found that white students were twice as likely as blacks to be in advanced mathematics courses. This study, however, found that the differences could be explained by accounting for test scores, grades, prior track placement, and socioeconomic status (S. Kelly 2009). A more recent nationally representative study found that African Americans and Latinos were underrepresented in advanced sophomore math classes in a large number of schools. Moreover, black and Latino students at those schools had lower average GPAs and rates of university enrollment (Muller, Riegle-Crumb, Schiller, Wilkinson, and Frank 2010).

In addition to within-school differences, there are also disparities between schools. Schools that are predominantly white are more

An honors Earth sciences class at a public high school in Massachusetts, 2013.

likely to have advanced placement classes than primarily black and Latino schools. The differential opportunities that black, Latino, and Native American students have to take advanced classes have important impacts on their overall academic achievement and college success rates (Kao and Thompson 2003).

Social and Cultural Capital and Schooling

Sociologists of education also often turn to social and cultural capital as explanations for the achievement gap. **Social capital** refers to the relationships and networks that students have, whereas **cultural capital** describes the cultural resources a student has at his or her disposal. Put simply, social capital is *who* you know, whereas cultural capital is *what* you know. Students who know many people who have had educational success—parents, uncles, aunts, and cousins with college degrees—will have more information and resources at their disposal than students whose social networks primarily include high school dropouts or people with no schooling at all. This social capital will play a role in a student's ability to succeed. In a similar fashion, students with access to dominant cultural capital—the norms, values, and cultural knowledge valued in the school—will have more chances for success than students whose families are not part of the dominant culture.

Based on their research with Mexican-origin students in the Bay Area, sociologists Ricardo Stanton-Salazar and Sanford M. Dornbusch (1995) argue that adolescents require supportive ties with **institutional agents** in order to be successful in school. An institutional agent is a person who occupies a position of power and is able to access or negotiate resources for students. These institutional agents can be family or community members as well as school personnel. An institutional agent can be a high school counselor who helps a student find financial aid, an alumnus of a local college who serves as a mentor to a student and helps him or her fill out college applications, or a high school teacher who writes a college recommendation for a student. These institutional agents constitute a form of social capital that permits students to reach their educational goals. Working-class youth have less of this necessary form of social capital, which makes reaching their educational goals more difficult.

Most schools in the United States make some effort to recognize the multicultural nature of the nation. Nevertheless, people whose culture and experiences are part of the dominant culture are in charge of most schools. Children whose families are part of the dominant culture thus have an inherent advantage, as they do not have to learn the codes and norms of the dominant culture in order to be successful in school. Moreover, the school does not devalue their experiences and culture.

The concept of cultural capital draws from the work of French sociologist Pierre Bourdieu (1984), who argued that the dominant group in a society makes its preferences, tastes, and norms appear to be superior to those of the nondominant group. He describes the power of the dominant group to do this as **symbolic violence**, as the dominant group creates a context in which the norms, values, and tastes of other groups are labeled as inferior. An example of this symbolic violence in the United States is the idea that the standard form of English spoken by middle-class white Americans is an indication of intelligence and eloquence, whereas the forms of English that working-class African Americans speak to one another is an indication of ignorance. The dominant group—middle-class whites—sets the standards.

What all this means for education is that children who grow up in homes where Standard English is spoken can speak this language in school and receive praise for their intelligence and eloquence. Meanwhile, children raised in homes where other forms of English or other languages are spoken must learn new languages and accents in school, and their teachers may tell them not to speak the way their parents do at home. The act of telling children that the way their parents speak is inferior and unacceptable in a school environment can amount to symbolic violence.

Scholars such as Michéle Lamont and Annette Lareau (1988, 164) define **cultural capital** as "widely shared, legitimate culture made up of high-status cultural signals (attitudes, preferences, behaviors, and goods) used in direct or indirect social and cultural exclusion." Other scholars, however, contend that all people have cultural capital, not solely those who belong to the dominant group. Sociologist Prudence Carter (2003) explains that nondominant cultural capital refers to those cultural resources and tastes that people who do not belong to the dominant group use to gain authenticity as a member of their group. For example, African American youth may use nondominant cultural capital such as knowledge of the latest underground hip-hop music to signify their cultural authenticity. In this way, nondominant cultural capital also has an instrumental use—even though that use may not gain the youth very much in terms of dominant society.

In a 2003 study, Prudence Carter interviewed African American youth in New York, who explained to her that they used different ways of talking at home and at school because they knew that speaking Standard English would be valued in a school setting. Her interviewees felt compelled to **codeswitch**, or change from the language they used at home to Standard English in order to succeed in school and be upwardly mobile. Carter posits that the use of African American speech codes at home and in the streets is critical to African American youths' sense of self, yet that these linguistic codes are devalued at school and in places of formal employment.

Carter's interviewees pointed to dress, musical, and speech styles as the most salient cultural indicators of what it means to be authentically black. Carter, however, found that there was a certain amount of tension involved in these students' navigation of their home and school identities. Students told her that they could easily navigate the different cultural markers and language of the two environments. However, in some cases, the youth "sensed that their cultural presentations of selves negatively influenced teachers' evaluations" (150). Black youth who wish to maintain cultural authenticity have to work hard to maintain an appropriate balance. However, middle-class white youth whose families and communities value dominant cultural capital do not have to worry about this particular balancing act. As Carter explains, the black youth she worked with

> *perceived that teachers evaluated them as deficient based on the teachers' and the schools' standards of cultural decorum. They understood that most Whites with whom they came into contact used Standard English primarily, the language that facilitates success in U.S. schools (although it is not a sufficient condition by itself). At the same time, they did not believe their own speech styles to be incompatible with school success. (151)*

Although most teachers have good intentions, the reality is that teachers are members of our society and, like all of us, are inundated with media images that reinforce stereotypes. The prevalence of stereotypes about blacks and criminality, for example, influences how teachers respond to black boys who misbehave. This, in turn, affects their schooling outcomes. Ann Arnett Ferguson (2001) offers a poignant example from a school in California where a white teacher compared black children who didn't return library books to "looters." Instead of seeing the children as careless or forgetful, the teacher resorted to racialized stereotypes of black men as thieves. Ferguson argues that cultural representations of black men as criminals serve to **adultify** black boys in the eyes of teachers. Thus, instead of seeing black boys as "just being boys" when they misbehave, teachers were inclined to say things such as "that boy has a jail cell with his name on it."

Hidden Curricula and the School-to-Prison Pipeline

Schools are sites of socialization and learning: students learn to become members of society and develop the skills necessary to be successful. The official curricula of schools include subjects such as math, science, history, and, increasingly, test-taking skills. Schools are also meant to function as sorting mechanisms: students who work hard and perform well will become the future leaders of society. Some education scholars argue that there is also a **hidden curriculum**, in that the school curriculum is designed to reflect the cultural hegemony and ensure the class interests of the dominant group. From this perspective, schools also function as sorting mechanisms, but not according to merit. Instead, schools reproduce race and class inequality. Schools that primarily serve the working class teach students to follow rules and take orders, whereas schools that primarily serve the middle and upper class teach creativity and independence. The idea behind this hidden curriculum is that schools are designed to transform working-class students into diligent workers who do not question authority, whereas middle- and upper-class students are taught to be creative and motivated leaders. Because of racial disparities in income and wealth, this structure means that black and Latino students are more likely to attend schools that have a coercive authority structure (Bowles and Gintis 1976).

Schools that have high numbers of black and Latino children reproduce racial inequality through rules and punishment. Students are evaluated not only on their achievement, but also on their ability to conform to rules. Punishment for rule breaking becomes a mechanism of social differentiation and normalization. The disciplinary techniques used by schools create children who are labeled as "good," "bad," "gifted," and "troublemakers," and children are judged on their ability to conform to school rules (A. Ferguson 2001, 52).

voices

Moesha

Prudence Carter's (2003) work introduces us to a young African American woman named Moesha, who had recently graduated from high school, found an entry-level job, and taken a few college courses. Moesha was what Carter calls a "cultural straddler," in that she was able to use "black" cultural capital as well as dominant cultural capital, depending on the situation. Despite her ability to codeswitch quite fluently, Moesha perceived that there are tensions between dominant and "black" cultural capital.

Moesha explained to Carter in an interview:

> We're [African Americans are] not ignorant; there are just certain ways that we talk to each other. It might not seem right, but that doesn't mean we're dumb. See I know people who can act ignorant [clownish] as anything, but they are also smart, and they can also talk in an intelligent way. It's just that when you talk with your friends, you talk in a certain way. Or when you're at work or wherever you're at, you have to act intelligent.

Later, Moesha explained how these ideas were carried over into the school setting:

> There were like certain teachers, they would give you attitude for no reason. And you're like . . . I didn't do anything. But for me, it was only like for certain friends that I had [who] were outspoken, and me I was very passive. I'd let whoever say whatever. And [my friends] weren't like that. I guess . . . for my friends, I didn't like the way that the teacher would talk to them. I had friends that . . . were very smart. They were very, very smart, and the teachers think that because they are a certain way, and they act a certain way, that they are not smart. And that's not true. They are; they are very smart. It's important that you learn about people.

Even though Moesha had learned that she was expected to use Standard English and deferential modes of behavior in school to gain the teacher's favor, she recognized that these expectations also meant that students who were more outspoken were mistreated.

It is also important to think about the fact that whereas white, middle class students can use the same speech styles and behavioral mannerisms at home and at school, children from working-class and non-white communities are expected to alter their behavior when at school. This puts a certain burden on students who do not hail from the dominant culture. In addition, it sends home a strong message when a teacher tells a student that the way he or she (and his or her parents) speaks at home is "ignorant."

Source: Carter 2003.

This focus is a crucial part of what some scholars call the **school-to-prison pipeline**—a set of practices that leads to children being funneled from public schools into the juvenile and criminal justice system. Factors contributing to this pipeline include a rise in suspension rates across the country and increased policing of and arrests within schools. These practices build up over the course of a child's educational career and have pernicious effects on black and Native American youth in particular. Across all age groups, starting with preschool, black students are three times more likely than white students to be suspended from school, and Native American students are twice as likely as white students to be suspended. Relatedly, black and Native American students are also twice as likely as other students to be subject to a school-related arrest (U.S. Department of Education, Office for Civil Rights 2014).

CONCLUSION AND DISCUSSION

In the United States, 28 percent of adults over the age of twenty-five have a bachelor's degree. With the changing labor market and growing inequality, postsecondary education has become increasingly important. An individual's opportunities for financial stability increasingly depend on completing college.

In this chapter, we have explored the various dimensions of educational inequality. There are various sociological explanations for why American Indians, Latinos, and African Americans are only about half as likely as white adults to have a college degree. Some of these reasons are historical; the parents of many people of color did not have college degrees because of extreme barriers to higher education in the past. There are also socioeconomic explanations. For example, it is more difficult to attend college if you are in a financially precarious situation, and whites have, on average, higher incomes than other groups. There are also structural and cultural explanations for racial disparities in educational outcomes.

What do we do with all of this information? Many fantastic public schools across the country continue to be primarily or exclusively white. Meanwhile, there are vastly underresourced and even dangerous schools that primarily serve black, Latino, and Native American youth. What does it say about us as a nation that we do not give truly equal opportunities to children from disadvantaged backgrounds?

How has your cultural capital affected your educational experience? Reflect on the extent to which you have had access to dominant versus non-dominant cultural capital and how that has shaped your education. Drawing from the readings and your own experiences, describe an idea for how youth without access to dominant cultural capital could excel academically.

THINKING ABOUT **RACIAL JUSTICE**

Key Terms

Brown v. Board of Education 141
affirmative action 149
legacy admissions 150
"model minority" myth 151
achievement gap 153
oppositional culture 154
acting white 154
social capital 157
cultural capital 157
institutional agent 157
symbolic violence 158
codeswitching 159
adultify 160
hidden curriculum 160
school-to-prison pipeline 162

Check Your Understanding

OBJECTIVE 6.1

Examine the history of educational inequality in the United States.

- The United States has a long history of educational inequality. In the early twentieth century, Native American, African American, and Mexican American children were relegated to separate and inferior schools. Segregation was outlawed in 1954, yet it has produced lingering effects.

Q What were Indian schools, and what were the conditions like in those schools?

Q On what basis could plaintiffs in the *Brown v. Board of Education* case argue that schools were not "separate but equal"?

Q Why did it take so long for schools to become integrated after the 1954 *Brown v. Board of Education* decision?

OBJECTIVE 6.2

Analyze the dimensions of racial inequality in our educational system.

- Educational disparities among racial and ethnic groups are evident at each level of the educational system.

Q How has educational attainment across racial and ethnic groups changed over time?

Q What is the relationship between school segregation and poverty?

Q Why have schools begun to resegregate since 1991?

OBJECTIVE 6.3

Evaluate the continuing gap in the educational achievements of white, Asian, black, Native American, and Latino students.

- Asian and white students tend to do better on tests, have higher GPAs, and have higher rates of college completion than African American, Native American, and Latino students.

Q What theoretical explanations do sociologists offer for the achievement gap?

Q What is the difference between social and cultural capital? How are social and cultural capital related to educational success?

Critical Thinking

1. Explain and reflect on the tension some youth face between maintaining cultural authenticity and being perceived as serious students. How much does this resonate with your personal experience?
2. How do racial ideologies play a role in reproducing racial inequalities within the school system? Specify which racial ideologies you are referring to and how they are connected to inequality.
3. Which explanation for the achievement gap do you find most convincing? Why?
4. To what extent do you think that black children do less well in school than white children because of the desire not to be perceived as "acting white"? On what empirical basis do you make your arguments?
5. How are social and cultural capital important for school success? How have social and cultural capital affected your own educational experiences?

7

INCOME AND LABOR MARKET INEQUALITY

CHAPTER OUTLINE

LEARNING OBJECTIVES

7.1 Explain the extent of income inequality by race, ethnicity, and gender.

7.2 Describe the dimensions of labor market inequality.

7.3 Examine how sociologists explain labor market inequality.

7.4 Understand how affirmative action works.

7.5 Assess the relationship between self-employment and labor market inequality.

The United States is one of the most unequal countries in the Western hemisphere. We have typically considered our Latin American neighbors to be more unequal than us, yet in 2013, by some measures, the United States had more income inequality than Mexico. Moreover, in the United States, inequality is mapped along race and gender lines, with African Americans and Latinos earning substantially less than whites.

We see this racial inequality not just in income but also in the labor market as a whole. In this chapter, we will take a closer look at income and labor market inequality and develop a deeper understanding of racial inequality in the United States today.

Studies of labor market discrimination and income inequality clearly show that men earn more than women and that white workers earn more than non-white workers, even accounting for differences in education, skills, years on the job, and productivity. Why are employers willing to pay a premium for white male workers? It seems as if in a capitalist society, employers should want to get the best worker they can for the lowest price. Yet the evidence suggests that employers routinely pass over highly qualified black and Latino candidates and offer raises and promotions to white candidates. Why do you think this is the case? Why are employers less likely to hire black and Latino candidates? Why are highly qualified Asians paid less than their white counterparts?

INCOME INEQUALITY BY RACE, ETHNICITY, AND GENDER

Before delving into inequalities among racial and ethnic groups, it is worth pointing out that in the United States, the difference in earnings between the richest and the poorest people has widened over the past few decades. Income inequality among Americans has increased in large part because of tremendous growth in the incomes of the highest earners and stagnation or decline in the incomes of the lowest earners. By 2007, the share of the national income held by the top 1 percent was higher than it had been since 1917 (Morris and Western 1999; McCall and Percheski 2010). You may recall the slogans of the "Occupy Wall Street" movement referring to this income (and wealth) disparity, such as: "We are the 99%."

Tensions over inequality in the United States have risen in recent years in response to rising inequality. In 2013, the richest 20 percent of the U.S. population earned sixteen times more, on average, than the poorest 20 percent. According to this method of calculating inequality, the United States compares unfavorably to both Mexico and Uruguay, as shown in Figure 7-1.

FIGURE 7-1

INEQUALITY IN THE AMERICAS

The higher the number, the greater the economic inequality, calculated by dividing the annual income of the richest 20 percent by the annual income of the poorest 20 percent.

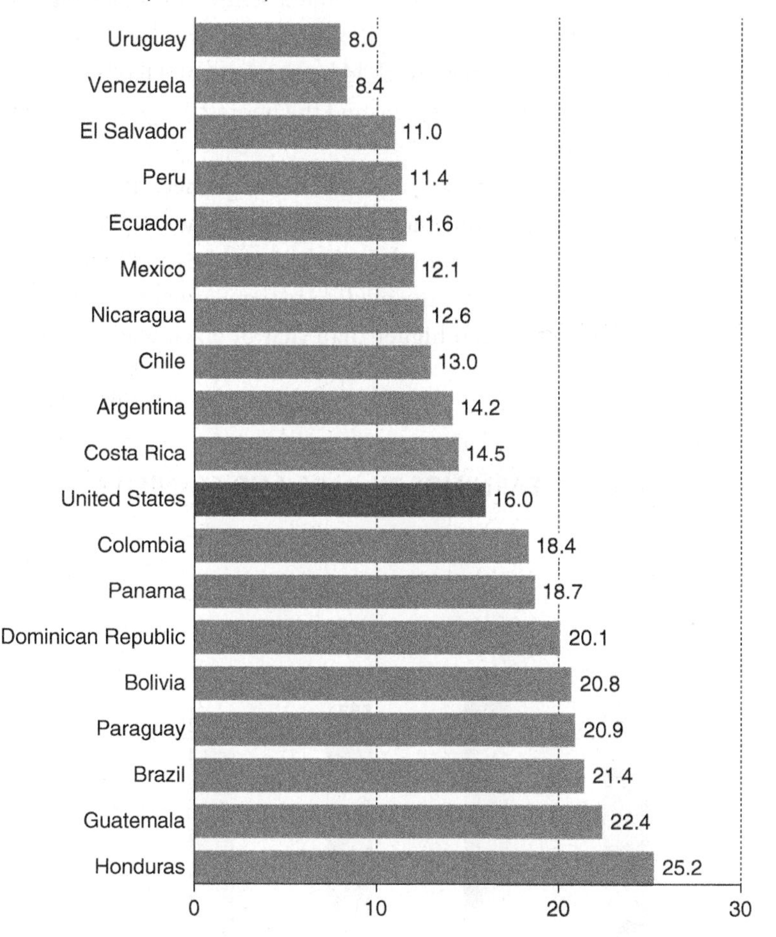

Source: U.N. Economic Commission for Latin America and the Caribbean and U.S. Census, cited by Isacson (2013).

By 2011, the United States was one of the most unequal advanced economies in the world in terms of income, with a Gini coefficient of 47.7. (By comparison, Norway's Gini coefficient was 23.) The **Gini coefficient** is a measure from 1 to 100, with 0 representing perfect equality (i.e., everyone earning exactly the same amount) and 100 representing perfect inequality (i.e., a single person having all the earnings) (International Labor Organization [ILO] 2013). This inequality is problematic both because it means that the United States has an increasingly large poor population and because inequality is related to a host of health and social problems, including high rates of low birth weight, homicide, mental illness, and violent crime (Wilkinson and Pickett 2009).

Compared with similar nations, the United States is the most unequal on a variety of other measures as well. In addition to having the highest Gini coefficient, it has the highest child poverty rate, and has the largest ratio between the richest 10 percent and the poorest 10 percent (Internationalcomparison.org 2014).

Overall inequality is exacerbated by earnings inequality distributed along racial and ethnic lines. In the United States today, Asians have the highest median earnings, followed by whites and then blacks and Hispanics (Figure 7-2). The median income of white workers in the United States has been higher than that of black workers for as

FIGURE 7-2

MEDIAN WEEKLY EARNINGS BY RACE AND ETHNICITY, 2013

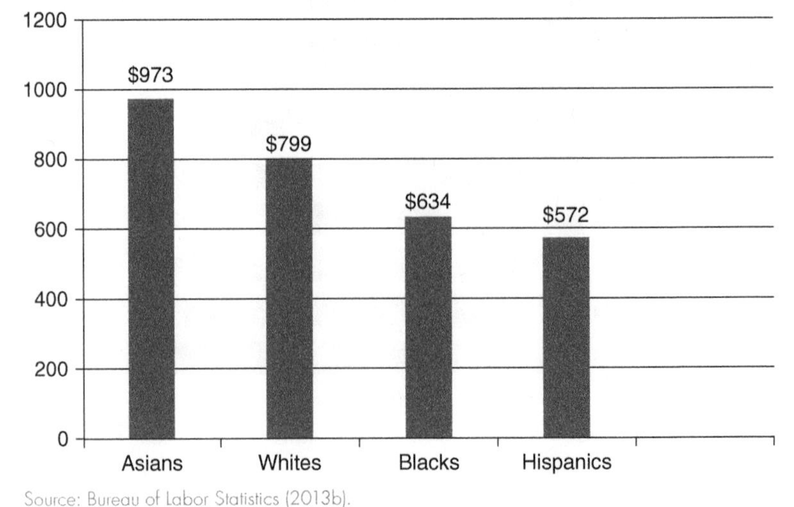

Source: Bureau of Labor Statistics (2013b).

long as we have kept track of income data. Such differences in earnings by group are called the **earnings gap**. Sociologists provide a wide array of explanations for this gap, and we will go over many of them later in this chapter.

How does income inequality by race and ethnicity further break down by gender? As we see in Figure 7-3, the largest difference in income is between Asian men—whose median weekly earnings were $1,092 in 2013, and Hispanic women—whose median weekly earnings were $525 per week. Notably, the gender income gap between Asian men and Asian women is also one of the largest, with Asian men earning 40 percent more than Asian women.

Figure 7-3 does not include Native Americans. However, researchers have found that Native Americans have lower average earnings than whites, and that these differences also vary by gender. In 2000, the average yearly earnings for white men were $49,634. In contrast, Native American men earned, on average, $29,954—just 60 percent of white men's earnings. White women had average yearly earnings of $27,749, compared with $21,103 for Native American women (Huyser, Sakamoto, and Takei 2009).

FIGURE 7-3

MEDIAN WEEKLY EARNINGS BY RACE AND ETHNICITY AND GENDER, 2013

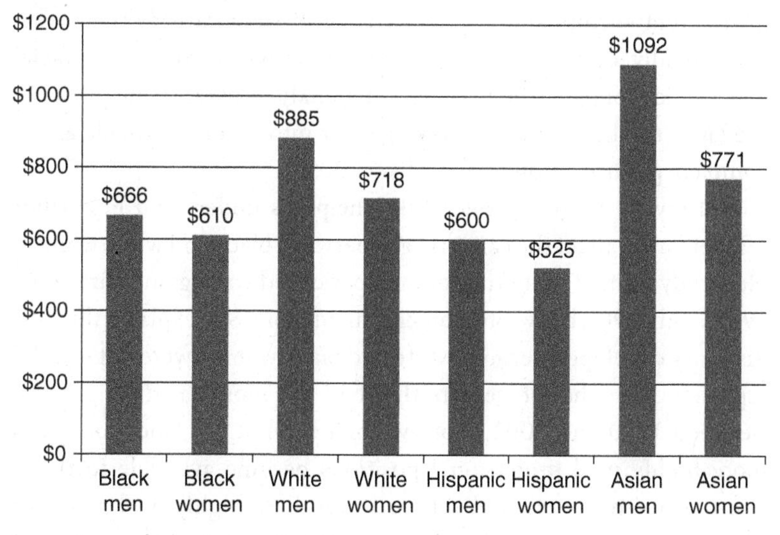

Source: Bureau of Labor Statistics (2013b).

In addition to the earnings gap, sociologists have identified a **wage gap**, which refers to the differences in hourly earnings among groups. Whereas the earnings gap refers to overall income regardless of hours worked, the wage gap refers only to the difference in the amount earned per hour worked. To understand earnings and wage gaps by group, we need to account for broader forces at work in the labor market.

DIMENSIONS OF RACIAL DISPARITIES IN THE LABOR MARKET

Disparities in earnings and wages are tied to many facets of the labor market, including unemployment rates, promotion practices, and employment stability. The wage gap is a reflection of how much people are paid per each hour of work, yet labor market inequality also includes differences in yearly and lifetime earnings. For example, black women are at a higher risk of unemployment than white women, meaning they are even more economically disadvantaged than the wage gap suggests (Pettit and Ewert 2009). Is it harder for people from some racial or ethnic groups to obtain jobs? Are some groups less likely to be promoted? Are some groups less likely to be in stable employment? All of these factors are relevant to understanding the extent of labor market disparities.

Disparities among Women

First, let's look at how gender plays a role. Men and women often work in different sectors and frequently have distinct career trajectories. Additionally, earnings differences by gender within and across racial and ethnic groups can be striking. Thus, analyses of racial inequality in the labor market that do not take gender into account provide an incomplete picture (Browne and Misra 2003).

A study by Raine Dozier (2010) helps us understand how labor market forces affect the earnings gap between black and white women. Her study found that both groups experienced wage gains during the 1980s and 1990s, but white women gained more. She explains that this disparity developed because white and black women were not equally represented in the job sectors that had the most earnings growth. Between 1980 and 2002, more women entered the labor force and more highly paid professional positions became available to them. White women were more likely to attain these highly paid positions and thus gain more than their black counterparts.

Black, white, and Latina women have different labor market outcomes, and these vary further by level of education. Among high school graduates aged eighteen to twenty-four, 61 percent of white women are employed, compared with 52 percent of blacks and 55 percent of Hispanics. The trends are distinct for college graduates: 86 percent of black female college graduates are employed, compared with 82 percent of white female college graduates and 77 percent of Hispanic female college graduates. Overall, black female college graduates are less disadvantaged relative to their white counterparts than are low-skilled black women (Alon and Haberfeld 2007).

These disparities continue over the length of time spent in the workforce. We can see this by looking at wage differentials over time. For unskilled women, defined as women with a high school degree or less who do not have a skilled trade, first entering the labor market, the average hourly rate (in 1995 dollars) does not vary greatly by race and ethnicity: $6.28 for black women, $6.42 for white women, and $6.67 for Hispanic women. However, by the fourteenth year in the labor market, white and Hispanic women are doing, on average, a lot better, with an average pay of $10.04 and $9.34 per hour, respectively. In contrast, after fourteen years of work, unskilled black women earn, on average, only $7.48 per hour. Whereas the earnings of white and Hispanic women in low-skill jobs tend to increase over time, this is not the case for black women. These data show that the human capital advantage of work experience is less for black women than for white and Hispanic women, even though black women with college degrees experience other labor market advantages (Alon and Haberfeld 2007).

Disparities among Latinos and Asian Americans

Given the tremendous diversity within the Latino and Asian American populations, it can be helpful to break these groups down by national origin when analyzing economic disparities. In 2010, there were more than 17 million Asians in the United States. Six national origin groups accounted for about 89 percent of all Asian Americans: Chinese, Filipinos, Indians, Koreans, Vietnamese, and Japanese. Of these groups, Indians had the highest median household income ($88,000), followed by Filipinos ($75,000), Japanese ($65,390), Chinese ($65,400), Vietnamese ($53,400), and Koreans ($50,000). These differences have some correlation with education: only 26% of Vietnamese in the United States have college degrees, compared with 70% of

Indians (Figure 7-4). The relationship between education and income becomes clearer when we look at individual earnings, as shown in Figure 7-5. The median earnings of Indians are $65,000 per year, compared with $35,000 for Vietnamese. The Hmong had the lowest median earnings in 2010—$28,866—and the lowest levels of education, with only 14% having a bachelor's degree or higher.

In a study using data from the 2000 U.S. census, Emily Greenman and Yu Xie (2008) looked at full-time, year-round workers between the ages of twenty-five and fifty-five. They found that among men, four groups had higher earnings than white men: Chinese, Asian Indians, Koreans, and Japanese. However, among women, in addition to those four groups, Cuban women and Filipina women also out-earn their

FIGURE 7-4

COLLEGE EDUCATION RATES AMONG ASIAN AMERICAN ADULTS BY NATIONAL ORIGIN GROUP, 2010

(% with a bachelor's degree or higher)

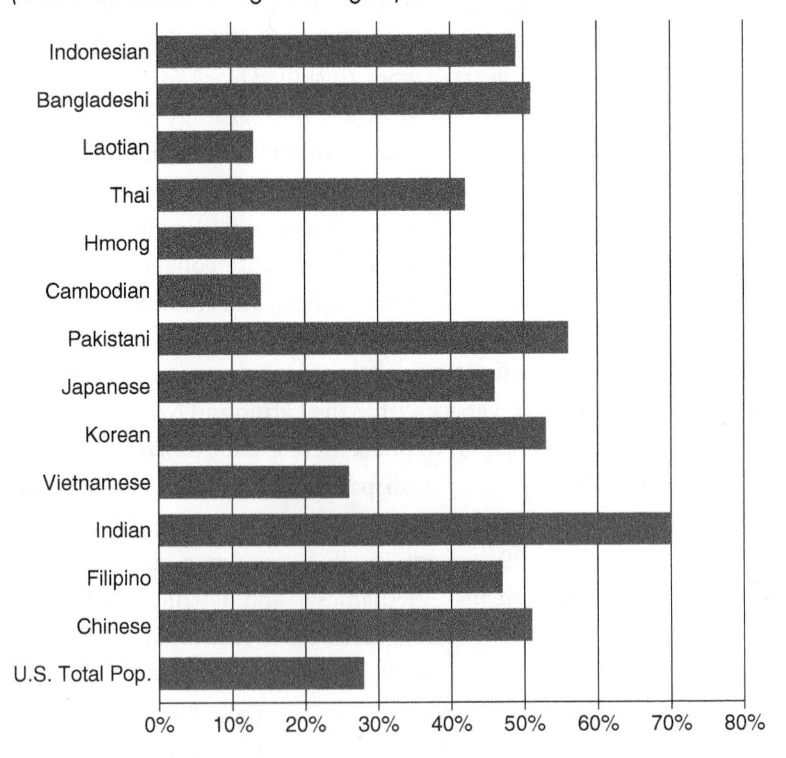

Source: Pew Research Center, 2013.

FIGURE 7-5

MEDIAN INDIVIDUAL EARNINGS AMONG ASIAN AMERICAN ADULTS BY NATIONAL ORIGIN GROUP, 2010

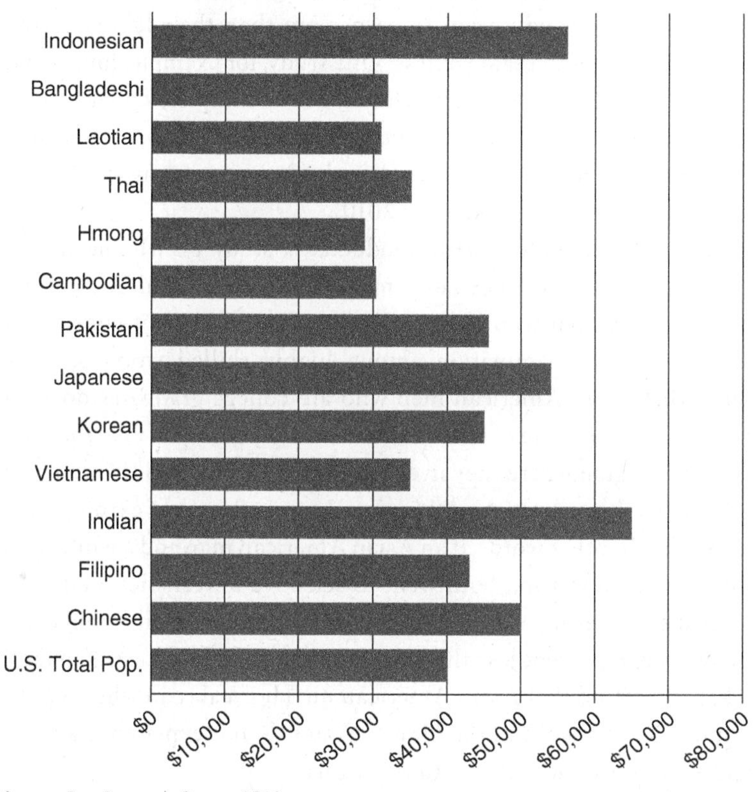

Source: Pew Research Center, 2013.

white counterparts. Overall, Greenman and Xie found that white women earn seventy-one cents for each dollar that white men earn, and that white women have the largest gender disadvantage of all of the racial and ethnic groups. Korean women, for example, earned eighty-six cents for each dollar that Korean men earned, and black and Filipina women earned eighty-four cents for each dollar that their male counterparts earned. These results show that it is not the case that race and gender are additive factors in the labor market. Instead, racism and sexism operate in distinct ways for different ethnic and racial groups.

Asian American men have the highest average earnings in the United States. Does this mean they do not face discrimination? Not necessarily. Many sociologists have pointed out that Asians earn more than whites, but that their average earnings should actually be even higher, because Asians have higher average educational attainment than whites. Because of how our society is organized, we should expect people with more education to earn more than their less educated counterparts, not the same or less. One study, for example, found that over half of Asians born in the United States complete college, compared with less than a third of whites. Asians are also more likely than other groups to major in areas that have higher pay, such as science and engineering (Kim and Sakamoto 2010).

Kim and Sakamoto (2010) conducted a study on whether Asian American men experience labor market discrimination. Their study included only men who were college graduates. Thus, it considered labor market discrimination among highly skilled workers. They found that Asian American men who are college graduates do earn more than their white counterparts. However, once you take into account the region where they live, their field of study, and their college type, native-born Asian American men have an 8 percent earnings disadvantage. In other words, if an Asian American man and a white man both live in New York, both went to selective universities, and both studied engineering, we could expect that the Asian man would earn, on average, 8 percent less than the white man. In contrast, Kim and Sakamoto found that Asian American men born abroad who went to school and now work in the United States do not experience a labor market disadvantage relative to white men.

Another study conducted in 2008, however, did find that foreign-born Asian men earn less than similarly qualified white men. Using data from the 2000 census, Qingfang Wang (2008) explored earnings disparities between U.S.-born whites and blacks and foreign-born Hispanics and Asians, looking at men and women separately. Wang found that foreign-born Hispanic black women have the lowest average annual earnings, and that Asian American and white men had the highest earnings, according to the raw data. However, once we take into account age, educational attainment, employment hours, and English proficiency, the disparities decline. Holding these factors constant, white men still earn the most, but the Asian advantage declines substantially, with foreign-born Asian men earning $5,600 less than black men and $15,000 less than white men annually. These analyses show that the higher earnings of foreign-born Asian men are due in large part to their higher educational levels. By the same token, the relative prosperity of white men and women is due to an unmeasured advantage in the labor market over non-whites.

Underemployment, Unemployment, and Joblessness

Earnings inequality is compounded by unemployment rates. Earnings data do not factor in unemployed people, who may not be taking home any income. It is thus important to consider the effects of unemployment and underemployment on the bigger picture. These rates vary significantly by race and ethnicity, as shown in Figure 7-6. Since 1970, the unemployment rate for blacks has been about twice that for whites.

Wage differentials in the labor force provide us with a limited view of overall inequality, as analyses of the earnings gap account only for people who are actually working. Thus, the finding that the earnings gap between whites and blacks has decreased since 1980 may not be as promising as it seems in terms of racial equality, as we will see. The Bureau of Labor Statistics counts people as unemployed when they do not have a job and have actively looked for work in the previous month. Thus, as many people do not work and have given up looking for work, the unemployment rate is only one measure of joblessness (University of California Berkeley Labor Center 2013).

The jobless rate is therefore higher than the unemployment rate, which only includes people actively looking for employment. The

FIGURE 7-6

UNEMPLOYMENT RATE BY RACE/ETHNICITY, 1973–2013

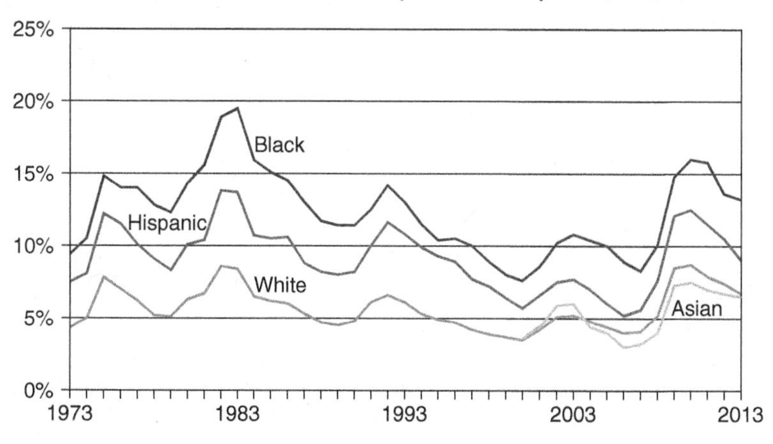

Sources: Freeman (2011); Bureau of Labor Statistics (2013b).

employment-population ratio can be a useful tool for analyzing racial disparities in the labor market. Instead of measuring unemployment, this ratio estimates the probability that a person of working age is employed, factoring in those who are not looking for work. Some of the individuals considered as being outside the labor force are students, others are homemakers, and still others are retired or disabled (University of California Berkeley Labor Center 2013).

The labor market prospects of black and Latino workers look even bleaker if we take **underemployment** into account. The underemployment category includes jobless workers actively seeking work, people who are working part-time yet are available to work full-time, and those who have looked for work in the past year yet are not actively seeking employment. In 2013, 19 percent of Latino workers and 22 percent of black workers met this definition of underemployed, compared with 12 percent of white workers (see Figure 7-7).

The 2 million people in the criminal justice system are also mostly outside the labor force, yet they are not included in the official counts of the unemployed. In 1999, a third of black men aged twenty-two to

FIGURE 7-7

UNDEREMPLOYMENT RATE OF WORKERS AGED 16 OR OLDER, BY RACE/ETHNICITY, 2000–2013

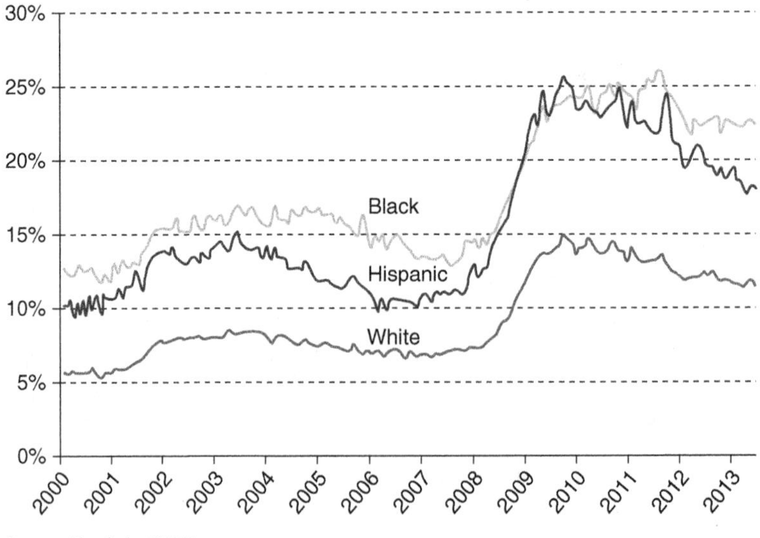

Source: Shierholz (2013).

voices

Jarred

Jarred, a forty-nine-year-old African American grandfather, has been out of work for over a year. Unemployment is financially and emotionally taxing. His story is similar to that of many African American men who live in deindustrialized cities—those where factories have closed down and manufacturing jobs have severely declined.

Jarred's first job began shortly after he graduated from high school. He worked at a turkey farm for four years. He feels fortunate to have secured his second job in the better-paid manufacturing sector, where his father also worked, at a local turbine factory. He worked there for fourteen years, until a large-scale layoff in the 1980s—a time when many factories that provided good jobs to working-class men were closing.

After the layoff, Jarred was unemployed for nine months before securing another job. This job was also in the manufacturing sector and provided a living wage. Jarred was the only African American man in the plant where he worked. He remained there for four years before being laid off again.

When factories closed in the 1980s, many workers found themselves unemployed after having worked decades at the same factory.

(continued)

voices *continued.*

Jarred

After his latest layoff, Jarred not only has trouble supporting his two children and three stepchildren, but also feels emotionally drained. He explained to Kenlana Ferguson, who interviewed him:

> Being unemployed [is] . . . rough. Now, I've been out of work since October 28th of last year, and it's a degrading feeling. . . . If you don't watch it, it'll ruin your manhood because it comes to the point where you just feel like you worked all those years for nothing at all. . . . I just want to keep building on what I've already worked for. . . .
>
> My wife and I have three grandkids living with us full time. So, a family that size and you're going from $60 grand a year to $15,900. It's a big loss.

Jarred's wife is disabled, and her disability check is not enough to support their family. He continues to look for work, but his chances are relatively low, given that he is nearly fifty years old and there are many other men in the town where he lives who have also been laid off and are looking for work. The chances of his finding a well-paying manufacturing job are even slimmer, as most of those jobs have moved overseas—and are not so well-paying anymore.

Source: Adapted from K. Ferguson 2012.

thirty were jobless or incarcerated, compared with only 13 percent of their white counterparts (Western and Pettit 2005). As one example of how the incarceration rate affects the jobless rate, we can consider another study by Western and Pettit (2002) that looked at the percentages of black and white high school dropouts with jobs. The study found that without taking the incarcerated population into account, 50 percent of black high school dropouts aged twenty-two to thirty had jobs, compared with 80 percent of white high school dropouts. Factoring in the incarcerated population, however, this percentage dropped to less than 30 percent for black male high school dropouts, compared with over 60 percent for their white counterparts (Figure 7-8; Western and Pettit 2002).

Western and Pettit (2005) found that the gains in black men's wages between 1980 and 1999 must be assessed in light of the large numbers

FIGURE 7-8
EMPLOYMENT PERCENTAGES OF MALE HIGH SCHOOL DROPOUTS, AGED 22 TO 30, BY RACE AND EDUCATION HISTORY, 1980 AND 1999

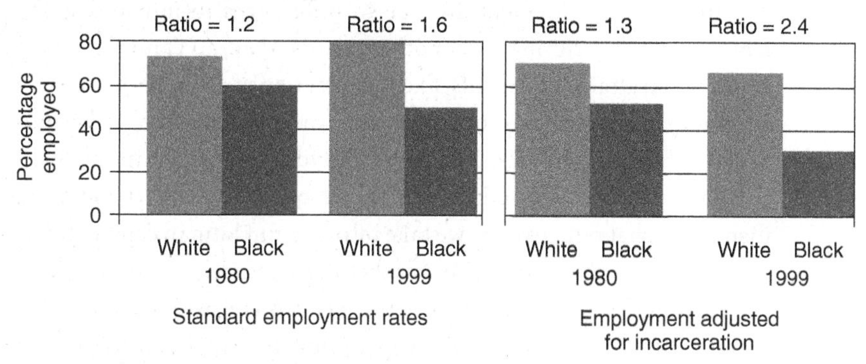

Source: Western and Pettit (2002).

of black men who went to prison and became jobless during that same time period. Incarceration is an important factor in assessing labor market inequality for black men. If we look at labor market inequality without taking into account incarceration rates, we will have an incomplete picture, because large numbers of black men are effectively taken out of the labor market by imprisonment.

One in three black men born in the twenty-first century can expect to spend time in prison during his lifetime (Mauer and King 2007). While incarcerated, people are either unemployed or employed at extremely low wages, as the minimum wage does not apply to prison labor. Moreover, the effects of imprisonment endure after incarceration. People who spend time in prison often have trouble finding work once released because of the stigma of a criminal record (Pager 2007). They also are likely to earn less than people who have not been to prison, as their time in prison takes them out of the labor market, rendering them incapable of gaining work experience during this time. In a recent study, Lyons and Pettit (2011) explored how spending time in prison affects wage trajectories for black and white men. They found that there was relatively little difference between black and white men's wage growth prior to incarceration, but that after incarceration, black men's wages grew at a 21 percent slower rate than the wages of their white counterparts.

SOCIOLOGICAL EXPLANATIONS FOR INCOME AND LABOR MARKET INEQUALITY

One question that arises from these disparities is whether the gaps in earnings and employment are due to differences in human capital, labor market discrimination, or other factors. **Human capital** refers to educational attainment, skills, and job experience. Scholars who study labor market disparities often measure earnings gaps while taking into account human capital differences. The idea is that an individual's earnings should be based on his or her qualifications. If there are disparities that remain once we take into account human capital differences, we can argue that labor market discrimination plays a role in the earnings gap. Studies of the earnings gap consistently show that about 10 to 20 percent of this gap cannot be explained by human capital differences. Sociologists often consider the unexplained gap to be an indicator of labor market discrimination (Pager, Western, and Bonikowski 2009).

Field research or audit studies are another way to measure labor market discrimination, particularly in terms of hiring. In these studies, researchers send out people with similar qualifications but different racial and ethnic identities to apply for existing jobs in order to find out if racial identity plays a role in employers' hiring decisions.

To understand the relative prosperity of whites and Asian Americans versus blacks and Hispanics, we have to look at individual factors such as average educational levels and structural factors such as changes in the labor market. During the 1980s, for example, wages increased for high-skilled jobs, there were declines in government sector work, many unionized jobs went overseas, and there was a rise in part-time and temporary work. These structural changes affected labor market disparities. Of course, individual and structural factors also work together. For example, blacks have, on average, lower educational attainment than Asian Americans, and this disparity has disadvantaged blacks in recent years because of diminished opportunities for low-skill work as a result of outsourcing.

Individual-Level Explanations

One way to explain the earnings gap among different racial groups in the United States is on an individual level. Some scholars argue that the earnings gap is due to individual human capital differences—for

voices

Francisco Pinto's Experiences in 3-D Jobs

Francisco Pinto is a fifty-eight-year-old, "1.5- generation" Mexican immigrant who grew up in Central Texas and Utah. He went to college in Texas, where he earned a bachelor's degree in geography. To pay the bills while in school, Francisco worked as a janitor. After graduating, he landed a job with Texas Parks and Recreation.

He spoke at length about the poor working conditions and racial discrimination he faced as a janitor in "3-D" employment—jobs that are dirty, dangerous, and difficult. These jobs include low-wage, low-skilled jobs such as bricklayer, roofer, doméstica [housekeeper], janitor, and car washer. In the Southwest, these gender-specific, low-skilled jobs are disproportionately performed by lower class Latinos/as, especially those of Mexican origin. Francisco explained:

> They would put all the mexicanos in the janitor crew to clean the elementary schools, which were horrible! They'd have parties . . . popcorn [everywhere]. We cleaned the bathrooms. . . . Man, kids would pee on the walls. . . . It'd take you hours to clean one room. And [the management company] only put mexicanos there. That school didn't pay the minimum wage, that's why all the mexicanos were put cleaning the schools. And my Anglo janitor friends would all get assigned to the Ford dealership; they'd go clean the telephone company and that kinda job.

In the Southwest, low-skilled jobs that are dirty, dangerous, and difficult ("3-D jobs") are disproportionately performed by lower-class Latinos/as, especially those of Mexican origin.

(continued)

voices *continued.*

Francisco Pinto's Experiences in 3-D Jobs

Francisco's perception of discrimination was borne out about a year later when a successful discrimination lawsuit was brought by the ACLU against the company he worked for. (He and the other Latino/a workers were each awarded $1,500.)

Because Mexican immigrants in America are disproportionately unauthorized, poor, and uneducated when compared with other immigrant minority groups in the United States, they are especially likely to experience a negative labor market or societal context that racializes dirty, dangerous, or difficult work as "Mexican" or "immigrant" work. Such work is associated with adverse physical working conditions and verbal abuse from employers or customers and is often rooted in an anti-immigrant sentiment or racial and ethnic discrimination.

Source: Valdez 2011, 47–49.

example, if Asian Americans have higher levels of education than blacks, we can expect them to have higher incomes.

In 2000, 32 percent of white men had completed college, compared with only 18 percent of black men. In that same year, the average annual earnings for black men was $33,614, compared with $50,132 for white men (Semyonov and Lewin-Epstein 2009). To what extent does educational attainment help explain why, overall, black men earned only two-thirds of what white men earned in 2000?

Sociologists Moshe Semyonov and Noah Lewin-Epstein (2009) examined the earnings gap between black men and white men by looking at individual-level characteristics such as age, marital status, immigrant status, region of residence, education, hours worked, and occupation. Using census data from between 1960 and 2000 to examine how inequalities have changed over time, they found that even when we take all of these characteristics into consideration, black men continue to have an earnings disadvantage. The good news is that the disadvantage has lessened over time among men with similar occupational and social statuses. In 1960, black men had an earnings penalty of 25 percent (meaning they earned 25 percent less than their white counterparts with similar backgrounds). This penalty declined to 10 percent in 1980 and was down to 4.2 percent in 2000. By 2000, black men earned 4 percent less than white men with similar backgrounds. For Semyonov and Lewin-Epstein, human capital and other individual-level characteristics explain most, but not all, of the earnings gap between white and black men.

Other studies have shown that factors other than individual-level characteristics account for earnings disparities among blacks, whites, and Hispanics. A study by McElroy and Darity (1999) compared the earnings of college-educated white, Hispanic, and black men and found that the white men earned, on average, $41,402, whereas the Hispanic men earned an average of $32,142, and the black men earned an average of $31,119. Moreover, even when blacks, Hispanics, and whites were in the same occupational category, whites earned more. For example, white males in professional and managerial occupations earned an average of $926 a week, whereas black males in that category earned an average of only $662 per week.

Racial discrimination in the labor market occurs when racial status plays a role in an employer's decision to deny a person a job, promotion, or raise. A survey conducted in 2001 found that more than one-third of blacks and nearly 20 percent of Latinos believed they had experienced labor market discrimination (Schiller 2004). Other studies have found that employers admit they are hesitant to hire black workers (Pager and Shepard 2008). One way of measuring labor market discrimination is to use statistics to identify systematic disparities between different groups. For example, if we compare the earnings of thirty-five-year-old college-educated white men to similarly situated black men and find a disparity, we can conclude that labor market discrimination plays a role in the earnings disparity. As previously mentioned, another method for uncovering discrimination involves the use of field experiments or audit studies in which researchers send equally qualified individuals out to apply for jobs and calculate the extent to which race or ethnicity affects employers' hiring practices. Each of these methodologies has revealed labor market discrimination (Pager and Sheperd 2008).

Marianne Bertrand and Sendhil Mullainathan (2004) conducted an extensive audit study to find out if employers discriminate against

African Americans. They created four résumés—two high-skill and two low-skill—to send to over 1,300 job ads in Chicago and Boston. To isolate the effect they were studying, they randomly assigned either an African American–sounding name (such as Lakisha Washington or Jamal Jones) or a white-sounding name (such as Emily Walsh or Greg Baker) to each résumé. They found that applicants with white-sounding names needed to send out about ten résumés to get a callback, whereas applicants with African American–sounding names needed to send about fifteen. This audit study shows that African Americans have a harder time securing employment than whites in part because employers often prefer white employees.

Both audit studies and studies of statistical discrimination clearly demonstrate that part of the earnings gap between whites and non-whites is due to many employers' preference for hiring whites. This preference may reflect conscious or unconscious bias. In addition to employer discrimination, there are structural factors that prevent some groups, particularly African Americans, from faring well in the U.S. labor market.

Structural Explanations

Some scholars have looked beyond individuals to explain the disparities between social groups in terms of larger structures. One prominent explanation for earnings disparities between black and white men points to the changing nature of U.S. cities, where the decline in manufacturing has meant the disappearance of work. This shift in the labor market has affected black men in particular because of their concentration in the manufacturing sectors of many major cities.

Deindustrialization, the shift from a manufacturing to a service economy, has affected working-class people in all racial and ethnic groups in the United States. After World War II, working families in the United States experienced newfound prosperity. Between 1950 and 1960, average incomes in the United States increased steadily. However, these increases began to level off, and by the 1970s, incomes for the working poor had stopped increasing. The average income for people with less than a high school diploma actually decreased from $30,015 in 1967 to $23,419 in 2010 (in constant 2010 dollars). One reason for the decreases in the average pay for low-skilled workers is deindustrialization. In 1950, 40 percent of all jobs were involved in producing goods. By 1997, less than 20 percent of all jobs were goods-producing (see Figure 7-9). Whereas historically,

FIGURE 7-9

THE CHANGING INDUSTRIAL COMPOSITION OF THE U.S. ECONOMY, 1980–2010

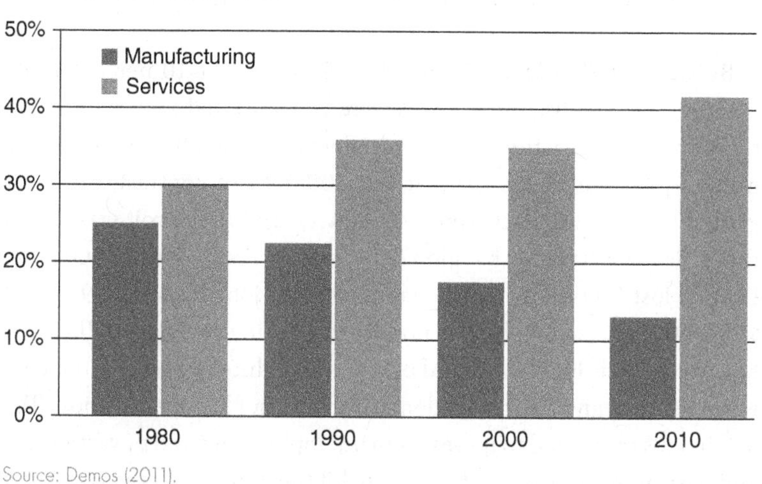

Source: Demos (2011).

manufacturing jobs often offered stable employment and a family wage, service-sector jobs are often temporary and part-time, and they offer lower wages. The decline in manufacturing was also accompanied by a decline in unionized jobs: in 1970, 27 percent of all workers in the United States were unionized, compared with only 15 percent in 1993. As unionized workers tend to earn more, the decline in unions has affected wage inequality (Morris and Western 1999). By 2011, only 11.3 percent of workers in the United States were unionized (ILO 2013).

In the 1950s, many urban African American families lived in poverty, but they were among the working poor, as described in the opening excerpt of this chapter. For example, in 1960, 69 percent of men over the age of fourteen who lived in the Black Belt region of the city of Chicago were regularly employed. By 1990, only 37 percent of men sixteen or over were regularly employed (C. Wilson 1996). This figure is even smaller if we take into account the incarcerated population, as discussed previously.

Up until the 1980s, many black men were employed in manufacturing jobs, which provided benefits and a family wage, permitting families to attain comfortable standards of living. Once these factories began to close, these comfortable lifestyles went with them. Black men were the hardest hit by this economic restructuring: Oliver and Shapiro (2006, 26) write that "from 1979 to 1984 one-half of black males in durable-goods manufacturing in five Great Lakes cities lost their jobs."

Between 1979 and 1985, the United States lost 10 percent of its manufacturing jobs. These losses were concentrated in certain areas, thereby enhancing their localized effects. The Midwest lost over a million jobs, and the Northeast lost 800,000. In contrast, the West gained 53,000 manufacturing jobs (Sassen 1990). Detroit was one of the cities hit hardest by global economic restructuring. Overall, Detroit lost 70 percent of its manufacturing jobs between 1969 and 1989. Detroit also lost half its population during this time. When the economic crisis hit Detroit and other cities, white residents often fled, whereas black and Latino residents often did not have that option. The loss in jobs translated to increases in unemployment and poverty rates, and African Americans and men were hit the hardest. By the end of the 1980s, over a third of all African Americans in Detroit lived in poverty, as did half of Detroit's black children (Kodras 1997).

What William Julius Wilson (1996) calls "the disappearance of work" in inner-city neighborhoods was largely a consequence of reduced demand for low-skilled labor in the manufacturing sector in the United States. This change in the economy—also called deindustrialization—was a consequence of at least three factors: (1) the computer revolution and the spread of new technologies that could replace low-skilled workers; (2) the growth in college enrollment, which increased the supply of high-skilled labor in the United States; and (3) increases in international trade, which allowed U.S.-based corporations to send jobs overseas. Manufacturing companies were able to move their operations abroad because of trade agreements negotiated between the United States and foreign governments.

These changes affected all low-skilled workers. However, African Americans were hit particularly hard because they were more likely to be low-skilled and to live in places that lost jobs to overseas outsourcing. In the 1990s, 40 percent of the workers in the apparel industry were African American, and many of these jobs went overseas. Furthermore, many of the new, higher-skilled jobs created by deindustrialization were located in the suburbs, far from where African Americans lived (C. Wilson 1996). The **spatial mismatch hypothesis** helps us understand why African Americans are having trouble getting employment in the current economy: many African Americans live in areas where there has been a reduction in work for low-skilled workers. The **skills mismatch hypothesis** offers a complementary explanation: African American men in particular often do not have the skills required to secure work in the current economy. Although there has been growth in employment sectors that require a college degree, many African American men do not have the qualifications for these jobs.

AFFIRMATIVE ACTION

In a profit-based economic system, wages should be determined by competition, and the most qualified people should get the available jobs. If there are lots of people with a certain skill set, wages will be lower for that job. In contrast, if there are fewer people, then wages should be higher. However, prior to the civil rights era, employers practiced overt discrimination: they refused to hire African Americans and paid them less than whites when they did hire them. Edna Bonacich (1976) explains that historic disparities between blacks and whites are due to a **split labor market**, which refers to a difference in the price of labor for two or more groups of laborers. For example, in 1927 in Virginia, the average daily pay rate for white bricklayers was $11.00, whereas it was $9.60 for blacks. Similarly, white cement workers earned an average of $6.33 per day, whereas blacks earned an average of $4.42. In addition to paying African Americans less, many companies refused to hire them. This seems somewhat illogical, as we would expect employers to want the lowest-paid workers they could find. However, racial discrimination is often not based on logic.

One story from the late 1950s is that of Thomas Bailey, a skilled brick-mason who had trouble finding steady work. When he applied for jobs, foremen often told him that he had to be a member of a union to work there. Yet when he applied for membership in the union, the business agent told him he could only be a member if he was actively working. Bailey, an African American, was caught in a bind. He had trouble getting steady work because the unions often refused to allow black men to join, and the unions controlled access to construction employment. When this issue came to the attention of local civil rights leaders, they pressured the union to allow Bailey to join. He eventually was let in but faced intimidation by other union members. Because of the widespread nature of cases like Bailey's, national leaders decided it was time to push for more systematic changes. The construction industry was one of the first targets, because it relied on federal contracts. The federal government had the power to require these companies to obey antidiscrimination laws as a condition of their contracts (Golland 2011).

One of the proposed solutions to labor market discrimination came to be known as "affirmative action." This term was first used in 1935 in the National Labor Relations Act, which specified that employers could not discriminate against union members or organizers. If they did, they would have to take affirmative action to remedy the effects of that discrimination (Skrentny 1996). Three decades later, Lyndon Johnson used the term in Executive Order 11246 (1965). In this order, Johnson called for federal contractors to "take affirmative action to ensure that applicants are employed, and that employees are treated during employment without regard to their race, color, religion, sex or national origin."

Because of this order and other civil rights legislation and rules, by the 1960s, federal contractors had to sign pre-award affirmative action agreements that contained provisions such as those ensuring that contractors would actively recruit a diverse workforce to complete the contract. Contractors also had to agree to sponsor non-white workers for apprenticeships and training. In this way, in towns and cities across the nation, African Americans and Latinos were able to secure employment in what had been a primarily white employment sector (Golland 2011).

Today, *affirmative action* refers to policies and procedures designed to combat ongoing discrimination in the workplace and in schools. Affirmative action policies aim to keep discrimination from occurring by requiring employers to be proactive in their attempts to diversify their employees. In addition, affirmative action policies require employers to be conscious of the racial and ethnic makeup of their employees in order to ensure a more diverse workforce (Skrentny 1996). The overarching goal of affirmative action in employment is to decrease the influence of racial discrimination on the employment prospects of people of color.

The government orders for contractors are one of four kinds of affirmative action in the United States, which are as follows:

1. Government orders regulating government contractors and subcontractors
2. Regulations requiring affirmation action by public employers

3. Court orders based on antidiscrimination law
4. Employers' voluntary human resources policies

Since 1965, companies that do business with the federal government have been required to meet affirmative action requirements. The U.S. Department of Labor website (n.d.) indicates that "for federal contractors and subcontractors, affirmative action must be taken by covered employers to recruit and advance qualified minorities, women, persons with disabilities, and covered veterans. Affirmative actions include training programs, outreach efforts, and other positive steps." What this means is that any company that works with the federal government has to show it is taking positive steps to maintain or increase the diversity of its employees. If a company is presented with two equally qualified employees—for example, a white man and a black woman—hiring the black woman is considered such a step. Federal law explicitly prohibits choosing a less qualified candidate on the basis of race.

In 1972, the Equal Opportunity Act created a provision that mandated that employers who have been found guilty of discrimination must implement affirmative action policies. Since 1965, hundreds of employers have implemented affirmative action voluntarily in their hiring and promotion strategies. Nevertheless, despite fifty years of affirmative action, African Americans, Latinos, and Asian Americans continue to experience labor market discrimination.

ENTREPRENEURSHIP AND SELF-EMPLOYMENT

Given the unequal conditions of the formal labor market, many racial and ethnic minorities turn to self-employment as a means to achieve the American Dream and to be their own bosses. Self-employment rates vary significantly among groups. In 2010, 13.5 percent of white men were self-employed, compared with 6.2 percent of African Americans, 34 percent of Israelis, 27 percent of Koreans, 10 percent of Mexicans, and 9 percent of Dominicans. Most sociologists explain these disparities in self-employment rates by pointing to differences in social and ethnic networks and human capital (Portes and Yiu 2013).

The self-employment strategy has worked better for some groups than others. Chinese and Cuban small-business owners, for example, tend to do better than their counterparts who are not self-employed. However, African American, Korean, and Mexican small-business owners often experience severe setbacks. Korean small-business owners, for example, often work eighty hours per week, rely on unpaid family member labor, and barely earn enough to get by.

The work of both Adia Harvey Wingfield (2008) and Zulema Valdez (2008a, 2011) adds complexity to traditional understandings of the **ethnic enclave economy**, which refers to clusters of small businesses that primarily serve people of the same ethnicity and work to facilitate the success of co-ethnics. The ethnic enclave economy has helped immigrants of certain national origins, such as Cubans, attain economic success in the United States. According to this framework, immigrants such as the Chinese, Cubans, Greeks, and Koreans have attained success in small-business ownership because of their high human capital, social networks, and close-knit ethnic communities. However, both Wingfield and Valdez use an intersectional framework to critique scholarship that explains small business success through ethnicity and culture by explaining how race, class, and gender also play a role in the success of small businesses.

Wingfield (2008) draws on the concept of a **racial enclave economy**, in which a business' success is both shaped and limited by the racial group membership of the business owner. She uses the example of black female owners of hair salons to elaborate on this concept. Valdez (2011) draws from interviews with restaurant owners of different ethnic origins to explain how race, class, and gender play a role in shaping the success of local businesses. She uses the concept of an **embedded market**—a market economy embedded within interlocking systems of oppression and privilege, such as "capitalism, patriarchy, and White supremacy"— to explain disparities in the success of small businesses (37). These systems of oppression affect an individual's possibilities for success as an entrepreneur. Whereas previous scholarship on ethnic enclaves might presume that Mexicans have similar options in the restaurant industry, Valdez explains that an upper-class male Mexican may be able to open a highly profitable Italian restaurant in a wealthy neighborhood, whereas a poor female Mexican may be limited to opening a taqueria in the barrio.

Valdez (2008b) conducted a national study in which she looked at four groups of entrepreneurs: white, Korean, Mexican, and black men. She found that 40 percent of the white owners earned over $75,000 a year, as did 25 percent of the Koreans, 20 percent of the Mexicans, and 17 percent of the black business owners. In contrast, nearly half of the black business owners earned less than $25,000 a year, as did 41 percent of the Mexicans, 33 percent of the Koreans, and 24 percent of the white male business owners. Her study found that this disparity can be explained in part by the fact that Korean and white small business owners are more likely to have higher educational levels than the Mexican and black business owners. Black and Mexican business owners with higher levels of education and more access to bank loans are able to do much better with their businesses. Nevertheless, as Wingfield (2008) notes, some African American women without college educations are able to do well for themselves in certain racial enclave economies, such as hair salons. Wingfield, however, further points out that the enclave places limits on the success of black female hair salon owners: they are able to do well, but their profits tend to plateau after about five years.

CONCLUSION AND DISCUSSION

Despite fifty years of affirmative action and scores of antidiscrimination laws and lawsuits, non-whites continue to be disadvantaged in the labor market. There are many reasons for this.

One reason is that it is difficult or even impossible to simply legislate away discrimination. Employers may be discriminating against non-whites and women unconsciously. As mentioned in Chapter Four, racial ideologies are often ingrained in our individual perceptions. A hiring manager may not be aware that he thinks that a white man is a "natural leader" because of entrenched stereotypes. He also may not realize that his presumptions that a black man is irresponsible or that a Latina is incapable of being professional are based on those individuals' races or ethnicities. In many ways, labor market discrimination will not disappear until racial stereotypes go away.

One reason for the earnings gap is structural: growth in certain industries and contraction in others is due to global forces that are beyond the control of a single government. Nevertheless, a government can provide training programs to get people up to speed and to work in emerging fields. This is an example of a race-neutral program that may help reduce racial disparities.

A related reason for this gap is that the labor market and the small-business market are structured by deeply entrenched inequalities, patriarchy, and racial divisions. Racial segregation in housing and schools, for example, leads to racially segregated social networks, which themselves reproduce preexisting inequalities. We will learn more about the interlocking nature of different systems of inequality in the next chapter, which focuses on structural racism.

Finally, as the United States continues to move off the charts in terms of inequality, it will be important to work toward ameliorating overall inequality while striving to reduce disparities among racial groups.

THINKING ABOUT RACIAL JUSTICE

Imagine if everyone in the United States, regardless of racial status, had an equal chance of being rich, middle class, or poor, but that the dimensions of income inequality did not change. Would that be racial justice? Keep in mind that, in that scenario, with so many poor people in the United States, millions of non-whites would continue to be poor. Reflect on the extent to which racial justice is tied to economic justice.

Key Terms

Gini coefficient 168
earnings gap 169
wage gap 170
employment-population ratio 176
underemployment 176
human capital 180
deindustrialization 184
spatial mismatch hypothesis 186
skills mismatch hypothesis 187
split labor market 187
ethnic enclave economy 190
racial enclave economy 190
embedded market 190

Check Your Understanding

OBJECTIVE 7.1

Explain the extent of income inequality by race, ethnicity, and gender.

- Overall income inequality in the United States is at a historic high. This inequality is exacerbated when we take racial, ethnic, and gender disparities into account.

Q How unequal is the United States compared to other countries?

Q What is the difference between the wage gap and the earnings gap? How do they represent different facets of inequality?

OBJECTIVE 7.2

Describe the dimensions of labor market inequality.

- A complete understanding of racial disparities in the labor market requires a consideration of gender, national-origin differences, incarceration rates, and unemployment rates.

Q What are some unique aspects of labor market inequality that arise when we take gender into account?

Q Why does the author argue that the incarcerated population should be included in counts of the unemployed?

Q To what extent are Asians advantaged or disadvantaged in the U.S. labor market?

OBJECTIVE 7.3

Examine how sociologists explain labor market inequality.

- Sociologists offer various explanations for labor market disparities that range from human capital disparities to employer discrimination and structural changes in the overall economy.

Q Why is it important to take human capital into account when measuring earnings disparities?

Q Of the explanations provided, which do you find most convincing for explaining the earnings disparities between black and white men?

OBJECTIVE 7.4

Understand how affirmative action works.

- Few employers have affirmative action policies in place. Those that do are required to take positive steps to ensure that their company does not practice racial discrimination and has a diverse workforce that reflects the working-age population of the United States.

Q How has affirmative action been implemented in the United States?

OBJECTIVE 7.5

Assess the relationship between self-employment and labor market inequality.

- Self-employment and entrepreneurship have worked well for some racial minority groups but not for others.

Q Which minority groups have benefited from affirmative action? Why?

Critical Thinking

1. How do the individual-level explanations for labor market disparities differ from the structural explanations? To what extent could these explanations work together?
2. Are audit studies a useful way to measure discrimination? Why or why not? What are the weaknesses and strengths of this approach?
3. What strategies do you think could be implemented to reduce the earnings penalty for non-white workers?

8

INEQUALITY IN HOUSING AND WEALTH

CHAPTER OUTLINE

LEARNING OBJECTIVES

8.1 Examine the historical reasons for housing and wealth inequalities in the United States.
8.2 Explain when and how residential segregation became a characteristic of U.S. cities.
8.3 Evaluate the extent of wealth inequality today.
8.4 Assess factors that are perpetuating and exacerbating wealth inequalities today.

Wealth inequality in the United States is staggering: 1 percent of Americans own nearly half of the wealth in this country (Norton and Ariely 2011). Despite these tremendous inequalities, the idea persists that if you work hard, you will succeed. This is an ideology deeply rooted in the American psyche and perpetuated through popular media and folklore. Many Americans believe they deserve what they have because they have worked hard. Yet many people work hard all of their lives and die with no assets. As writer and activist George Monbiot (2011) puts it, "If wealth was the inevitable result of hard work and enterprise, every woman in Africa would be a millionaire."

In this chapter, we will learn about wealth inequality—both overall inequality and inequality among racial and ethnic groups. **Wealth** is the sum total of a person's **assets**—cash in the bank and the value of all property, not only land but houses, cars, stocks and bonds, and retirement savings—minus debt. It is something built up over a lifetime and passed on to the next generation through inheritances.

In Chapter Seven, we learned about income inequality. Wealth inequality, as we will see, is both more entrenched and more severe. Most Americans think that wealth should be distributed more equally—even as they underestimate the true extent of the inequality. Most think that a fair distribution would mean a substantial amount of wealth for the middle class. The reality, however, is very different, with the middle class holding very little or no wealth and the poor having no wealth at all. These proportions—broken down into ideal, perceived, and actual distributions—are shown in Figure 8-1. As this figure shows, the United States is a highly unequal society in terms of wealth and is even more unequal than most of us realize. The top 20 percent of the population controls over 80 percent of the wealth (Norton and Ariely 2011).

When we add race into the equation, the numbers get starker. Black and Latino families in the United States own just five cents of wealth for each dollar white families own (Kochhar, Taylor, and Fry 2011). How do we explain such racial disparities in wealth?

As we will see, the reasons for these disparities run deeper than those for income disparities. Wealth inequality is related to income inequality, but wealth and income inequality function differently. The wealth inequality between whites and blacks, for example, is a result of historically embedded inequalities that go back to the time of

FIGURE 8-1

IDEAL, PERCEIVED, AND ACTUAL WEALTH DISTRIBUTION IN THE UNITED STATES

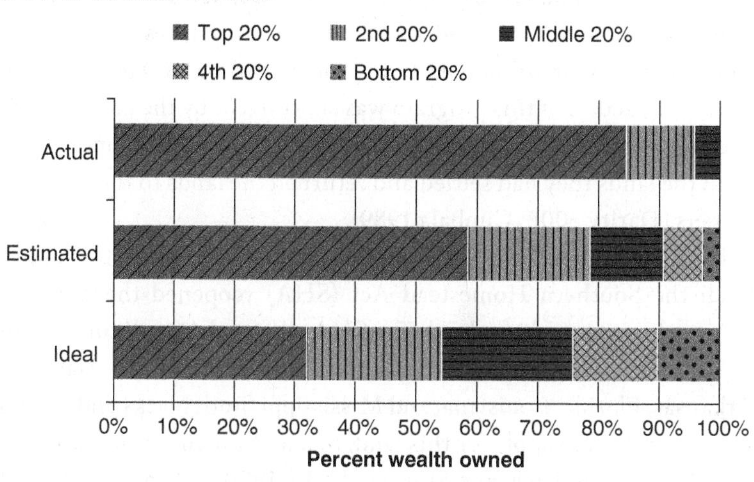

Source: Norton and Ariely (2011).

slavery, the Jim Crow era, and early twentieth-century housing policies. Today, it is perpetuated and even exacerbated by inequalities in homeownership, college attendance, inheritance, and unemployment rates. Homeownership, often considered the cornerstone of the American Dream, is one of the primary driving forces behind racial disparities in wealth. In this chapter, we will take a close look at the historical roots of wealth inequality, as well as contemporary trends, through the lens of race. We will begin with slavery, which set the stage for contemporary racial inequalities.

LAND OWNERSHIP AFTER SLAVERY

At the end of the Civil War, African-descended people who had been enslaved for generations were freed. Slaves had cleared the forests and made the land productive, generating wealth for southern landowners. They were at last given their freedom, but nothing more. Enslaved Africans played a tremendous role in creating prosperity for the United States, but their enslavement prevented them from accumulating any wealth.

Slaves were, by definition, unable to own any type of property. With freedom came limited possibilities for land ownership. In 1865, General William Sherman issued Special Field Order No. 15, which set aside land for former slaves in an area that traversed the coastal regions of South Carolina and Florida. Sherman's order specified that black families could settle on no more than forty acres of tillable land. The order, however, stopped short of conferring titles to the land. In less than a year, 40,000 ex-slaves had settled on 400,000 acres of land. The success of this program was short-lived: by the end of 1865, President Andrew Johnson had ordered the removal of former slaves from the lands they had settled and returned the lands to their former owners (Darity 2008; Cimbala 1989).

In 1866, former slaves were given another opportunity to acquire land: the Southern Homestead Act (SHA) reopened the door for former slaves to apply for land. The SHA allocated 46 million acres of public lands for homesteading in five southern states: Alabama, Arkansas, Florida, Louisiana, and Mississippi. Both blacks and whites were permitted to apply for this land, much of which was not productive (Canaday, Reback, and Stowe n.d.). By 1900, only one-quarter of southern black farmers owned their land (Oliver and Shapiro 2006). The rest eked out a living working for others or eventually made their way north to seek their fortunes in the cities there.

Although some black Americans found economic opportunities in northern cities, they were not able to reap the same advantages over time as their white counterparts. One of the main reasons for the inability of blacks to build wealth has been the creation of housing segregation within U.S. cities. **Residential segregation** happens when different groups of people are sorted into distinct neighborhoods.

RESIDENTIAL SEGREGATION

Today, most U.S. cities are heavily segregated, yet this was not the case during the nineteenth century. Urban residential segregation in the United States was created in the early twentieth century and has had pernicious consequences for the wealth portfolios of black Americans.

The century following emancipation saw dramatic changes in the demographics of the United States. In 1870, 80 percent of black Americans lived in the rural South. By 1970, this figure had reversed: 80 percent of black Americans had come to live in cities, equally divided between the North and the South. During the same period that black Americans were migrating to the North, European immigrants were arriving in U.S. cities.

At first, blacks in urban areas lived in close proximity to whites. Yet between 1900 and 1940, U.S. cities were transformed from having very little residential segregation to having high levels of it. In Kansas City, for example, residential segregation tripled between 1900 and 1930. By 1930, the typical black Chicagoan lived in a neighborhood that was over two-thirds black. In effect, the urban ghetto in the United States was created in the first two decades of the twentieth century (Massey and Denton 1993). How did this happen?

Part of the explanation is that African Americans moved into cities that had previously had small numbers of non-whites. The rise of segregation, however, was not an organic process: white residents created segregation and ensured that it persisted.

The Creation of Residential Segregation

A combination of three forces led to residential segregation: collective racial violence carried out by whites, federal housing programs and policies that exclusively benefited whites, and practices created and reinforced by the nascent real estate industry. We will examine each of these factors in turn.

Throughout the twentieth century—even well after the civil rights movements of the 1960s—white residents used racial violence to keep blacks out of primarily white neighborhoods (Gotham 2000; Lipsitz 2006). Whites engaged in cross burning and window breaking, and joined organized mobs in nearly every major northern city. There were hundreds of incidents of racial violence intended to prevent blacks from moving into white neighborhoods in Chicago, Detroit, Philadelphia, and other cities. In most cases, these violent actions went unpunished (Sugrue 2008).

The second reason for residential segregation we will examine here is the nature of federal housing programs and policies. Federal housing policies in the 1930s would solidify the line between whites and non-whites for decades to come.

The **Federal Housing Administration** (FHA) was established in 1934 with the purpose of bolstering the economy and, in particular, the construction industry. The FHA encouraged the building of new homes for people living in crowded tenements in inner cities by creating a new, government-backed mortgage system. Prior to the creation of the FHA, people had to come up with as much as half of the value of a home before purchasing it. The FHA created the conditions under which banks could loan people money to purchase homes with small down payments and at reasonable interest rates. The vast majority of new homes were built in city suburbs, where suburban living was enabled by the simultaneous construction of highways and the development of suburban services (Oliver and Shapiro 2006).

Banks used FHA guidelines to decide who should be permitted to borrow money. The 1938 *Underwriting Manual* of the FHA stated that "if a neighborhood is to retain stability, it is necessary that properties shall continue to be occupied by the same social and racial classes" (quoted in Oliver and Shapiro 2006). The *Manual* further recommended the implementation of restrictive covenants, which remained in place until they were outlawed in 1949. The *Manual* also endorsed a practice known as **redlining**, in which communities where loans were not recommended were outlined in red on a map. Those communities where loans were denied were primarily black.

Between 1933 and 1978, U.S. government policies enabled over 35 million families to increase their wealth through housing equity. As homeowners, millions of Americans were able to begin to accumulate the tax savings, home equity, economic stability, and other benefits associated with homeownership. White Americans benefited disproportionately from this shift for two primary reasons: (1) it was easier for white people to purchase homes, and (2) the homes that whites bought increased in value more rapidly than those purchased by blacks because of the perceived desirability of all-white neighborhoods. In addition, few women were able to benefit directly from these policies, as they did not have the financial stability to purchase homes on their own. Because of racial endogamy in marriages (marrying within one's race), white women benefited; their white husbands purchased homes, whereas black women received only the same paltry benefits as their husbands or hardly any at all if they were single (Oliver and Shapiro 2006).

The final factor we will examine that contributed to residential segregation was **racially restrictive covenants**—contractual agreements that prevent the sale or lease of property within an area to non-whites—created and reinforced by the real estate industry. By the 1920s, deeds in nearly every new housing development in the northern United States prevented the ownership or rental of houses in the development by anyone who was not white. From the 1930s until the 1960s, the guidelines of the National Association of Real Estate Boards prevented realtors from selling homes to non-whites in white areas (Sugrue 2008). Kevin Gotham (2000) argues that the primary motive for these covenants was economic: real estate investors wanted to ensure their profits, and they believed that racially stable and all-white neighborhoods were the most likely to increase in value over time.

Consider the case of Levittown, New York, an archetypal suburb where houses were available only to white families in 1948. A white couple born in the 1920s could have purchased a brand-new home there for $8,000, with no down payment, by taking advantage of the federal housing programs. In the 1960s, that family could use the home equity built up in that property to take out loans to pay for university for their children. And if the couple passed away in the 2000s, their children would inherit the home, in a neighborhood that is still 98 percent white, valued at $400,000. The opportunity to accumulate that kind of wealth was denied to black families, who were not permitted to purchase homes in Levittown. Eugene Burnett, for example, is a black Army veteran who tried to purchase a home in Levittown in 1949. When he put in an application, the agent told him that "the owners of this development have not as yet decided whether they're going to sell these homes to Negroes" (Lambert 1997). Those black families who were able to purchase homes did not see their real estate values climb in the same way. The average home value in the nearby, primarily non-white Central Islip is about a third of the value of a home in the primarily white Levittown.

In 1948, the Supreme Court declared racially restrictive covenants unenforceable. And in 1968, the passage of the Fair Housing Act made these covenants illegal. Once covenants became illegal, real estate agents developed new tactics to preserve residential segregation. One of the most common activities was **steering**, in which real estate agents would show homes in white neighborhoods only to whites and homes in black neighborhoods only to blacks. For these and other reasons, over sixty years after the passage of the Fair Housing Act, we still have high levels of residential segregation, exacerbating wealth inequality. Real estate agents continue to practice steering today, and the wealth generated by the properties purchased by whites who benefited from the housing policies of the 1930s and 1940s continues to be passed down within families.

One real estate developer built a half-mile-long wall in Detroit in 1940 to separate the black and white communities. Today, because of white flight, the wall separates one black community from another.

Discriminatory and Predatory Lending Practices

In 1977, the Community Reinvestment Act (CRA) was passed, encouraging federally insured banks to help meet the needs of low-income people and minorities and to end redlining. The Act mandates that bank regulatory agencies evaluate the extent to which banks are serving local communities. Since the passage of the law, low-income people of color have had more access to home loans. As of 2005, there had been $1.7 trillion in new loans to low-income areas (Friedman and Squires 2005). Even though the FHA's discriminatory housing programs have been discontinued, black and Latino families have continued to face disadvantages through contemporary discriminatory lending practices. On average, blacks are 2.7 times more likely than whites to be denied mortgages. Prospective homeowners who are denied mortgages have to either forgo the opportunity to accumulate wealth through homeownership or seek out a less favorable loan with a higher interest rate. In fact, black homeowners pay 0.54 percent higher interest rates than whites. This half-point differential adds up to tens of thousands of dollars over the course of a loan. The racial disparity in lending practices thus has far-reaching consequences. Bankers often claim that the reason blacks are more often denied loans is that they do not have the same creditworthiness as whites. Yet a study by the Federal Reserve Bank of Boston revealed that even when credit scores were taken into account, black and Latino mortgage applicants were still 60 percent more likely to be turned down than whites (Oliver and Shapiro 2006). Continued discrimination in home loans perpetuates the wealth inequality that was solidified with the FHA programs of the 1930s (Oliver and Shapiro 2006).

In the 1990s and early 2000s, bank lending became more predatory, particularly for blacks and Latinos. **Predatory lenders** traditionally include pawnshops, payday lenders, and check-cashing services that charge very high fees and interest rates. Following changes in lending laws, the late 1990s saw the rise of another type of predatory financial practice: **subprime loans**, or high-interest loans to people at high risk of defaulting. Black and Latino homeowners were much more likely than whites to receive loans with unfavorable conditions such as prepayment penalties and high interest rates. Between 1993 and 2000, the percentage of subprime mortgages in black and Latino neighborhoods rose from 2 percent to 18 percent. Overall, black and Latino families were about twice as likely as white families to receive subprime loans. By 2009, over 15 percent of subprime loans were in foreclosure (Dymski, Hernandez, and Mohanty 2013; Rugh and Massey 2010).

Segregation exacerbated the effects of the economic crisis for black families. Metropolitan areas with higher degrees of racial segregation had higher rates of foreclosure. Additionally, black families in highly segregated cities had been more likely to get subprime loans than their counterparts in less segregated cities. The higher rate of subprime loans in segregated cities was partly because unregulated mortgage brokers targeted black neighborhoods where regulated banks were less likely to have branches. Notably, more than half of all subprime loans made in the 2000s were for refinancing instead of purchasing new homes. When those homes in primarily black neighborhoods failed to appreciate in value as expected or decreased in value, families who had borrowed at high interest rates found themselves in financial trouble (Dymski, Hernandez, and Mohanty 2013; Rugh and Massey 2010).

voices

A Tale of Two Families

Chris and Peter Ackerman live with their three children in a suburb of Saint Louis, Missouri. With both holding middle-class occupations, their earnings in 2003 were over $80,000. A few years prior, they were able to purchase a starter home. Both of their parents had paid for their children's college education, meaning neither Chris nor Peter had any student loan debt. Furthermore, Peter's parents helped them with the down payment. When their three children were nearing school age, Chris and Peter decided to move out of their first home and into the suburbs. Their first home had increased in value, and they were able to use the equity from that home to purchase their second home, in the suburbs of Saint Louis. They chose to move in large part because they wanted to live in a district with good public schools. The community they live in is very similar to their own demographic profile—nearly all white and with an average annual income of $60,000 to $80,000. Chris and Peter had over $100,000 in net worth in 2003, placing them above the national average.

Chris and Peter have worked hard, yet they also have benefited from their parents' healthy economic standing. Their parents paid their college tuition and helped them to purchase their first home. This permitted them to live without being saddled by debt and to use their economic advantages to build their own wealth.

Judith and Steve Andrews are an African American family with a different story. Judith Andrews bought their home in the Vandeventer neighborhood of Saint Louis in 1982 for $1,500. The home was dilapidated, and she has since put about $30,000 into completely revamping it. In 1990, the average price for a home in the primarily black neighborhood where she purchased her house was $32,000. In 1994, Judith, who has a master's degree, married Steve, a paralegal. Together, they, like the Ackermans, earned about $80,000 in 2003. As Judith and Steve considered their options for sending their children to school, they saw their best choice to be private schools, which cost them $18,000 a year for both children. They took out a home equity loan to cover their expenses. By 2003, their house was worth about $70,000. In 2013, you could buy a three-bedroom, 1,500 square foot home built in 2001 in Vandeventer for $55,000.

If the Andrews' home had been in a primarily white Saint Louis neighborhood or suburb, it would have increased more in value between 1982 and 2003. Homes in the nearby suburb of Skinker, which is 88 percent white, and similar to the suburb where the Ackermans purchased their home, were valued well into the $300,000s in 2013. Furthermore, the public elementary school that serves Skinker was rated 10 on a scale of 1 to 10 by the national nonprofit GreatSchools. In contrast, homes in good condition in Vandeventer were selling for less than $20,000 in 2013, and the local school, Cole Elementary, was rated 1 on the same scale by GreatSchools, with less than 20 percent of students passing assessment tests.

Julie Andrews could have made a different decision about where to purchase a home in 1982. However, her story is part of a larger pattern in which African Americans are locked out of building home equity and having the opportunity to send their children to good public schools simply because their homes are in primarily black neighborhoods. Their children will likely need to take out loans if they attend college, and they will likely not be able to rely on their parents to help them out with a down payment on a home. And thus the cycle continues.

Source: Shapiro 2004, 27–29, 57–59. Supplemented by information from Zillow.com.

Neighborhood Segregation Today

Even though the housing policies that contributed to residential segregation have been repealed, neighborhood segregation persists today. How do we quantify it? One measure is the **dissimilarity index**, which describes the extent to which two groups—such as blacks and whites—are found in equal proportions in all neighborhoods. We can interpret this measure as the percentage of individuals in either group who would have to move to achieve perfect integration. Another tool for measuring segregation is the **isolation index**, which compares a neighborhood's demographics against citywide demographics. If, for example, a city is 30 percent black, yet blacks live in neighborhoods that are 50 percent black, the isolation index would be the difference, 20 percent.

Black-white segregation continues to have the highest national dissimilarity index. In 2000, the black-white **segregation index** was 67, whereas the Hispanic-white index was 52 and the Native American–white index was 47 (Lichter, Parisi, Grice, and Taquino 2007). The black-white segregation index is even higher in cities with large black populations, such as Detroit and Chicago. This index in 2010 was 80 for Detroit and 76 for Chicago. The average Detroit black resident lives in a neighborhood that is 81 percent black, and the average black person in Chicago lives in a neighborhood that is 67 percent black. Latinos and Asian Americans have remained somewhat less segregated from whites, with dissimilarity indexes of 48 and 41, respectively, in 2010 (Logan and Stults 2011).

According to data from the 2010 census, non-Hispanic whites make up 67 percent of the U.S. population. The average white person in a

What comes to mind when you see these two images of neighborhoods? Who do you think is more likely to live in these neighborhoods?

metropolitan area lives in a neighborhood that is 75 percent white, whereas the typical black person lives in a neighborhood that is 45 percent white and 45 percent black. The average Latino lives in a neighborhood that is 35 percent white, and the average Asian American lives in a neighborhood that is 49 percent white (see Figure 8-2). The only group that, on average, lives in a primarily white neighborhood is whites (Logan and Stults 2011).

Scholars sometimes refer to African Americans in urban areas as **hypersegregated** because of the notably high levels of segregation in

FIGURE 8-2

DIVERSITY EXPERIENCED IN EACH GROUP'S TYPICAL NEIGHBORHOOD, BY RACE/ETHNICITY, 2010

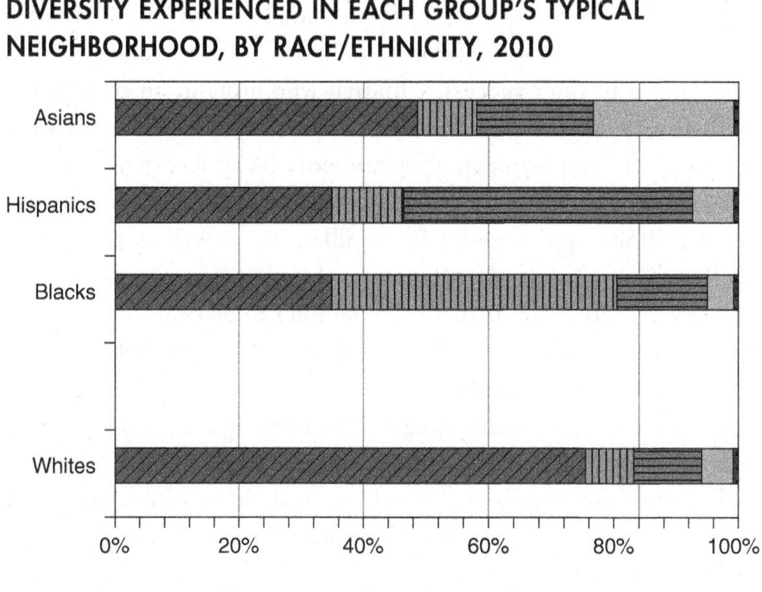

Source: Logan and Stults (2011).

these neighborhoods. In contrast, other racial and ethnic minorities tend not to experience such high levels of segregation. Studies show relatively low levels of Native American segregation in urban areas, especially compared to the levels experienced by African Americans (Wilkes and Iceland 2004). In 2000, 1.4 million Native Americans lived in rural areas—accounting for about a third of all Native Americans. Most of these rural Native Americans lived on Indian reservations, effectively separated from non–Native Americans. Outside of reservations, however, rural Native Americans have relatively low levels of segregation (Lichter et al. 2007).

Racial segregation poses a problem not just because people of different races have little contact with one another but because it exacerbates existing inequalities. Black and Latino families of all economic statuses are more likely than white families to live in neighborhoods with high poverty rates. Even affluent blacks and Latinos live in neighborhoods with fewer resources than those inhabited by poor whites (Logan 2013). Racial segregation often means concentrated poverty, which in turn leads to underresourced neighborhoods with poor public schools, high levels of crime, and high unemployment rates. High levels of racial segregation mean that black and Latino families are more likely than white families to live in neighborhoods that are inhospitable to their success. Children who grow up in segregated, high-poverty neighborhoods are much less likely to finish high school and to secure employment. They are more likely to experience violence growing up and to have children out of wedlock. Residential segregation limits opportunities for middle-class as well as poor black families (C. Z. Charles 2003). One of the most longstanding consequences of segregation is that black families in black neighborhoods are unable to build up home equity and therefore lag far behind white families in wealth accumulation.

As we have seen, racial segregation in housing is driven by formal and informal policies and practices. It is also affected by whites' preferences to live in primarily white neighborhoods. Most white Americans balk at the idea of living in a neighborhood with more than a few black families. Contrary to popular perceptions, residential segregation is not due to black Americans' preferences for living exclusively among other black Americans. Sociologists Maria Krysan and Reynolds Farley (2002) analyzed survey data from 2,000 black families in several cities and found that African Americans prefer racially diverse neighborhoods. In the study, the interviewers showed respondents fictional representations of five neighborhoods, ranging from all black to all white, and asked them to rank the neighborhoods in order of preference. They also asked respondents if they would not want to live in one of the fictional neighborhoods. Half of the black respondents chose the neighborhood that was evenly split between black and white as their most preferred neighborhood. Only 20 percent of the black respondents chose the neighborhood that was all black. African Americans in this survey expressed a strong preference for mixed neighborhoods. Although only 35 percent of African Americans were willing to be the first black family to move into a white neighborhood, nearly all of the respondents expressed willingness to move into a neighborhood if it was primarily white, so long as there were one or two other black families living there. In contrast, less than a third of white respondents indicated they were willing to move into a neighborhood that was evenly split between black and white families. The results from this study clearly show that African Americans are much more willing than whites to live in racially diverse neighborhoods.

WEALTH INEQUALITY

Racial segregation in housing is one of the driving factors behind wealth disparities among racial groups. On average, African Americans and Latinos have less than 8 percent of the wealth of whites (Figure 8-3). The disparities between the wealth portfolios of whites and Latinos and between those of whites and blacks are about twice as large today as they were prior to the recession that began in 2007, primarily as a result of residual effects from the related crisis in the housing market. The housing crisis wiped out all of the gains in wealth made by black and Latino families compared to whites since 1984, when the United States first began to track wealth inequality. In 2009, one-third of black and Latino households had zero or negative wealth (Kochhar, Fry, and Taylor 2011).

Let's briefly revisit the differences between income and wealth. Americans primarily use their income to live on a day-to-day basis: to pay the rent or mortgage, to buy food, to pay for school, and to pay bills and other necessities. Income differentials often translate into differences in standards of living. Wealth, by contrast, has a different functionality. Wealth includes an individual's accumulated assets, such as savings, home equity, stocks, and business ownership. People don't use wealth to

FIGURE 8-3

MEDIAN NET WORTH OF HOUSEHOLDS, 2005 AND 2009

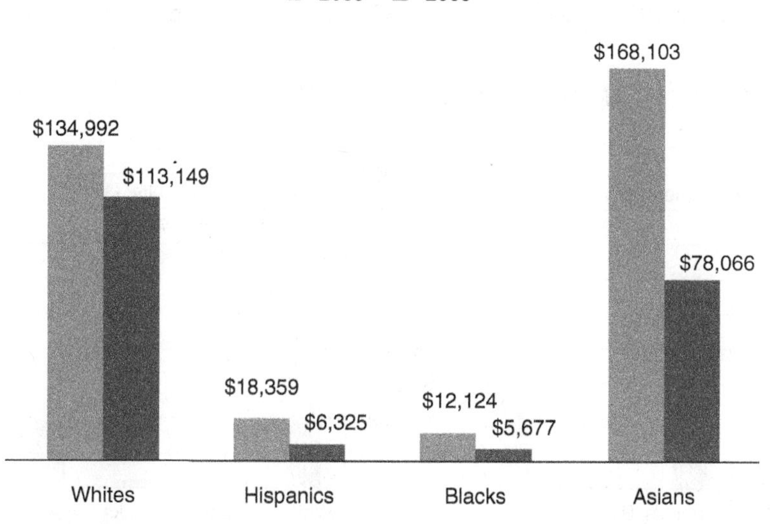

Source: Kochhar, Fry, and Taylor (2011).

pay for daily expenses (except in financial emergencies). Instead, wealth grants financial stability and is often used to ensure the financial success of future generations through inheritances. Oliver and Shapiro (2006, 175) contend that "wealth is money that is not typically used to purchase milk, shoes, or other necessities. . . . It is used to create opportunities, secure a desired stature and standard of living, or pass along a class status already obtained to a new generation." The vast discrepancies between black and white wealth, then, translate into the solidification of racial inequality across generations.

There are many reasons for wealth inequality. One of the main factors is inequality in home values and homeownership. In 2005, blacks and Latinos derived much greater proportions of their wealth from their homes than whites. Looking at the loss in average wealth for families between 2005 and 2009, it is clear that nearly all of the losses for all families came from losses in home equity (Figure 8-4). Since black and Latino families had almost no other wealth—an average of \$479 for Latino families and \$626 for black families—these households lost nearly all of their wealth as a result of the housing crisis (Kochhar et al. 2011).

In 2000, Native Americans were the racial group with the lowest average incomes. There is relatively little data on the wealth holdings of Native Americans. However, Jay Zagorsky (2006) was able to use data from the National Longitudinal Study of Youth to assess Native Americans' wealth holdings. He found that in 2000, the average Native American born between 1957 and 1965 had only \$5,700 in wealth, compared with the

FIGURE 8-4

AVERAGE WEALTH OF FAMILIES BY RACE/ETHNICITY

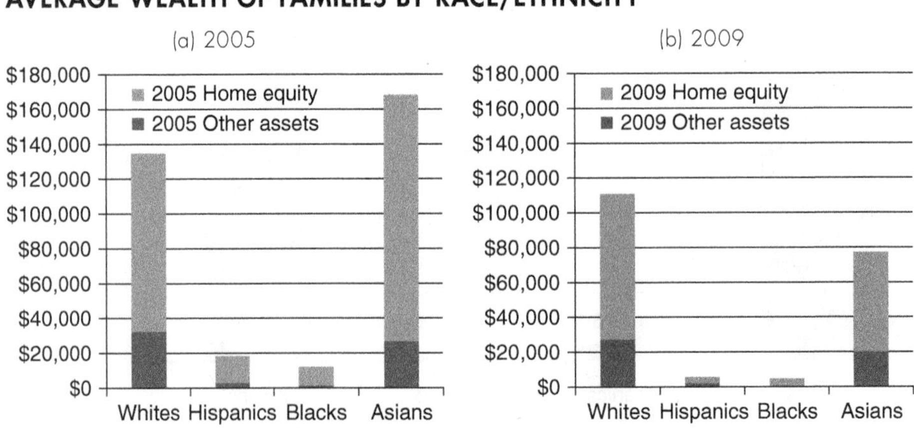

Source: Kochhar, Fry, and Taylor (2011).

$65,500 amassed by his or her white counterpart. He also found that only 43 percent of the Native Americans in this age group had bank accounts, compared with 65 percent of baby boomers overall. Only a third of Native American baby boomers owned homes, compared with 57 percent overall. Zagorsky (2006) found that Native Americans own fewer businesses, have lower rates of homeownership, and reside in homes with lower values than the average person living in the United States.

Inequality in Homeownership and Home Values

Using the 2001 American Housing Survey, Lauren Krivo and Robert Kaufman (2004) found that over 70 percent of white households owned their homes, compared with 46 percent of black households, 49 percent of Latino households, and 55 percent of Asian households. In addition, they found that white homeowners have more home equity than do blacks and Latinos. The median value of home equity for blacks was $52,882, and for Latinos it was $60,000. In contrast, the median home equity value for whites was $80,000. At $111,100, Asians had the highest average home equity. Moreover, blacks and Latinos were the most likely to have high-interest mortgages: 4 percent of whites had an interest rate higher than 9 percent, compared with nearly 11 percent of black homeowners and 7 percent of Latino homeowners. Asians were the least likely to have this kind of mortgage, with only 1.5 percent reporting high interest rates.

Between 2007 and 2009, blacks and Latinos were twice as likely as whites to experience foreclosures (Kochhar et al. 2011). Looking at home loans made between 2005 and 2008 reveals that 790 African Americans experienced a foreclosure by 2009 for each 10,000 loans, compared with 769 Hispanics and 452 whites. By 2010, 17 percent of Latino homeowners, 11 percent of African American homeowners, and 7 percent of non-Hispanic white homeowners had lost or were at imminent risk of losing their homes (Bocian, Li, and Ernst 2010). The recent housing crisis thus exacerbated preexisting inequalities in homeownership and home values.

Wealth Inequality beyond Homeownership

Families can have negative wealth if the total of their debts exceeds the total value of their assets. This situation has become increasingly common with the expansion of home equity loans and falling housing prices.

However, wealth includes factors beyond homeownership, such as stock holdings. When stock prices plummeted in 2007, black and Latino families lost the largest shares of their holdings. Latinos who owned stocks and mutual funds saw a 32 percent decline in their value between 2005 and 2009, and blacks saw a 71 percent decline in the same period. The stocks owned by whites fell only 9 percent, and those owned by Asians actually increased 19 percent during this same period (Kochhar et al. 2011).

High levels of debt also help explain wealth inequality. In 2002, over a quarter of black and Latino households had negative net worth, compared with 13 percent of white households. The numbers are even starker when we consider gender: nearly half of all black and Latina women had zero or negative wealth in 2007 (Kochhar et al. 2011).

EXPLAINING THE WEALTH GAP IN THE TWENTY-FIRST CENTURY

Rather than decreasing over time, inequalities among whites, blacks, and Latinos are increasing. The wealth gap between blacks and whites tripled between 1984 and 2009. In 2013, Thomas Shapiro, Tatjana Meschede, and Sam Osoro published a study that sought to explain why. Based on their examination of 1,700 households, these analysts attributed the wealth gap to five factors:

1. Years of homeownership
2. Household income
3. Years of unemployment
4. College education
5. Inheritances or financial support from family members

Notably, Shapiro and colleagues did not find the wealth gap to be a consequence of behavioral differences, such as consumption patterns or the propensity to build savings. It is also not solely a function of income differentials. Instead, the researchers were able to explain two-thirds of the wealth gap using these five factors. Years of homeownership accounted for 27 percent of the difference, household income for 20 percent, unemployment for 9 percent, and college education and inheritances for 5 percent each (Shapiro et al. 2013).

Figure 8-5 presents an explanation of the gap between black and white wealth. Many people would expect household income to account

FIGURE 8-5

HOW DO WE EXPLAIN THE BLACK/WHITE WEALTH GAP TODAY?

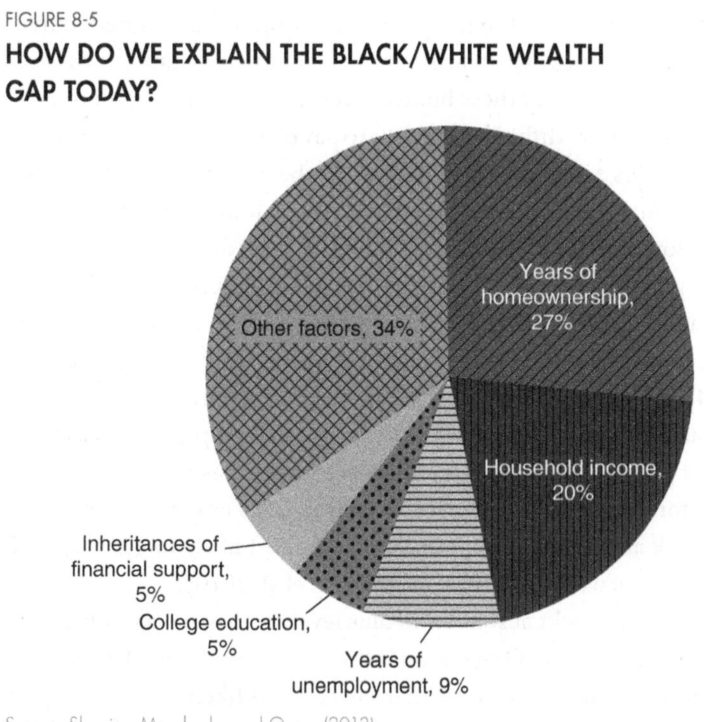

Source: Shapiro, Meschede, and Osoro (2013).

for the differences in wealth. However, as we have seen, income differences can explain only a portion of wealth inequalities. And although it is true that college education makes it easier to build up wealth, the fact that whites are more likely to be college educated accounts for only 5 percent of the differences in wealth between white and black households.

Years of homeownership accounted for the largest portion of the differences in wealth between white and black families. African American families tend to purchase homes later in life because they face more obstacles in doing so than whites. Further, black homeowners are less likely to build up equity over the years because of residential segregation, and white families are more likely to receive financial assistance in purchasing a home from their family members. Even though homeownership accounts for, on average, 53 percent of the wealth black families have, compared with 39 percent for whites, the return on investment in housing turns out to be far greater for white than for black households (Shapiro et al. 2013). Black families who are able to purchase homes face outright discrimination by real estate agents who continue to steer them to black neighborhoods and by lenders who quote them higher interest rates. The limited market potential for homes in primarily black neighborhoods inhibits the possibility for the value of these homes to increase, and the higher interest rates make it more difficult for blacks to pay off their mortgages quickly. These factors work together to reduce the home equity of blacks, thereby enhancing the wealth gap (Krivo and Kaufman 2004).

The foreclosure crisis of 2007–2009 further decimated black and Latino wealth portfolios. A study by the Center for Responsible Lending (Bocian et al. 2010) found that among recent borrowers, nearly 8 percent of black and Latino homeowners lost their homes, compared with 4.5 percent of whites. Nearly two-thirds of all foreclosures between 2005 and 2008 were on homes mortgaged using subprime loans, meaning that people with subprime loans were three times as likely to experience a foreclosure than people with conventional or government loans. And black and Latino borrowers were the most likely to get subprime loans with unfavorable conditions (Bocian et al. 2010).

Whites and blacks at similar income levels tend to have vastly different wealth portfolios. One reason is that whites are more likely to have jobs with benefits. This means that they are less likely to dip into their savings for medical emergencies and that their employers are more likely to be contributing to a retirement plan (Shapiro et al. 2013). Blacks also tend to be in more precarious employment situations and more likely to lose their jobs. When unemployment rose from 5.0 percent in December 2007 to 9.5 percent in June 2009, Latinos and blacks were hit the hardest, with black unemployment rates peaking at 15.6 percent and the Latino rate at 12.6 percent in 2009 (Kochhar et al. 2011).

The 2013 study by Shapiro and his colleagues found that 36 percent of white households inherited some money over the twenty-five-year period under study, compared with only 7 percent of black households. Moreover, the inheritances black households received were, on average, only about 10 percent of the amount inherited by white households. Inheritances are thus another important part of the legacy of inequality in this country.

CONCLUSION AND DISCUSSION

In this chapter, we have seen how wealth inequalities are entrenched and complex. Married white couples with college educations are well positioned to accumulate wealth over the course of their lives. However, married black couples with the same levels of education consistently earn less money and have much less wealth. Wealth provides a safety net for emergencies, such as serious medical issues or the loss of a job. This means that comfortably middle-class black families are at a much greater risk of descending into poverty than similarly placed white families. Not all white families have wealth, but historical racial disparities in the United States, as well as ongoing discriminatory practices, ensure that white families are more likely to accumulate wealth than black and Latino families.

Wealth also provides opportunities and allows families to invest in their future and to take risks. Families with substantial home equity can use that to finance their children's college educations. Families with significant savings and a wide social net can use those to take risks and invest in business opportunities. In these and other ways, wealth begets more wealth. For this reason, wealth inequality is hard to overcome.

Nevertheless, wealth researchers such as john a. powell (2008), and Melvin Oliver and Thomas Shapiro (2006) make a case for **asset-based social policies** that are designed to help narrow the wealth gap. These researchers contend that the FHA policies of the early twentieth century set the stage for the wealth gap, and that now the United States has the responsibility of reversing that trend by setting up proactive policies. These policies could include individual-level assistance in buying homes as well as larger-scale efforts such as improvements to transportation and investments in neighborhoods. For example, if the local, state, or federal government invested money in a working-class black neighborhood by building a transportation hub, transforming empty lots into parks, and revitalizing the business district, this would increase property values and provide job opportunities for the local community, thereby enhancing their wealth portfolios. It would take enormous investments to reverse the trend, but that is primarily because of the decades of investment the federal government has put into white communities.

Between 1933 and 1978, federal government policies enabled over 35 million families to purchase homes in new suburban areas. As a direct consequence of these policies, these families will pass on trillions of dollars of wealth to their children through accumulated home equity. Nearly all of these families are white, meaning that non-white Americans have been locked out of this tremendous wealth-generating federal program. Today, most black families have no wealth to pass on to their children. For this reason, many activists contend that it is time for the federal government to enact new wealth-generating programs that, unlike past programs, are not exclusive to white Americans (Oliver and Shapiro 2006).

THINKING ABOUT RACIAL JUSTICE

Some people argue that responses to the foreclosure crisis in the United States should be framed in the context of racial justice. To what extent do you think this is true? Draw from the materials in this chapter to make your case.

Key Terms

wealth 196
assets 196
residential segregation 198
Federal Housing Administration (FHA) 199
redlining 200
racially restrictive covenants 200
steering 201
predatory lender 203
subprime loan 203
dissimilarity index 205
isolation index 205
segregation index 205
hypersegregation 206
asset-based social policy 215

Check Your Understanding

OBJECTIVE 8.1

Examine the historical reasons for housing and wealth inequalities in the United States.

- Enslaved African Americans were unable to accumulate wealth. Once freed, their opportunities for land ownership were limited.

Q What does slavery have to do with contemporary wealth inequalities?

Q What is the difference between wealth and income? Why is this difference important in studies of racial inequality?

OBJECTIVE 8.2

Explain when and how residential segregation became a characteristic of U.S. cities.

- Residential segregation was created in the early twentieth century by white residents who desired homogenous neighborhoods, profit seeking by the real estate industry, and federal housing programs that were exclusively available to whites.

Q What factors contributed to the creation of residential segregation?

OBJECTIVE 8.3

Evaluate the extent of wealth inequality today.

- On average, African Americans and Latinos have less than 8 percent of the wealth of whites. The housing crisis has exacerbated racial inequalities in wealth.

Q How is residential segregation related to the racial wealth gap?

Q What programs and policies have contributed to the racial wealth gap, and in what ways?

OBJECTIVE 8.4

Assess factors that are perpetuating and exacerbating wealth inequalities today.

- Black families with similar incomes as white families have substantially less wealth. This is because wealth is not solely a function of income differentials. The disparity is also attributable to years of homeownership, years of unemployment, college education, and inheritances.

Q Why and how did the wealth gap between whites and other groups change between 2005 and 2009?

Q What factors have exacerbated the wealth gap in the twenty-first century?

Critical Thinking

1. What distinct social challenges stem from overall wealth inequality and the racial wealth gap?
2. In the United States, why does the idea endure that if you work hard, you will get ahead?

3. Have any of the federal programs mentioned in this chapter helped your family accumulate wealth? How has your family's race, class, and immigration history played a role in the accumulation of wealth in your family?
4. Why is racial segregation problematic? Provide at least three separate reasons.
5. To what extent would narrowing the racial income gap contribute to narrowing the racial wealth gap?
6. How would asset-based social policies work in practice? Could they work?

9

RACISM AND THE CRIMINAL JUSTICE SYSTEM

CHAPTER OUTLINE

LEARNING OBJECTIVES

9.1 Examine the rise of mass incarceration in the United States and its relation to the criminalization of drugs.

9.2 Assess the extent to which institutional racism operates in the criminal justice system.

9.3 Evaluate how the rise of mass incarceration is tied to large-scale economic trends.

9.4 Examine the consequences of mass incarceration for people who are not currently behind bars.

Writing at the turn of the twentieth century, W. E. B. DuBois likened the prison system to "slavery in private hands" (1904, 2). He explained that with the end of slavery, the numbers of black convicts in the South rose substantially, in large part because of vagrancy laws passed in the aftermath of emancipation. African Americans' testimonies in courts were largely ignored, and any accusation by whites could result in conviction. Southern states, however, were not able to build prisons fast enough to house these new convicts. Thus a convict-lease system was born whereby convicts could be leased to the highest bidder to work as slaves. This practice was legal because the Thirteenth Amendment allows forced labor as a punishment for crime. Notably, in our present system, states still can (and do) force prisoners to work for little or no pay.

Convict leasing was a system of both free labor and social control. Today, prisons do not function to the same extent as a source of unpaid labor, yet the element of social control persists. Similar to slavery and Jim Crow laws, incarceration is a racialized form of social control in that it disproportionately affects black, Latino, and Native American people. One place we can see this is in the lifelong stigma attached to being labeled a felon. As Michelle Alexander (2010) explains, this stigma makes various forms of racial discrimination legal. Felons face discrimination in housing, employment, and access to social services.

This chapter elaborates on these and other ways in which mass incarceration acts as a tool of social control, and how this crime control strategy has disproportionately affected people of color. The evidence presented makes it clear that mass incarceration not only is ineffective at preventing crime, but also has been particularly detrimental to communities of color and to poor people across the United States. This chapter begins with a discussion of mass incarceration and then moves to an analysis of institutionalized racism in the criminal justice system. It concludes with a consideration of the economic and collateral consequences of mass incarceration.

The United States has more people in prison than any other country in the world and today incarcerates people at a higher rate than at any other time in history. Our crime rate, however, is not higher than that of other countries or than it has been historically. Why, then, are so many Americans behind bars? The answer lies in the United States' use of mass incarceration as a strategy to reduce crime and particularly to fight illicit drug use. Yet mass incarceration has not been effective at reducing crime and illicit drug use. It has, however, destroyed families and communities and exacerbated racial inequality in that the primary victims of intensified law enforcement efforts have been people of color.

MASS INCARCERATION IN THE UNITED STATES

An understanding of the racially disparate consequences of the criminal justice system in the United States must first begin with an exploration of the uniqueness of this system. The United States is distinctive among wealthier nations in terms of its liberal use of the prison system. While drugs such as marijuana and cocaine have been decriminalized in Western Europe, the United States has enhanced the punishments for the use of illicit drugs. Repeat offender laws and mandatory sentencing have meant that in the United States, many people spend years behind bars for nonviolent crimes. Because of these laws' racially disparate implementation and character, their impact is visible to a greater degree in communities where blacks and Latinos reside.

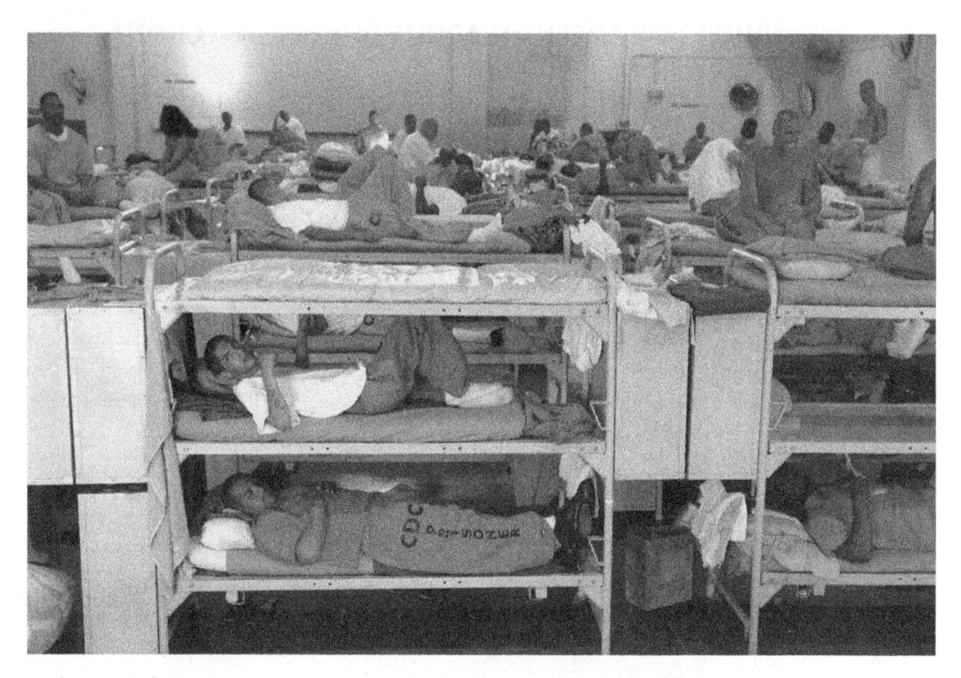

In the United States, prisons are crowded with nonviolent offenders.

The Rise of Mass Incarceration

Mass incarceration is a relatively new phenomenon in the United States and marks a divergence from the attitudes of the mid-twentieth century. At that time, Americans tended to view incarceration as an ineffective means of controlling crime and searched for other solutions to reduce it. Prison was seen as a last resort, and the Federal Bureau of Prisons planned to close large prisons in Kansas, Washington, and Georgia. In 1970, Congress voted to eliminate nearly all federal mandatory minimum sentences for drug offenders, as most Americans viewed drug addiction as a problem of public health, not criminal justice (Alexander 2010).

Just ten years later, this mindset—that drugs are a public health problem and prisons are barbaric—was pushed to the margins as a policy of mass incarceration took off. As shown in Figure 9-1, the U.S. incarceration rate was about 1 per 1,000 residents for almost the entire twentieth century up until the 1970s. That rate doubled between 1972 and 1984, and again between 1984 and 1994. By the end of the

FIGURE 9-1

NUMBER OF AMERICAN ADULTS UNDER CORRECTIONAL SUPERVISION, 1980–2009

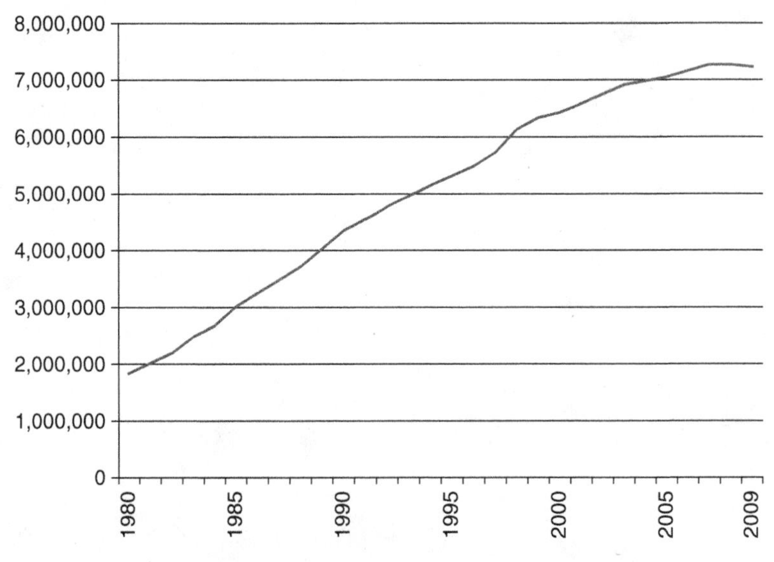

Source: Bureau of Justice Statistics (2009).

twentieth century, the United States had an unprecedented number of inmates: over 2 million, more than ten times the number of U.S. inmates at any time prior to the 1970s. In 2009, over 7.2 million people were on probation or parole or in jail or prison—3.1 percent of all U.S. adult residents, or one in every thirty-two adults (Glaze 2010). The increase in incarceration cannot be explained by a rise in crime, as crime rates have remained fairly steady (Wacquant 2009). Incarceration rates have soared because the laws have changed, making a wider variety of crimes punishable by incarceration and lengthening sentences for those incarcerated.

Mass Incarceration in a Global Context

The United States stands alone in its rate of incarceration. In 2012, 716 of every 100,000 residents were incarcerated—a much higher rate than in Western European countries. The incarceration rate in Western Europe ranges from 24 per 100,000 residents in Liechtenstein to 122 per 100,000 in Luxembourg (Walmsley 2013). Our prison population also dwarfs that of larger countries, including China, in terms of sheer numbers. In 2012, the United States had 2,228,424 people behind bars. The next largest incarcerated population was in China, with 1,701,344 prisoners, followed by Russia, Brazil, and India. The so-called "War on Drugs" in the United States accounts for much of this disparity. In most other developed countries, a first-time drug offense leads to no more than six months in jail, and rehabilitation is used more often than criminalization as a response. In the United States, the typical mandatory minimum sentence in federal court for a first-time drug offense is five or ten years (Alexander 2010). At the state level, there are even more extreme examples: in Florida, illegal possession of the painkiller hydrocodone (one of the most frequently prescribed drugs in the United States) leads to a twenty-five-year mandatory minimum sentence (Mascharka 2001). With more people in jail on drug charges for longer periods of time, the U.S. incarceration rate continues to rise above and beyond that of other countries. As shown in Figure 9-2, Russia is the only European country that has an incarceration rate remotely close to that of the United States. The United States has an incarceration rate seven times higher than that of other developed countries such as Japan, South Korea, and Denmark.

FIGURE 9-2

INCARCERATION RATES PER 100,000 POPULATION IN DEVELOPED COUNTRIES, 2005

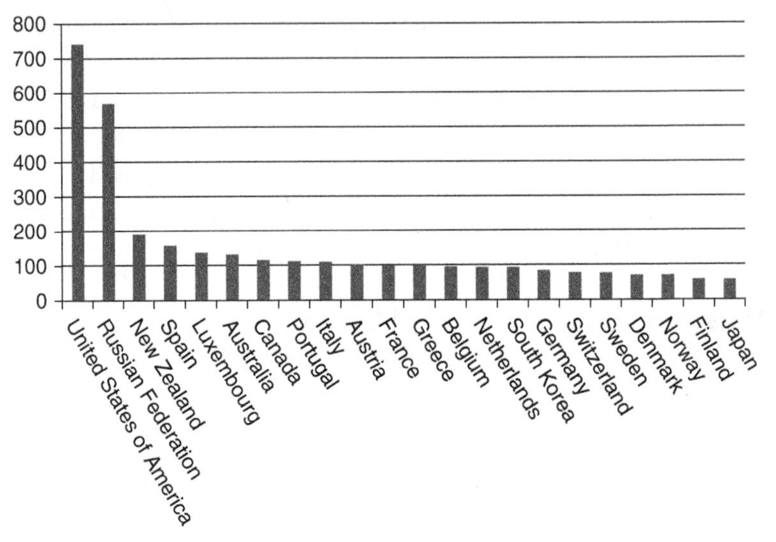

Source: Walmsley (2013).

Race and Mass Incarceration

When we consider the U.S. incarceration rate in light of race, the picture becomes even more unsettling. In 2008, less than one-third of the population of the United States was black or Latino. In that same year, blacks and Latinos made up 58 percent of the nation's prison population (Sabol, West, and Cooper 2009). In 2009, the imprisonment rate of white males was 487 per every 100,000 in the population, as compared to compared to 1,193 per 100,000 Latino males, and 3,110 per 100,000 black males. Black males were six times as likely to be incarcerated as white males in 2009 (West and Sabol 2010). Figure 9-3 shows these rates by race and gender in 2007.

Much of the disparity is due to imprisonment for drug crimes, even though people of all races use and sell drugs at similar rates (Alexander 2010). This disparity has increased over time. In 1975, the ratio of black to white arrests for drug crimes was 2 to 1. By 1990, the ratio was 5 to 1, even though there is no evidence that blacks began to use or sell drugs at higher rates than whites during this period (Wacquant 2009).

By the end of the twentieth century, black men were seven times more likely than white men to go to prison. Over the course of a black

FIGURE 9-3

ESTIMATED NUMBER OF (A) MALE AND (B) FEMALE INMATES BY RACE PER 100,000 RESIDENTS, 2007

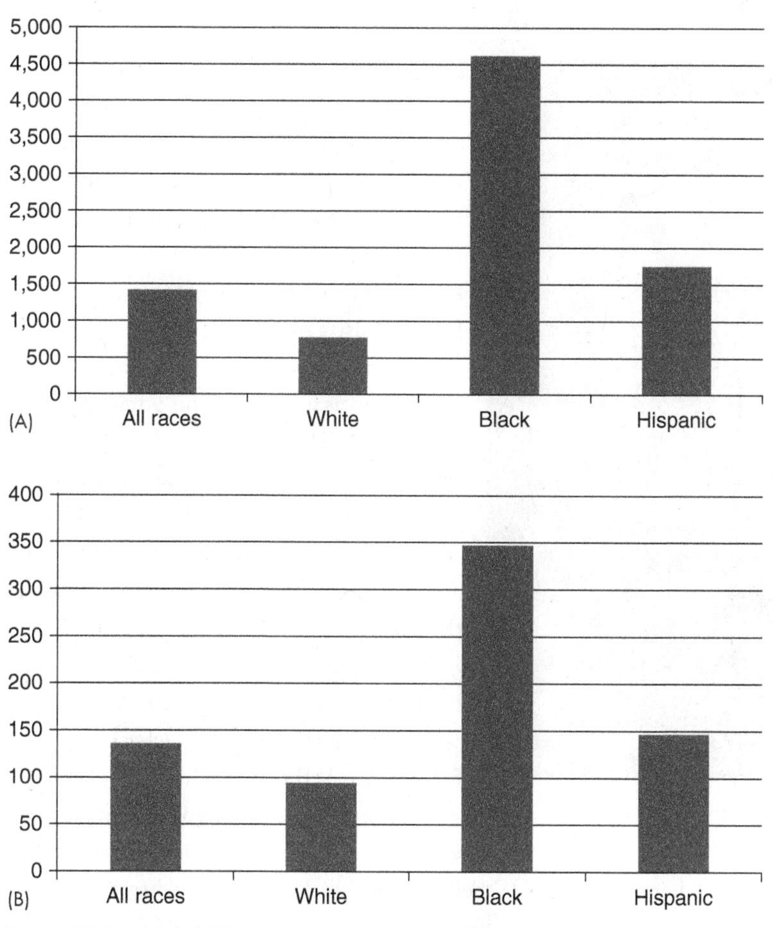

Source: West and Sabol (2010).

man's life, he is more likely to go to prison than to get a bachelor's degree or join the military. Whereas a white man is ten times more likely to get a college degree than to go to prison, a black man is nearly twice as likely to end up in prison than to finish college. Imprisonment has become an expected life outcome for some black men: nearly 60 percent of black male high school dropouts born between 1965 and 1969 will be incarcerated at some point in their lives. In contrast, only about 11 percent of white male high school dropouts born in the same period will be incarcerated (Western 2006).

Kemba Smith

Kemba Smith.

Kemba Smith grew up in an upper-middle-class home in Richmond, Virginia. When she completed high school in 1989, she decided to attend a historically black university, Hampton University. In her second year, she met and fell in love with Peter Hall, a well-known and popular man on campus. Peter Hall was also a major drug dealer. At first, Kemba was impressed with his cars, clothes, and money, as well as with his popularity. After they had been dating for a while, Peter became abusive toward Kemba. She began to fear for her life as well as her family's lives and felt compelled to do whatever Peter Hall asked her to do, even if it meant transgressing the law.

She stayed with him and eventually became pregnant with their son. When she was seven months pregnant, Peter Hall was found dead. At the time of his death, Hall was being pursued by the police on drug and murder charges, and Kemba was implicated in some of those charges by virtue of their relationship. Kemba turned herself in and pleaded guilty to charges of money laundering, conspiracy to sell drugs, and false statements, even though she had never handled or used cocaine and received little benefit from its sale. She pleaded guilty because the prosecutor told her she would receive a reduced sentence. Instead, Kemba was sentenced to twenty-four years in jail under the mandatory sentencing laws and was forced to give birth to her son in prison. She stayed in prison for nearly seven years, until national advocacy efforts finally led to President Clinton commuting her sentence.

Source: Copeland 2000.

The Inefficacy of Mass Incarceration

Incarceration has emerged as the most popular crime control strategy in the United States. However, there is limited evidence that incarceration is an effective strategy to control crime. One piece of evidence demonstrating its ineffectiveness can be seen in state-level incarceration trends. Between 1998 and 2003, some states greatly increased the number of people they sent to prison, while other states did not. The average decrease in crime rates in these states was similar. Higher rates of incarceration did not translate into more substantial declines in states' crime rates (R. King, Mauer, and Young 2005).

Incarceration has had a limited impact on crime rates for two reasons. First of all, it is just one of many factors that influence crime rates: changes in the economy, fluctuations in the drug market, and community-level responses often have more pronounced effects. Second, there are diminishing returns from incarceration: incarcerating repeat violent offenders takes them off the streets and thus reduces crime, whereas incarcerating nonviolent offenders has a minimal effect on crime rates (King et al. 2005).

It is thus remarkable that crime rates have been steady or declining since the 1970s, yet arrest and incarceration rates have soared in that same time period. Incarceration rates have gone up even as crime rates have decreased and (presumably) there are fewer people to incarcerate. Figures 9-4 and 9-5 provide a visual representation of how violent

FIGURE 9-4

VIOLENT CRIME RATE: ADJUSTED VICTIMIZATION RATE PER 1,000 PERSONS AGED 12 OR OLDER, 1973–2009

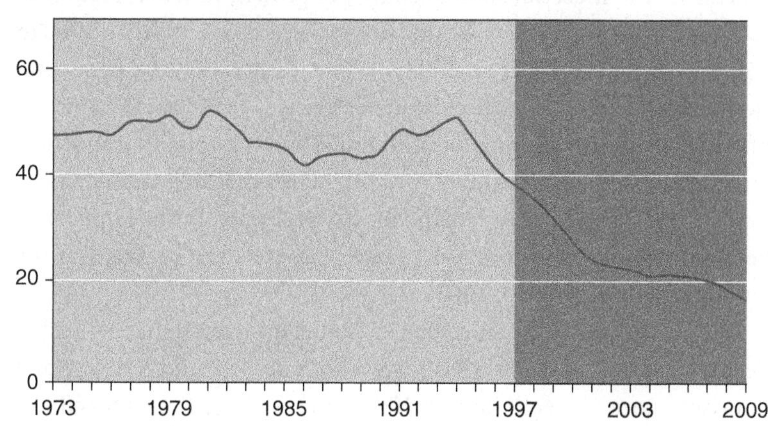

Source: Bureau of Justice Statistics (2010).

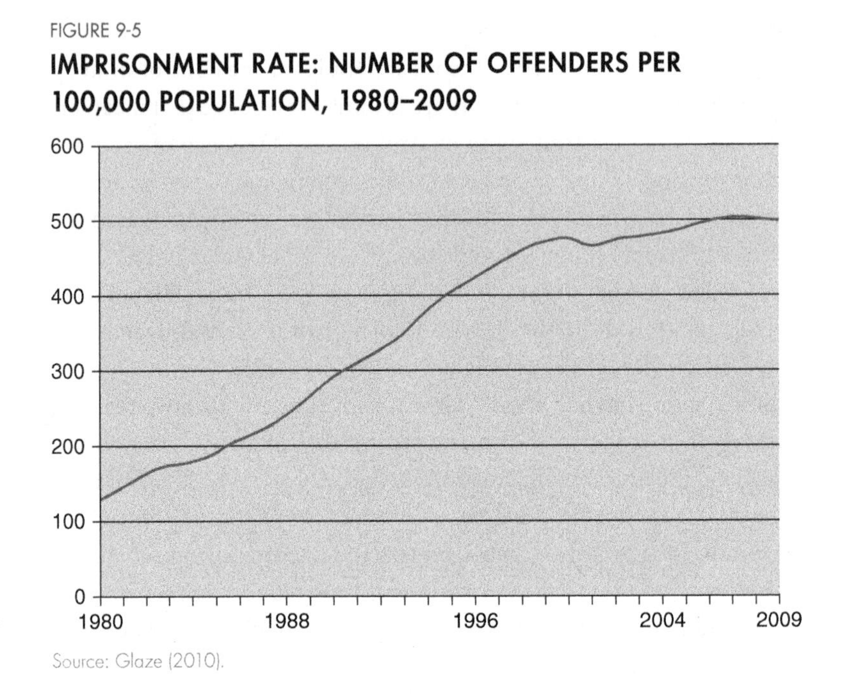

FIGURE 9-5

IMPRISONMENT RATE: NUMBER OF OFFENDERS PER 100,000 POPULATION, 1980–2009

Source: Glaze (2010).

crime rates remained fairly steady and then decreased while incarceration rates continued to increase.

Despite the low efficacy of imprisoning nonviolent offenders, this is the segment of the prison population that has grown the fastest, and drug arrests are on the rise (Figure 9-6). Between 1970 and 2000, incarceration rates in the United States increased five-fold, in large part because of legislation designed to fight drugs. As such, drug offenders represent "the most substantial source of growth in incarceration in recent decades, rising from 40,000 persons in prison and jail in 1980 to 450,000 today" (King et al. 2005, 6). The irony is that the incarceration of drug offenders is a highly ineffective way to reduce the amount of illegal drugs sold in the United States. When street-level drug sellers are incarcerated, they are quickly replaced by other sellers, since what drives the drug market is demand for drugs. Incarcerating large numbers of drug offenders has not ameliorated the drug problem in the United States (King et al. 2005).

Despite the lack of evidence that increased incarceration rates lead to decreased crime (Lynch 1999), we continue to build prisons and imprison more people (Gilmore 2007), and we have not changed our policies in response to substantial evidence that being tough on crime

FIGURE 9-6

ADULT DRUG ARRESTS, 1970–2006

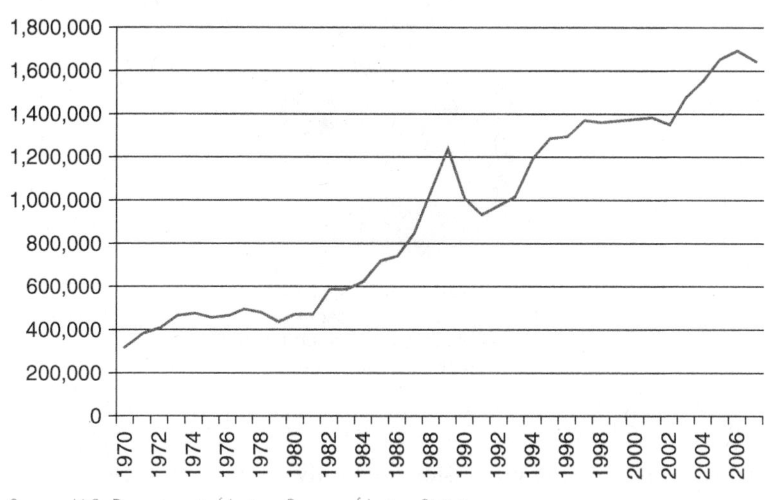

Source: U.S. Department of Justice, Bureau of Justice Statistics.

does not lead to safer communities. Politicians who invest money in the criminal justice system can claim to their constituents that they are serious about law enforcement. This strategy creates the impression that they have crime victims' interests at heart and has become essential for winning electoral campaigns (Simon 2007). In 1998, political activist and scholar Angela Davis pointed out: "Mass incarceration is not a solution to unemployment, nor is it a solution to the vast array of social problems that are hidden away in a rapidly growing network of prisons and jails. However, the great majority of people have been tricked into believing in the efficacy of imprisonment, even though the historical record clearly demonstrates that prisons do not work" (1998, 3). The emergence of mass incarceration as a solution to social ills can be attributed primarily to the War on Drugs, as we will see.

Mass Incarceration and the War on Drugs

To understand why black men are imprisoned at seven times the rate of white men and why the United States imprisons more people than any other country in the world requires a consideration of the War on Drugs, which is largely responsible for the explosion in incarceration rates since 1980. Whereas 41,000 people were behind bars for a drug offense in 1980, about a half a million were in 2010. Many people are incarcerated for low-level drug crimes. In 2005, 80 percent of drug

FIGURE 9-7

DRUG SALES VERSUS DRUG POSSESSION ARRESTS, 2007

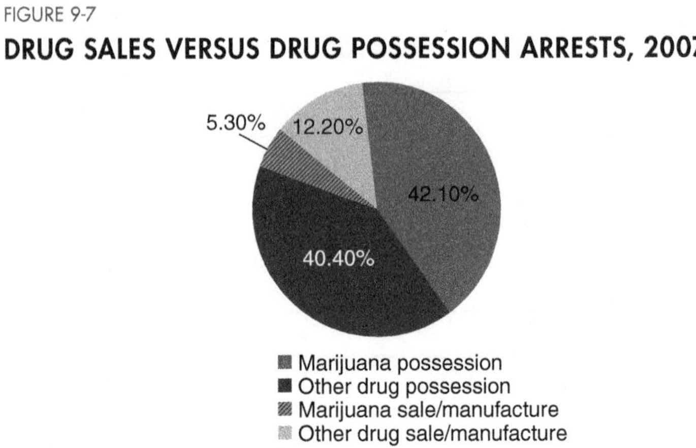

Source: Alexander (2010).

arrests were for drug possession, and only 20 percent were for drug sales (Alexander 2010; Figure 9-7).

Zealous enforcement of drug laws disproportionately affects people of color, even though whites are actually more likely to use and sell drugs. In the United States, black men are sent to prison on drug charges at thirteen times the rate of white men, yet five times as many whites as blacks use illegal drugs (Alexander 2010). According to results from the National Household Survey on Drug Abuse, white youth aged twelve to seventeen are more likely than blacks to have sold illegal drugs (Alexander 2010). These data are based on self-reports, yet they are confirmed by more objective data: white youth are about three times as likely as their African American counterparts to end up in an emergency room for drug-related emergencies. Whites who use and abuse drugs most often buy their drugs from white sellers, just as blacks who use drugs buy from black sellers (Alexander 2010).

Law enforcement agents cannot fully enforce drug laws because drug use and selling are too widespread. More than half of the people in the United States have violated drug laws at some point in their lives, yet relatively few have been punished for it. In any given year, about 10 percent of American adults violate drug laws. As law enforcement agents have neither the resources nor the mandate to prosecute every lawbreaker, they must be strategic with their resources and enforcement tactics. Because of stereotypes that drug law violators are black, combined with the relatively weak political power of poor black communities, law enforcement agents have targeted open-air drug markets in poor black communities instead of the places where whites use and sell drugs (Alexander 2010).

Crack cocaine is often portrayed as public enemy number one in the War on Drugs. It is thus remarkable that crack cocaine hit the streets in 1985, yet the War on Drugs began three years earlier, in 1982. When President Ronald Reagan officially declared the War on Drugs, less than 2 percent of Americans viewed drugs as the most important problem facing the nation. Public opinion changed drastically after the War on Drugs was launched in 1982 and crack cocaine became an urban problem in 1985. A media frenzy broke out over the problems of crackheads, crack babies, and crack whores. The media often racialized the crack problem as a black problem by showing images of black people in connection with stories about crack cocaine (Alexander 2010).

The penalties that emerged for possession and sale of crack cocaine were the harshest drug penalties in U.S. history. When the Anti-Drug Abuse Act was passed in 1988, it meted out a five-year mandatory minimum sentence for simple possession of crack. This was unprecedented: prior to this legislation, one year of imprisonment was the maximum sentence one could receive for possession of any amount of any drug (Alexander 2010). Along with the federal laws, states began to pass stricter laws, including "three strikes," "truth in sentencing," and "zero tolerance" legislation, which led to a huge upswing in incarceration rates. By 1996, nearly three-quarters of all people admitted to state prisons were nonviolent offenders with relatively minor convictions (Ladipo 2001).

At the federal level, three major laws were passed in 1984, 1986, and 1988 that marked the beginning of a new era in criminal justice:

- The **1984 Crime Control Act** established mandatory minimum sentences and eliminated federal parole.
- The **Anti-Drug Abuse Act of 1986** imposed even more mandatory minimum sentences. Most significantly, it set a five-year mandatory minimum sentence for offenses involving 100 grams of heroin, 500 grams of cocaine, or 5 grams of crack cocaine.
- The **Anti-Drug Abuse Act of 1988** included a five-year mandatory minimum sentence for simple possession of crack cocaine, with no evidence of intent to sell. Prior to 1988, one year of imprisonment had been the maximum penalty for possession of any amount of any drug.

Race, Class, Gender, and Mass Incarceration

Mass incarceration has led to the filling of jails with black and Latino working-class and poor men. Mass incarceration is thus evidently raced, classed, and gendered. However, an intersectional analysis requires a consideration not only of the numbers of blacks, Latinos, and men behind bars, but also of how mass incarceration affects people in different social locations differently. When we look at women, for example, it becomes clear that there are three specific ways that mass incarceration has directly affected women in distinct ways from men:

1. There were very few women behind bars prior to 1970, meaning that incarceration is a relatively new phenomenon for women. Incarceration rates for women rose dramatically in the context of the War on Drugs. Between 1970 and 1997, the population of women in prison rose more than twelve-fold, from 5,600 to 75,000. With the addition of the 35,000 women in jails, there were about 100,000 women incarcerated by the late 1990s. By 2000, the sum total of women in prison or jails, on probation, or on parole was one million (Covington and Bloom 2003). Similar to men, women of color are incarcerated at a higher rate than white women. In 1990, black women were three times as likely as white women to be incarcerated, and Latina women were twice as likely (Zatz 2000).
2. Women are more likely than men to have been the primary caregivers prior to being incarcerated. This means that the incarceration of women often has a more direct and immediate effect on their children.
3. Women are more likely than men to have experienced physical or sexual abuse. One study found that nearly 80 percent of women prisoners had experienced some form of abuse in their lives. Many of the women serving time for violent crimes are in jail for retaliating against their abusers (Covington and Bloom 2003).

INSTITUTIONAL RACISM IN THE CRIMINAL JUSTICE SYSTEM

Racial disparities in incarceration rates are a classic example of institutional racism. As discussed in Chapter Seven, institutional racism is the creation of racial disparities as a result of institutional practices and policies that distribute resources, power, and advantages to whites.

Racial inequalities in law enforcement are institutionalized at every level of the criminal justice process, from stops to arrests to charges to sentencing to release. Blacks and Latinos are more likely to be arrested than whites. They are more likely to be charged, more likely to be convicted, more likely to be given a longer sentence, and more likely to face the death penalty. The cumulative effect of these disparities at each stage of the process creates a situation in which black men are seven times more likely than white men to be put behind bars.

Racial Profiling

The propensity of police officers to pull over African Americans more often than whites is so prevalent that the moniker "driving while black" has emerged to explain this phenomenon. In the early 1990s, statistician John Lamberth (1994) conducted a detailed investigation of police stops on the New Jersey Turnpike. This study provided convincing evidence that police officers engage in **racial profiling**, the use of race or ethnicity as grounds for suspicion. Lamberth's study revealed that only 13 percent of all cars on the New Jersey Turnpike had a black driver or passenger but that 35 percent of those stopped on the turnpike were black, and 73.2 percent of those arrested were black. Blacks were much more likely than whites to be stopped, even though blacks and whites violated traffic laws at almost exactly the same rate. Studies in other states have revealed similar results: police officers are more likely to pull over African American drivers than white drivers. In Maryland, an American Civil Liberties Union (ACLU) study found that 75 percent of drivers along Interstate 95 were white, but between January 1995 and September 1996, 73 percent of the motorists that Maryland state police searched were black (Harris 1999). Racial profiling also extends to Hispanics: a study in Volusia County in Florida, for example, revealed that blacks and Hispanics were more likely to be pulled over and much more likely to be searched once pulled over than whites (Mauer 1999).

One poignant story is that of Charles and Etta Carter, an elderly African American couple. In 1997, on their fortieth wedding anniversary, they were stopped by Maryland state troopers, who proceeded to search their car. The officers brought in drug-sniffing dogs, which destroyed much of the contents of their car, including their daughter's wedding dress. At the end of the long, humiliating search, no drugs were found and no ticket was issued (Harris 1999). The Carters believe they were subject to racial profiling—that the police officers pulled them over and searched their car because they were black. They argue that had they been white, it is very unlikely the police would have pulled them over and subjected them to this humiliating search.

Racial profiling happens on street corners as well as highways, where police officers stop and frisk blacks and Latinos much more frequently than they do whites. African Americans make up 13 percent of the U.S. population and 14 percent of illegal drug users in this country. However, they account for 37 percent of the people arrested for drug offenses, in part because blacks are more likely to be stopped and frisked than whites (Mauer 2009). In New York City, for example, one study found that blacks account for half of all people stopped by the police, even though they make up only a quarter of the New York City population (Gelman, Fagan, and Kiss 2007). Once stopped, New York police officers are more likely to frisk blacks and Latinos than whites. According to data provided by the New York Police Department (NYPD), between 1998 and 2008, NYPD officers frisked 85 percent of blacks and Latinos that they stopped, compared with only 8 percent of whites (New York City Bar Association 2013). A study in Seattle revealed similar results. Seventy percent of people in Seattle are white, and the majority of those who sell and use drugs in Seattle are white. However, blacks represent nearly two-thirds of all those arrested for drug offenses (Barnes and Chang 2012). This is primarily because police officers tend to target predominantly black neighborhoods in criminal law enforcement operations.

Sentencing Disparities

Blacks and Latinos are more likely to be arrested than whites. An arrest is just the first point of entry into the criminal justice system, where blacks and Latinos are likely to continue to find the odds stacked against them. A recent study of federal offenders, for example, found that blacks and Latinos are likely to be sentenced to longer prison terms than whites, even after taking into account the severity of the charges. In contrast, whites are more likely than blacks to get no prison time when that option is available. This study also found that the disparities between sentences for whites and non-whites are most evident in drug trafficking cases (Mustard 2001).

Although more whites are convicted of drug felonies than blacks, more blacks are admitted to prison. This disparity is related to the differing severity of sentences that blacks and whites receive in courts of law. Overall, blacks are sent to prison on drug charges at nearly twelve times the rate of whites, even though, as mentioned previously, blacks and whites use and sell drugs at about the same rates (Alexander 2010). One of the main reasons for this disparity is that police officers target open-air drug markets in black neighborhoods yet often ignore the widespread usage of narcotics in primarily white suburban areas and on college campuses. Because whites are less likely to be arrested for drug offenses, they are less likely to be charged, convicted, or sentenced to prison for drug offenses. This means that harsh penalties for drug offenses have had a disproportionate impact on people of color.

As the War on Drugs advanced in the 1970s, discretionary power was increasingly taken away from judges out of fear that they might be soft on crime. One of the trends in sentencing reform has been the introduction of mandatory minimum sentences and mandatory guidelines for calculating prison sentences (Simon 2007). The implementation of mandatory prison terms for certain drug crimes has had a disproportionate impact on African Americans. The 1986 Anti-Drug Abuse Act established mandatory prison terms of five years for possession or sale of 5 grams of crack cocaine or 500 grams of powder cocaine. This sentencing disparity is emblematic of how drug law enforcement has meted out different sentences to blacks and whites. Between 1986 and 2006, more than 80 percent of people sentenced to prison for crack cocaine were black (Mauer 2007). This is especially remarkable when we consider that two-thirds of regular crack cocaine users are either white or Latino (Mauer 2009). The 1986 act is one of many pieces of legislation that set mandatory minimum sentences, which have disproportionately affected African Americans. Blacks are 21 percent more likely than whites to receive a mandatory minimum sentence when facing an eligible charge, and black drug defendants are 20 percent more likely than white drug defendants to be sentenced to prison (Mauer 2009).

The Ultimate Sentence: Racial Disparities in the Death Penalty

As a black man accused of killing a white man, Troy Davis had the odds against him. A study conducted in California found that people accused of killing whites are over three times more likely to be sentenced to death than those who kill African Americans (American

voices

Troy Davis

Troy Davis.

On September 21, 2011, the state of Georgia executed Troy Davis, an African American man who was raised in Savannah, Georgia, where he was a coach for the Savannah Police Athletic League. His father was a former police officer.

In 1991, Troy Davis was convicted of the murder of Mark MacPhail, a white off-duty police officer. There is no physical evidence connecting Davis to the crime scene. A murder weapon has never been found. The conviction is based primarily on eyewitness accounts, even though seven of the nine witnesses who were not police officers have recanted their testimonies since Davis's original conviction. Amnesty International, the NAACP, and several other groups demanded clemency. Several prominent leaders, including Jimmy Carter, Desmond Tutu, and Pope Benedict XVI called for a closer examination of the evidence.

Supporters of Troy Davis protested outside of the execution grounds right up until the moment of his execution. Many of them claimed there was too much doubt about his guilt for the state to proceed. One of the original jurors, Brenda Forrest, declared on CNN: "If I knew then what I know now, Troy Davis would not be on death row. The verdict would be 'not guilty.'" Troy Davis's sister claims that the witnesses were coerced and threatened with jail time. Another witness, Benjamin Gordon, alleged that he had been coerced by police to implicate Davis. In addition, Gordon signed a statement in 2008 that claimed he actually had seen another person shoot the officer. Because of these and other testimonies, Davis's supporters contended there was too much doubt for Davis to be executed.

Source: Thomson 2011.

Civil Liberties Union 2003). Another study examined all death penalty cases since 1977, when the death penalty was reinstated, and found that although whites accounted for about half of all murder victims, 80 percent of all death penalty cases involved white victims (American Civil Liberties Union 2003). In addition, between 1976 and 2002, only twelve people were executed for crimes in which the defendant was white and the victim black, compared with the 178 black defendants who were executed after having been convicted of killing a white person (American Civil Liberties Union 2003).

Between 1977 and 2010, more than 1,200 people were executed in the United States. Remarkably, more than 130 people were released from death row after being found innocent. In recent years, the death penalty has come under increasing scrutiny. New Mexico and New Jersey have abolished the death penalty, and death sentences have decreased since their peak in the 1990s. In addition, the U.S. Supreme Court has abolished the death penalty for minors and mentally retarded people (Amnesty International 2010).

THE ECONOMICS OF MASS INCARCERATION

Mass incarceration is a consequence of laws passed at both the state and the federal levels. Before the election of Ronald Reagan as president, however, keeping street crime in check had traditionally been the responsibility not of federal law enforcement but of state and local law enforcement. To fulfill Reagan's campaign promise to fight crime, his administration poured money into federal law enforcement agencies, and Congress passed federal laws that enhanced the punishments for drug-related offenses.

California led the states in prison buildup. Between 1977 and 2007, the California State Assembly passed more than 1,000 laws extending and toughening prison sentences (Wacquant 2009). The California state prison population increased five-fold between 1982 and 2000, even though the crime rate peaked in 1980 and declined thereafter (Gilmore 2007). Notably, California's incarceration rate increased *after* the crime rate had begun to decrease. California had built only twelve prisons between 1852 and 1964, yet built twenty-three major new prisons between 1984 and 2004 (Gilmore 2007). What happened? Why did California engage in this massive prison-building project? Why did the legislature pass so many anti-crime laws?

The answers to these questions can be found through a consideration of the economic restructuring that California underwent leading up to this period. During World War II, much of California's prosperity had been tied directly to defense contracts: people from across the country flocked to California to secure well-paying jobs building defense machinery. After the war, California invested in education and technology to ensure that defense contracts would continue, and it endeavored to make itself uniquely able to provide research, development, and manufacturing for the Department of Defense (DoD). DoD contracts continued to come in until the 1980s, but they contributed to the splitting of the labor market into high-skilled, well-paid technology jobs on one hand and low-skilled, poorly paid jobs on the other (Gilmore 2007).

The restructuring of California's economy led to increases in unemployment, poverty, and inequality. By the 1980s, California was a highly unequal state, with high poverty rates, high housing costs, and high unemployment rates while also being home to some of the wealthiest people in the nation. Over the next fifteen years, its economy continued to change, with increasing numbers of low-paid manufacturing and service jobs and fewer high-paid manufacturing jobs. Childhood poverty rates had increased 25 percent between 1969 and 1979, and they continued to soar over the next decade, increasing another 67 percent between 1980 and 1995, such that by the end of the twentieth century, one in four children in California lived in poverty (Gilmore 2007). Beset with social problems, the California legislature attempted to use mass incarceration as a solution to poverty, unemployment, and inequality. Prisons serve the dual purpose of providing employment to tens of thousands of Californians and locking away a good proportion of the surplus labor force.

The economic restructuring in California mirrored that of the rest of the country, as did cuts in government spending. When Ronald Reagan took office in 1980, he implemented **Reaganomics**, a set of economic policies that involved heavy cuts to a wide variety of social programs across the country. Christian Parenti (1999, 40–41) explains: "In 1982 alone, Reagan cut the real value of welfare by 24 percent, slashed the budget for child nutrition by 34 percent, reduced funding for school milk programs by 78 percent, urban development action grants by 35 percent, and educational block grants by 38 percent." These enormous cuts in social spending disproportionately affected low-wage people of color in urban areas (Figure 9-8).

Neoliberalism is a label for the ideology that open markets, liberalized trade, and privatization are the keys to economic success. Neoliberalism is based on the idea that the state's primary role is to protect property rights, free markets, and free trade, not to hand out social services to its citizens. Under this ideology, the needs of the poor are left to the market, because the state does not intervene or provide any social assistance. Although neoliberalism demands that the state cut back its social services, there is one area of the state that tends to grow when these policies are implemented: its coercive arm (i.e., the police force and the military). Insofar as neoliberalism diminishes

FIGURE 9-8

STATE SPENDING GROWTH FOR HIGHER EDUCATION AND CORRECTIONS, 1987–2007

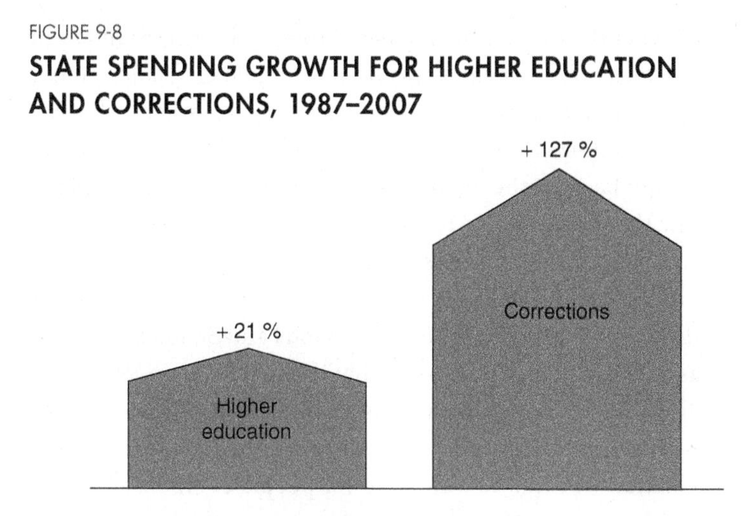

Source: Pew Charitable Trust (2008).

opportunities and services for the poor, the state must ensure that working-class and poor people do not pose a threat to the rich. Government cutbacks in social services often lead to dissent and increases in crime. The state responds by strengthening the police force and the military. Under neoliberalism, "forms of surveillance and policing multiply: in the United States incarceration became a key state strategy to deal with problems arising among discarded workers and marginalized populations. The coercive arm of the state is augmented to protect corporate interests and, if necessary, to repress dissent" (Harvey 2005, 77).

As discussed in Chapter Seven, at the same time as the government began to cut social spending, companies began to **outsource** manufacturing, moving jobs once held by Americans overseas, where cheaper labor could be found. This practice, part of the larger process of **deindustrialization**, led to the impoverishment of cities such as Chicago and Detroit. Detroit was hit particularly hard: it lost half of its population in the 1980s. In Detroit as well as other cities across the country, the War on Drugs kicked off at the same time that inner-city communities were experiencing a dramatic economic crisis. Well-paying, stable blue-collar jobs disappeared, leaving unemployment, as well as social unrest, in their wake (Alexander 2010). This social unrest in turn led to the expansion of the criminal justice system, which was designed to manage and contain the underclass created by neoliberal economic policies.

In 2009, after thirty years of prison building, California found itself with a massive prison system it was no longer able to finance, and it began to release some prisoners to cut costs. It is remarkable that the first cuts in California's prison system after thirty years of buildup were made not because the prison system was failing to reduce crime, but because the state could no longer afford to finance a prison system larger than that of most countries in the world.

In late 2014, California voters passed the Proposition 47 ballot initiative, also known as the Safe Neighborhoods and Schools Act. This Act reclassifies drug and theft crimes that involve less than $950 from felonies to misdemeanors, which translates into shorter sentences for offenders. The Center on Juvenile and Criminal Justice estimates that this proposition will lead to 40,000 fewer people being incarcerated each year. Shortly after the proposition was announced, county officials in places such as San Bernardino began to express concern that they may no longer have access to the low-level inmates they need to operate their wildfire programs (Barragan 2014). This is just one example of the many ways that incarceration has become entrenched in California beyond the physical presence of prisons.

Private Prisons

Another item in the neoliberal toolkit is privatization. With massive cutbacks in state spending, the private sector can compete in arenas where the state used to operate, and the prison system is no exception. It is not surprising, then, that the Corrections Corporation of America (CCA) was awarded its first government contract in 1984, at the same time that neoliberal economic policies were being implemented. During the 1990s, the CCA began to see substantial profits, and by 1998 its stock prices had hit $44 a share. The CCA was doing so well that at the end of the twentieth century, the company began to build speculative prisons—"excess prison space for inmates who did not yet exist" (P. Wood 2007, 232)—with the expectation that the prison population would continue to grow.

At the beginning of the twenty-first century, however, rates of incarceration leveled off, and the CCA faced serious problems. Its stock values fell from $44 in 1998 to a mere $0.18 in December 2000. By 2001, the CCA had 8,500 empty beds and was over a billion dollars in debt (P. Wood 2007). Its rival, Wackenhut, also saw its stock lose a third of its value between 1998 and 2001 (Berestein 2008). Both companies had reinvested their immense profits in new prisons that were now sitting empty, and funding options seemed bleak.

Because states had cut back funding for prisons, the CCA looked to the federal government. Its federal lobbying expenses increased from $410,000 in 2000 to $3 million in 2004, and these efforts appear to have paid off. Not only has the CCA been awarded lucrative federal contracts in recent years to build new prisons, but the government has increased its rate of immigrant detention, leaving no doubt that newly built prisons can be kept full. Business has been booming for the CCA (Golash-Boza 2012).

The CCA has been able to obtain favorable government contracts in part because of its ties to current and former elected officials. The former head of the Federal Bureau of Prisons, J. Michael Quinlan, is one of the CCA's top executives. Both the CCA and its competitor Wackenhut have dominated the private prison sector because of their political influence. As Wood notes, "both benefit from extensive and intimate connections with state and local politics and the public corrections sector as well as from the usual interlocking directorships with other corporations in prison services, construction, the media and finance" (2007, 231). The enormous public and private investment in the criminal justice system has led some scholars to argue that we now have a prison-industrial complex.

The Prison-Industrial Complex

The **prison-industrial complex** (PIC) refers to the vast network of prisons, jails, courts, police officers, and other elements that purport to reduce the amount of criminal activity in our society. The PIC is a "self-perpetuating machine": the enormous investment in prisons, jails, and law enforcement, combined with the perceived political benefits of crime control, have led to policies such as mandatory minimum sentences that ensure that more people are sentenced to prison, thereby creating the need for more prison beds (Brewer and Heitzeg 2008, 637). A core feature of the idea of the PIC is that prisons are not built solely to house criminals; instead, a confluence of interests has led to the building of more prisons, the enactment of harsher laws, and the mass incarceration of poor people. Those constituencies with interests in mass incarceration include the media, private contractors, politicians, state bureaucracies, and private prisons (Davis 1998; Gilmore 2007; Schlosser 1998; Do Valle, Huang, and Spira 2006).

Ideas of racial otherness play an important role in the demonization of criminals. This otherization allows politicians to play on public fears and portray these groups as threatening public safety. As Michael Welch argues, the punitive drug control legislation passed in the last decades of the twentieth century to control crime and immigration is "not only poorly formulated, but also unjust and discriminatory against the poor and people of color" (2002, 14). Welch further contends that these laws are passed in the context of a "moral panic, a turbulent and exaggerated response to a putative social problem" (8).

The PIC relies on the production of criminals through repressive laws and the policing of communities to fill the prisons it builds (Richie 2005). The creation of increasingly strict crime laws is partly due to campaign tactics used by politicians who aim to play on fears regarding crime to capture more votes. One of the most famous examples of a politician using the fear of crime as a campaign tactic is the "Willie Horton" case. In the 1988 presidential race, George Bush's campaign played on white Americans' fear of crime and racial prejudices against blacks through the use of an ad that featured "Willie Horton." William Horton, a young black man, had escaped from prison while on a weekend pass. He then "kidnapped and brutally assaulted a white couple in their home, raping the woman and stabbing the man" (Mendelberg 1997). An ad that featured this story and a mugshot of Horton was used by the Bush campaign to portray the opposing party as being lax on crime. This ad was part of Bush's successful campaign to keep the presidency in Republican hands. This is just one of many examples of politicians using fears about crime for political gain. Notably, the Willie Horton case used both the fear of crime and the fear of black men to push forward a political agenda.

The PIC has come into being because it serves the interests of powerful groups in our society. Politicians have used a tough-on-crime approach to gain votes. The mass media have highlighted local crime in order to attract viewers (Chermak 1994). Rural areas have turned to building prisons to boost local economic development—over two-thirds of the prisons built in California between 1982 and 1998 were built on formerly irrigated agricultural land that had ceased production (Gilmore 2007, 105–106). Finally, private prisons have cashed in on growing rates of incarceration (Brewer and Heitzeg 2008; Schlosser 1998; Do Valle et al. 2006). For these reasons, not because of excessive rates of criminality, we now have over 2 million people behind bars in the United States, over ten times as many as we did prior to the 1970s. Mass incarceration of poor people has generated profits for private prisons and political capital for politicians, yet has not made this country any safer (Hattery and Smith 2006).

BEYOND INCARCERATION: COLLATERAL CONSEQUENCES

Incarceration affects most directly the 2.3 million people behind bars. It also has a great impact on the 7 million people under criminal justice supervision. Because of the lifelong stigma associated with a felony, mass incarceration also affects the 12 million felons in the United States long after they have been released from prison. Incarceration not only influences the lives of these 19 million people who have been directly involved in the criminal justice system: it also has an impact on their children, spouses, and communities. The collateral consequences of mass incarceration are indeed wide-ranging.

The Impact of Mass Incarceration on Families and Children

African American men have been disproportionately affected by mass incarceration. More African Americans are under criminal justice supervision today than were enslaved in 1850 (Alexander 2010). However, the effects of mass incarceration are not limited to these men: their mothers, wives, and children also suffer from the collateral consequences of mass incarceration. When a family member is incarcerated, often legally innocent people have to change their behavior, expectations, and living arrangements in response to the loss of a family member or friend. They also may suffer emotional or health-related consequences (Comfort 2007). Children are the most obvious victims of the incarceration of adults. Comfort reports that "an estimated 1.1 million jail and prison inmates in the United States are parents to 2.3 million children; 90 percent of these parents are fathers" (2007, 274).

Parental imprisonment deepens racial inequality insofar as black and Latino children are disproportionately its victims (Wildeman 2009). Black and Latino children face trauma and disadvantage because of parental incarceration more often than do white children (Wildeman 2009). The incarceration of a parent—usually a father—often has financial consequences for a household. This is particularly the case when the father was working, as men often are the primary or only breadwinner in a family unit. Families with an incarcerated member often have to change residence because of the loss of an income. Relocating affects family members' access to neighborhood support networks, and children may be forced to change schools (Geller, Garfinkel, Cooper, and Mincy 2009).

Some mothers choose to maintain a relationship with the incarcerated fathers of their children. However, doing so requires resources and often puts a financial strain on families, especially if they are poor (Woldoff and Washington 2008). The loss of a parent has economic costs, but there may be other costs as well. When one parent is incarcerated, the other parent may have less time and money to invest in his or her children. In addition, older siblings may find themselves with new responsibilities, from caring for younger siblings to housework to the need to seek outside employment (Foster and Hagan 2009). The stigma associated with the incarceration of parents may also be a source of shame for children (Foster and Hagan 2009).

Although women are less likely to be incarcerated than men, female prisoners are more likely to have been primary caregivers for their children. The incarceration of women thus often means that children's lives are drastically altered, as they frequently find themselves in a new home, either with their father for the first time or with their grandparents. In 1999, about 126,000 children in the United States had a mother in prison. In many of these cases, children end up in foster homes in the absence of any willing relative. When children are placed in foster care, parents face losing their children permanently. The 1997 Adoption and Safe Families Act (ASFA) mandates the termination of parental rights once a child has spent more than fifteen months in foster care (Covington and Bloom 2003).

Children with incarcerated parents have been found to suffer mental health problems such as depression, anxiety, and aggressiveness. Some even exhibit symptoms of posttraumatic stress disorder. These problems are exacerbated when a parent is incarcerated because of child or spousal abuse (Comfort 2007). Foster and Hagan (2009, 191) have "found strong evidence that the imprisonment of fathers has negative causal consequences for children." They further contend that economic disadvantages are only one of many that children of the incarcerated face: children also suffer educational and emotional disadvantages when their parents are incarcerated.

The Lifelong Stigma of a Felony: "The New Jim Crow"

There were about 12 million felons in the United States in 2005, and about 600,000 of them had been released from prison that same year. These former inmates face both legal and social exclusion. When a person is released from prison, he or she must not only figure out how to start anew with few resources, but also deal with life as a felon. In the United States, it is illegal to discriminate against people because of race, color, or national origin. However, it is perfectly legal to discriminate against a person because of a felony record. Felons can be excluded from employment, housing, voting, public benefits, and jury service. In many major cities, three-quarters of African American men have criminal records and are subject to legalized discrimination (Alexander 2010). Legal scholar Michelle Alexander (2010, 38) argues, "Today a criminal freed from prison has scarcely more rights, and arguably less respect, than a freed slave or a black person living 'free' in Mississippi at the height of Jim Crow."

Having a felony also makes it difficult for people to get jobs. Sociologist Devah Pager (2007) deployed a field experiment to find out how severe the stigma of a felony record is for people released from prison and whether the stigma varies racially. Pager sent two white applicants to apply for 150 jobs. She assigned them identical credentials, except that in some cases, the white applicant had a criminal record, and in other cases the white applicant did not have a criminal record. She found that the white person with the criminal record received a callback subsequent to a job application 17 percent of the time. In contrast, the white person without a criminal record received a callback 34 percent of the time. In other words, not having a criminal record doubled the chances of a callback for the white jobseeker.

Then, Pager sent out a pair of black jobseekers to apply for 200 jobs. In their case, the jobseeker with a criminal record received a callback in only 5 percent of cases, as compared with the non-felon, who received a callback in 14 percent of cases. What is notable here is that (1) a white felon had a better chance of getting a callback than a black non-felon; (2) a white felon was one-half as likely as a white non-felon to get a callback, whereas a black felon was only one-third as likely as a black non-felon to get a callback; and (3) black felons got callbacks only 5 percent of the time, meaning that, on average, they would have to apply for twenty jobs just to get one callback, whereas white non-felons would have to apply for only three.

Callback Percentages for Job Applicants in Pager's Study

	Black Men	White Men
FELONS	5%	17%
NON-FELONS	14%	34%

These findings led Pager to argue that because of stereotypes about black criminality, employers tend to think that a black person with a criminal record is a criminal, whereas they are more likely to see a white person with a criminal record as someone who made a mistake but is essentially a good person. Pager refers to incarceration or a felony on the record as a "negative credential" insofar as it makes it more difficult for felons to get jobs. Because of this negative credential, about 75 percent of people released from prison are unable to find work in the first year after their release.

Sociologist William Julius Wilson (2009) has argued that discrimination is no longer a determining factor for black Americans and that instead, inequality between blacks and whites can be explained largely by structural changes in the economy. Devah Pager's findings indicate that individual-level discrimination also plays a role in blacks' relatively high rates of unemployment. For African Americans, the mark of a felony on the record makes it very difficult to find employment. In addition, this mark does not go away with time.

CONCLUSION AND DISCUSSION

Legal scholar Michelle Alexander (2010) has recently made the case that mass incarceration is the civil rights issue of the twenty-first century. She contends that because incarceration has become a common life event for African Americans, and because it is legal to discriminate against felons, our criminal justice system systematically denies rights and opportunities to African Americans, effectively replacing openly racist policies of the past. According to Alexander, "today it is perfectly legal to discriminate against criminals in nearly all the ways that it was once legal to discriminate against African Americans. Once you're labeled a felon, the old forms of discrimination—employment discrimination, housing discrimination, denial of the right to vote, denial of educational opportunity, denial of food stamps and other public benefits, and exclusion from jury service—are suddenly legal" (2010, 2). As discussed previously, she even goes so far as to contend that "today a criminal freed from prison has scarcely more rights, and arguably less respect, than a freed slave or a black person living 'free' in Mississippi at the height of Jim Crow" (138). What do you think? Is mass incarceration the "New Jim Crow"?

Mass incarceration has been condoned by American voters because crime control is considered a crucial element of a safe society. However, the evidence presented in this chapter makes it clear that mass incarceration is not an effective crime control strategy. Moreover, the consequences of zealous law enforcement have been felt more deeply in already-disadvantaged communities. What if, instead of creating a safer society, mass incarceration has instead been the root cause of poverty, violence, and instability in U.S. cities?

The incarceration rate appears to have leveled off in recent years, largely because the global economic crisis has obliged states to cut back expenditures—the highest of which are related to criminal justice. In short, states do not have the budgets to incarcerate more people. But the question of whether we will witness yet another turn in the history of criminal justice is an open one.

THINKING ABOUT **RACIAL JUSTICE**

The United States has the largest prison population in the world, and black men are dramatically over-represented in our prisons. What role does racism play in this process? More broadly, what would prisons look like in a racially just society? Does the devaluation of black lives make it possible for the United States to have the largest prison system in the world? Or is our society punitive independent of racial ideologies?

Key Terms

1984 Crime Control Act 231
Anti-Drug Abuse Act of 1986 231
Anti-Drug Abuse Act of 1988 231
racial profiling 233
Reaganomics 238
neoliberalism 238
outsourcing 239
deindustrialization 239
prison-industrial complex 241

Check Your Understanding

OBJECTIVE 9.1

Examine the rise of mass incarceration in the United States and its relation to the criminalization of drugs.

- The United States has one of the highest incarceration rates in the world. Moreover, black and Latino men are disproportionately affected by harsh crime control policies.

Q Explain the trends in property crime and violent crime rates between 1970 and 2000. Compare these trends to incarceration rates. What differences do you see?

Q How do incarceration rates in the United States compare to those of other developed countries?

Q What are three reasons African American men are seven times more likely than white men to be incarcerated?

OBJECTIVE 9.2

Assess the extent to which institutional racism operates in the criminal justice system.

- The high rates of incarceration for black and Latino men can be traced to racial profiling and sentencing disparities. Racial ideologies of black male criminality have serious implications for the lives of African American men.

Q To what extent are disparities in the criminal justice system reflective of institutional racism in the United States?

OBJECTIVE 9.3

Evaluate how the rise of mass incarceration is tied to large-scale economic trends.

- Mass incarceration came about at the same time that inner cities began to lose jobs. There are profit motivations behind private prisons, and certain groups have benefited economically from mass incarceration.

Q How is economic restructuring related to incarceration and crime rates?

Q What is the prison-industrial complex?

Q What role might individual discrimination play in maintaining the high incarceration rates for African Americans?

OBJECTIVE 9.4

Examine the consequences of mass incarceration for people who are not currently behind bars.

- Mass incarceration affects the 2 million people behind bars and the 7 million people under criminal justice supervision. It also affects the 12 million felons in the United States and their families and children.

Q What are some barriers felons face when released from prison?

Q What are some ways that imprisonment affects prisoners' families?

Critical Thinking

1. What roles do individual and institutionalized racism play in maintaining the high rates of incarceration for African Americans?
2. What are some of the ways that mass incarceration affects men and women differently?
3. Why do you think police officers are more likely to conduct drug raids in low-income, black neighborhoods than in wealthier, primarily white neighborhoods?

10

HEALTH INEQUALITIES, ENVIRONMENTAL RACISM, AND ENVIRONMENTAL JUSTICE

CHAPTER OUTLINE

LEARNING OBJECTIVES

10.1 Examine the racial history of health disparities in the United States.

10.2 Describe health disparities in the United States by race and ethnicity today.

10.3 Assess the effects of environmental racism.

10.4 Examine movements for environmental justice.

Thus far we have examined racial inequalities in education, in the labor market, in housing, and in the criminal justice system. The accumulated disadvantages for non-whites, what Joe Feagin (2001) calls "systemic racism," are also found in the areas of health and the environment. Racial inequalities in the United States diminish not only opportunities for non-whites, but also the most valuable asset we have—our time on earth. A twenty-five-year-old African American can expect to live five years less than a twenty-five-year-old white American. Blacks and Latinos are much more likely than whites to live in neighborhoods with toxic waste facilities. How do we begin to make sense of the cost of racial inequality when we learn that racism literally kills?

In this chapter, we will explore the complexities of racial inequalities in health and the environment. This discussion will shed light on why blacks have lower life expectancies than whites, as well as a host of other facts related to health disparities. We will continue to consider the effects of racial ideologies by asking, How have unequal health outcomes been explained in the past, and how do these explanations relate to changing racial ideologies over time?

THE HISTORY OF HEALTH DISPARITIES IN THE UNITED STATES

Disparities in life expectancy for blacks and whites in the United States are not new. Medical treatment of African Americans during and since slavery has been at best subpar and at worst deadly. It is not difficult to imagine that the lives of people of African descent were devalued in the past, but a look into the history of health disparities and medical care also gives us insight into present-day inequalities.

Involuntary Experimentation on African Americans

During slavery in the United States, medical care was brutal and ineffective for most people. Slaves in particular suffered in innumerable ways under the care of physicians, and they had no option to refuse treatment. The accounts that remain about the treatment of slaves by southern doctors provide a window into some of the brutality slaves endured. One account is that of John Brown, who escaped from slavery and lived to tell his story.

In 1847, a former slave who had been known as "Fed" escaped to England, where he took on the name John Brown. In his memoir, Brown describes how he was subjected to medical experimentation in Georgia in the 1820s and 1830s. Dr. Thomas Hamilton had cured Brown's former master of an illness and, in exchange, asked to perform experiments on a slave. John Brown describes several sets of experiments Dr. Hamilton performed on him. The first was to subject him to extreme levels of heat in order to find a treatment for sunstroke. The next set involved letting him bleed every day. Then Dr. Hamilton burned Brown in an effort to see how deep his black skin went. Brown explained that Dr. Hamilton "also tried experiments upon me, which I cannot dwell upon" (quoted in Washington 2006, 54). We can only imagine what those experiments involved.

Dr. Hamilton's tactics, unfortunately, were not an isolated case. The famed American doctor James Marion Sims (1813–1883) is sometimes called the father of American gynecology. A lesser-known fact about Dr. Sims is that he used involuntary subjects—many of them enslaved African Americans—for experiments. During the nineteenth century, vesicovaginal fistulas (abnormal passages connecting the bladder and the vagina that often developed as a result of childbirth) were a serious problem for women of all races. In developing a cure for the fistulas, Dr. Sims carried out a series of painful operations on enslaved women.

Sims convinced the owners of eleven female slaves with the condition to lend the slaves to him for treatment. It took Dr. Sims scores of experimental operations to arrive at his cure: silver sutures to prevent infection. One of the slaves, named Anarcha, was seventeen when she came under his care in 1844. She developed a fistula and a torn vagina after a forceps-induced birth to a stillborn baby. Sims repeatedly sewed up Anarcha's vagina, yet it became infected every time, and he had to painfully reopen the wounds. Sims knew about anesthesia but refused to administer it to Anarcha or to the ten other women. When Sims began his experiments, he worked with several other doctors who helped him hold down the women as he performed the surgeries. Within a year, however, all the other doctors left, as they could not bear to hear the screams of the women. From then on, the enslaved women had to hold one another down as Sims operated without anesthesia. In 1849, Sims at last announced that he had found the cure and succeeded in repairing Anarcha's fistula. It remains unclear whether he repaired the fistulae of the other ten enslaved experimental subjects. This example is one of many situations in which treatments that would primarily benefit whites who could afford a doctor were first tried in an experimental fashion on slaves (Washington 2006).

The practice of using involuntary black experimental subjects continued after slavery and involved both live and dead bodies. In 1989, construction workers in Augusta, Georgia, uncovered nearly 10,000 human bones and skulls beneath what was once the Medical College of Georgia. This discovery led to an appalling finding: in the nineteenth century, doctors at the Medical College of Georgia had ordered porters at the college to remove bodies from nearby cemeteries for medial dissection. Most were removed from an African American burial ground. Overall, 75 percent of the bones belonged to African Americans, even though blacks made up less than half of the local population. When Harriet Washington (2006) researched the grave-robbing, she discovered that faculty at the Medical College had sent a slave called Grandison Harris to pull bodies from graves. Harris continued to work at the Medical College and to rob African American graves until his death in 1911.

Involuntary experimentation continued well into the twentieth century. One infamous example is the Tuskegee syphilis experiment. In 1932, the Public Health Service (PHS) and the Tuskegee Institute in Alabama recruited nearly 400 poor black men for a study of the long-term effects of syphilis. They determined that the men had syphilis but did not give them this diagnosis, instead telling them they would be treated for "bad blood," a nonspecific, nonmedical term. Unable to afford healthcare, these men agreed to participate in the study in exchange for free medical exams, free meals, and burial insurance. Rather than treating the men for syphilis, the PHS doctors used the study to determine what untreated syphilis would do to the body. When it finally came to an end in 1972, the unethical study had involved a total of 624 participants and lasted for four decades (Reverby 2009).

Another area of research in which blacks were disproportionately affected is the experimental use of radiation. In 1945, an African American truck driver named Ebb Cade was in a serious accident. When he arrived at the hospital in Oak Ridge, Tennessee, doctors determined that he would not survive his injuries. Unbeknown to Cade, the doctors were under contract with the U.S. Atomic Energy Commission and had been waiting for a moribund patient so that they could test the effects of plutonium, a radioactive element used in nuclear weapons and reactors. Without Cade's consent, they injected him with plutonium. The doctors' expectation was that Cade would soon die, but they hoped to keep him alive long enough to see the effects of the high dose of radiation on his body. In order to do so,

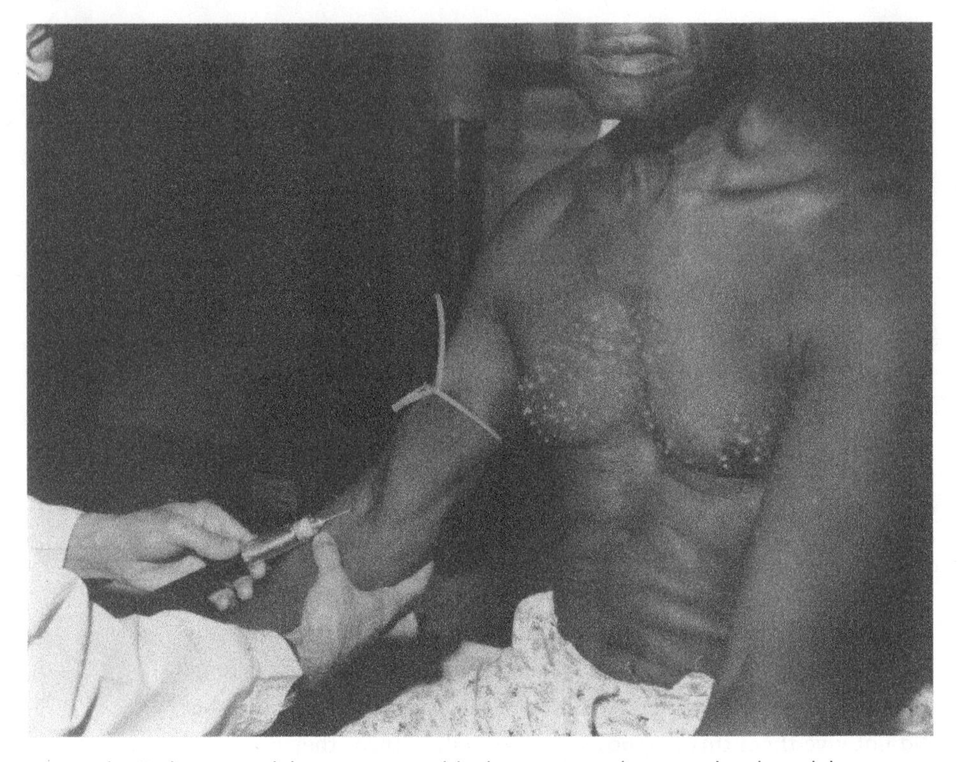

During the Tuskegee syphilis experiment, black men were diagnosed with syphilis yet were neither treated for it nor told they had it.

they extracted bone chips and pulled fifteen of his teeth. Cade recovered, however, and escaped from the hospital six months later. He returned to his home in Greensboro, North Carolina, where he died in 1953 of heart disease, unrelated to his injection (Washington 2006).

In 1953, the U.S. Department of Defense adopted the **Nuremberg Code**. Under this policy, any research subject had to be provided with information about the nature, duration, and purpose of the research before participating in it. Subjects also had to be informed that their participation in any research project was voluntary. Despite this order, approximately fifty more experimental radiation treatments on uninformed subjects occurred during the 1960s and 1970s (Washington 2006).

Free Blacks as Mentally and Physically Unfit

The 1840 U.S. census indicated that free blacks suffered from far worse mental health than either whites or enslaved blacks, reporting that whereas only 1 in 1,558 (enslaved) blacks in the South were "idiot or insane," 1 in 144 (free) blacks in the North fell into this category. People who defended slavery used these numbers to argue that blacks were incapable of self-government. These writers portrayed slavery as necessary to protect whites from mentally unstable blacks as well as to protect blacks from themselves (Washington 2006).

A few statisticians took it upon themselves to review the 1840 census data and found enormous statistical errors. For example, they found towns that reported having only three blacks total yet six insane blacks. Once these errors were made public, the U.S. Congress ordered a review. However, William A. Weaver, the originator of the census, was the person appointed to examine it; he of course declared the census to be error-free (Washington 2006).

Whites used pseudoscience to justify slavery on the basis that blacks were physically stronger than whites and that blacks would suffer mentally if they were freed. Yet "scientific" studies were also used during the postslavery era to argue that blacks were physically weak. Many pundits predicted the eventual demise of the black race based on physical unfitness. It was true that blacks were more likely to suffer from diseases. However, instead of blaming poor living conditions, lack of sanitation, and poverty for blacks' illnesses, scientists often chose to blame blacks' presumed inherent defects.

One of the most pernicious consequences of the widespread belief that blacks were physically unfit was compulsory surgical sterilization. In the early to mid-twentieth century, hundreds of thousands of black girls and women were subjected to involuntary sterilization. Women who went to the doctor for other reasons, such as an appendectomy, would later discover that they had been sterilized without their permission. In some areas of the South, involuntary sterilization of black women was so common that it became known as a "Mississippi appendectomy" (Washington 2006).

Sterilization was not unique to African Americans, and it continues to the present day. Thomas Volscho (2010) offers the concept of **sterilization racism**, which he defines as those health care policies and practices that attempt to control the reproductive capacities of women of color. Volscho argues that Native American, Latina, and black women are more likely to be sterilized than white women because health care providers see these women as incapable of controlling their own reproductive capacities. Volscho found that over a third of American Indian women had undergone a tubal sterilization in 2004, as did 30 percent of African American women. In contrast, only 19 percent of white women had undergone this procedure. Moreover, Volscho found that black and Native American women are more likely to undergo sterilization than white women even when looking only at women with similar characteristics, including marital status, income, education, and health insurance. Both Volscho (2010) and Elena Gutiérrez (2008) argue that these women are more likely to be sterilized because of stereotypes about non-white women as breeders and unfit mothers.

When we look back in history and then at our medical care system today, it is clear that disparities between whites and non-whites persist. How we decide to explain these disparities is a matter of racial ideology. Is the low life expectancy of blacks a result of their genetic makeup, or is it a result of social factors such as poverty and isolation? Is it a result of direct racial discrimination by doctors, or is it a result of institutional racism? The facts of racial inequalities are clear. For sociologists, the task is to explain them.

EXPLAINING HEALTH DISPARITIES BY RACE AND ETHNICITY TODAY

African Americans at every age are more likely than any other racial group to die, as shown in Figure 10-1. They are twice as likely as whites

FIGURE 10-1

AGE-ADJUSTED DEATH RATE BY RACE/ETHNICITY, 2009

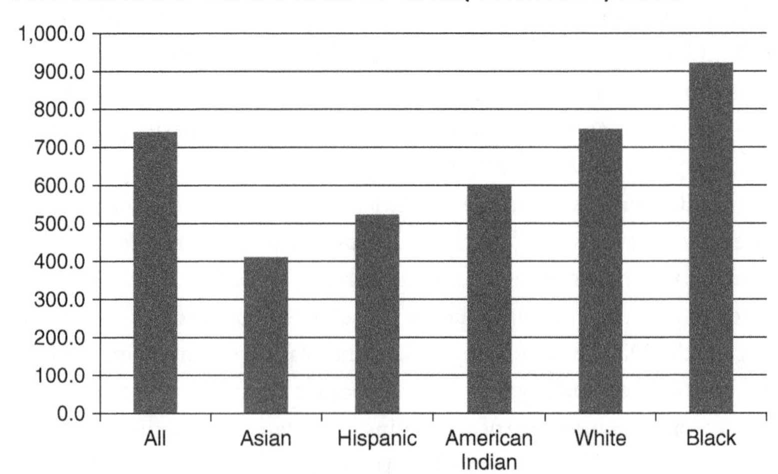

Source: Centers for Disease Control and Prevention (2011).

to die of diabetes, five times as likely to die of homicide, and eight times as likely to die of AIDS. Overall, blacks have a 32 percent higher age-adjusted death rate than whites for all causes and can expect to live about six years less than whites (American Sociological Association 2005). Sociologists have offered a range of theories to explain these and other health disparities by race and ethnicity, as we will explore in this section.

Socioeconomic Status and Health Disparities by Race/Ethnicity

First, we should note that health disparities are clearly linked to socioeconomic status. These disparities are evident in our earliest records and have been found in every country where they have been examined: people with higher incomes live longer, healthier lives. Moreover, it is not just poverty that affects health—relative poverty is also important. One way this relationship can be seen is through a comparison of life expectancies in Japan and Great Britain. In 1970, these two countries had similar life expectancies and similar levels of inequality. Over the next two decades, inequality increased dramatically in Great Britain while it narrowed in Japan. By 1990, Japan had the highest life expectancy in the world, while Great Britain's had declined (D. Williams and Collins 1995).

Every step up in income and wealth translates into an increased likelihood of having good health. However, once we begin to parse these outcomes by race, a different story emerges. African Americans do not experience the same health gains as whites do by virtue of an increase in socioeconomic status—though they do experience some health gains. There is clearly a relationship between health and socioeconomic status, but these factors work in different ways across racial and ethnic lines.

Black/white disparities do not disappear as African Americans gain more education and income. In 2008, for example, the low birth rate for black women without a high school education was 60 percent higher than it was for white women with a similar background and level of education. In contrast, the infant mortality rate for black women with a college education was 78 percent higher than it was for white women with a college education. Whereas the disparities among white women, Asian women, Native American women, and Latina women narrowed with higher levels of education, the gap actually expanded for black women (Centers for Disease Control 2011).

FIGURE 10-2

LOW BIRTH WEIGHT AMONG MOTHERS 20 YEARS OF AGE OR OLDER, BY RACE/ETHNICITY AND EDUCATION OF MOTHER, 2008

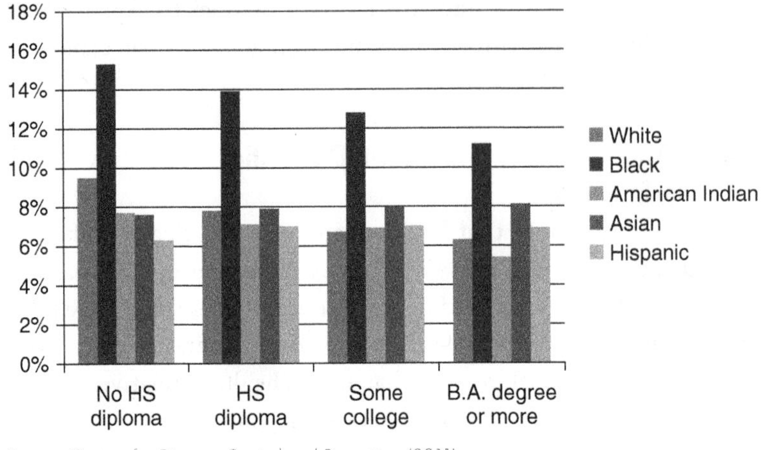

Source: Centers for Disease Control and Prevention (2011).

Studies of birth weight by race/ethnicity and level of education reveal a similar pattern. Babies born with low birth weight are at a higher risk for death, making birth weight an important factor for health scholars to consider. As shown in Figure 10-2, in 2008, blacks with college degrees were more likely than whites, Hispanics, and Asians with less than a high school education to have low birth-weight babies.

One example of health outcomes that vary by race is illustrated by the story of Jasmine Zapata, an African American medical student at the University of Wisconsin. Jasmine, studying to be a doctor, knew the importance of proper prenatal care. She neither smoked nor drank during her pregnancy and carefully followed her doctor's advice. When she felt pain in her abdomen during her twenty-fifth week of pregnancy, Jasmine knew something was wrong. When she began to bleed profusely, she mentally prepared herself to lose the baby. Jasmine's daughter, Aameira, was born shortly afterward. Weighing just over a pound, her daughter miraculously survived. Jasmine was overjoyed but couldn't help but wonder why her daughter was born prematurely (Johnson and Ghose 2011). This is a question researchers continue to ponder: Why do African American women have poorer birth outcomes than white women? Furthermore, why is it the case that health outcomes for African Americans do not improve with higher levels of income and education? If socioeconomic status alone does not explain these disparate outcomes by race and ethnicity, what does? Sociologists and public health scholars have put forth several different explanations, which we will consider next.

Segregation and Health

David Williams and Chiquita Collins (2001) argue that racial residential segregation is the primary cause of black/white health disparities because it affects the educational opportunities of children, concentrates poverty and resources, and forces many African Americans to live in environments that are unhealthy on a variety of levels. Williams and Collins suggest that segregation has adverse health outcomes for blacks because it creates "pathogenic residential conditions"—unsafe streets where people are scared to exercise, have few opportunities to buy fresh produce, see more advertisements for alcohol and tobacco, and live with higher rates of violent crime. One study in Baltimore, for example, found that neighborhoods with a high percentage of African Americans are more likely to have liquor stores than are white communities (LaVeist and Wallace 2000). People living in disadvantaged neighborhoods also have higher incidences of heart disease, diabetes, obesity, tuberculosis, infant mortality, and hypertension.

Availability of healthy food is one way that segregation can affect health outcomes. A study in New York compared East Harlem, which is 6 percent white, with the Upper East Side, which is 84 percent white. East Harlem has the highest prevalence of diabetes and obesity in New York City, whereas the Upper East Side has the lowest. The researchers who carried out the study wanted to know if stores in these neighborhoods carried foods that doctors recommend for people with diabetes. They surveyed stores to find if they had diet soda, 1 percent or fat-free milk, high-fiber bread, fresh fruit, and fresh vegetables. They found that Upper East Side stores were three times as likely to carry all of the recommended food items as East Harlem stores (Horowitz, Colson, Hebert, and Lancaster 2004).

Persons of low socioeconomic status, blacks, and Latinos all have higher obesity rates than the general population. One possible explanation for this is that they live in areas that promote obesity. Public health scholars have found that people who live close to supermarkets and have safe places to exercise are less likely to be obese. Low-income and non-white people are more likely to live far from supermarkets with healthy produce and closer to fast food outlets and convenience stores. They are also more likely to live in areas where crime is higher, making it less safe to walk around the neighborhood. By concentrating poverty and people of color, segregation can contribute to higher levels of obesity in these groups (Lovasi, Hutson, Guerra, and Neckerman 2009).

American Indians, African Americans, and Hispanics are about twice as likely as whites to be diagnosed with diabetes (Isaac 2013). These disparities are closely related to diet. What people eat is a result of their personal food preferences as well as what food is available where they live. The Tohono O'odham and Pima Indians of southern Arizona have the highest rate of Type 2 diabetes in the world—nearly 50 percent of the people in their community have diabetes. A century ago, there were almost no cases of diabetes among these American Indian tribes. What happened? The film *Bad Sugar* explains that the Tohono O'odham diet changed when the government cut off their irrigation water supply, preventing them from growing their own food. Instead of growing and eating the food they had eaten for centuries, they consumed food from the U.S. Commodity Supplemental Food Program (Adelman 2008). Prior to 1999, this program included no fresh produce. When the Tohono O'odham people began to consume large amounts of white flour, shortening, sugar, and canned foods, their diabetes rate skyrocketed. We see similar patterns, although not as drastic, in black and Latino neighborhoods, which have high concentrations of fast food restaurants and corner stores selling many more packaged, processed foods than fresh produce. Diet is influenced by what food is available, and what we eat affects our health outcomes.

The Effects of Individual Racism on the Health of African Americans

To explain why African Americans have the worst health outcomes on nearly every measure, some scholars point to racial discrimination. They argue that African Americans are disproportionately exposed to racial discrimination, that discrimination can produce stress, and that stress can lead to negative health outcomes. When African Americans experience discrimination, their responses may include anger, resentment, fear, frustration, and other stress responses. Scientists have found that these responses cause the adrenal gland to produce hormones that inhibit immune responses and increase vulnerability to disease (Clark, Anderson, Clark, and Williams 1999).

Although African Americans have higher levels of most physical ailments, it turns out they have lower levels of mental illness. Public health scholar James Jackson and his colleagues (Jackson, Knight, and Rafferty 2010) offer an explanation for this. They contend that African Americans have developed coping strategies that enable them to deal with stress (such as that related to individual racism), but that these same coping strategies ultimately have negative physical health outcomes. For example, many African Americans are confronted with stressful conditions such as poverty, crime, poor housing, and racial discrimination. In response, many engage in unhealthy behaviors such as smoking, alcohol use, and overeating of fatty foods to alleviate stress. Jackson and his colleagues found that African Americans are likely to eat comfort foods to deal with stress because fatty foods inhibit the release of certain hormones and do provide short-term stress relief. However, the consumption of these foods leads to long-term health problems, obesity, stroke, and cardiovascular disease. They argue that the consumption of comfort foods does help reduce stress in the short term, thus leading to lower levels of mental illness, but has long-term physical effects.

One effect of eating to cope with stress is obesity. About half of all African American women are obese; the rate for white women, by contrast, is 30 percent. Christie Malpede and her colleagues (2007) explored the extent to which weight-related beliefs and attitudes are linked to obesity among black and white women. When the researchers asked black women how being black affected their weight, the most common responses included the consumption of unhealthy foods and lack of exercise. In contrast, white women responded that being a white woman meant that they had distorted expectations of body type, that they thought their success depended on being thin and beautiful, and that they had negative body images. Overall, black women talked more about food choices, and white women talked more about body image when asked about their weight-related beliefs.

Life-Course Perspectives on African American Health

Health inequality increases with age across a range of outcomes. As blacks get older, they get progressively less healthy than whites and more likely to have an untimely death. Whereas black youth have fairly similar health outcomes to white youth, there is more divergence as they age. Older black adults have significantly higher levels of daily function limitations and disability than do older whites. Because of this, scholars have offered **life-course perspectives**, which focus on how health outcomes change over the life course, to explain health disparities. Two of the most accepted life-course explanations are the **cumulative disadvantage perspective** and the **weathering hypothesis**. The first explanation focuses on how disadvantages accumulate over the life course, and the second focuses on how constant exposure to stress accelerates health declines for blacks (Thorpe and Kelley-Moore 2012).

The cumulative disadvantage perspective provides a framework to explain the increasing divergence between black and white health outcomes. It focuses on the fact that many health conditions are related to stressors that accumulate over the life course. These stressors include poor nutrition, discrimination, and living in disadvantaged neighborhoods (Thorpe and Kelley-Moore 2012).

Scholars who adopt the weathering perspective contend that the health status of blacks declines more quickly than that of whites as a consequence of long-term exposure to unhealthy conditions. According to this perspective, black Americans age more quickly than whites because of the social, economic, and environmental conditions they face. The focus in this perspective is on the effects of sustained stressors—constant discrimination, financial stress, family crises, and fear—which can wear down the body in tangible ways (Thorpe and Kelley-Moore 2012).

Jan Warren-Findlow (2006) interviewed black women with early-stage heart disease to better understand how the weathering perspective could be applied to their lives. She found that two-thirds of the women she interviewed were taking antidepressants or anti-anxiety medication as a response to high levels of stress. All of the women talked about being stressed for reasons such as family problems, neighborhood violence, and financial strain. One woman explained that the stress of living "one paycheck away from homelessness" was "killing" her. Warren-Findlow argues that high levels of stress over the life course of these African American women contributed to their development of heart disease and the worsening of their condition.

A recent study found that although blacks and Mexican Americans have worse health outcomes than whites overall, Mexican Americans do not experience cumulative disadvantage or weathering in the same way that African Americans do. Instead, Mexican Americans' higher likelihood of having serious medical conditions does not increase with age (Brown, O'Rand, and Adkins 2012).

Culture and Health

Is simply being or becoming an American bad for your health? It seems it might be, as the United States ranks fairly low for a country in the developed world on a wide range of health indicators. Moreover, immigrants often have better health than their native-born counterparts. In the United States, foreign-born women have substantially better pregnancy outcomes than women born in the United States. Gopal Singh and Stella Yu (1996) found that foreign-born women have lower infant mortality rates, lower rates of low birth weight, and lower rates of teenage births than their counterparts born in the United States. However, their study found some important variations. The reduced risk for infant mortality is most pronounced among Cuban immigrants—compared with Cubans born in the United States, they have 39 percent lower risk. Black immigrants also are 25 percent less likely to experience infant mortality than native-born blacks. Overall, foreign-born blacks, Cubans, Mexicans and Chinese have lower risks for infant mortality and low birth weight than their native-born counterparts.

Health outcomes for Latinos compare favorably with those of other groups on a wide variety of measures. As shown in Figure 10-1, in 2009, the age-adjusted death rate for Latinos was lower than that of all groups except Asians, and Latina women had the lowest rates of low birth-weight babies in 2008. And even though Latinos have, on average, a lower socioeconomic status than whites, they have comparable infant mortality rates (Lara, Gamboa, Kahramanian, Morales, and Bautista 2005). Scholars have come up with many explanations for this phenomenon, which is known as the **Hispanic Paradox**.

One hypothesis to explain the Hispanic Paradox is that many Hispanics are immigrants and have better health behaviors than native-born Americans. There is some support for this explanation, but the results are mixed. Mariaelena Lara and her colleagues (2005), for example, found that Latinos who are more acculturated into U.S. society are more likely to engage in unhealthy behaviors such as eating unhealthy foods, smoking, and drinking alcohol. In contrast, there were positive factors associated with **acculturation**, or the process by which immigrants adopt the behaviors and preferences of the host society: more acculturated Latinos were more likely to go to the doctor, get preventative care, be screened for cancer, and have health insurance. Overall, the researchers found that acculturation has negative effects in terms of health behaviors, but positive effects in terms of health care usage and access.

Research by Edna Viruell-Fuentes (2007), however, challenges these findings on acculturation. Viruell-Fuentes acknowledges that Mexican immigrants often have better health outcomes than Mexican Americans, yet she argues that this is because Mexican Americans are more attuned to racial discrimination in the United States and that this discrimination leads to stress, which has negative effects on their health. Viruell-Fuentes's interviews with Mexican immigrants and Mexican Americans shed light on the differences between these two groups. Mexican immigrants are likely to live in ethnic enclaves, where they have few interactions with non-Mexicans and thus are less likely to experience discrimination. In contrast, Mexican Americans experience persistent discrimination, exclusion, and "othering" beginning in elementary school. Mexican Americans recounted to Viruell-Fuentes that they grew up feeling angry about being excluded by white Americans. This exclusion was alienating and psychologically straining. Viruell-Fuentes argues that these stressors—not acculturation—can explain why Mexican Americans have worse health outcomes than Mexican immigrants.

Genetics, Race, and Health

Although most social scientists accept that there is no biological basis for dividing humans into distinct racial groups, it can be hard to fully divorce ourselves from the idea that there are races and that they are distinct. Some medical researchers continue to hunt for genetic explanations for racial disparities in disease rates. One example is the Genetics of Asthma Lab. It is certainly true that black and Latino children are more likely to suffer from asthma than white children. Most scholars, however, would attribute that disparity to the fact that black and Latino children are more likely to live in highly polluted areas. A 2007 report entitled *Toxic Wastes and Race at Twenty—1987–2007: Grassroots Struggles to Dismantle Environmental Racism in the United States* (Bullard 2007) used 2000 census data and databases of hazardous waste facilities to find out if there were racial disparities in the location of toxic waste facilities. The authors discovered that "people of color make up the majority of those living in neighborhoods within two miles of hazardous waste facilities, and toxic neighborhoods have twice the percentage of minorities as nontoxic neighborhoods." Despite substantial evidence linking asthma and unhealthy air, some scientists insist on searching for genetic explanations for these and other disparities. What could their motive be?

A primary motive for seeking genetic explanations is profit potential. If diseases have genetic causes, corporations can design personalized medicine to cure them. In contrast, there is no profit to be found in addressing deep structural inequalities that contribute to health disparities. In *Fatal Invention,* Dorothy Roberts (2011) explains how race is increasingly being used as a proxy for genetics to explain health disparities. Rather than blame structural inequality for poor health outcomes for people of color, researchers point to race and genetics.

Myths that "black" diseases exist may also motivate some researchers to seek genetic explanations for racial disparities in health. Many people, for example, believe that sickle cell disease is a black disease, but this is not true. Sickle cell disease is common wherever malaria is common. Thus, you can find sickle cell disease in parts of Africa as well as in parts of Europe, Oceania, India, and the Middle East—all regions where malaria is common (Piel et al. 2013). In contrast, large swaths of Africa are unaffected by both malaria and sickle cell disease. If doctors were to look for sickle cell disease only in black patients, they would risk the lives of many other patients who also are vulnerable to the disease.

In terms of health outcomes, race is often used as a stand-in for a more precise genetic explanation. For example, if researchers find that a certain glaucoma drug works better for blacks, the most likely explanation is that the drug actually works better for people with dark eyes and thus could be harmful for blacks with light eyes. Or a drug found to require a low dose for Asians could be related to weight, not to Asian ancestry. When scientists find that drugs work better for some races than others, or in different doses depending on race, these racial explanations are most likely explained by another factor. Racial dosing and racial prescribing are imprecise and potentially harmful, because race is always a stand-in for another, more precise explanation (D. Roberts 2011).

ENVIRONMENTAL RACISM

As discussed earlier, African Americans and Latinos are more likely to live in neighborhoods where they have less access to fresh produce, parks, jogging trails, and healthy foods. In addition, people of color and poor people are also more likely to live close to places that can directly damage their health—toxic waste dumps, highly polluted freeways, and other environmental hazards. In this way, health disparities can be linked directly to **environmental racism**: institutional policies and practices that differentially affect the health outcomes or living conditions of people and communities based on race or color. The disparities between the living conditions of white and non-white communities are clear.

In the United States, poor people and people of color are more likely to be exposed to environmental hazards. Black children are five times more likely than white children to have lead poisoning. More than 68 percent of African Americans live within thirty miles of a coal-fired power plant, compared with 56 percent of white Americans. In 2000, neighborhoods with hazardous waste facilities were, on average, 56 percent non-white, and neighborhoods without such facilities were 30 percent non-white. In the southeastern region of the United States—the area once dominated by slaves and slave-owners—three out of four of the largest hazardous waste landfills can be found in majority black areas (Checker 2006). As shown in Figure 10-3, neighborhoods with hazardous waste facilities—called host areas—have, on average, higher percentages of people of color than non-host areas.

The placement of hazardous waste facilities affects community health. The lack of basic plumbing also has serious consequences and renders communities vulnerable to a host of diseases. In 1950, 27 percent of houses in the United States lacked complete plumbing facilities. By 2000, this percentage had dropped to 0.64 percent—a great improvement. However, nearly 700,000 households, representing 1.7 million people in the United States, continued to live without complete plumbing facilities in 2000. The lack of plumbing continues to

FIGURE 10-3

PERCENTAGES OF PEOPLE OF COLOR LIVING IN NEIGHBORHOODS WITH AND WITHOUT TOXIC WASTE FACILITIES, IN STATES WITH THE LARGEST DISCREPANCIES, 2007

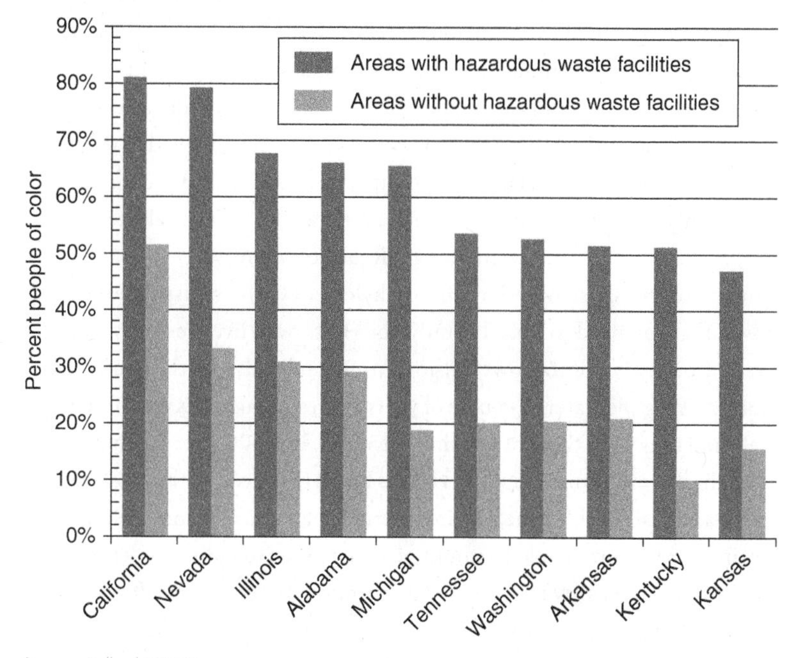

Source: Bullard (2007).

disproportionately affect non-whites. In 2000, 0.47 percent of whites lived without plumbing, compared with 1.1 percent of blacks; 1.47 percent of Hispanics; and 4.41 percent of American Indians and Alaska Natives, primarily concentrated on reservations (Rural Community Assistance Partnership n.d.).

Faced with these disparities, communities around the United States have fought to have their communities cleaned up and to gain better access to clean air, water, and soil. These struggles can be contentious, and the possible outcomes are not always clear. What does a community do when it realizes that a toxic waste dump is in its backyard? Should everyone leave? They can't, in good conscience, sell their properties, so are they stuck? As profiled in the "Voices" box in this chapter, the struggles of the Holt family in Dickson, Tennessee, put a human face on widespread environmental injustices.

voices

The Holt Family of Dickson, Tennessee

Dickson, Tennessee, is a town of 12,244 located about thirty-five miles west of Nashville. In 1946, the city of Dickson purchased seventy-four acres of land to be the city's open, unlined dump. In 1964, the Scovill-Schrader automotive company opened a plant that manufactures automotive tire valves and gauges, producing a large amount of hazardous waste. It is no coincidence that both of these hazardous waste sites were opened in the primarily black neighborhood of Eno Road. Dickson County covers nearly 500 square miles. In 2000, the town was only 4.5 percent African American. However, the only cluster of solid waste facilities in the county is located in the Eno Road community.

In 1988, government officials discovered trichloroethylene (TCE)—a suspected carcinogen—in a well that belonged to a black family, the Holts, who lived just fifty-four feet from the Dickson County Landfill. However, government officials told the family that they could continue drinking the water. A couple of years later, similar levels were found in a white family's well, and they were told not to drink the water. By 2000, every member of the Holt family had health problems, including various forms of cancer. In that same year, the Holt family well was retested. This time, Environmental Protection Agency officials found twenty-four times the recommended amount of TCE in the Holt family's drinking water. At that point, the family was given access to city drinking water—years after white families had been provided with that option.

In 2008, the Holt family filed a lawsuit against the Dickson City and Dickson County governments, seeking redress for the harm inflicted on their family by the contaminated water and racial discrimination. In 2011, the family reached a settlement with the city and county governments for over $5 million. In addition, they were awarded a $1.75 million settlement for racial discrimination, since the county had responded to complaints by white residents, but not by black residents.

This type of legal victory is relatively rare, as it can be hard to prove that disparities are the result of racial discrimination. Despite the difficulties involved in bringing lawsuits, movements for environmental justice have sprung up around the country.

Source: *Bullard 2007, 2012.*

MOVEMENTS FOR ENVIRONMENTAL JUSTICE

The struggles for better conditions in one's neighborhood have become known as the movement for **environmental justice**. Many scholars locate the beginning of the environmental justice movement in the 1980s, when primarily non-white communities began to come together and insist on their right to live in non-toxic neighborhoods. Melissa Checker (2006) traces this activism back to earlier struggles to get city services in low-income and primarily black communities. Dorceta Taylor (2009) agrees and argues that blacks' fights for lead screening, Chicano and Filipino struggles against the use of pesticides in agriculture, and Native Americans' battles for fishing rights in the 1950s and 1960s are all part of the movement for environmental justice. Environmental justice movements fight for causes ranging from the creation of parks and open spaces to clean-up efforts by toxic waste producers to clean air and water and other initiatives to improve the health and quality of life in neighborhoods.

Melissa Checker (2006) conducted an in-depth study of Hyde Park, a black community near Augusta, Georgia, that has long struggled for environmental justice. In 1970, Hyde Park residents won a two-year struggle to get sewage, paved roads, and running water in their community. In many ways, this was both an environmental battle and a battle against racism, as the conditions in the neighborhood during heavy rains were toxic, and the white neighborhoods had long had adequate city services.

In Hyde Park, the struggle for environmental justice is clearly linked to the fight for civil rights. In the late 1960s, Hyde Park residents formed an organization called the Hyde and Aragon Park Improvement Committee (HAPIC) to fight for better services for their neighborhood. This same organization survived over many decades and evolved into a movement for environmental justice during the 1990s, when it became clear that many of the nearby factories were emitting toxic chemicals and poisoning the community. Residents of Hyde Park became increasingly incensed as a junkyard in their neighborhood continued to expand—at times practically into their backyards—and when dust from a ceramics factory left white powder sprinkled on their cars and smelly waters filled their ditches during heavy rains.

Residents began to tie these environmental hazards to high rates of disease and death in their small community of 250 people. For Hyde Park residents, the environmental hazards were evident in the fact that whereas they once were able to grow bountiful gardens, their plots became less productive after the factories and junkyards moved in. In 1991, researchers from the University of Georgia confirmed their suspicions when they found elevated levels of arsenic and chromium in the local soil and produce and warned residents not to eat the produce from their gardens.

Residents of Hyde Park near Augusta, Georgia, faced a long struggle for environmental justice as factories and junkyards polluted their community.

Around that same time, residents of the neighboring Virginia subdivision filed a lawsuit against Southern Wood Piedmont—the local wood-processing plant—for contamination. Although the neighborhoods are very close and the same water travels between them, the primarily white residents of the Virginia subdivision did not include Hyde Park residents in their lawsuit.

Hyde Park residents decided to file their own lawsuit in 1991. When the Environmental Protection Agency (EPA) tested the air, water, and soil in Hyde Park, they found weak evidence of contamination. However, when HAPIC commissioned its own studies, a neuropsychologist found a high degree of neurological abnormalities among residents, and a dermatologist found a high rate of arsenical keratosis. For Hyde Park residents, it was clear that they had a high number of health issues and that their neighborhoods were toxic and filled with smelly air and water. EPA testers, however, were unable to find conclusive evidence of a connection between contamination and their illnesses. In all, Hyde Park residents filed three separate lawsuits between 1991 and 1995. One was dismissed, and fifteen years later, the other two were still pending. At the end of the twentieth century, Hyde Park residents were finally able to secure government grants to clean up the toxic waste near their neighborhood and to clear out a junkyard. The struggle for a clean environment, however, continues (Checker 2006).

How is the fight for environmental justice in Hyde Park tied to race? Many of the residents of Hyde Park interpret their experiences through a racial lens: the failure of the local, state, and federal governments to respond to their need is part of a history of exclusion that African Americans have faced since slavery. Additionally, African Americans are more likely than whites to live in toxic neighborhoods—meaning that we can tie their plight to structural racism in the United States insofar as environmental rules, laws, and policies reproduce historical racial disparities.

The struggle in Hyde Park is decidedly local: residents of this Georgia community experienced the direct effects of the emission of toxins by industrial facilities that were right in their community. They won a small victory when some of the toxic waste was cleaned up. But where did that waste go? It is conceivable that it went to another country. Ninety percent of the hazardous waste in the world is produced in industrialized nations such as the United States, Japan, and European countries. Much of it is eventually shipped to Latin America, the Caribbean, South and Southeast Asia, and Africa. In some cases, environmental clean-up in the United States can have detrimental effects on poor countries that accept the hazardous waste in exchange for much-needed cash (Pellow 2007).

The United States has only 5 percent of the world's population yet generates 19 percent of the world's waste. The waste output of residents of the United States is the highest in the world. Within the United States, there is continued controversy over what to do with the waste. One solution is to incinerate it. However, this produces incinerator ashes, which also must be disposed of. In 1986, the mayor of Philadelphia found himself with 15,000 tons of incinerator ash, and nowhere to dump it. Local environmental activists had succeeded in closing the Kinsley landfill, and Philadelphia found itself with tons of ash. The city contracted a local company to get rid of the ash, which in turn handed it over to Amalgamated Shipping, a company headquartered in the Bahamas. The shipping company loaded the ashes onto the *Khian Sea,* and the ship set sail for the Bahamas on September 5, 1986. However, officials in the Bahamas refused to accept the toxic waste, which then traveled to the Dominican Republic, Honduras, Guinea-Bissau, Puerto Rico, Bermuda, and the Dutch Antilles. Each port refused to accept the waste. Finally, in December 1987, the boat landed at Gonaives, Haiti, where the captain was able to work out an agreement with the military regime, in part because he told them the ash was fertilizer. The crew succeeded in unloading 3,700 tons of ash onto the beach before local activists and authorities became suspicious and were able to stop the dumping. The ship left Haiti, leaving the ashes on the beach. The *Khian Sea* continued its journey, unable to get rid of the waste. The ship's captain later admitted he dumped the ashes in the middle of the Indian Ocean several months later. But, the 3,700 tons of ash dumped on the beaches of Gonaives still remained. It took years of local and international activism until the toxic ash was finally removed from Haiti in April 2000.

The story of the *Khian Sea* is part of a story of global environmental injustice. Wealthier countries consume more resources than poorer ones and thus produce more waste. This global inequality is exacerbated when wealthy countries dump their waste in poorer countries. These inequalities are also drawn along racial lines: Western European countries and the United States attempt to dump their waste in Africa and the Caribbean.

CONCLUSION AND DISCUSSION

During the time of slavery, medical professionals had no qualms about using slaves as involuntary subjects in medical experiments. We no longer live in such brutal times, but the legacy remains. One hundred and fifty years after the abolition of slavery, whites continue to receive better medical care than blacks. Moreover, it is hard to say that white and black lives are equally valued when black life expectancy continues to be much lower than that of whites.

The ability to breathe clean air, eat healthy food, have access to good medical care, and spend time outside all lead to better health outcomes. In this way, the movement for environmental justice is intimately tied to the fight against health disparities.

Outright disregard for black lives informed the decisions made by industry and local leaders in the early twentieth century to place toxic waste facilities in primarily non-white neighborhoods. These same sentiments meant that black neighborhoods and towns were often the last to receive sewage infrastructure and piped water in their homes. By 2000, most communities had clean water, but non-white households continue to be the most likely to lack basic services.

Social scientists and public health scholars have provided us with the data we need to see the persistence of these disparities. These scientific studies leave little room for doubt that white Americans, on average, have better access to clean air and water and healthy communities than do non-white Americans. People of color in the United States and around the world are the most likely to have to contend with the health and environmental consequences of toxic dumping.

How do we explain these disparities? In each chapter, we have seen how racial ideologies help explain and justify inequalities. When looking at health and the environment, we can also uncover ideologies that serve this purpose, such as the misconception that African Americans are not interested in healthy eating and exercise. Such ideologies blame African Americans for their high prevalence of heart disease and diabetes while overlooking the structural reasons for health disparities, such as the lack of fresh vegetables and safe places to exercise in black neighborhoods.

One of the core values of the United States is that everyone should have an equal opportunity to flourish. How does the ideology of equal opportunity coexist with the reality that non-whites have less access than whites to education, jobs, and good health? How is this discord related to racial ideologies?

THINKING ABOUT **RACIAL JUSTICE**

WORLDWIDE, PEOPLE WITH higher standards of living have longer and healthier lives. In the United States, African Americans are on average not as healthy as whites with similar incomes. How do we think about racial justice given this context? What would racial justice look like in terms of our health and environment?

Key Terms

Nuremberg Code 254
sterilization racism 255
life-course perspective 262
cumulative disadvantage perspective 262
weathering hypothesis 262
Hispanic Paradox 263
acculturation 263
environmental racism 266
environmental justice 269

Check Your Understanding

OBJECTIVE 10.1

Examine the racial history of health disparities in the United States.

- During and even following slavery, black people were subjected to involuntary experimentation that was often brutal and had no therapeutic effects.
- Pseudoscientists described black people as physically and mentally unfit, and many black women were sterilized as a result.

Q What is involuntary experimentation?

Q Why was the Nuremberg Code important?

OBJECTIVE 10.2

Describe health disparities in the United States by race and ethnicity today.

- African Americans have lower life expectancies than whites, and racial disparities in health can be found from the womb to the deathbed. Many of these disparities are due to structural and individual-level discrimination.

Q Describe the differences in infant mortality rates for black and white women.

Q How are health disparities related to segregation?

Q Why has diabetes become a problem for Native Americans?

Q How can racial discrimination affect health?

Q What is a life-course perspective on health disparities?

Q What is the Hispanic Paradox?

OBJECTIVE 10.3

Assess the effects of environmental racism.

- Black and Latino neighborhoods are more likely to host toxic waste facilities than white neighborhoods. These facilities have negative health outcomes for the residents.

Q How prevalent is environmental racism?

Q What are some of the issues with genetic explanations for health disparities?

LEARNING OBJECTIVE 10.4

Examine movements for environmental justice.

- The fight for clean neighborhoods has come to be called the environmental justice movement.

Q How did environmental justice movements get started?

Q How is the fight against toxins in Hyde Park related to race and racism?

Critical Thinking

1. Why is it important to understand the history of health injustice in the United States?
2. How does our understanding of health disparities change when we take into account both race and socioeconomic status?
3. Is segregation at the root of health disparities? Or are there more deeply rooted causes? Explain your position.
4. What role do you think acculturation plays in explaining the Hispanic Paradox?
5. Why do you think blacks and Latinos are more likely to live near hazardous waste facilities? To what extent is this likelihood related to structural racism?
6. How are racial ideologies used to explain persistent health disparities?

GLOSSARY

1851 Indian Appropriations Act Legislation that created reservations for Native Americans and provided funds for tribes to relocate to these communal lands.

1871 Indian Appropriations Act Legislation that declared that the U.S. government would no longer sign treaties with Native American tribes.

1882 Chinese Exclusion Act The first major piece of immigration legislation; it was overtly racist in that it specifically prohibited Chinese laborers from entering the United States.

1965 Immigration and Nationality Act Legislation that put an end to the racially biased quotas set forth in the 1924 Oriental Exclusion Act and the Immigration Act of 1924. It set a universal quota of 20,000 immigrants for every country in the world.

1984 Crime Control Act This act established mandatory minimum sentences and eliminated federal parole.

1986 Immigration Reform and Control Act (IRCA) A series of immigration provisions that (1) offered a legalization option for undocumented workers living in the United States and (2) imposed sanctions on employers who hired undocumented workers.

abstract liberalism The first of Bonilla-Silva's "frames" of color-blind racism. It involves using liberal ideas such as equality of opportunity or freedom of choice to explain or justify racial inequality.

acculturation A process by which immigrants adopt the behaviors and preferences of the host society.

achievement gap The disparate educational outcomes of whites, Asians, blacks, Latinos, and Native Americans.

acting white A term used to refer to non-whites who are perceived as behaving in ways associated with white people.

adultify When a teacher or other authority figure interprets children's behavior as if they were adults.

affirmative action Policies and procedures designed to combat ongoing discrimination in schools and the workplace.

Anti-Drug Abuse Act of 1986 This act imposed even more mandatory minimum sentences. Most significantly, it set a five-year mandatory minimum sentence for offenses involving 100 grams of heroin, 500 grams of cocaine, or 5 grams of crack cocaine.

Anti-Drug Abuse Act of 1988 This act included a five-year mandatory minimum sentence for simple possession of crack cocaine, with no evidence of intent to sell.

Anti-Terrorism and Effective Death Penalty Act (AEDPA) of 1996 Legislation that, among other provisions, eliminated judicial review of some deportation orders and required mandatory detention for many non-citizens.

asset-based social policy Proactive policy, at either the individual or structural level, designed to help narrow the wealth gap.

assets Cash in the bank and the value of all property, not only land but also houses, cars, stocks and bonds, and retirement savings.

assimilation The incorporation of ethnic minority groups into the mainstream.

beauty queue A concept explaining how sexism and racism interact to create a queue of women ranging from the lightest to the darkest, in which the lightest get the most resources.

biological racism The idea that whites are genetically superior to non-whites.

biracial buddy A character type of a Westernized Asian man who uses ancient Japanese or Chinese knowledge to help whites.

bracero program A U.S. government program that brought in temporary workers from Mexico between 1942 and 1964.

Brown v. Board of Education of Topeka, Kansas Landmark 1954 U.S. Supreme Court decision in which the court determined that separate educational facilities were inherently unequal and in violation of the Fourteenth Amendment of the U.S. Constitution.

Butterfly A stereotype of an Asian woman who is a demure, devoted, and submissive wife.

Cantina Girl A stereotype of a Latina as an available sexual object.

capitalism A profit-based economic system that produces inequality.

Chinese Exclusion Act Legislation that denied Chinese laborers entry to the United States.

codeswitching The practice of alternating between Standard English and another variety of English used at home or with friends.

colonialism The practice of acquiring political control over another country, occupying it with settlers, and exploiting it economically.

color-blind ideology An ideology in which race is not explicitly acknowledged, but individual prejudices, acts of racial discrimination, and structures of inequality work to benefit whites.

color-blind racism A racial ideology that explains contemporary racial inequality as the outcome of nonracial dynamics, such as market dynamics, naturally occurring phenomena, and non-whites' supposed cultural limitations.

colorism The idea that, within races, lighter is better.

controlling images Raced, gendered, and classed depictions in the media that shape people's ideas of what African Americans are and are not.

craniometry The measurement of skulls.

cultural capital Cultural resources that offer social and other benefits.

cultural racism A way of thinking that attributes disadvantaged racial groups' lack of prosperity to their behavior and culture, rather than to structural factors.

cumulative disadvantage perspective A framework used to explain the increasing divergence between black and white health outcomes that focuses on how disadvantages accumulate over the life course.

deindustrialization The process of decline in industrial activity in a region or economy that involves a shift from a manufacturing to a service economy.

diaspora A dispersion of people from their original homeland.

racial discrimination The practice of treating people differently on the basis of their race.

dissimilarity index Measure that describes the extent to which two groups—such as blacks and whites—are found in equal proportions in all neighborhoods.

Dragon Lady A stereotype of an Asian woman as a sinister, crafty, and destructive seductress.

earnings gap Differences in annual earnings among racial groups.

embedded market A market economy embedded within interlocking systems of oppression and privilege.

employment-population ratio An estimate of the probability that a person of working age is employed, factoring in those who are not looking for work.

enlightened racism The idea that the United States is a land of opportunity and that African Americans could do better if they only tried harder.

environmental justice Efforts to ensure the right to live in non-toxic neighborhoods, regardless of race.

environmental racism Institutional policies and practices that differentially affect the health outcomes or living conditions of people and communities based on race or color.

erotic capital A concept linking the attractiveness and sensuality of a woman to her skin color.

ethnic enclave economy Clusters of small businesses that primarily serve people of the same ethnicity and work to facilitate the success of co-ethnics.

ethnicity A group identity based on notions of similar and shared history, culture, and kinship.

eugenics The practice of controlled breeding to increase the occurrence of desirable characteristics in a population.

Federal Housing Administration (FHA) Government agency established in 1934 with the purpose of bolstering the economy and, in particular, the construction industry.

Gini coefficient A measure of inequality, with 0 representing perfect equality and 100 representing perfect inequality.

global color hierarchy A worldwide system in which white (or light) skin is privileged and people—especially women—strive to become lighter.

hidden curriculum Underlying curriculum designed to reflect and promote the interests of the dominant class.

Hispanic Paradox The observation that even though Latinos have, on average, a lower socioeconomic status than whites, they have comparable health outcomes to whites.

human capital Educational attainment, skills, and job experience.

hypersegregation Instances of notably high levels of segregation.

hypodescent The idea that having any amount of black ancestry makes you black.

Illegal Immigration Reform and Immigrant Responsibility Act (IIRIRA) of 1996 Legislation under which legal permanent residents face mandatory deportation if they are convicted of "aggravated felonies."

Immigration Act of 1924/Johnson–Reed Act Legislation that greatly reduced U.S. immigration from southern and eastern Europe by introducing quotas, or limits on the number of people from these countries who were allowed entry.

Indian Removal Act of 1830 Act that enabled the administration of U.S. president Andrew Jackson to use military power to displace at least 70,000 Native Americans, killing tens of thousands in the process.

individual racism When one person discriminates against another on the basis of race or ethnicity.

institutional agent A person who occupies a position of power and is able to access or negotiate resources for others.

institutional racism Policies, laws, and institutions that reproduce racial inequalities.

intelligence testing The attempt to measure intellectual ability using scientific measures.

isolation index Measure that compares a neighborhood's demographics against citywide demographics.

Jezebel A name with biblical origins that has come to signify a stereotypically oversexed or hypersexual black woman.

Jim Crow laws A system of laws passed in the late 1800s denying nonwhites equality.

legacy admissions The practice of giving preference to the children of alumni in university admissions.

legal permanent resident A foreign national who is granted the right to remain in the United States and who will be eligible for naturalization after a period of three to five years.

life-course perspective A framework used to explain how health outcomes change over the life course.

Mammy A stereotypical image of a black maid.

McCarran Internal Security Act A 1950 U.S. law designed to combat Communism. It required members of the Communist Party in the United States to register with the federal government, and it allowed for the deportation of foreign nationals who were members of the Communist Party.

meme An idea, image, video, or phrase that spreads in a culture.

mestizo A Latin American classification of people of European and indigenous ancestry.

"model minority" myth The stereotype that Asians are the racial minority group that has "made it" in the United States.

mulatto The progeny of blacks and whites; a class of mixed-race people who are darker than whites but lighter than blacks.

nativism The presumed superiority of native-born citizens, favoring the allocation of resources to them over immigrants and promoting a fear of foreign cultures.

naturalization The process whereby people become citizens of a country where they do not have birthright citizenship.

Naturalization Act of 1790 The first piece of U.S. legislation relating to the foreign-born, stating that only free white persons who had lived in the United States for at least two years were eligible for citizenship.

neoliberalism The ideology that open markets, liberalized trade, and privatization are the keys to economic success.

new racism An ideology in which it is not acceptable to make overtly racist statements, yet racial inequality persists.

Nuremberg Code Policy adopted by the U.S. Department of Defense in 1953 under which research subjects have to be informed that participation is voluntary and be provided with information about the nature, duration, and purpose of the research.

Operation Wetback Massive roundups of Mexicans by the U.S. Border Patrol from 1950 to 1954.

oppositional culture Signithia Fordham and John Ogbu's (1986) thesis that black children receive signals from both the white and black communities that lead them to reject schooling as a route to success.

Oriental Exclusion Act of 1924 Legislation that expanded the Chinese Exclusion Act and prohibited most immigration from Asia to the United States.

outsourcing The practice of moving jobs once held by Americans overseas, where cheaper labor can be found.

pardo A Brazilian census category meaning "brown."

patriarchy A system of oppression that ensures male dominance in terms of power and property.

Personal Responsibility and Work Opportunity Reconciliation Act (PRWORA) of 1996 Legislation that denied government services and benefits to legally present migrants.

pigmentocracy A society in which blacks, Asians, and Latinos have different social statuses according to their skin color.

predatory lender A pawnshop, payday lender, or check cashing service that charges very high fees and interest rates.

prejudice The belief that people belong to distinct races and that these racial groups have innate hierarchical differences that can be measured and judged.

prison-industrial complex The vast network of prisons, jails, courts, police officers, and other elements that purport to reduce the amount of criminal activity in our society.

race A social construction to describe a group of people who share physical and cultural traits as well as a common ancestry.

racial democracy A society in which color and ethnic differences do not affect life chances.

racial enclave economy An economy in which a business' success is both shaped and limited by the racial group membership of the business owner.

racial formation As defined by Michael Omi and Howard Winant (1994), "the sociohistorical process by which racial categories are created, inhabited, transformed, and destroyed."

racial ideology A set of principles and ideas that (1) divides people into racial groups and (2) serves the interests of one group.

racial microaggression Daily, commonplace insults and racial slights that cumulatively affect the psychological well-being of people of color.

racial profiling The use of race or ethnicity as grounds for suspicion.

racial project As defined by Michael Omi and Howard Winant (1994), a way of giving meaning to racial categories through cultural representations and social structures.

racially restrictive covenants Contractual agreements that prevent the sale or lease of property within an area to non-whites.

racism (1) The belief that races are populations of people whose physical differences are linked to significant cultural and social differences and that these innate hierarchical differences can be measured and judged. (2) The practice of subordinating races believed to be inferior.

Reaganomics The economic policies of former U.S. president Ronald Reagan, involving heavy cuts to a wide variety of social programs across the country.

redlining A practice from the 1938 *Underwriting Manual* of the Federal Housing Authority in communities where home loans were not recommended were outlined in red on a map. Those communities where loans were denied were primarily African American.

residential segregation The separation of different groups of people into distinct neighborhoods.

rhetorical strategy Way of expressing ideas to justify racial prejudices and discriminatory actions.

Sapphire One of the main characters on the television show *Amos 'n' Andy*; the caricature of an angry black woman.

school-to-prison pipeline a national trend where children are funneled out of public schools and into the juvenile and criminal justice systems.

scientific racism The use of science or pseudoscience to justify racial inequality or to promulgate racial prejudice or discrimination.

segregation index Measure that describes the percentage of 88 percent non-whites who would have to move in order for the city to be fully residentially integrated.

skills mismatch hypothesis The hypothesis that African American men in particular often do not have the skills required to secure work in the current economy.

skin-color privilege The privilege of being considered more beautiful, intelligent, and otherwise superior as a result of having lighter skin.

skin-color stratification A system in which resources such as income and status are distributed unequally according to skin color.

slave codes Laws enacted in the 1660s that clearly spelled out the differences between African slaves and European indentured servants.

social capital Relationships and networks that offer social and other benefits.

social construction An idea or way of viewing people based not on biological differences but on social perceptions.

sociological theory of racism Sociological explanation for how racial inequality is created and reproduced.

spatial mismatch hypothesis The hypothesis that many African Americans live in areas where there has been a reduction in work for low-skilled workers.

split labor market A difference in the price of labor for two or more groups of laborers.

steering A practice by which real estate agents show homes in white neighborhoods only to whites and homes in black neighborhoods only to blacks.

sterilization racism Racist health care policies and practices that attempt to control the reproductive capacities of women of color.

structural racism Inter-institutional interactions across time and space that reproduce racial inequality.

subprime loan High-interest loan to someone at high risk of defaulting.

Suffering Señorita A stereotype of a Latina who suffers physical harm while protecting her Anglo love interest.

symbolic violence As described by Pierre Bourdieu (1984), the power of a socially dominant group to make its preferences, tastes, and norms appear to be superior to those of the nondominant group.

systemic racism As defined by Joe Feagin (2001), a diverse assortment of racist practices, encompassing daily microaggressions, deep-seated inequalities, historical inequalities, and anti-black ideologies.

Trails of Tears The forced displacement of the Cherokee of Georgia, the Apalachicola of Florida, the Peoria of Illinois, the Shawnee of Ohio, and a host of other tribes.

underemployment A category including jobless workers actively seeking work, people who are working part-time yet are available to work full-time, and those who have looked for work in the past year yet are not actively seeking employment.

Vamp A stereotype of a Latina who uses devious and cunning stratagems to get what she wants.

wage gap Differences in hourly earnings (wages) among racial groups.

wage of whiteness As defined by W. E. B. DuBois in 1936, psychological benefits that white workers received by aligning with the dominant group, their white bosses.

wealth The sum total of a person's assets minus debt. Wealth is built up over a lifetime and passed on to the next generation through inheritances.

weathering hypothesis A framework used to explain the increasing divergence between black and white health outcomes that focuses on how constant exposure to stress accelerates health decline for blacks.

white privilege The advantages associated with being categorized as white.

white supremacy A system of racial stratification that places whites at the top of the hierarchy.

REFERENCES

Adelman, Larry. 2008. *Unnatural Causes*. California Newsreel: San Francisco, CA.

Ainsworth-Darnell, James, and Douglas Downey. 1998. Assessing the oppositional culture explanation for racial/ethnic differences in school performance. *American Sociological Review* 63 (4): 536–553.

Ajrouch, Kristine, and Amaney Jamal. 2007. Assimilating to a white identity: The case of Arab Americans. *International Migration Review* 41 (4): 860–879.

Ajrouch, Kristine J., and Abdi M. Kusow. 2007. Racial and religious contexts: Situational identities among Lebanese and Somali Muslim immigrants. *Ethnic and Racial Studies* 30 (1): 72–94.

Alameda County Public Health Department. 2008. *Life and Death from Unnatural Causes: Health and Social Inequity in Alameda County*. http://www.acphd.org/media/53628/unnatcs2008.pdf.

Alcoff, Linda Martín. 2000. Is Latina/o identity a racial identity? In *Hispanics/Latinos in the United States: Ethnicity, Race, and Rights*, ed. Jorge Gracia and Pablo de Greiff, 23–44. New York: Routledge.

Alexander, Michelle. 2010. *The New Jim Crow*. New York: New Press.

Allen, Theodore. 1994. *The Invention of the White Race*. New York: Verso.

Alon, Sigal, and Yitchak Haberfeld. 2007. Labor force attachment and the evolving wage gap between white, black, and Hispanic young women. *Work and Occupations* 34 (4): 369–398.

Alsultany, Evelyn. 2008. The prime-time plight of Arab Muslim Americans after 9/11. In *Race and Arab Americans Before and After 9/11: From Invisible Citizens to Visible Subjects*, ed. Amaney A. Jamal and Nadine Christine Naber, 204–227. Syracuse, NY: Syracuse University Press.

Alvarez, R. Michael, and Tara L. Butterfield. 2000. The resurgence of nativism in California? The case of Proposition 187 and illegal immigration. *Social Science Quarterly* 81 (1): 167–179. http://www.polmeth.wustl.edu/media/Paper/alvar97d.pdf.

American Civil Liberties Union (ACLU). 2003. *Race and the Death Penalty*. https://www.aclu.org/capital-punishment/race-and-death-penalty.

American Immigration Lawyers Association. 2010. *Case No. CIV-10-1061-SRB*. http://www.aila.org/content/default.aspx?docid=32246.

American Sociological Association. 2005. *Race, Ethnicity, and the Health of Americans*. ASA Series on How Race and Ethnicity Matter. http://www2.asanet.org/centennial/race_ethnicity_health.pdf.

Amnesty International. 2010. USA increasingly isolated as the world turns against death penalty. *Amnesty International*, October 8. http://www.amnesty.org/en/news-and-updates/usa-increasingly-isolated-world-turns-against-death-penalty-2010-10-08.

Anderson, James, and Dara N. Byrne. 2004. *The Unfinished Agenda of* Brown v. Board of Education. Hoboken, NJ: J. Wiley & Sons.

Aoki, Keith. 1998. No right to own? The early twentieth-century "Alien Land Laws" as a prelude to internment. *Boston College Third World Law Journal* 19 (1): 37–72.

Aranda, Elizabeth M., and Guillermo Rebollo-Gil. 2004. Ethnoracism and the "sandwiched" minorities. *American Behavioral Scientist* 47 (7): 910–927.

Avila, José Luis, Carlos Fuentes, and Rodolfo Tuirán. 2000. Tiempos de estancia de los trabajadores temporales en los Estados Unidos: Situación actual y perspectivas (Length of stay of temporary workers in the United States: Current Situation and Perspectives). In La situación demográfica de México, 2000. Mexico: Consejo Nacional de Población. http://www.portal.conapo.gob.mx/publicaciones/sdm/sdm2000/13Migracion.pdf.

Baker, Wayne, Sally Howell, Amaney Jamal, Ann Chih Lin, Andrew Shryock, Ron Stockton, and Mark Tessler. 2003. *Preliminary Findings from the Detroit Arab American Study*. Ann Arbor, MI: Inter-University Consortium for Political and Social Research. http://www.ns.umich.edu/Releases/2004/Jul04/daas.pdf.

Balderrama, Francisco E., and Raymond Rodriguez. 2006. *Decade of Betrayal: Mexican Repatriation in the 1930s*. Albuquerque: University of New Mexico Press.

Balogun, Oluwakemi M. 2012. Cultural and cosmopolitan: Idealized femininity and embodied nationalism in Nigerian beauty pageants. *Gender & Society* 26 (3): 357–381.

Barnes, Mario, and Robert Chang. 2012. Analyzing stops, citations, and searches in Washington and beyond. *Seattle University Law Review* 25:673.

Barragan, James. 2014. Prop. 47 leaves future of California inmate fire crews uncertain. *Los Angeles Times,* November 12. http://www.latimes.com/local/california/la-me-san-bernardino-inmate-firecrew-20141112-story.html#page=1.

Basu, Moni. 2009. Black in America: It's not just about the color of your skin. *In America* (CNN), December 9. http://inamerica.blogs.cnn.com/2012/12/09/black-in-america-its-not-just-about-the-color-of-your-skin/.

Beck, Cheryl Tatano. 2001. Predictors of postpartum depression: An update. *Nursing Research* 50 (5): 275–285.

Berestein, Leslie. 2008. Detention dollars: Tougher immigration laws turn the ailing private prison sector into a revenue maker. *San Diego Tribune,* May 4.

Berg, Charles R. 2002. *Latino Images in Film: Stereotypes, Subversion, and Resistance*. Austin: University of Texas Press.

Berger, Bethany R. 2009. Red: Racism and the American Indian. *UCLA Law Review* 56:591–656.

Bertrand, Marianne, and Sendhil Mullainathan. 2004. Are Emily and Greg more employable than Lakisha and Jamal? A field experiment on labor market discrimination. *American Economic Review* 94 (4): 991–1013.

Bird, Elizabeth. 1999. Gendered construction of the American Indian in popular media. *Journal of Communication* 49 (3): 61–83.

Blodget, Harry. 2012. You'll feel differently about George Zimmerman and the Trayvon Martin shooting after you read this. *Business Insider,* April 25. http://www.businessinsider.com/george-zimmerman-before-the-trayvon-martin-shooting-2012-4#ixzz1t90NcZoO.

Bocian, Debbie Gruenstein, Wei Li, and Keith S. Ernst. 2010. *Foreclosures by Race and Ethnicity: The Demographics of a Crisis*. Washington, DC: Center for Responsible Lending.

Bonacich, Edna. 1976. Advanced capitalism and black/white race relations in the United States: A split labor market interpretation. *American Sociological Review* 41:34–51.

Bonczar, Thomas. 2003. *Prevalence of Imprisonment in the U.S. population, 1974–2001*. Bureau of Justice Statistics Special Report. http://www.bjs.gov/index.cfm?ty=pbdetail&iid=836.

Bonilla-Silva, Eduardo. 1997. Rethinking racism: Toward a structural interpretation. *American Sociological Review* 62 (3): 465–480.

———. 2013. *Racism Without Racists: Color-Blind Racism and the Persistence of Racial Inequality in America.* Lanham, MD: Rowman & Littlefield.

Bonilla-Silva, Eduardo, and David R. Dietrich. 2009. The Latin Americanization of U.S. race relations: A new pigmentocracy. In *Shades of Difference: Why Skin Color Matters,* ed. Evelyn Nakano Glenn, 40–60. Palo Alto, CA: Stanford University Press.

Booth, Alison L., Andrew Leigh, and Elena Varganova. 2010. Does racial and ethnic discrimination vary across minority groups? Evidence from a field experiment. Discussion Paper Series No. 4947. Bonn, Germany: Forschungsinstitut zur Zukunft der Arbeit [Institute for the Study of Labor].

Borman, Kathryn M., Tamela M. Eitle, Deanna Michael, David J. Eitle, Reginald Lee, Larry Johnson, Deirdre Cobb-Roberts, Sherman Dorn, and Barbara Shircliffe. 2004. Accountability in a postdesegregation era: The continuing significance of racial segregation. *American Educational Research Journal* 41 (3): 605–631.

Bourdieu, Pierre. 1984. *Distinction: A Social Critique of the Judgment of Taste.* New York: Routledge.

Bourricaud, François 1975. Indian, mestizo and cholo as symbols in the Peruvian system of stratification. In *Ethnicity: Theory and Experience,* ed. Nathan Glazer and Daniel Moynihan, 350–387. Cambridge, MA: Harvard University Press.

Bowles, Samuel, and Herbert Gintis. 1976. *Schooling in capitalist America.* Vol. 57. New York: Basic Books.

Bowser, Frederick P. 1974. *The African Slave in Colonial Peru, 1524–1650.* Stanford, CA: Stanford University Press.

Brewer, Rose M., and Nancy Heitzeg. 2008. The racialization of crime and punishment: Criminal justice, color-blind racism, and the political economy of the prison industrial complex. *American Behavioral Scientist* 51 (5): 625–644.

Brodkin, Karen. 1998. *How Jews Became White Folks and What That Says About Race in America.* New Brunswick, NJ: Rutgers University Press.

———. 2005. How Jews became white folks. In *White Privilege: Essential Readings on the Other Side of Racism,* 2nd ed., ed. Paula S. Rothenberg, 41–54. New York: Worth.

Brooks, Roy L. 2009. *Racial Justice in the Age of Obama.* Princeton, NJ: Princeton University Press.

Brooks, Siobhan 2010. Hypersexualization and the dark body: Race and inequality among black and Latina women in the exotic dance industry. *Sexuality Research and Social Policy* 7 (2): 70–80.

Brown, Tyson H., Angela M. O'Rand, and Daniel E. Adkins. 2012. Race-ethnicity and health trajectories: Tests of three hypotheses across multiple groups and health outcomes. *Journal of Health and Social Behavior* 53 (3): 359–377.

Brown v. Board of Education. 347, U.S. 483 (1954). Appeal from the United States District Court for the District of Kansas. Online at: http://caselaw.lp.findlaw.com/scripts/getcase.pl?court=US&vol=347&invol=483.

Browne, Irene, and Joya Misra. 2003. The intersection of gender and race in the labor market. *Annual Review of Sociology* 29:487–513.

Bullard, Robert D. 2007. *Toxic Wastes and Race at Twenty—1987–2007: Grassroots Struggles to Dismantle Environmental Racism in the United States.* Report prepared for the United Church of Christ Justice & Witness Ministries.

———. 2012. Earth Day 2012: Toxic environmental racism in Tennessee threatens family. *Racism Review,* April 22. http://www.racismreview.com/blog/2012/04/22/earth-day-2012-toxic-environmental-racism-in-tennessee-threatens-family/.

Bureau of Justice Statistics. 2009. Correctional populations in the United States, 2009; prisoners in 2009; jail inmates at midyear 2009—statistical tables; and probation and parole in the United States, 2009. Table 348. Washington, DC: U.S. Department of Justice. http://www.census.gov/compendia/statab/2012/tables/12s0348.pdf.

———. 2010 National Crime Victimization Survey, violent crime trends, 1973–2009. *Key Facts at a Glance*. Washington, DC: U.S. Department of Justice. http://bjs.ojp.usdoj.gov/content/glance/tables/viortrdtab.cfm.

Bureau of Labor Statistics. 2012. Economic report 2012. Table B-42. Civilian unemployment rate, 1965–2011. Washington, DC: U.S. Department of Labor. http://www.gpo.gov/fdsys/granule/ERP-2012/ERP-2012-table42/content-detail.html.

———. 2013a. American Time Use Survey summary. Washington, DC: U.S. Department of Labor. http://www.bls.gov/news.release/atus.nr0.htm.

———. 2013b. Median weekly earnings, second quarter 2013. *Editor's Desk*, July 24. Washington, DC: U.S. Department of Labor. http://www.bls.gov/opub/ted/2013/ted_20130724.htm.

Burgess, Melinda C. R., Karen E. Dill, S. Paul Stermer, Stephen R. Burgess, and Brian P. Brown. 2011. Playing with prejudice: The prevalence and consequences of racial stereotypes in video games. *Media Psychology* 14 (3): 37–41.

Calavita, Kitty. 2000. The paradoxes of race, class, identity, and "passing": Enforcing the Chinese Exclusion Acts, 1882–1910. *Law & Social Inquiry* 251:1–40.

Canaday, Neil, Charles Reback, and Kristin Stowe. n.d. *The Southern Homestead Act: Race, Literacy, and Learning*. http://history.appstate.edu/sites/history.appstate.edu/files/Neil%20Canaday.pdf.

Carson, Clayborne 1981. *In Struggle: SNCC and the Black Awakening of the 1960s*. Cambridge, MA: Harvard University Press.

Carter, Prudence L. 2003. Black cultural capital, status positioning, and schooling conflicts for low-income African American youth. *Social Problems* 50 (1): 136–155.

Cave, Alfred. 2003. Abuse of power: Andrew Jackson and the Indian Removal Act of 1830. *Historian* 65 (6): 1330–1353. http://onlinelibrary.wiley.com/doi/10.1111/j.0018-2370.2003.00055.x/full.

Centers for Disease Control and Prevention. 2011. Table 10. Low Birthweight Live Births Among Mothers 20 Years of Age and Over, by Detailed Race, Hispanic Origin, and Education of Mother: United States, Selected Reporting Areas 2007 and 2008. http://www.cdc.gov/nchs/data/hus/2011/010.pdf.

Charles, Christopher A. D. 2009. Skin bleachers' representations of skin color in Jamaica. *Journal of Black Studies* 40 (2): 153–170.

———. 2011. The derogatory representations of the skin bleaching products sold in Harlem. *Journal of Pan African Studies* 4 (4): 117–141.

Charles, Camille Zubrinsky 2003. The dynamics of racial residential segregation. *Annual Review of Sociology* 29:167–207.

Checker, Melissa. 2006. *Polluted Promises: Environmental Racism and the Search for Justice in a Southern Town*. New York: New York University Press.

Chermak, Steven M. 1994. Body count news: How crime is presented in the news media. *Justice Quarterly* 11 (4): 561–582.

Churchill, Ward. 2002. *Struggle for the Land: Native North American Resistance to Genocide, Ecocide, and Colonization*. New York: City Lights.

Cimbala, Paul A. 1989. The Freedmen's Bureau, the freedmen, and Sherman's grant in reconstruction Georgia, 1865–1867. *Journal of Southern History* 55 (4): 597–632.

Clark, Rodney, Norman B. Anderson, Vernessa R. Clark, and David R. Williams. 1999. Racism as a stressor for African Americans: A biopsychosocial model. *American Psychologist* 54 (10): 805–816.

Cochran, David Carroll 1999. *The Color of Freedom: Race and Contemporary American Liberalism*. Albany: SUNY Press.

Collins, Patricia Hill. 2004. *Black Sexual Politics*. New York: Routledge.

Collins, Randall. 2004. Lenski's power theory of economic inequality: A central neglected question in stratification research. *Sociological Theory* 22 (2): 219–228.

Comfort, Megan. 2007. Punishment beyond the legal offender. *Annual Review of Law & Social Sciences* 3:271–296.

Committee on the Elimination of Racial Discrimination (CERD) Working Group on Health and Environmental Health. 2005. *Unequal Health Outcomes in the United States: Racial and Ethnic Disparities in Health Care Treatment and Access, the Role of Social and Environmental Determinants of Health, and the Responsibility of the State*. Report to the UN Committee on the Elimination of Racial Discrimination. http://www.prrac.org/pdf/CERDhealthEnvironmentReport.pdf.

Copeland, Libby. 2000. Kemba Smith's hard time. *Washington Post*, February 13. http://www.washingtonpost.com/wp-dyn/articles/A46891-2000Feb13.html.

Cornell, Stephen, and Douglas Hartmann. 1998. *Ethnicity and race: Making identities in a changing world*. Thousand Oaks: Pine Forge Press.

Covington, Stephanie, and Barbara Bloom. 2003. Gendered justice: Women in the criminal justice system. In *Gendered Justice: Addressing Female Offenders*, ed. Barbara E. Bloom, 3–24. Durham, NC: Carolina Academic Press.

Crenshaw, Kimberle. 1991. Mapping the margins: Intersectionality, identity politics, and violence against women of color. *Stanford Law Review* 43 (6): 1241–1299.

Dalton, Harlon. 2005. Failing to see. In *White Privilege: Essential Readings on the Other Side of Racism*, 2nd ed., ed. Paula S. Rothenberg, 15–18. New York: Worth.

Dalmage, Heather. 2000. *Tripping on the Color Line: Black-White Multiracial Families in a Racially Divided World*. New Brunswick, NJ: Rutgers University Press.

Daniels, Jessie. 2008. Race, civil rights, and hate speech in the digital era. In *Learning Race and Ethnicity: Youth and Digital Media*, ed. Anna Everett, 129–154. Cambridge, MA: MIT Press.

Darity, William. 2008. "Forty Acres and a Mule in the 21st Century" *Social Science Quarterly* 89: 3: 656–664.

Davis, Angela. 1998. Masked racism: Reflections on the prison industrial complex. *Colorlines* 2. http://www.colorlines.com/article.php?ID=309&p=1.

Demos. 2011. *The Great Unraveling: A Portrait of the Middle Class*. http://www.demos.org/sites/default/files/publications/Great_Unraveling_MiddleClass_Demos.pdf.

Diamond, Sara. 1996. Right-wing politics and the anti-immigration cause. *Social Justice* 23 (3): 154–169.

Dorman, Jacob S. 2011. Skin bleach and civilization: The racial formation of blackness in 1920s Harlem. *Journal of Pan African Studies* 4 (4): 47–80.

Do Valle, Alice, Vanessa Huang, and Mari Spira. 2006. The prison industrial complex: A deliberation. *International Feminist Journal of Politics* 8 (1): 130–144.

Dow, Mark. 2005. *American Gulag: Inside U.S. Immigration Prisons*. Berkeley: University of California Press.

Dowell v. Board of Education of Oklahoma City Public Schools, 778 F. Supp. 1144 (W.D. Okla. 1991).

Dozier, Raine. 2010. Accumulating disadvantage: The growth in the black–white wage gap among women. *Journal of African American Studies* 14 (3): 279–301.

D'Souza, Dinesh. 2009. Obama and post-racist America. *Townhall.com*, January 28. http://townhall.com/columnists/dineshdsouza/2009/01/28/obama_and_post-racist_america/page/full.

Duany, Jorge. 1998. Reconstructing racial identity: Ethnicity, color, and class among Dominicans in the United States and Puerto Rico. *Latin American Perspectives* 25:147–172.

Du Bois, William Edward Burghardt, ed. 1904. *Some Notes on Negro Crime, Particularly in Georgia*. Atlanta: Atlanta University Press.

Dymski, Gary, Jesus Hernandez, and Lisa Mohanty. 2013. "Race, gender, power, and the US subprime mortgage and foreclosure crisis: A meso analysis." *Feminist Economics* 19: 3: 124–151.

Eckstein, Susan, and Lorena Barberia. 2002. Grounding immigrant generations in history: Cuban Americans and their transnational ties. *International Migration Review* 36 (3): 799–837.

Edwards, Korie, Katrina Carter-Tellison, and Cedric Herring. 2004. For richer, for poorer, whether dark or light: Skin tone, marital status, and spouse's earnings. In *Skin Deep: How Race and Complexion Matter in the "Color-Blind" Era*, ed. Cedric Herring, Verna M. Keith, and Hayward Derrick Horton, 65–81. Urbana and Chicago: University of Illinois Press.

eMarketer. 2013. Digital set to surpass TV in time spent with US media. *eMarketer*, August 1. http://www.emarketer.com/Article/Digital-Set-Surpass-TV-Time-Spent-with-US-Media/1010096#Ecc1XKrIcD8corwo.99.

Everett, Anna, and S. Craig Watkins. 2008. The power of play: The portrayal and performance of race in video games. In *The Ecology of Games: Connecting Youth, Games, and Learning*, ed. Katie Salen, 141–166. Cambridge, MA: MIT Press.

Eze, Emmanuel Chukwudi, ed. 1997. *Race and the Enlightenment*. Cambridge, MA: Blackwell.

Feagin, Joe. 2001. *Racist America: Roots, Current Realities, and Future Reparations*. New York: Routledge.

Feagin, Joe, and Sean Elias. 2013. Rethinking racial formation theory: A systemic racism critique. *Ethnic and Racial Studies* 36 (6): 931–960.

Feagin, Joe R., and Karyn D. McKinney. 2003. *The Many Costs of Racism*. Lanham, MD: Rowman & Littlefield.

Ferguson, Ann Arnett. 2001. *Bad Boys: Public Schools in the Making of Masculinity*. Ann Arbor: University of Michigan Press.

Ferguson, Kenlana R. 2012. In their own words: The lived experiences of unemployed African American men. Ph.D. diss., Western Michigan University. http://scholarworks.wmich.edu/cgi/viewcontent.cgi?article=1083&context=dissertations.

Field, Tiffany. 2008. Postpartum depression effects on early interactions, parenting, and safety practices: A review. *Infant Behavior and Development* 33:1–6.

Foner, Nancy. 2008. Gender and migration: West Indians in comparative perspective. *International Migration* 47 (1): 3–29.

Fordham, Signithia, and John U. Ogbu. 1986. Black students' school success: Coping with the "burden of acting white." *Urban Review* 18 (3): 176–206.

Foster, Holly, and John Hagan. 2009. The mass incarceration of parents in America: Issues of race/ethnicity, collateral damage to children, and prisoner reentry. *Annals of the American Academy of Political and Social Science* 623 (1): 179–194.

Fragomen, Austin T., and Steven Bell. 2007. *Immigration Fundamentals: A Guide to Law and Practice*. New York: Practicing Law Institute.

Frank, Reanne, Ilana Redstone Akresh, and Bo Lu. 2010. Latino immigrants and the U.S. racial order: How and where do they fit in? *American Sociological Review* 75 (3): 378–401.

Frankenberg, Ruth. 1993. *White Women, Race Matters: The Social Construction of Whiteness*. Minneapolis: University of Minnesota Press.

———. 1997. *Displacing Whiteness: Essays in Social and Cultural Criticism*. Durham, NC: Duke University Press.

Franklin, John Hope. 1974. *From Slavery to Freedom*. New York: Alfred A. Knopf.

Franklin, John Hope, and Alfred A. Moss. 2000. *From Slavery to Freedom: A History of African Americans*, 8th ed. New York: Alfred A. Knopf.

Freeman, Donald. G. 2011. "On (not) Closing the Gaps: The Evolution of National and Regional Unemployment Rates by Race and Ethnicity" Sam Houston State University Department of Economics and International Business Working Paper Series. Working Paper No. 11-01 Online at: http://www.shsu.edu/~tcq001/paper_files/wp11-01_paper.pdf.

Friedman, Samantha, and Gregory D. Squires. 2005. "Does the community reinvestment act help minorities access traditionally inaccessible neighborhoods?." *Social Problems* 52: 2: 209–231.

Frost, Peter. 2006. Skin color preference in sub-Saharan Africa. *Evo and Proud*, December 21. http://evoandproud.blogspot.com/2006/12/skin-color-preference-in-sub-saharan.html.

Fry, Richard, and Paul Taylor. 2013. *Hispanic High School Graduates Pass Whites in Rate of College Enrollment*. Washington, DC: Pew Research Center, Pew Hispanic Center. http://www.pewhispanic.org/files/2013/05/PHC_college_enrollment_2013-05.pdf.

Gamoran, Adam. 2001. American schooling and educational inequality: A forecast for the 21st century. *Sociology of Education* 74:135–153.

García, Maria Elena. 2005. *Making Indigenous Citizens: Identities, Education, and Multicultural Development in Peru*. Stanford, CA: Stanford University Press.

Garrison, Vivian, and Carol I. Weiss. 1979. Dominican family networks and United States immigration policy: A case study. *International Migration Review* 13:264–283.

Geller, Amanda, Irwin Garfinkel, Carey E. Cooper, and Ronald B. Mincy. 2009. Parental incarceration and child well-being: Implications for urban families. *Social Science Quarterly* 90 (5): 1186–1202.

Gelman, Andrew, Jeffrey Fagan, and Alex Kiss. 2007. An analysis of the New York City police department's "stop-and-frisk" policy in the context of claims of racial bias. *Journal of the American Statistical Association* 102:479.

Gilmore, Ruth. 2007. *Golden Gulag: Prisons, Surplus, Crisis and Opposition in Globalizing California*. Berkeley: University of California Press.

Glaze, Lauren. 2010. Correctional population in the United States, 2009. *Bureau of Justice Statistics Bulletin* December. http://www.bjs.gov/content/pub/pdf/cpus09.pdf.

Glennie, Alex, and Laura Chappell. 2010. Jamaica: From diverse beginning to diaspora in the developed world. *Migration Information Source*. http://www.migrationpolicy.org/article/jamaica-diverse-beginning-diaspora-developed-world.

Glover, Nii-Odoi. 2010. Chipped away. In *12 Angry Men: True Stories of Being a Black Man in America Today*, ed. Gregory S. Parks and Matthew Hughey, 71–86. New York: New Press.

Godfrey, Phoebe C. 2008. The "other white": Mexican Americans and the impotency of whiteness in the segregation and desegregation of Texan public schools. *Equity & Excellence in Education* 41 (2): 247–261.

Golash-Boza, Tanya. 2010. "Had they been polite and civilized, none of this would have happened": Discourses of race and racism in multicultural Lima. *Latin American and Caribbean Ethnic Studies* 5 (3): 317–330.

———. 2011a. *Yo Soy Negro: Blackness in Peru*. Gainesville: University Press of Florida.

———. 2011b. Treat them like criminals. *Social Scientists on Immigration Policy*, November 8. http://stopdeportationsnow.blogspot.com/2011/11/treat-them-like-criminals.html.

———. 2012. *Immigration Nation: Raids, Detentions, and Deportations in the United States*. Boulder, CO: Paradigm.

Golash-Boza, Tanya, and William Darity, Jr. 2008. Latino racial choices: The effects of skin colour and discrimination on Latinos' and Latinas' racial self-identifications. *Ethnic and Racial Studies* 31 (5): 899–934.

Golash-Boza, Tanya, and Pierrette Hondagneu-Sotelo. 2013. "Latino immigrant men and the deportation crisis: A gendered racial removal program." *Latino Studies* 11: 3: 271–292.

Golland, David. 2011. *Constructing Affirmative Action: The Struggle for Equal Employment Opportunity*. Lexington: University Press of Kentucky.

Gómez, Christina. 2008. Brown outs: The role of skin color and Latinas. In *Racism in the 21st Century: An Empirical Analysis of Skin Color*, ed. Ronald E. Hall, 193–204. New York: Springer.

Gómez, Laura. 1992. The birth of the "Hispanic" generation: Attitudes of Mexican-American political elites toward the Hispanic label. *Latin American Perspectives* 19 (4): 45–58.

Gonzales, Juan L., Jr. 1986. Asian Indian immigration patterns: The origins of the Sikh community in California. *International Migration Review* 20:40–54.

Gotham, Kevin Fox. 2000. Urban space, restrictive covenants and the origins of racial residential segregation in a US city, 1900–50. *International Journal of Urban and Regional Research* 24 (3): 616–633.

Gould, Stephen Jay. 1996. *The Mismeasure of Man*. New York: W. W. Norton & Company.

Graham, Richard, ed. 1990. *The Idea of Race in Latin America, 1870–1940*. Austin: University of Texas Press.

Gray, Herman. 1995. *Watching Race: Television and the Struggle for "Blackness."* Minneapolis: University of Minnesota Press.

Greenman, Emily, and Yu Xie. 2008. Double jeopardy? The interaction of gender and race on earnings in the United States. *Social Forces* 86 (3): 1217–1244.

Guerrero, Ed. 1993. *Framing Blackness*. Philadelphia: Temple University Press.

Guillory, Raphael M. 2009. American Indian/Alaska Native college student retention strategies. *Journal of Developmental Education* 33 (2): 14–40. http://homepages.se.edu/native-american-center/files/2012/04/American-Indian-Alaska-Native-College-Student-Retention-Strategies1.pdf.

Gutiérrez, Elena R. 2008. *Fertile Matters: The Politics of Mexican-Origin Women's Reproduction*. Austin: University of Texas Press.

Hamamoto, Darrell. 1994. *Monitored Peril: Asian Americans and the Politics of TV Representation*. Minneapolis and London: University of Minnesota Press.

Hamilton, Nora, and Norma Stoltz Chinchilla. 1991. Central American migration: A framework for analysis. *Latin American Research Review* 26:75–110.

Haney-Lopez, Ian. 2006. *White by Law: The Legal Construction of Race*. New York: New York University Press.

Harper, Shaun R., and Sylvia Hurtado. 2007. Nine themes in campus racial climates and implications for institutional transformation. *New Directions for Student Services* 120:7–24.

Harper, Shaun R., Ryan J. Davis, David E. Jones, Brian L. McGowan, Ted N. Ingram, and C. Spencer Platt. 2011. Race and racism in the experiences of black male resident assistants at predominantly white universities. *Journal of College Student Development* 52 (2): 180–200.

Harris, David A. 1999. *Driving While Black: Racial Profiling on Our Nation's Highways*. American Civil Liberties Union Special Report. Washington, DC: American Civil Liberties Union. https://www.aclu.org/racial-justice/driving-while-black-racial-profiling-our-nations-highways.

Harris-Perry, Melissa V. 2011. *Sister Citizen: Shame, Stereotypes, and Black Women in America*. New Haven, CT: Yale University Press.

Hart, Carl L. 2014. *High Price: A Neuroscientist's Journey of Self-Discovery That Challenges Everything You Know About Drugs and Society.* Harper: New York.

Harvey, David 2005. *A Brief History of Neoliberalism.* New York: Oxford University Press.

Harvey Wingfield, Adia, and Joe R. Feagin. 2010. *Yes We Can? White Racial Framing and the 2008 Presidential Campaign.* New York: Routledge.

Hattery, Angela, and Earl Smith. 2006. The prison industrial complex. *Sociation Today* 4 (2). http://www.ncsociology.org/sociationtoday/v42/prison.htm.

Hernandez, Kelly Lytle. 2010. *Migra: A History of the U.S. Border Patrol.* Berkeley and Los Angeles: University of California Press.

Hernández, Ramona. 2004. On the age against the poor: Dominican migration to the United States. *Journal of Immigrant & Refugee Services* 2 (1–2): 87–107.

Herrnstein, Richard, and Charles Murray. 1994. *The Bell Curve.* New York: The Free Press.

Hersch, Joni. 2008. Skin color, immigrant wages, and discrimination. In *Racism in the 21st Century: An Empirical Analysis of Skin Color,* ed. Ronald E. Hall, 77–92. New York: Springer.

Herskovitz, Melville. 1928. *The American Negro: A Study in Racial Crossing* New York: Knopf.

Hochschild, Jennifer, and Vesla Weaver. 2007. The skin color paradox and the American racial order. *Social Forces* 86 (2): 643–670.

Hoefer, Michael, Nancy F. Rytina, and Christopher Campbell. 2007. *Estimates of the Unauthorized Immigrant Population Residing in the United States: January 2006.* Department of Homeland Security, Office of Immigration Statistics.

Hondagneu-Sotelo, Pierrette. 1994. *Gendered Transitions: Mexican Experiences of Immigration.* Berkeley: University of California Press.

———. 1995. Women and children first: New directions in anti-immigrant politics. *Socialist Review* 251:169–190

Horowitz, Carol R., Kathryn A. Colson, Paul L. Hebert, and Kristie Lancaster. 2004. Barriers to buying healthy foods for people with diabetes: Evidence of environmental disparities. *American Journal of Public Health* 94 (9): 1549–1554.

Howell, Elizabeth A., Pablo A. Mora, Carol R. Horowitz, and Howard Leventhal. 2005. Racial and ethnic difference in factors associated with early postpartum depressive symptoms. *Obstetrics & Gynecology* 105 (6): 1442–1450.

Human Rights Watch. 2009. *Forced Apart (By the Numbers): Non-Citizens Deported Mostly for Non-Violent Offenses.* New York: Human Rights Watch. www.hrw.org/node/82173.

Humes, Karen R., Nicholas A. Jones, and Roberto R. Ramirez. 2011. "Overview of race and Hispanic origin: 2010." US Census Bureau. Online at: http://www.census.gov/prod/cen2010/briefs/c2010br-02.pdf.

Hunt, Darnell M. 2005. Black content, white control. In *Channeling Blackness: Studies on Television and Race in America,* ed. D. M. Hunt, 267–302. New York: Oxford University Press.

Hunter, Margaret. 2005. *Race, Gender, and the Politics of Skin Tone.* New York: Routledge.

———. 2007. The persistent problem of colorism: Skin tone, status, and inequality. *Sociology Compass* 1 (1): 237–254.

Hurwitz, Michael. 2011. The impact of legacy status on undergraduate admissions at elite colleges and universities. *Economics of Education Review* 30.3: 480–492.

Huyser, Kimberly R., Arthur Sakamoto, and Isao Takei. 2009. The persistence of racial disadvantage: The socioeconomic attainments of single-race and multi-race Native Americans. *Population Research and Policy Review* 29 (4): 541–568.

Immigration Law Group @ Baurkot & Baurkot. 2011. *Robert Bautista v. Attorney General of the United States of America: Third Circuit Court Indefinitely Stops Dominican Immigrant's*

Deportation in Recent Decision. http://www.jdsupra.com/legalnews/third-circuit-court-indefinitely-stops-d-90641/

Inda, Jonathan Xavier. 2006. *Targeting Immigrants: Government, Technology, and Ethics*. New York: John Wiley & Sons.

Internationalcomparison.org. 2014. International comparisons. http://www.internationalcomparison.org/intl_comp_files/sheet006.htm.

Independent School District v. Salvatierra, 284 U.S. 580, 52 S. Ct. 28, 76 L. Ed. 503 (Supreme Court 1931).

International Labor Organization. 2013. *World of Work Report: Repairing the Economic and Social Fabric*. Geneva: International Institute for Labor Studies.

Isaac, Lydia A. 2013. Defining health and health care disparities and examining disparities across the life span. In *Race, Ethnicity, and Health: A Public Health Reader*, eds. Thomas LaVeist and Lydia A. Isaac, 11–33. San Francisco, CA: Jossey-Bass Publishers Inc.

Isacson, Adam. 2013. Adam Isacson's Latin America Blog. *Adam Isacson's Latin American Blog*, January 22. http://thisisadamsblog.com/post/41220961868/take-the-annual-income-of-the-wealthiest-20.

Jackson, James S., Katherine M. Knight, and Jane A. Rafferty. 2010. Race and unhealthy behaviors: Chronic stress, the HPA axis, and physical and mental health disparities over the life course. *American Journal of Public Health* 100 (5): 933–939.

Jacobson, Matthew. 1998. *Whiteness of a Different Color*. Cambridge, MA: Harvard University Press.

Jacobson, Robin Dale. 2008. *The New Nativism: Proposition 187 and the Debate Over Immigration*. Minneapolis: University of Minnesota Press.

Jefferson, Thomas. 1787. *Notes on the State of Virginia*. Digireads.com Publishing, 2004.

Jhally, Sut, and Justin Lewis. 1992. *Enlightened Racism: The Cosby Show, Audiences and the Myth of the American Dream*. Boulder, CO: Westview.

Johnson, Kevin. 2004. *The "Huddled Masses" Myth: Immigration and Civil Rights*. Philadelphia: Temple University Press.

———. 2005. The forgotten "repatriation" of persons of Mexican ancestry and lessons for the "War on Terror." Fifteenth Annual Dyson Distinguished Lecture. White Plains, NY: Pace Law School.

Johnson, Mark, and Tia Ghose. 2011. Is stress to blame for preterm births? *Milwaukee Journal Sentinel*, April 16. http://www.jsonline.com/news/health/119987024.html.

Jones, David S. 2003. Virgin soils revisited. *William and Mary Quarterly* 60 (4): 703–742.

Joppke, Christian. 1998. Why liberal states accept unwanted immigration. *World Politics* 50:266–293.

Jordan, Winthrop. 1968. *White over Black*. Chapel Hill: University of North Carolina Press.

Kahlenberg, Richard D. 2010. *Affirmative action for the rich: Legacy preferences in college admissions*. New York: Century Foundation Press.

Kandaswamy, Priya. 2012. Gendering racial formation. In *Racial Formation in the Twenty-First Century*, ed. D. M. HoSang, O. LaBennett, and L. Pulido, 23–43. Berkeley: University of California Press.

Kao, Grace, and Jennifer S. Thompson. 2003. Racial and ethnic stratification in educational achievement and attainment. *Annual Review of Sociology* 29 (1): 417–442.

Keith, Verna. 2009. A colorstruck world: Skin tone, achievement, and self-esteem among African American women. In *Shades of Difference: Why Skin Color Matters*, ed. Evelyn Nakano Glenn, 25–39. Palo Alto, CA: Stanford University Press.

Keller, Gary D. 1994. *Hispanics and United States Film: An Overview and Handbook*. Tempe, AZ: Bilingual Review Press.

Kelly, Gail P. 1986. Coping with America: Refugees from Vietnam, Cambodia, and Laos in the 1970s and 1980s. *Annals of the American Academy of Political and Social Science* 487:138–149.

Kelly, Sean. 2009. The black-white gap in mathematics course taking. *Sociology of Education* 82 (1): 47–69.

Kennedy, Randall. 2011. *The Persistence of the Color Line: Racial Politics and the Obama Presidency*. New York: Random House.

Khan, Aisha. 2009. Caucasian, Coolie, black, or white? Color and race in the Indo-Caribbean diaspora. In *Shades of Difference: Why Skin Color Matters*, ed. Evelyn Nakano Glenn, 95–113. Palo Alto, CA: Stanford University Press.

Kim, ChangHwan, and Arthur Sakamoto. 2010. Have Asian American men achieved labor market parity with white men? *American Sociological Review* 75 (6): 934–957.

King, C. Richard, and Charles Fruehling Springwood. 2001. *Beyond the Cheers: Race as Spectacle in College Sport*. Albany: SUNY Press.

King, Marsha. 2008. Tribes confront painful legacy of Indian boarding schools. *Seattle Times*, February 3. http://courses.washington.edu/divrspol/class readings/Tribes painful legacy.pdf.

King, Ryan, Marc Mauer, and Malcolm C. Young. 2005. *Incarceration and Crime: A Complex Relationship*. Washington, DC: The Sentencing Project. http://www.sentencingproject.org/doc/publications/inc_iandc_complex.pdf.

Knight, Alan. 1990. Racism, revolution, and *indigenismo*: Mexico, 1910–1940. In *The Idea of Race in Latin America*, ed. Richard Graham, 71–113. Austin: University of Texas Press.

Kochhar, Rakesh, Richard Fry, and Paul Taylor. 2011. *Wealth Gaps Rise to Record Highs Between Whites, Blacks and Hispanics*. Washington, DC: Pew Research Center.

Kodras, Janet E. 1997. The changing map of American poverty in an era of economic restructuring and political realignment. *Economic Geography* 73.1: 67–93.

Kopacz, Maria, and Bessie Lee Lawton. 2011a. Rating the YouTube Indian: Viewer ratings of Native American portrayals on a viral video site. *American Indian Quarterly* 35 (2): 241–257.

———. 2011b. The YouTube Indian: Portrayals of Native Americans on a viral video site. *New Media and Society* 13 (2): 330–349.

Kpanake, Lonzozou, Maria Teresa Munoz Sastre, and Etienne Mullet. 2009. Skin bleaching among Togolese: A preliminary inventory of motives. *Journal of Black Psychology* 36 (3): 350–368.

Krivo, Lauren, and Robert Kaufman. 2004. Housing and wealth inequality: Racial-ethnic differences in home equity in the United States. *Demography* 41 (3): 585–605.

Krysan, Maria, and Reynolds Farley. 2002. The residential preferences of blacks: Do they explain persistent segregation? *Social Forces* 80 (3): 937–980.

Ladipo, David. 2001. The rise of America's prison-industrial complex. *New Left Review* 7:109–123.

Lambert, Bruce. 1997. At 50, Levittown contends with its legacy of bias. *New York Times*, December 28. http://www.nytimes.com/1997/12/28/nyregion/at-50-levittown-contends-with-its-legacy-of-bias.html.

Lamberth, John. 1994. *Revised Statistical Analysis of the Incidence of Police Stops and Arrests of Black Drivers: Travelers on the New Jersey Turnpike Between Exits or Interchanges 1 and 3 from the Years 1988 Through 1991*. http://www.lamberthconsulting.com/uploads/new_jersey_study_report.pdf.

Lamont, Michéle, and Annette Lareau. 1988. Cultural capital: Allusions, gaps and glissandos in recent theoretical developments. *Sociological Theory* 6 (2): 153–168.

Lara, Marielena, Cristina Gamboa, M. Iya Kahramanian, Leo S. Morales, and David E. Hayes Bautista. 2005. Acculturation and Latino health in the United States: A review of the literature and its sociopolitical context. *Annual Review of Public Health* 26:367–397.

LaVeist, Thomas A., and John M. Wallace. 2000. Health risk and inequitable distribution of liquor stores in African American neighborhood. *Social Science & Medicine* 51 (4): 613–617.

Lavelle, Kristen, and Joe Feagin. 2006. Hurricane Katrina: The race and class debate. *Monthly Review* July/August: 1–15.

Lee, Erika. 2002. The Chinese exclusion example: Race, immigration, and American gate-keeping, 1882–1924. *Journal of American Ethnic History* 21 (3): 36–62.

Lee, Jennifer. 2008. A post-racial America? Multiracial identification and the color line in the 21st century. *Social Sciences* 30:13–31.

Lee, Jennifer, and Frank D. Bean. 2004. America's changing color lines: Immigration, race/ethnicity, and multiracial identification. *Annual Review of Sociology* 30 (1): 221–242.

Lee, Sharon M. 1993. Racial classifications in the US census: 1890–1990. *Ethnic and Racial Studies* 16:75–94.

Lewis, Amanda E. 2004. What group? Studying whites and whiteness in the era of color-blindness. *Sociological Theory* 22 (4): 623–646.

Lewis, Kelly M., Navit Robkin, Karie Gaska, and Lillian Carol Njoki. 2011. Investigating motivations for women's skin bleaching in Tanzania. *Psychology of Women Quarterly* 35 (1): 29–37.

Lichter, Daniel T., Domenico Parisi, Steven Michael Grice, and Michael C. Taquino. 2007. National estimates of racial segregation in rural and small-town America. *Demography* 44 (3): 563–581.

Lindsay, Matthew. 1998. Reproducing a fit citizenry: Dependency, eugenics, and the law of marriage in the United States, 1860–1920. *Law & Social Inquiry* 23 (3): 541–585.

Linnæus, C. 1735. *Systema naturæ, sive regna tria naturæ systematice proposita per classes, ordines, genera, & species*. Lugduni Batavorum.

Lippard, Cameron D. 2011. Racist nativism in the 21st century. *Sociology Compass* 5 (7): 591–606.

Lipsitz, George. 2006. *The Possessive Investment in Whiteness: How White People Profit from Identity Politics*. Philadelphia: Temple University Press.

Littlefield, Daniel, and James Parins, eds. 2011. *Encyclopedia of American Indian Removal*. Santa Barbara, CA: Greenwood.

Liu, John M., Paul M. Ong, and Carolyn Rosenstein. 1991. Dual chain migration: Post-1965 Filipino immigration to the United States. *International Migration Review* xxv: 3: 487–513.

Logan, John R. 2011. *Separate and Unequal: The Neighborhood Gap for Blacks, Hispanics and Asians in Metropolitan America*. Project US2010 Report. http://www.hispanicallyspeakingnews.com/uploads/documents/normal-docs/BrownhousingStudy.pdf.

Logan, John R. 2013. The persistence of segregation in the 21st century metropolis. *City & Community* 12 (2): 160–168.

Logan, John R., and Brian J. Stults. 2011. *The Persistence of Segregation in the Metropolis: New Findings from the 2010 Census*. Project US2010. http://www.s4.brown.edu/us2010/Data/Report/report2.pdf.

Lopez, Mark Hugo, and Susan Minushkin. 2008. *National Survey of Latinos: Hispanics See Their Situation in US Deteriorating; Oppose Key Immigration Enforcement Measures*. Washington, DC: Pew Hispanic Center.

Lovasi, Gina, Malo A. Hutson, Monica Guerra, and Kathryn M. Neckerman. 2009. Built environments and obesity in disadvantaged populations. *Epidemiologic Reviews* 31:7–20.

Lynch, Michael. 1999. Beating a dead horse: Is there any basic empirical evidence for the deterrent effect of imprisonment? *Crime, Law and Social Change* 31:347–362.

Lyons, Christopher J., and Becky Pettit. 2011. Compounded disadvantage: Race, incarceration, and wage growth. *Social Problems* 58 (2): 257–280.

Malpede, Christie Z., Lori F. Greene, Stephanie L. Fitzpatrick, Wendy K. Jefferson, Richard M. Shewchuk, Monica L. Baskin, and Jamy D. Ard. 2007. Racial influences associated with weight-related beliefs in African American and Caucasian women. *Ethnicity & Disease* 17 (1): 1.

Marks, Jonathan. 2004. Review of *Race: The Reality of Human Differences,* by Vincent Sarich and Frank Miele. *Common Review* 3 (2): 42–44.

Marr, Carolyn. n.d. Assimilation through education: Indian boarding schools in the Pacific Northwest. University of Washington Digital Collections. http://content.lib.washington.edu/aipnw/marr.html.

Marx, Anthony W. 1996. Race-making and the nation state. *World Politics* 48 (2): 180–208.

Mascharka, Christopher. 2001. Mandatory minimum sentences: Exemplifying the law of unintended consequences. *Florida State University Law Review* 28:935–975. http://www.law.fsu.edu/journals/lawreview/downloads/284/Masharka2.pdf.

Massey, Douglas, and Nancy Denton. 1993. *American Apartheid: Segregation and the Making of the Underclass.* Cambridge, MA: Harvard University Press.

Massey, Douglas S., Jorge Durand, and Nolan J. Malone. 2002. *Beyond Smoke and Mirrors: Mexican Immigration in an Era of Economic Integration.* New York: Russell Sage Foundation.

Master, Maureen. 2003. *Due Process for All: Redressing Inequities in the Criminal Provisions of the 1996 Immigration Laws.* United States Conference of Catholic Bishops. Office of Migration and Refugee Policy Staff Paper.

Maston, Cathy, and Erica Smith. 2010. Estimated Drug Arrests by Age, 1970–2007. *Uniform Crime Reports in the United States.* Washington, DC: Federal Bureau of Investigation.

Mauer, Marc. 1999. *The Crisis of the Young African American Male and the Criminal Justice System.* Washington, DC: The Sentencing Project. http://www.sentencingproject.org/doc/publications/rd_crisisoftheyoung.pdf.

———. 2007. Racial impact statements as a means of reducing unwarranted sentencing disparities. *Ohio State Journal of Criminal Law* 5 (19): 19–46. http://www.sentencingproject.org/doc/publications/rd_racialimpactstatements.pdf.

———. 2009. *Testimony of Marc Mauer, Executive Director, the Sentencing Project.* Washington, DC: The Sentencing Project. http://www.sentencingproject.org/doc/dp_crack_testimony.pdf.

Mauer, Marc, and Ryan S. King. 2007. *Uneven Justice: State Rates of Incarceration by Race and Ethnicity.* Washington, DC: The Sentencing Project. http://www.sentencingproject.org/doc/publications/rd_stateratesofincbyraceandethnicity.pdf.

McCall, Leslie, and Christine Percheski. 2010. Income inequality: New trends and research directions. *Annual Review of Sociology* 36 (1): 329–347.

McElroy, Susan W., and William A. Darity. 1999. Labor market discrimination by race. In *Readings in Black Political Economy,* ed. John Whitehead and Cobie Kwasi Harris, 123–139. Dubuque, IA: Kendall/Hunt.

McNeal, Laura R. 2009. The re-segregation of public education now and after the end of *Brown v. Board of Education. Education and Urban Society* 41 (5): 562–574.

Mellon, James, ed. 2002. *Bullwhip Days: The Slaves Remember: An Oral History.* New York: Grove.

Mendelberg, Tali. 1997. Executing Hortons: Racial crime in the 1988 presidential campaign. *Public Opinion Quarterly* 61:134–157.

Mendez v. Westminister School District, 64 F. Supp. 544 (S.D. Cal. 1946).

Menjívar, Cecilia. 2000. *Fragmented Ties: Salvadoran Immigrant Networks in America.* Berkeley: University of California Press.

———. 2011. *Enduring Violence: Ladina Women's Lives in Guatemala.* Berkeley: University of California Press.

Merskin, Debra. 2007. Three faces of Eva: Perpetuation of the hot-Latina stereotype in *Desperate Housewives. Howard Journal of Communications* 18 (2): 133–151.

Miele, Frank, and Vincent Sarich. 2004. *Race: The Reality of Human Differences* Boulder, CO: Westview Press.

Migration Policy Institute. 2012. "U.S. Immigrant Population and Share over Time, 1850-Present" Online at: http://www.migrationpolicy.org/programs/data-hub/charts/immigrant-population-over-time?width=1000&height=850&iframe=true.

Min, Pyong Gap. 1990. Problems of Korean immigrant entrepreneurs. *International Migration Review* 24:436–455.

Mitchell, Gerald. 2012. Why focusing on black males is necessary to address high African-American unemployment. *The Grio,* March 9. http://thegrio.com/2012/03/09/black-unemployment-why/.

Mohideen, Ismath. 2009. The fair skin battle. *Brown Girl Magazine.* http://browngirlmagazine.com/2009/02/the-fair-skin-battle/.

Monbiot, George. 2011. The self-attribution fallacy. *George Monbiot,* November 7. http://www.monbiot.com/2011/11/07/the-self-attribution-fallacy/.

Monk-Turner, Elizabeth, Mary Heiserman, Crystle Johnson, Vanity Cotton, and Manny Jackson. 2010. The portrayal of racial minorities on prime time television: A replication of the Mastro and Greenberg study a decade later. *Studies in Popular Culture* 32 (2): 101–114.

Montagu, Ashley. 1997. *Man's Most Dangerous Myth: The Fallacy of Race,* 6th ed. Walnut Creek, CA: AltaMira.

Morawetz, Nancy. 2000. Understanding the impact of the 1996 deportation laws and the limited scope of proposed reforms. *Harvard Law Review* 113 (8): 1936–1962.

Morgan, Edmund. 1975. *American Slavery, American Freedom: The Ordeal of Colonial Virginia.* New York: W. W. Norton and Co.

Morris, Martina, and Bruce Western. 1999. Inequality in earnings at the close of the twentieth century. *Annual Review of Sociology* 25 (1): 623–657.

Moss, Kirby. 2003. *The Color of Class: Poor Whites and the Paradox of Privilege.* Philadelphia: University of Pennsylvania Press.

Moynihan, Daniel Patrick. 1965. *The Negro Family: The Case for National Action,* Washington, D.C., Office of Policy Planning and Research, U.S. Department of Labor.

Muller, Chandra, Catherine Riegle-Crumb, Kathryn S. Schiller, Lindsey Wilkinson, and Kenneth A. Frank. 2010. Race and academic achievement in racially diverse high schools: Opportunity and stratification. *Teachers College Record* 112 (4): 1038.

Murguia, Edward, and Rogelio Saenz. 2002. An analysis of the Latin Americanization of race in the United States: A reconnaissance of color stratification among Mexicans. *Race and Society* 5 (1): 85–101.

Murguia, Edward, and Edward Telles. 1996. Phenotype and schooling among Mexican Americans. *Sociology of Education* 69 (October): 276–289.

Murphy, Katy. 2013. Affirmative action ban at UC, 15 years later. *San Jose Mercury News*, June 24. http://www.mercurynews.com/ci_23516740/affirmative-action-ban-at-uc-15-years-later.

Museus, Samuel D., and Peter N. Kiang. 2009. Deconstructing the model minority myth and how it contributes to the invisible minority reality in higher education research. *New Directions for Institutional Research* 142:5–15.

Mustard, David B. 2001. Racial, Ethnic, and Gender Disparities in Sentencing: Evidence from the US Federal Courts. *Journal of Law and Economics* 44 (1): 285–314.

Nadal, Kevin L., Yinglee Wong, Katie Griffin, Julie Sriken, Vivian Vargas, Michelle Wideman, and Ajayi Kolawole. 2011. Microaggressions and the multiracial experience. *International Journal of Humanities and Social Science* 1 (7): 36–44. http://www.ijhssnet.com/journals/Vol._1_No._7_[Special_Issue_June_2011]/6.pdf.

Nagata, Donna K. 1991. The transgenerational impact of the Japanese internment: Clinical issues in working with the children of former internees. *Psychotherapy Theory Research & Practice* 28 (1): 121–128.

National Center for Education Statistics. 2010. *Digest of Education Statistics*. http://nces.ed.gov/programs/digest/.

National Hispanic Foundation for the Arts. 2001. *Prime Time for Latinos: Report II: 2000–2001 Prime Television Season*. http://www.hispanicarts.org/Media/REPORT2.pdf.

New York City Bar Association. 2013. *Report on the NYPD's Stop and Frisk Policy*. http://www2.nycbar.org/pdf/report/uploads/20072495-StopFriskReport.pdf.

Ng, Wendy. 2002. *Japanese American Internment During World War II: A History and Reference Guide*. Westport, CT: Greenwood.

Ngai, Mae. 2004. *Impossible Subjects: Illegal Aliens and the Making of Modern America*. Princeton, NJ: Princeton University Press.

Ngo, Bic, and Stacey J. Lee. 2007. Complicating the image of model minority success: A review of Southeast Asian American education. *Review of Educational Research* 77 (4): 415–453.

Noel, Jana. 2002. Education toward cultural shame: A century of Native American education. *Educational Foundations* 16 (1): 19–32.

Nopper, Tamara K. 2011. Barack Obama's community organizing as new black politics. *Political Power and Social Theory* 22:51–73.

Norton, Michael I., and Dan Ariely. 2011. Building a better America—one wealth quintile at a time. *Perspectives on Psychological Science* 6 (1): 9–12.

Ocampo, Anthony C. 2014. Are second-generation Filipinos "becoming" Asian American or Latino? Historical colonialism, culture and panethnicity. *Ethnic and Racial Studies* 37 (3): 425–445.

Oliver, Melvin, and Thomas Shapiro. 2006. *Black Wealth/White Wealth: A New Perspective on Racial Inequality*. New York: Routledge.

Omi, Michael, and Howard Winant. 1994. *Racial Formation in the United States from the 1960s to the 1990s*, 2nd ed. New York: Routledge.

Orfield, Gary. 2009. *Reviving the Goal of an Integrated Society: A 21st Century Challenge*. Los Angeles: Civil Rights Project/Proyecto Dereches Civile at UCLA. http://civilrightsproject.ucla.edu/research/k-12-education/integration-and-diversity/reviving-the-goal-of-an-integrated-society-a-21st-century-challenge/orfield-reviving-the-goal-mlk-2009.pdf.

Orfield, Gary, and Chungmei Lee. 2004. *Brown at 50: King's Dream or Plessy's Nightmare?* Cambridge, MA: Harvard University Civil Rights Project. http://civilrightsproject.ucla.edu/research/k-12-education/integration-and-diversity/brown-at-50-king2019s-dream-or-plessy2019s-nightmare/orfield-brown-50-2004.pdf.

Pager, Devah. 2007. *Marked: Race, Crime, and Finding Work in an Era of Mass Incarceration.* Chicago: University of Chicago Press.

Pager, Devah, and Hana Shepherd. 2008. The sociology of discrimination: Racial discrimination in employment, housing, credit, and consumer markets. *Annual Review of Sociology* 34:181–209.

Pager, Devah, Bruce Western, and Bart Bonikowski. 2009. Discrimination in a low-wage labor market: A field experiment. *American Sociological Review* 74 (5): 777–799.

Parameswaran, Radhika, and Kavitha Cardoza. 2009. Melanin on the margins: Advertising and the cultural politics of fair/light/white beauty in India. *Journalism & Communication Monographs* 11 (3): 213–274.

Parenti, Christian. 1999. *Lockdown America: Police and Prisons in the Age of Crisis.* New York: Verso.

Park, Jane Chi Hyun. 2010. *Yellow Future: Oriental Style in Hollywood Cinema.* Minneapolis: University of Minnesota Press.

Pellow, David Naguib. 2007. *Resisting Global Toxins: Transnational Movements for Environmental Justice.* Cambridge, MA: MIT Press.

Perez, Louis. 2003. *Cuba and the United States: Ties of Singular Intimacy,* 3rd ed. Athens and London: University of Georgia Press.

Pettit, Becky, and Stephanie Ewert. 2009. Employment gains and wage declines: The erosion of black women's relative wages since 1980. *Demography* 46 (3): 469–492.

Pew Charitable Trust. 2008. *One in 100: Behind Bars in America 2008.* http://www.pewtrusts.org/en/research-and-analysis/reports/2008/02/28/one-in-100-behind-bars-in-america-2008.

Pew Hispanic Center. 2006. *Cubans in the United States.* http://pewhispanic.org/files/factsheets/23.pdf.

Pew Research Center. 2006. *Increasingly, Americans Prefer Going to the Movies at Home.* May 16. http://pewresearch.org/assets/social/pdf/Movies.pdf.

———. 2013. *The Rise of Asian Americans.* April 4. http://www.pewsocialtrends.org/files/2013/04/Asian-Americans-new-full-report-04-2013.pdf.

Pfeifer, Michael James. 2006. *Rough Justice: Lynching and American Society, 1874–1947.* Champaign: University of Illinois Press.

Piel, Frédéric B., Anand P Patil, Rosalind E. Howes, Oscar A. Nyangiri, Peter W. Gething, Mewahyu Dewi, William H. Temperley, Thomas N. Williams, David J. Weatherall, and Simon I. Hay 2013. Global epidemiology of sickle haemoglobin in neonates: A contemporary geostatistical model-based map and population estimates. *The Lancet* 381, no. 9861: 142–151. DOI: 10.1016/S0140-6736(12)61229-X.

Pierre, Jemima. 2008. "I like your colour!" Skin bleaching and geographies of race in urban Ghana. *Feminist Review* 90 (1): 9–29.

Plyler v. Doe. 457 U.S. 202 (1982). United States Supreme Court. Online at: http://caselaw.lp.findlaw.com/scripts/getcase.pl?court=US&vol=457&invol=202.

Plessy v. Ferguson, 163 U.S. 537, 16 S. Ct. 1138, 41 L. Ed. 256 (1896).

Pomerantz, Dorothy. 2011. The highest-paid men in entertainment. *Forbes,* September 12. http://www.forbes.com/sites/dorothypomerantz/2011/09/12/the-highest-paid-men-in-entertainment/.

Pon, Gordon, Kevin Gosine, and Doret Phillips, D. 2011. Immediate response: Addressing anti-native and anti-black racism in child welfare. *International Journal of Child, Youth, and Family Studies* 2 (3/4): 385–409.

Portes, Alejandro, and Jessica Yiu. 2013. Entrepreneurship, transnationalism, and development. *Migration Studies* 1 (1): 75–95.

Portes, Alejandro., Patricia Fernandez-Kelly, and William Haller. 2005. Segmented assimilation on the ground: The new second generation in early adulthood. *Ethnic and Racial Studies* 28 (6): 1000–1040.

Portes, Alejandro, and Ruben G. Rumbaut. 2006. *Immigrant America: A portrait.* Berkeley, CA: University of California Press.

powell, john a. 2008. Structural racism: Building upon the insights of John Calmore. *North Carolina Law Review* 86:791–816.

Quan, Adán. 2005. Through the looking glass: U.S. aid to El Salvador and the politics of national identity. *American Ethnologist* 32 (2): 276–293.

Quijano, Anibal. 2000. Coloniality of power and Eurocentrism in Latin America. *International Sociology* 15 (2): 215–232.

Rajgopal, Shoba Sharad. 2010. "The daughter of Fu Manchu": The pedagogy of deconstructing the representation of Asian women in film and fiction. *Meridians* 10 (2): 141–162.

Reeves, Terrance J., and Claudette E. Bennett. 2004. *We the People: Asians in the United States,* vol. 17. Washington, DC: U.S. Department of Commerce, Economic and Statistics Administration, U.S. Census Bureau.

Reimers, David M. 1981. Post–World War II immigration to the United States: America's latest newcomers. *Annals of the American Academy of Political and Social Science* 454 (1): 1–12.

Restall, Matthew. 2000. Black conquistadors: Armed Africans in early Spanish America. *The Americas* 57 (2): 171–205.

Reverby, Susan. 2009. *Examining Tuskegee: The infamous syphilis study and its legacy.* Chapel Hill: University of North Carolina Press.

Richie, Beth. 2005. Queering anti-prison work: African American lesbians in the juvenile justice system. In *Global Lockdown: Race Gender and the Prison-Industrial Complex,* ed. Julia Sudbury, 73–85. New York: Routledge.

Roberts, Dorothy. 2011. *Fatal Invention: How Science, Politics, and Big Business Re-Create Race in the Twenty-First Century.* New York: New Press.

Robinson, Eugene. 1999. *Coal to Cream: A Black Man's Journey Beyond Color to an Affirmation of Race.* New York: Free Press.

Rockquemore, Kerry Ann, and Patricia Arend. 2002. Opting for white: Choice, fluidity and racial identity construction in post civil-rights America. *Race and Society* 5 (1): 49–64.

Rockquemore, Kerry Ann, and David L. Brunsma. 2002. Socially embedded identities: Theories, typologies, and processes of racial identity among black/white biracials. *Sociological Quarterly* 43 (3): 335–356.

Rodríguez, Clara. 1997. *Latin Looks: Images of Latinas and Latinos in the U.S. Media.* Boulder, CO: Westview.

———. 2000. *Changing Race: Latinos, the Census, and the History of Ethnicity in the United States.* New York: New York University Press.

Roediger, David R. 1999. *The Wages of Whiteness: Race and the Making of the American Working Class.* New York: Verso.

Rondilla, Joanne L. 2009. Filipinos and the color complex: Ideal Asian beauty. In *Shades of Difference: Why Skin Color Matters,* ed. Evelyn Nakano Glenn, 63–80. Palo Alto, CA: Stanford University Press.

Rondilla, Joanne L., and Paul Spickard. 2007. *Is Lighter Better? Skin-Tone Discrimination Among Asian Americans.* Lanham, MD: Rowman & Littlefield.

Roscigno, Vincent, and James Ainsworth-Darnell. 1999. Race, cultural capital, and educational resources: Persistent inequalities and achievement returns. *Sociology of Education* 72 (3): 158–178.

Roth, Wendy D. 2005. The end of the one-drop rule? Labeling of multiracial children in black intermarriages. *Sociological Forum* 20 (1): 35–67.

Rugh, Jacob S., and Douglas S. Massey. 2010. "Racial segregation and the American foreclosure crisis." *American Sociological Review* 75 (5): 629–651.

Ruiz, Vicki L. 2001. South by southwest: Mexican Americans and segregated schooling. *OAH Magazine of History* 15 (2): 23–27.

Rural Community Assistance Partnership. n.d. *Still Living Without the Basics in the 21st Century: Analyzing the Availability of Water and Sanitation Services in the United States.* http://win-water.org/reports/RCAP_full_final.pdf.

Rytina, Nancy. 2011. *Estimates of the Legal Permanent Resident Population in 2010.* Washington, DC: Office of Immigration Statistics, Policy Directorate, U.S. Department of Homeland Security.

Sabol, William, Heather West, and Matthew Cooper. 2009. Prisoners in 2008. *Bureau of Justice Statistics Bulletin.*Washington, DC: U.S. Department of Justice. http://www.bjs.gov/content/pub/pdf/p08.pdf.

Saleem, Muniba. 2008. Effects of stereotypic video game portrayals on implicit and explicit attitudes. M.S. thesis, Iowa State University.

Sanchez, George. 1997. Face the nation: Race, immigration, and the rise of nativism in late twentieth century America. *International Migration Review* 31 (4): 1009–1030.

San Miguel, G. 1983. The struggle against separate and unequal schools: Middle class Mexican Americans and the desegregation campaign in Texas. *History of Education Quarterly* 23 (3): 343–359.

Saperstein, Aliya. 2012. Capturing complexity in the United States: Which aspects of race matter and when? *Ethnic and Racial Studies* 35 (8): 1484–1502.

Saraswati, Ayu. 2010. *Cosmopolitan* whiteness: The effects and affects of skin-whitening advertisements in a transnational women's magazine in Indonesia. *Meridians* 10 (2): 15–41.

———. 2012. "Malu": Coloring shame and shaming the color of beauty in transnational Indonesia. *Feminist Studies* 38 (1): 113–140.

Sassen, Saskia. 1990. *The Mobility of Labor and Capital: A Study in International Investment and Labor Flow.* London: Cambridge University Press.

Schiller, Bradley. 2004. *The Economics of Poverty and Discrimination*, 9th ed. Upper Saddle River, NJ: Pearson Prentice Hall.

Schlosser, Eric. 1998. The prison-industrial complex. *Atlantic Monthly*, December.

Semyonov, Moshe, and Noah Lewin-Epstein. 2009. The declining racial earnings' gap in United States: Multi-level analysis of males' earnings, 1960–2000. *Social Science Research* 38 (2): 296–311.

Sethi, Kapil. 2000. Branding brides and grooms in India: An analysis of matrimonial advertising in India 1967–1997. *McCann Erickson's Consumer Insights*, May. http://www.brandingasia.com/columns/mccannerickson5.htm.

Shaheen, Jack. 1997. *Arab and Muslim Stereotyping in American Popular Culture.* Washington, DC: Center for Muslim-Christian Understanding.

Shapiro, Thomas M. 2004. *The Hidden Cost of Being African American: How Wealth Perpetuates Inequality.* New York: Oxford University Press.

Shapiro, Thomas, Tatjana Meschede, and Sam Osoro. 2013. *The Roots of the Widening Racial Wealth Gap: Explaining the Black-White Economic Divide.* Institute on Assets and Social Policy, February. http://www.naacpldf.org/files/case_issue/Shapiro racialwealthgapbrief.pdf.

Shierholz, Heidi. 2013. Roughly One in Five Hispanic and Black Workers Are "Underemployed." Economic Policy Institute. August 22. Online at: http://www.epi.org/publication/roughly-hispanic-black-workers-underemployed/.

Siddle Walker, Vanessa. 2000. Valued segregated schools for African American children in the South, 1935–1969: A review of common themes and characteristics. *Review of Educational Research* 70:253–285.

Simon, Johnathan. 2007. *Governing Through Crime: How the War on Crime Transformed American Democracy and Created a Culture of Fear.* New York: Oxford University Press.

Singh, Gopal K., and Stella M. Yu. 1996. Adverse pregnancy outcomes: Differences between U.S. and foreign-born women in major U.S. racial and ethnic groups. *American Journal of Public Health* 86 (6): 837–843.

Skrentny, John D. 1996. *The Ironies of Affirmative Action: Politics, Culture, and Justice in America.* Chicago: University of Chicago Press.

Small, Stephen. 1999. The contours of racialization. In *Race, Identity, and Citizenship: A Reader,* ed. Rodolfo D. Torres, Luis F. Mirón, and Jonathan Xavier Inda, 47–64. New York: Blackwell.

Smedley, Audrey. 2007. *Race in North America: Origin and Evolution of a Worldview,* 3rd ed. Boulder, CO: Westview.

Smith, Andrea. 2012. Indigeneity, settler colonialism, white supremacy. In *Racial Formation in the Twenty-First Century,* ed. Daniel Martinez HoSang, Oneka LaBennett, and Laura Pulido, 66–90. Berkeley: University of California Press.

Smith, Jay Scott. 2012. Detroit immigrant fights to be classified as black. *The Grio,* September 4. http://thegrio.com/2012/09/04/detroit-immigrant-wants-to-be-classified-as-black/#bmb=1.

Snowden, Frank. 1970. *Blacks in Antiquity.* Cambridge, MA: Harvard University Press.

———. 1983. *Before Color Prejudice: The Ancient View of Blacks.* Cambridge, MA: Harvard University Press.

Solorzano, Daniel, Miguel Ceja, and Tara Yosso. 2000. Critical race theory, racial microaggressions, and campus racial climate: The experiences of African American college students. *Journal of Negro Education* 69 (Winter/Spring): 60–73.

Span, Christopher M. 2002. "I must learn now or not at all": Social and cultural capital in the educational initiatives of formerly enslaved African Americans in Mississippi, 1862–1869. *Journal of African American History* 87:196–206.

Spiro, Jonathan. 2008. *Defending the Master Race: Conservation, Eugenics, and the Legacy of Madison Grant.* Burlington: University of Vermont Press.

Stannard, David E. 1993. *American Holocaust: The Conquest of the New World.* New York: Oxford University Press.

Stanton-Salazar, Ricardo D., and Sanford M. Dornbusch. 1995. Social capital and the reproduction of inequality: Information networks among Mexican-origin high school students. *Sociology of Education* 68 (April): 116–135.

Stephens, Dionne P., and Paula Fernández, P. 2011. The role of skin color on Hispanic women's perceptions of attractiveness. *Hispanic Journal of Behavioral Sciences* 34 (1): 77–94.

Stout, Mary A. 2012. *Native American Boarding Schools.* Santa Barbara, CA: ABC-CLIO.

Subramanian, Ram, and Alison Shames. 2013. *Sentencing and Prison Practices in Germany and the Netherlands: Implications for the United States.* Vera Institute of Justice. http://www.vera.org/sites/default/files/resources/downloads/european-american-prison-report-v3.pdf.

Sue, Christina A. 2009. The dynamics of color: Mestizaje, racism and blackness in Veracruz, Mexico. In *Shades of Difference: Why Skin Color Matters*, ed. Evelyn Nakano Glenn, 114–128. Palo Alto, CA: Stanford University Press.

Sue, Derald Wing., Jennifer Bucceri, Annie I. Lin, Kevin L. Nadal, and Gina C. Torino. 2007. Racial microaggressions and the Asian American experience. *Cultural Diversity & Ethnic Minority Psychology* 13 (1): 72–81.

Sugrue, Thomas. 2008. *The Unfinished History of Racial Segregation*. http://www.prrac.org/projects/fair_housing_commission/chicago/sugrue.pdf.

Szasz, Ferenc. 1967. The New York slave revolt of 1741: A re-examination. *New York History* 48 (3): 215–230.

Tahmahkera, Dustin. 2008. Custer's last sitcom: Decolonized viewing of the sitcom's "Indian." *American Indian Quarterly* 32 (3): 324–351.

Tatum, Beverly Daniel. 2003. *"Why Are All the Black Kids Sitting Together in the Cafeteria?" and Other Conversations About Race*. New York: Basic Books.

Taylor, Dorceta E. 2009. *The Environment and the People in American Cities, 1600s to 1900s: Disorder, Inequality, and Social Change*. Durham, NC: Duke University Press.

Telles, Edward E. 2004. *Race in Another America: The Significance of Skin Color in Brazil*. Princeton, NJ: Princeton University Press.

Telles, Edward E., and Liza Steele. 2012. *Pigmentocracy in the Americas: How Is Educational Attainment Related to Skin Color?* Americas Barometer Insight Series 73. Princeton, NJ: PERLA: The Project on Ethnicity and Race in Latin America.

Thomas, Lynn M. 2009. Skin lighteners in South Africa: Transnational entanglements and technologies of the self. In *Shades of Difference: Why Skin Color Matters*, ed. Evelyn Nakano Glenn, 188–210. Palo Alto, CA: Stanford University Press.

Thomson, Charles. 2011. Strange fruit still falling in the southern states: The unjust execution of Troy Davis. *Charles Thomson*, September 11. http://www.charles-thomson.net/strangefruit.html.

Thorpe, Roland, Jr., and Jessica A. Kelley-Moore. 2012. Life-course theories of race disparities: A comparison of the cumulative dis/advantage theory perspective and the weathering hypothesis. In *Race, Ethnicity, and Health: A Public Health Reader*, ed. Thomas Laveist and Lydia Isaac, 355–374. San Francisco: Jon Wiley & Sons.

Todorov, Tzvetan. 1984. *The Conquest of America: The Question of the Tther*. Norman: University of Oklahoma Press.

Torok, John, 2004. Ideological deportation: The case of Kwong Hai Chew. Available at http://ssrn.com/abstract=462500 or http://dx.doi.org/10.2139/ssrn.462500.

Trennert, Robert A. 1982. Educating Indian girls at nonreservation boarding schools, 1878–1920. *The Western Historical Quarterly* 13: 3: 271–290.

Tumlin, Karen, and Wendy Zimmerman. 2003. *Immigrants and TANF: A Look at Immigrant Welfare Recipients in Three Cities*. Occasional Paper No. 69. Urban Institute. http://www.urban.org/UploadedPDF/310874_OP69.pdf.

Ture, Kwame, and Charles Hamilton. 1967. *Black Power: Politics of Liberation in America*. New York: Random House.

Twine, France Winddance. 1998. *Racism in a Racial Democracy: The Maintenance of White Supremacy in Brazil*. New Brunswick, NJ: Rutgers University Press.

Tyson, Karolyn. 2002. Weighing in: Elementary-age students and the debate on attitudes toward school among black students. *Social Forces* 80 (4): 1157–1189.

University of California Berkeley Labor Center. 2013. *Black Employment and Unemployment in November 2013*. Data brief. http://laborcenter.berkeley.edu/blackworkers/monthly/bwreport_2013-12-06_64.pdf.

University of California Regents v. Bakke. 438 U.S. 265, 98 S. Ct. 2733, 57 L. Ed. 2d 750 (1978).

U.S. Department of Education, Office for Civil Rights. 2014. *Data Snapshot: School Discipline*. Issue Brief No. 1, March. http://www2.ed.gov/about/offices/list/ocr/docs/crdc-discipline-snapshot.pdf.

U.S. Department of Homeland Security, Office of Immigration Statistics. 2009. Yearbook of Immigration Statistics. Online at: https://www.dhs.gov/xlibrary/assets/statistics/yearbook/2009/ois_yb_2009.pdf.

U.S. Department of Homeland Security, Office of Immigration Statistics. 2010. Yearbook of Immigration Statistics. Online at: https://www.dhs.gov/xlibrary/assets/statistics/yearbook/2010/ois_yb_2010.pdf.

U.S. Department of Labor. n.d. *Hiring*. http://www.dol.gov/dol/topic/hiring/affirmativeact.htm.

U.S. Sentencing Commission. 1995. *Public Hearing on Proposed Guideline Amendments*. http://www.src-project.org/wp-content/uploads/2009/08/ussc_publiccomment_19950314.pdf.

Vaid, Jyotsna. 2009. Fair enough? Color and the commodification of self in Indian matrimonials. In *Shades of Difference: Why Skin Color Matters*, ed. Evelyn Nakano Glenn, 148–165. Palo Alto, CA: Stanford University Press.

Valdez, Zulema. 2008a. Beyond ethnic entrepreneurship: An embedded market approach to group affiliation in American enterprise. *Race, Gender & Class* 15 (1): 156–169. http://escholarship.org/uc/item/8c8206b6.pdf.

———. 2008b. The effect of social capital on white, Korean, Mexican and black business owners' earnings in the US. *Journal of Ethnic and Migration Studies* 34 (6): 955–973.

———. 2011. *The New Entrepreneurs: How Race, Class and Gender Shape American Enterprise*. Palo Alto, CA: Stanford University Press.

Van den Berghe, Pierre. 1974. The Use of Ethnic Terms in the Peruvian Social Science Literature. In *Class and Ethnicity in* Peru, ed. Pierre van den Berghe, 12–22. Leiden, The Netherlands: E. J. Brill.

Vardi, Nathan. 2011. America's most affluent neighborhoods. *Forbes*, January 18. http://www.forbes.com/2011/01/18/americas-most-affluent-communities-business-beltway.html.

Vargas, Ramon Antonio. 2011. Fourth marijuana conviction gets Slidell man life in prison. *Times Picayune*, May 5.

Vickerman, Milton. 1999. *Crosscurrents: West Indian Immigrants and Race*. New York: Oxford University Press.

Vidal-Ortiz, Salvador. 2004. On being a white person of color: Using autoethnography to understand Puerto Ricans' racialization. *Qualitative Sociology* 27 (2): 179–203.

Viruell-Fuentes, Edna. 2007. Beyond acculturation: Immigration, discrimination, and health research among Mexicans in the United States. *Social Science & Medicine* 65:1524–1535.

Volscho, Thomas W. 2010. Sterilization racism and pan-ethnic disparities of the past decade: The continued encroachment on reproductive rights. *Wicazo Sa Review* 25 (1): 17–31.

Wacquant, Loïc. 2009. *Punishing the Poor: The Neoliberal Government of Social Insecurity*. Durham, NC: Duke University Press.

Wade, Peter. 1993. *Blackness and Race Mixture: The Dynamics of Racial Identity in Colombia*. Baltimore: Johns Hopkins University Press.

———. 1997. *Race and Ethnicity in Latin America*. Chicago: Pluto.

Walmsley, Roy. 2013. *World Prison Population List*, 10th ed. International Centre for Prison Studies. http://prisonstudies.org/sites/prisonstudies.org/files/resources/downloads/wppl_10.pdf.

Walters, Pamela Barnhouse. 2001. Educational access and the state: Historical continuities and discontinuities in racial inequality in American education. *Sociology of Education* Extra Issue: 35–49.

Wang, Qingfang. 2008. Race/ethnicity, gender and job earnings across metropolitan areas in the United States: A multilevel analysis. *Urban Studies* 45 (4): 825–843.

Warren, Jonathan W., and France Winddance Twine. 1997. White Americans, the new minority? Non-blacks and the ever-expanding boundaries of whiteness. *Journal of Black Studies* 28 (2): 200–218.

Warren-Findlow, Jan. 2006. Weathering: Stress and heart disease in African American women living in Chicago. *Qualitative Health Research* 16 (2): 221–237.

Washington, Harriet. 2006. *Medical Apartheid: The Dark History of Medical Experimentation on Black Americans from Colonial Times to the Present.* New York: Random House.

Watras, Joseph. 2004. Progressive education and Native American schools, 1929–1950. *Educational Foundations* 18:81–105.

Weismantel, Mary. 2001. *Cholas and Pishtacos: Stories of Race and Sex in the Andes.* Chicago: University of Chicago Press.

Welch, Michael. 2002. *Detained: Immigration Laws and the Expanding INS Jail Complex.* Philadelphia: Temple University Press.

Wellman, David T. 1993. *Portraits of White Racism*, 2nd ed. Cambridge and New York: Cambridge University Press.

Wendel, Carrie. 2013 The social contexts and construction of emotional distress in new parents. Unpublished manuscript, University of Kansas.

West, Heather, and William Sabol. 2010. *Prisoners in 2009.* Bureau of Justice Statistics. http://www.bjs.gov/content/pub/pdf/p09.pdf.

Western, Bruce. 2006. *Punishment and Inequality in America.* New York: Russell Sage Foundation.

Western, Bruce, and Becky Pettit. 2002. Beyond crime and punishment: Prisons and inequality. *Contexts* 1 (3): 37–43.

———. 2005. Black-white wage inequality, employment rates and incarceration. *American Journal of Sociology* 111 (2): 553–578.

White, Fredrick. 2012. Ubiquitous American Indian stereotypes in television. In *American Indians and Popular Culture: Media, Sports, and Politics*, ed. Elizabeth DeLaney Hoffman, 1:135–150. Santa Barbara, CA: ABC-CLIO.

White, Michael J., Ann E. Biddlecom, and Shenyang Guo. 1993. Immigration, naturalization, and residential assimilation among Asian Americans in 1980. *Social Forces* 72 (1): 93–117.

Wildeman, Christopher. 2009. Parental imprisonment, the prison boom, and the concentration of childhood disadvantage. *Demography* 46 (2): 265–280.

Wilder, JeffriAnne. 2010. Revisiting "color names and color notions": A contemporary examination of the language and attitudes of skin color among young black women. *Journal of Black Studies* 41 (1):184–206.

Wilkes, Rima, and John Iceland. 2004. Hypersegregation in the twenty-first century. *Demography* 41 (1): 23–36.

Wilkins, Amy C. 2004. Puerto Rican wannabes: Sexual spectacle and the marking of race, class, and gender boundaries. *Gender & Society* 18 (1): 103–121.

Wilkinson, Richard G., and Kate E. Pickett. 2009. Income inequality and social dysfunction. *Annual Review of Sociology* 35 (1): 493–511.

Williams, David R., and Chiquita Collins. 1995. U.S. socioeconomic and racial differences in health: Patterns and explanations. *Annual Review of Sociology* 21 (1): 349–386.

———. 2001. Racial residential segregation: A fundamental cause of racial disparities in health. *Public Health Reports* 116 (5): 404–416.

Williams, Eric. 1944. *Capitalism and Slavery*. Chapel Hill: University of North Carolina Press.

Wilson, Carter. 1996. *From Slavery to Advanced Capitalism*. Thousand Oaks, CA: Sage.

Wilson, William Julius. 1996 *When Work Disappears: The World of the New Urban Poor.* New York: Vintage.

Wilson, William Julius. 2009. *More Than Just Race: Being Black and Poor in the Inner City Issues of Our Time*. New York: W. W. Norton & Company.

Winant, Howard. 2000. Race and race theory. *Annual Review of Sociology* 26: 169–185.

Wing, Jean Yonemura. 2007. Beyond black and white: The model minority myth and the invisibility of Asian American students. *Urban Review* 39 (4): 455–487.

Wingfield, Adia Harvey. 2008. *Doing Business with Beauty: Black Women, Hair Salons, and the Racial Enclave Economy*. Lanham, MD: Rowman & Littlefield.

Wise, Tim. 2005. Membership has its privileges: Thoughts on acknowledging and challenging whiteness. In *White Privilege: Essential Readings on the Other Side of Racism*, 2nd ed., ed. Paula S. Rothenberg, 119–123. New York: Worth.

———. 2008. *White Like Me: Reflections on Race from a Privileged Son*. Berkeley, CA: Counterpoint.

———. 2010. *Colorblind: The Rise of Post-Racial Politics and the Retreat from Racial Equity*. San Francisco: City Lights.

Woldoff, Rachael A., and Heather M. Washington. 2008. Arrested contact: The criminal justice system, race, and father engagement. *Prison Journal* 88 (2): 179–206.

Wollenberg, Charles. 1974. *Mendez v. Westminster*: Race, nationality, and segregation in California schools. *California Historical Quarterly* 53 (4): 317–332.

Wood, Forrest G. 1991. *The Arrogance of Faith: Christianity and Race in America from the Colonial Era to the Twentieth Century*. Boston: Northeastern University Press.

Wood, Phillip J. 2007. Globalization and prison privatization: Why are most of the world's for-profit adult prisons to be found in the American South? *International Political Sociology* 1:222–239.

Yamamoto, Eric. 2009. *Interracial Justice: Conflict and Reconciliation in Post–Civil Rights America*. New York: New York University Press.

Yancey, George A. 2003. *Who Is White? Latinos, Asians, and the New Black/Nonblack Divide*. Boulder, CO: Lynne Rienner.

Yosso, Tara J., Laurence Parker, Daniel G. Solorzano, and Marvin Lynn. 2004. From Jim Crow to affirmative action and back again: A critical race discussion of racialized rationales and access to higher education. *Review of Research in Education* 28 (1): 1–25.

Zagorsky, Jay. 2006. Native Americans' wealth. In *Wealth Accumulation in Communities of Color in the United States*, ed. Jessica Gordon Nembhard and Ngina S. Chiteji, 133–154. Ann Arbor: University of Michigan Press.

Zatz, Marjorie. 2000. The convergence of race, ethnicity, gender, and class on court decision-making: Looking toward the 21st century. *Criminal Justice* 3:503–552. https://www.ncjrs.gov/criminal_justice2000/vol_3/03j.pdf.

Zinn, Howard. 2010. *A People's History of the United States*. New York: HarperCollins.

Zolberg, Aristide R. 2009. *A Nation by Design: Immigration Policy in the Fashioning of America*. Cambridge, MA: Harvard University Press.

CREDITS

PHOTO CREDITS

p. 8: Time & Life Pictures/Getty Images; p. 36: © So-CoAddict; p. 49: Lawrence Journal-World Photo; p. 66: P20: 1208, Extension Bulletin Illustrations Photograph Collection, courtesy OSU Archives; p. 101: The Kobal Collection at Art Resource, NY; p. 105: Courtesy of Emma Halling; p. 120: Photographs and Prints Division, Schomburg Center for Research in Black Culture, The New York Public Library, Astor, Lenox, and Tilden Foundations; p. 124: © epa european pressphoto agency b.v./Alamy; p. 131: Kristina Robinson © 2014 BlackStar Creative. Photo by Noelle Théard; p. 133: AP Photo/People; p. 143: Copyright Bettmann/Corbis/AP Images; p. 156: Boston Globe via Getty Images; p. 177: Yali Shi/Fotolia; p. 181: gustoledo/Fotolia; p. 202: ASSOCIATED PRESS; p. 206 (top): Thomas Northcut/Getty Images; p. 206 (bottom): Denis Jr. Tangney/Getty Images; p. 221: AP Photo/California Department of Corrections, File; p. 226: Photo by Brad Barket/Getty Images; p. 236: AP Photo/The Savannah Morning News, File; p. 254: Courtesy of the National Archives at Atlanta; p. 270 (left): Reproduced by permission of the American Anthropological Association from Anthropology News, Volume 46, Issue 6, page 43, September 2005. Not for sale or further reproduction; p. 270 (right): © Corey Perrine/Augusta Chronicle/ZUMAPRESS.com

FIGURE CREDITS

Figure 2-1: Rakesh Kochhar, Richard Fry and Paul Taylor. "Wealth Gaps Rise to Record Highs Between Blacks, Whites, Hispanics." Pew Research Center, Washington, D.C. (July 26, 2011). http://www.pewsocialtrends.org/2011/07/26/wealth-gaps-rise-to-record-highs-between-whites-blacks-hispanics/, accessed on January 17, 2014; **Figure 3-1**: Migration Policy Institute, 2012; **Figure 3-2**: DHS OIS; **Figure 3-3**: DHS OIS; **Figure 3-4**: DHS OIS 2011; **Figure 3-5**: DHS OIS; **Figure 3-6**: DHS OIS 2009; **Figure 4-1a**: Kopacz and Lawton 2011, Monk-Turner et al. 2010; **Figure 4-1b**: U.S. Census; **Figure 6-1**: adapted from Orfield and Lee (2004); **Figure 6-2**: National Center for Education Statistics; **Figure 6-3**: National Center for Education Statistics; **Figure 7-1**: U.N. Economic Commission for Latin America and the Caribbean and U.S. Census; **Figure 7-2**; Bureau of Labor Statistics, 2013. http://www.bls.gov/news.release/pdf/wkyeng.pdf; **Figure 7-3**; Bureau of Labor Statistics, 2013. http://www.bls.gov/news.release/pdf/wkyeng.pdf; **Figure 7-4, 7-5**: "The Rise of Asian Americans." Pew Research Center, Washington, D.C. (April 4, 2013); **Figure 7-6**: Freeman 2011 and Bureau of Labor Statistics; **Figure 7-7**: Shierholz, Heidi, Economic Policy Institute, August 2013. http://www.epi.org/publication/roughly-hispanic-black-workers-underemployed/; **Figure 7-8**: Western and Pettit (2002); **Figure 7-9**: Demos, 2011; **Figure 8-1**: Norton, Michael I. and Dan Ariely 2011. "Building a Better America—One Wealth Quintile at a Time." *Perspectives on Psychological Science* 6: 9 DOI: 10.1177/1745691610393524; **Figure 8-2**: John R. Logan and Brian Stults, 2011. "The Persistence of Segregation in the Metropolis: New Findings from the 2010 Census" Census Brief prepared for Project US2010.

http://www.s4.brown.edu/us2010; **Figure 8-3, 8-4a, 8-4b**: Rakesh Kochhar, Richard Fry and Paul Taylor. "Wealth Gaps Rise to Record Highs Between Blacks, Whites, Hispanics." Pew Research Center, Washington, D.C. (July 26, 2011). http://www.pewsocialtrends.org/2011/07/26/wealth-gaps-rise-to-record-highs-between-whites-blacks-hispanics/, accessed on January 17, 2014; **Figure 8-5**: Shapiro, Meschede, and Osoro 2013; **Figure 9-1**: Bureau of Justice Statistics http://bjs.ojp.usdoj.gov/index.cfm?ty=tp&tid=11; **Figure 9-2**: International Centre for Prison Studies http://www.prisonstudies.org/info/worldbrief/wpb_stats .php?area=all&category=wb_poprate; **Figure 9-3**: Bureau of Justice Statistics; **Figure 9-4**: Bureau of Justice Statistics, http://bjs.ojp.usdoj.gov/content/glance/viort.cfm; **Figure 9-5**: Bureau of Justice Statistics, http://bjs.ojp.usdoj.gov/content/glance/incrt .cfm; **Figure 9-6**: Bureau of Justice Statistics; **Figure 9-7**: Alexander (2010); **Figure 9-8**: The Pew Charitable Trusts, http://www.pewcenteronthestates.org/uploadedFiles/8015PCTS_Prison08_FINAL_2-1-1_FORWEB.pdf; **Figure 10-1**: CDC 2011, Table 24, http://www.cdc.gov/nchs/hus/black.htm; **Figure 10-2**: CDC 2011, http://www.cdc.gov/nchs/data/hus/2011/010.pdf; **Figure 10-3**: United Church of Christ, 2007, http://www.ucc .org/justice/pdfs/toxic20.pdf

TEXT CREDITS

Chapter 1, p. 18: "Voices" excerpts from Bullwhip Days copyright © 1988 by James Mellon. Used by permission of Grove/Atlantic, Inc. Any third party use of this material, outside of this publication, is prohibited; Chapter 2, p. 36: "Voices" excerpt from The Microaggressions Project (www.microaggressions.tumblr.com), Eds. Lu, Vivian Chenxue and Zhou, David Wei; Chapter 4, p. 105: "Voices" excerpt printed with permission from Emma Halling; Chapter 5, p. 124: "Voices" excerpt from Ismath Mohideen for Brown Girl Magazine; Chapter 5, p. 130: Courtesy CNN; Chapter 7, p. 181: "Voices" excerpt from The New Entrepreneurs: How Race, Class, and Gender Shape American Enterprise by Zulema Valdez. Copyright © 2011 by the Board of Trustees of the Leland Stanford Jr. University. All rights reserved. Used with the permission of Stanford University Press, www.sup.org.

INDEX